TO MY FATHER,

HARRY DERBER,

AND TO THE MEMORY OF MY MOTHER

This book is possible only because of the writings of numerous earlier scholars and practitioners, who are cited throughout the text. I am especially indebted to three graduate students who devoted long hours to extracting and analyzing materials from the vast literature that is relevant to the subject. They are William Berger, David Levin, and Frank Schmieder. I am also grateful to Professor Irving Bernstein of the University of California at Los Angeles for several valuable suggestions and to my colleagues, W. E. Chalmers, Phillips Garman, Archie Green, and Martin Wagner, who contributed helpful ideas to earlier articles which served as testing grounds for this book.

Finally, I wish to express my appreciation to Mrs. Dorothy Wetzel for the preparation of the Index, to Peter Frey for his skilled aid in locating numerous library sources, and to Miss Anice Duncan and her staff for excellent typing services.

MILTON DERBER
Institute of Labor and
Industrial Relations
University of Illinois

CONTENTS

SECTION I

INTRODUCTION

CHAPTER 1

THE FRAMEWORK

INDUSTRIAL RELATIONS may be viewed from many angles: (1) as an economic process involving the allocation of human resources and the distribution of income; (2) as a system of rule-making, in which rule-makers develop working rules to guide future decisions and behavior; (3) as a struggle for power among classes, interest groups, or rival leaders; (4) as a conflict system in which the focus is on developing procedures for the resolution of conflicts; (5) as a small society with a distinctive culture, role structure, and communications network; (6) as a socio-psychological matrix of motivations, needs, desires, and expectations of the people involved and their abilities to satisfy them; or (7) as a process of administration or management involving the coordination of diverse interests at various levels of an organization.

The view underlying this study—one held by a number of the early scholars in the field including John R. Commons and William M. Leiserson—perceives industrial relations as a method of government with a formal role structure, machinery for rule-making and administration, and a system of due process for the orderly resolution of conflicts. Just as a political entity must be governed to satisfy certain needs and desires (such as order, defense, postal service, or economic welfare) of its citizens or

3

its controlling elite, so an industrial entity (an establishment, company, or industry) must be governed to produce goods or services and to satisfy the needs and desires of its participants for security, income, or status. Decisions must be made and executed effectively with respect to such matters as the location of the enterprise, the kinds of products or services to be provided, the recruitment and assignment of personnel, the methods of operation, the conditions of employment, and the distribution of economic rewards.

Like political entities, industrial units may be governed through a variety of structures and in a variety of styles. The following rather simplistic forms are illustrative:

1. *Autocracy* or *bossism*—strict control by one individual or a few persons in which the leader makes rules and gives orders that the others are expected to obey.

2. *Paternalism*—a benevolent form of autocracy based on the "one big family" view in which the "father" knows what is best.

3. *Bureaucracy*—a system emphasizing specialization, a hierarchy of authority, a set of formal rules, and impersonality.

4. *Scientific management* or *technocracy*—rule by experts and the law of the one best way.

5. *Democracy*—either direct rule by the many or rule through representatives in which rule-makers are subject to the control of the many.

This study deals with the last of these forms of industrial government—industrial democracy.

The reasons for singling out industrial democracy as a theme for historical analysis are threefold. First, the study of American labor-management history reveals the idea of industrial democracy as a major motivating force of many workers, union leaders, and reformers. Only the economic theme (the desire for more money, job security, improved living standards) seems to match it in importance. Second, my own value system places a high premium on the realization of the idea in the United States and elsewhere. Third, the nature and implications of industrial democracy have not been fully explored and assessed. Troublesome questions remain unanswered, such as whether industrial democracy is compatible with a mass technological, bureaucratic society; how much worker participation in decision-making is possible without serious interference with productive efficiency; what environmental conditions are most conducive to making industrial democracy work; whether democracy in the workplace also requires democracy within management and employee organizations; whether individuals are really happier and better able to fulfill their expectations and desires in a democratic setting than under any other system.

Two additional preliminary statements are necessary. *Industrial democracy* is a value-laden term, particularly when contrasted with an apparently neutral term like *industrial government*. This may be a disadvantage because it can produce bias and complicate discussion. On the other hand, the threat of bias may be an asset because it compels the researcher as well as his audience to confront and make explicit the problem of values which exists in every social or historical study. If we examine carefully the variants of industrial government previously outlined, it soon becomes clear that all of them are premised on different perceptions of human nature and society and on different sets of values as to how industry should be run and what it should achieve. The system of autocracy has implicit in it, for example, the right of owners or managers to govern their property as they see fit and the belief that governmental responsibility is best performed by a leadership elite. Scientific management attaches supreme weight to the value of maximum or optimal efficiency. Democracy values highly the ideas of equal citizenship and respect for individual dignity.

An equally serious problem arises out of the fact that the words *industrial democracy* connote different things to different persons. It is often uncertain just what is meant by the term. The reader's own views may distort the intended meaning. To minimize the risk of such misinterpretation, it will be necessary to examine in some detail the possible dimensions of the term and to make explicit the author's own operational definition.

History of the Term [1]

The oldest reference to industrial democracy which I have been able to find in American sources is attributed to Albert Gallatin, secretary of the treasury under Thomas Jefferson and James Madison, who introduced in his New Geneva, Pennsylvania, glassworks a profit-sharing plan with the statement: "The democratic principle on which this nation was founded should not be restricted to the political process but should be applied to the industrial operation as well."[2] This statement is believed to have been made about 1797. The same idea is reflected in a variety of early nineteenth-century reports on employer-employee relationships as well as in expressions like *social freedom, industrial liberty, social democracy,* and *economic democracy.* This volume, however, starts its account and analysis with the end of the Civil War rather than an earlier date because it was not until after 1865 that the problems of labor and industry replaced the slavery issue as the major issue of controversy in the nation.

The term *industrial democracy,* as such, has an interesting history of usage. From 1887, when it is first found, to the turn of

[1] The United Nations Educational, Scientific, and Cultural Organization has been concerned with the meaning of the word *democracy* since 1947. For an elaborate historical treatment of European concepts see Jens A. Christophersen, *The Meaning of Democracy as Used in European Ideologies from the French to the Russian Revolution* (Olso: Universitètsforlaget, 1966).

[2] *Profit Sharing Trends* (Chicago: Council of Profit Sharing Industries, March-April 1959), p. 3.

the century, when it was in rather common use, it appears sporadically and with very different meanings. For example, a brief article in the January 1887 issue of the short-lived monthly, *Work and Wages,* under the heading of "Industrial Democracy," chastised organized labor for coercing unorganized labor and concluded that "the weakness and limitation of democracy, whether in the political or industrial sphere, is not essentially different from the weakness and limitation of aristocracy. A majority may be as despotic as a minority." In November 1887 the progressive businessman, N. O. Nelson, labeled his profit-sharing plan a form of industrial democracy in a speech to the American Association of Social Science. In 1889 the dean of labor historians, Richard T. Ely, defined industrial democracy as "self-rule, self-control, the self-direction of the masses in their efforts to gain a livelihood . . . industrial self-government" which he found in "pure" or "productive" cooperation.[3]

In the same year, Henry D. Lloyd, a law-trained economist and journalist and one of the most eloquent of the social reformers, stated in a Chicago speech extolling the labor movement: "They seek today to add to political democracy industrial democracy."[4] In the following year, in another speech entitled "The New Independence" he clearly enunciated the theme of industrial democracy without using the term. In 1893 in an address to the annual convention of the American Federation of Labor, he hailed industrial democracy as the inevitable sequel to political democracy:

> The pioneers who saw a generation ago the thread that would lead
> us through the labyrinth and into the free air have now become
> a multitude. That thread is the thread of democracy, whose princi-

[3] Richard T. Ely, *An Introduction to Political Economy* (New York: Eaton and Mains, 1889), pp. 236–239.

[4] Henry D. Lloyd, *Men, the Workers* (New York: Doubleday, Page and Co., 1909), p. 40.

ples must and will rule wherever men co-exist, in industry not less surely than in politics. It is by the people who do the work that the hours of labour, the conditions of employment, the division of the produce is to be determined. It is by them the captains of industry are to be chosen, and chosen to be servants, not masters. It is for the welfare of all that the coordinated labour of all must be directed. Industry, like government, exists only by the cooperation of all, and like government, it must guarantee equal protection to all. This is democracy, and democracy is not true only where men carry letters or build forts, but wherever they meet in common efforts.[5]

Obviously influenced by Lloyd's train of thought, *The Encyclopedia of Social Reform*, edited by the Reverend William D. P. Bliss in 1897, contained, in an article on "Democracy," a section labeled "Need of Industrial Democracy" which included excerpts from Lloyd's AFL paper and from the nonsocialist writing of George Gunton.[6]

In much the same spirit, in August 1890 the Reverend Lyman Abbott wrote an article for the magazine *The Forum* entitled "Industrial Democracy" which depicted industrial democracy as the ultimate stage in industrial evolution, succeeding slavery, feudalism, individualism, or free competition of unorganized industry, and the wages system or the control of organized industry by oligarchic captains of industry. For Abbott, industrial democracy signified the implementation of two basic principles: (1) that each worker should receive the entire value of his produce, and (2) that the wealth of the nation comes from the people and should be administered by the people.

[5] Ibid., p. 91. This paper was so favorably received by the AFL convention that they voted to reprint it in an edition of 20,000 copies for general distribution: *Report of Proceedings of Thirteenth Annual Convention of American Federation of Labor*, December 11–19, 1893 (New York: Concord Co-operative Printing Co., 1894), p. 24.

[6] William D. P. Bliss, ed., *The Encyclopedia of Social Reform*, 2nd ed. (New York and London: Funk & Wagnalls Co., 1898), pp. 485–486.

A contemporary, Reverend N. P. Gilman, one of the leading students and proponents of profit-sharing (his favored form of industrial partnership), viewed the stirrings of industrial democracy with some concern.

> The varied, perpetual, and innumerable labor troubles of our time mean fundamentally this one thing—that the democratic spirit has invaded the industrial world ... universal suffrage and political democracy have forcibly suggested, not to workingmen only, but also to many of the more prosperous classes a false analogy between government and industry. If the one can be carried on by counting hands, then why not the other? Why should there not be industrial democracy as well as political democracy? Why should not the factory and counting room be conducted on republican principles? Why not, indeed, except for the one fact that human nature has not been developed on the line of uniformity of mind and equality of talent.[7]

In contrast, Henry C. Adams, in his presidential address to the American Economic Association in December 1896, undertook to demonstrate that "industrial liberty" could not be realized under existing industrial conditions without workers obtaining some form of property right in industry, and that without such a right, it would not be reasonable to expect the workers to exhibit a sense of responsibility in industry. He saw this new industrial right evolving through collective bargaining and the formal labor contract.

Far more important and influential than any of these writings was the classic British work of Sidney and Beatrice Webb, *Industrial Democracy*, first published in book form in 1897. At least three extensive reviews appeared in American journals in

---

[7] Reprinted in *Report of the U.S. Industrial Commission,* 14 (Washington, D.C.: Government Printing Office, 1901):366. This language appeared originally in N. P. Gilman's major book, *Socialism and the American Spirit* (Boston: Houghton Mifflin Co., 1893), pp. 295–296.

1898 and 1899, and there were a half dozen briefer book notices.[8] For the Webbs, industrial democracy seemed to have two meanings. One was the institution of trade unionism per se. The other was the ultimate ideal—the Fabian socialist society—in which industry would be governed on a functional basis: consumers to determine *what* products industry should produce, managers to determine *how* goods were to be produced, and unions to determine the *conditions* of production, with the State playing a partnership role in every enterprise in order to protect the interests of the community as a whole.

By 1902 the U.S. Industrial Commission was treating industrial democracy as a term well imbedded in the jargon of industrial relations. In its final report a page-and-a-half section was entitled "Democracy in Industry," and the conclusion was reached that "by the organization of labor, and by no other means, it is possible to introduce an element of democracy in the government of industry. By this means only the workers can effectively take part in determining the conditions under which they work. This becomes true in the fullest and best sense only when employers frankly meet the representatives of the workmen and deal with them as parties equally in the conduct of affairs."[9]

From this point on we can trace the use of the words *industrial democracy* in a growing crescendo so that by 1918–1919 it appeared to be one of the most widely used terms in industrial relations. John Leitch called his employee representation system "industrial democracy." The railroad union journal supporting the Plumb Plan for the nationalization of the railroads was called

---

[8] See, in particular, the *Journal of Political Economy*, 7 (March 1899); the *Yale Review*, 7 (November 1898); and the *Political Science Quarterly*, 13 (December 1898). *The American Fabian*, a monthly published between 1895 and 1899, devoted little attention to the practical government of industry. Apart from a reprint of a review of the Webbs' book, the term *industrial democracy* was found only once up to 1899.

[9] *Report of the U.S. Industrial Commission*, 14:805.

"Railroad Democracy." In 1921 the Intercollegiate Socialist Society became the League for Industrial Democracy. Father Joseph Husslein's Catholic history and analysis in 1920 was called "Democratic Industry." This pattern of use prevailed through the mid-twenties. In 1925 department store executive Edward A. Filene wrote: "A hundred and one books and a flood of articles have been written during the last few years about industrial democracy."[10] Then the flow slackened and particularly in the bleak years of the Great Depression (1929-1933), the attention of scholars as well as practitioners of industrial relations turned in other directions. Economic survival took precedence.

During the New Deal era and in the two decades following World War II, *industrial democracy* lost its earlier popularity as a working term. Nonetheless, significant references to industrial democracy continued, and the ideas bearing on industrial democracy received enlarged and more sophisticated treatment by practitioners as well as scholars. Speeches of Senator Robert Wagner are a prime example. Another is the book entitled *The Dynamics of Industrial Democracy* by Clinton S. Golden and Harold J. Ruttenberg, two top steelworker union officials. As a different type of illustration, President Truman's postwar labor-management conference in 1945 foundered because of an inability of the competing interest groups to reach agreement on the scope of issues in which unions could legitimately share decision-making power with managements. The Landrum-Griffin amendments to the National Labor-Management Relations Act in 1959 were mainly concerned with the internal democratization of unions. The Fund for the Republic, sponsored by the Ford Foundation, conducted a major inquiry into the relations of institutions (including corporations and unions) to the individual member. "Management rights," "participation in decision-making," "democracy within unions," "human

[10] Edward A. Filene, *The Way Out* (New York: Doubleday, Page and Co., 1925), p. 128.

relations in industry"—these and related terms were widely discussed. Thus, whether explicitly stated or not, the idea of industrial democracy has been a subject of deep concern in the United States throughout the past century and promises to be a subject of continued concern in the foreseeable future.

A Definition of Industrial Democracy

The genesis of industrial democracy clearly is attributable to the transfer of ideas about democracy in the city-state and the nation-state to democracy in industry. Superficially, the analogy seems valid and the transfer seems appropriate; but deeper consideration warns against too literal a translation. Important differences exist.

There are at least three different ways of conceptualizing the idea of democracy. One is by "pure theory," the development of an abstraction which rigorously pursues the full implications of the term "government of the people, by the people, and for the people." This abstraction is not intended to represent the real world or to be realizable in practice. It is an "ideal type" in Max Weber's terminology. Its value lies in its identification of certain strategic variables and of the suggested interconnections among them as a basis for studying the real world. A second way of conceptualizing is by formulating a general model with properties which are sufficiently close to real world practice as to warrant the label "realistic theory." Although not often realized in fact, the model may be realizable under optimal conditions. Thus it may serve as a guide for action as well as for thought. A third approach to conceptualizing democracy is to take some actual example as the norm and compare other cases with it. This approach is essentially a variant of the second. Its chief difficulty lies in the selection of the exemplary case which inevitably will involve unique conditions. The second of these three modes of thought therefore seems to be most appropriate for this study.

In the political sphere, democracy in its broadest sense connotes government by the many rather than by the few or by one. This may be interpreted in several ways. It may mean that governmental policies and rules are made by the many or that they are subject to the control of the many, or that they are subject to consent by the many. Obviously direct rule-making by the many is possible only in small governmental units, like the New England village or the Israeli kibbutz, numbering at most some hundreds of inhabitants and rarely exceeding a thousand. In large-scale units, government rules *must* be made by representatives selected by the citizenry at large.

Representative democracy is clearly a different process than direct democracy. In direct democracy, the basic principle is one person, one vote, and the majority rules. Although the voice of one citizen may be more influential than another on various issues, each rule is determined by the casting of equal votes. In a representative system, except for an unusual general referendum, the rules are determined by the voting of the chosen representatives, not by the citizenry at large. The latter are limited to voting for their representatives. This generates the problem of the relationship between the citizens and the representatives: Can representatives be "controlled" by their constituencies or must representative democracy be mainly government by consent—i.e., government in which the citizens have the option of displacing their representatives on periodic or other given occasions if they are not satisfied with their performance, but cannot otherwise affect the rule-making process by voting.[11] The political party system, with the designation of candidates by party mechanisms rather than through direct popular nominating

[11] Sartori's distinction between a "governing democracy" and a "governed democracy" is relevant here. See Giovanni Sartori, *Democratic Theory* (New York: Frederick A. Praeger, 1965), chapter 5.

procedures, makes even the selection of representatives by a majority of the citizens doubtful. Where the party leaders or activists select the candidates, the citizens are given a very limited choice—in effect, as between parties. Control by the many becomes remote and tenuous.

Democratic government becomes even more difficult to characterize when the focus is shifted from the legislative process of rule-making to the executive and administrative processes. In most units of government, the election process applies mainly to the chief executive and a few other high officials. The heads of departments, boards, and commissions are usually appointed by the chief executive but thereafter exercise considerable discretion in rule-making. The impact of the citizens on these administrative rules is at best indirect, the greatest influence being exercised by organized interest groups which may or may not represent a majority of the body politic. In a parliamentary democracy the political party and its effective leadership may be held ultimately responsible, and the citizens may at some point effect a change in the party through the majority voting process. In a system of divided authority and loose party discipline, as in this country, the citizen's control is much more limited.

These few observations on the political process suggest that the model of democracy expressed in the phrase "government by the many" assumes meaning in the modern mass society only when further reduced to such terms as: the right of all citizens to vote for representatives who will serve as the rule-makers; majority rule as the basis for selecting representatives as well as in voting by representatives on rule-making issues; and opportunity for citizens to exercise control over their representatives, at least to the degree of replacing undesired representatives by majority vote.

To make this conception of political democracy work, however, several supplemental standards are needed. These may be summarized as follows:

1. Access to information (i.e., a minimum of secrecy in governmental affairs) to develop an informed and knowledgeable citizenry, and to promote accountability by representatives to their constituents.

2. Provision for the rights of freedom of thought and speech, including the right to dissent from strongly established majority views.

3. Protection of minorities against arbitrary rule by the majority, such as unfair obstructions to opposition groups in their efforts to become the new majority through the ballot box.

4. Due process of law for all citizens so that the power of the government is not exercised in an arbitrary and unjust or discriminatory fashion.

This concept of political democracy rests on a set of postulates which may be summed up in the phrase "respect for the dignity of man" or in the propositions of the Declaration of Independence that "all men are created equal; that they are endowed by their Creator with certain unalienable rights; that among these are life, liberty, and the pursuit of happiness." Twentieth-century thinkers, like Lasswell and Fromm, have elaborated this view of democracy in terms of the creative development of the human personality. Padover refers to it as "a way of life."

There follows from this underlying conception a number of further attributes of political democracy:

1. Equal rights under law for all citizens so that there is no discrimination because of race, religion, sex, nationality, or other personal characteristics.

2. Equal opportunity for individuals so that each can develop and advance in society in accordance with his native abilities and his exertions.

3. Minimum standards of education, health, safety, employment, income, and leisure so that distinctions among citizens are restrained.

4. A sense of responsibility on the part of each citizen to fulfill his role creditably, to function in a lawful and orderly manner, and to assume an active, participatory role in the affairs of the community.

It is a relatively easy step to move from such an elaborated idea of political democracy to a comparable idea of industrial democracy. In the words of Samuel Gompers, "the old political democracy is the father of this new industrial democracy. Like government, industry must guarantee equal opportunities, equal protection, equal benefits and equal rights to all."[12] But the analogy must be used with considerable caution and in a restricted manner.

The differences and similarities between political democracy (the democratic government of a state) and industrial democracy (the democratic government of an enterprise) are brought out by comparing the two in terms of various aspects of the governmental process.

source of power
—the sovereignty of the democratic state (i.e., the power to rule or govern) lies ultimately in the will or consent of the citizens, since they have the power by majority vote to displace the rule-makers.

—the sovereignty of the democratic enterprise is divided among several discrete entities—the "controllers" of the owning-managing interest (i.e., majority stockholders and/or managers who obtain the support or consent of the stockholding majority); the nonmanagement employees through their labor organizations; and the State which, subject to constitutional limitations, has powers to regulate the enterprise in the interest of the general welfare. Under certain conditions, customers, suppliers, or creditors may also claim a share in the sovereignty of the enter-

[12] *American Federationist*, 26 (May 1919), 5:399. This language is very close to that used by Henry Lloyd in 1893.

prise, but usually they operate through management "behind the scene" rather than as a discrete entity in the governing process.

leaders and rule-makers
—political parties, reflecting diverse interest groups, compete for the right to govern in the State.
—stockholders, managers, and unions are the principal competitors for power in the enterprise.
But whereas the political parties are competing for the same positions of power and the victory of one means the defeat of the other, the actors in the enterprise fill separate roles and their competition is limited to how decision-making is to be shared.

manner of rule-making
—the rules or laws of a state are made by the political leadership of the majority party if the executive and legislative bodies are dominated by the same party. If power is divided among the parties or if the party leadership does not have effective control of the party representatives, an elaborate process of compromise and logrolling among factions and individuals is required. Legislative decisions, however, are based on majority vote of the legislators.
—the rules of an enterprise are made, on the one hand, by top management and, on the other hand, by collective bargaining between management and labor organizations. Agreement, voluntary or coerced, rather than majority rule is the method. The majority rule principle applies only when a negotiated agreement is referred back to the rank and file membership of the employee organization for approval.

organizational aims
—the goals of the democratic state are to promote the general welfare of the citizenry and to defend the interests and integrity of the state in relations with other states.
—the goals of the enterprise are to produce goods and services

for a profit and to survive and grow in the face of market competition. The democratic enterprise, like the democratic state, is concerned to advance the economic, social, and psychological needs, desires, and conditions of its members (i.e., the employees).

relation of individual to organization
—the citizen ordinarily sees his relation to the state as enduring for a lifetime. He expects the state to protect his way of life and to provide an environment which will enable him and his family to satisfy their economic, social, and other goals.
—the employee is concerned mainly with the job opportunities and rewards provided by the enterprise. The relationship is not necessarily an enduring one (although it may be), and the loyalty to a trade, craft, or profession may be stronger than to the enterprise.

We turn then to the development of the meaning of industrial democracy with the idea of political democracy as a guiding light but not as a prototype—and with the premise of a private ownership system of most of the industrial enterprises in which an owning-managerial interest is clearly distinguishable from the employee interest. The central question is: How should the rule-making power of the enterprise be distributed between the owning-managerial interest and the employee interest and, in relevant cases, the governmental interest. Bilateralism or even trilateralism in rule-making, however, is not sufficient for democracy in the workplace. Collusion among organizational leaders is not uncommon, and even if there are antagonistic or countervailing power groups, the democratic rights of the individual may be obstructed or ignored. Safeguards, therefore, must be provided for due process, freedom of dissent, the opportunity for a minority to seek to become a new majority if it so desires, and the equal treatment of every employee within the network of rules. Finally, the democratic model calls for an atmosphere and set of procedures which will afford each employee a chance to participate as creatively as he can, and to the degree he desires, in the governmental process.

Thus my operational definition of industrial democracy *in the American context* rests on the following principles:

1. *Representation.* Both employers and employees have the right, if they so desire, to form organizations and to choose representatives who will act in their behalf in the government of an enterprise or industry. Employee representatives are chosen by majority vote of an appropriate constituency on the principle of one man, one vote. (In a system of private ownership of industry, employer representation is determined by financial rather than electoral considerations.)

2. *Participation.* Employees have a voice, directly or through their representatives, in the determination of the rules relating to their terms and conditions of employment.

3. *Equal rights and opportunities.* All employees have equal rights as citizens of the enterprise and equal protection under the rules. Discrimination because of race, religion, sex, nationality, or other personal characteristics unrelated to the requirements of a job is prohibited.

4. *Right of dissent.* The rights of freedom of speech and orderly opposition to the formal leaders are protected.

5. *Due process.* Individuals or groups may raise complaints over the interpretation or application of existing rules and have ready access to effective procedures which assure them of a fair hearing and a just decision.

6. *Responsibility.* The parties live up to their contractual duties and responsibilities in an orderly and lawful manner.

7. *Minimum standards.* Socially acceptable minimum terms and standards of employment are provided.

8. *Information.* All needed information, including an accounting of funds, consistent with the external relationships of the enterprise, is provided to the interested parties.

9. *Personal dignity.* The dignity of every individual in the enterprise is respected.

This model of industrial democracy is a conception derived from American experience and American thought. It is "realistic" in the sense that it is realizable under American conditions. It can be used as a basis for the study of the past as well as a tool for prediction about the future.

The model, however, is descriptive rather than analytical. It can serve as a standard for comparisons in the real world. But it does not help to explain why either past or present forms of industrial government conform to it or deviate from it. For purposes of causal or diagnostic analysis, a broader conceptual framework is needed—one that takes into account the values and goals of the participants and the environmental context in which they interact. Some values are clearly compatible with industrial democracy, others are not; some environmental conditions are congenial and others are barriers.

Although it may not be possible to provide a completely satisfactory framework at this time, several of the key ingredients of the framework can be suggested:

1. *Attitudes.* For industrial democracy to take hold and survive, there must be a "will" among the participants to make it work. If owners or managers are hostile, or if employees in significant numbers are uninterested or apathetic, the chances of success are greatly reduced.

2. *Abilities.* More than any other form of industrial government, industrial democracy requires a body of literate and competent employees who understand, as well as desire, the functioning of democratic processes and who are both willing and able to assume the responsibilities of democratic participation.

3. *Local community climate.* The values of a community invariably carry over into its industrial establishments. If the socio-

psychological climate of the community embodies democratic values and is reflected in democratic practices, industrial democracy is more likely to emerge.

4. *Political system.* The distribution of political power in the greater society is likely to affect the distribution of power within industry. If interests favoring industrial democracy achieve sufficient political power, they can be expected to enact laws conducive to industrial democracy at the enterprise level.

5. *Economic situation.* Economic adversity in the short run may result in a climate of opinion favorable to industrial democracy, but in the longer run, industrial democracy can survive only if the economic situation of the enterprise is capable of providing socially acceptable minimum employment standards and economic benefits to all participants in the enterprise.

6. *Technology.* This factor is usually viewed as a barrier to industrial democracy on the grounds that it leads to large bureaucratic organizations in which the worker is an insignificant cog performing a limited and specialized job so that he cannot envisage the wholeness of the undertaking and therefore cannot function in a creative and psychologically healthy manner. It is often blamed for the worker's alienation from his work, from society, and from himself. But technology has also served to lighten man's physical labor, to reduce work hours, to increase the standard of life. Thus whether it diminishes or enhances industrial democracy would appear to depend on how the technology is used. Does man master the machine to achieve a better life or does he let the machine dominate and regulate him?

If the weight of these variables, on balance, is favorable to democratic thought and practice, industrial democracy can be expected to flourish; if not, the reverse will occur—other forms of industrial government will dominate. Which combinations of elements are most congenial and which are less so pose one of the challenges behind this study.

A Sketch of the Remainder of the Volume

In succeeding chapters, we shall apply these ideas about industrial democracy to the history of American thought and experience since the end of the Civil War. We shall trace the evolution of present-day elements of industrial democracy in the United States, integrating ideas and practice. This evolution may be divided into five main periods which will serve as the organizational frame for the discussion. In the first period, from 1865 to the turn of the century, the central theme seems to be a frenetic search for a workable model, with numerous concepts in competition and multiple diverse experiments. During the second period, from about 1898 to the end of World War I, the collective bargaining model of industrial democracy crystallized. In the course of crystallization, it met and beat back severe challenge from several socialist and syndicalist models. About 1915, and particularly after 1920, an even more serious challenger appeared in the form of welfare capitalism and the employee-representation plan. The third period, from 1920 to the Great Depression of 1929–1933, deals with this confrontation and the eventual elimination of the employer-dominated system. With the New Deal, government assumed a new and complex role in industrial democracy. The process of gestation of this role is the story of the fourth period from 1933 to 1945. In the two decades since 1945 the trilateral characteristics of the system have elaborated under a rule of law which may justify the concept of a fifth, and still incomplete, period.

In tracing this hundred years of evolution, we shall also search for an explanation of the forces at work. Hopefully this will enable us not only to explain the pattern of events but also to assess the survival ability of the current dominant model and the possible direction of future changes.

Industrial Democracy versus Individualism

The idea of industrial democracy may be contrasted with the doctrine of individualism which long dominated practice as well as thought in the United States. The latter was described by one of its staunchest proponents, Walter Gordon Merritt, under the rubric of industrial liberty.

> Industrial liberty has been recognized and protected by our legislatures and courts in ways unknown to other nations. We have placed our faith in man, rather than in groups and classes, and decreed that every man shall be free to live his own life and carve his own destiny, free from private obstruction.[13]
>
>   .   .   .   .
>
> It became an accepted belief in this country that the public has substantial interest in the freedom of men to work and engage in business. No artificial barrier shall be allowed to drive any man from his trade or any line of merchandise from the market and thus impair the consumer's sovereign right of choice. Industrial freedom is a public necessity. . . . We encourage men to combine and associate, for that is a part of individual liberty, but when their conduct turns aside from the normal pursuit of their own ends or seeks by artificial or unnatural processes to obstruct the action, or curtail the liberties of others, then such conduct becomes not an assertion of liberty, but an interference with liberty. We believe in collective self-help, but collectivism must be born of cooperation and not of coercion. We believe in voluntary associations but oppose involuntary associations.[14]

Herbert Hoover expressed the same thesis in the concluding speech of his 1928 campaign for the Presidency. Hoover stated:

[13] Walter Gordon Merritt, *The Struggle for Industrial Liberty* (New York: League for Industrial Rights, 1922), p. 4.
[14] Ibid., p. 8.

[The American system] is founded upon a particular conception of self-government in which decentralized local responsibility is the very base. Further than this, it is founded upon the conception that only through ordered liberty, freedom and equal opportunity to the individual will his initiative and enterprise spur on the march of progress. And in our insistence upon equality of opportunity has our system advanced beyond all the world. . . .

Nor do I wish to be misinterpreted as believing that the United States is free-for-all and devil-take-the-hindmost. The very essence of equality of opportunity and of American individualism is that there shall be no domination by any group or combination in this Republic, whether it be business or political. On the contrary, it demands economic justice as well as political and social justice. It is no system of laissez-faire.[15]

The chief support of this doctrine of individualism was provided by the court system and especially by the U.S. Supreme Court until its dramatic reversal of policy in 1937. In decision after decision the Court declared unconstitutional legislative efforts to scrap the theory that the individual male adult employee was the bargaining equal of the individual employer. In *Lochner* v. *New York* (1905) the majority opinion held:

There is no reasonable ground for interfering with the liberty of person or the right of free contract, by determining the hours of labor, in the occupation of a baker. There is no contention that bakers as a class are not equal in intelligence and capacity to men in other trades or manual occupations, or that they are not able to assert their rights and care for themselves without the protecting arm of the state, interfering with their independence of judgment and of action. . . . Statutes of the nature of that under review, limiting the hours in which grown and intelligent men may labor

---

[15] Quoted in J. Rogers Hollingsworth and Bell I. Wiley, eds., *American Democracy: A Documentary Record*, vol. 2: 1865–1961 (New York: Thomas Y. Crowell Co., 1962), pp. 236, 238.

to earn their living, are mere meddlesome interferences with the rights of the individual. . . .[16]

And in *Adkins* v. *Children's Hospital* (1923), the majority wrote:

That the right to contract about one's affairs is a part of the liberty of the individual protected by this clause [due process clause of Fifth Amendment], is settled by the decisions of this Court and is no longer open to question. [Citations omitted.] Within this liberty are contracts of employment of labor. In making such contracts, generally speaking, the parties have an equal right to obtain from each other the best terms they can as the result of private bargaining. . . .[17]

It is not necessary here to trace the subtleties and qualifications of the Supreme Court in interpreting the doctrine of individualism. Suffice it to say that during the first seventy years of the century covered in this study, the Court showed little sympathy for the ideas of industrial democracy with which we are primarily concerned. Court opinions will consequently receive much less attention than they would otherwise merit in a study of industrial government in the United States.

[16] 198 U.S. 45, 57, 61.
[17] 261 U.S. 525, 545.

SECTION **II**

SEARCH FOR A MODEL, 1865–1897

CHAPTER 2

LABOR'S REACTIONS
TO UNRESTRAINED
CAPITALISM

R APID CHANGE has been a characteristic of life in the United States throughout most of its history, but no period surpassed the last third of the nineteenth century in this respect. From the standpoint of industrial government, hardly a single relevant environmental factor failed to undergo drastic transformation. A newly industrializing nation with about a 35 million population became the industrial and economic giant of the world with a population of about 75 million. A society of small owner-operated workshops and factories dependent on the skilled artisan evolved into a system of mass production utilizing large numbers of unskilled laborers and dominated by huge trusts under the control of finance capitalists. Since political affairs of both the states and the federal government were largely in the hands of the business leaders, private enterprise was permitted virtually free play and the phenomenal growth process was consequently accompanied by violent, unregulated

In the preparation of this section, I am greatly indebted to David Levin, who served as my research assistant and wrote a comprehensive M.A. thesis, entitled "The Idea of Industrial Democracy in America, 1865–1900," under my supervision.

fluctuations in economic conditions. In comparison with the countries of Europe from which its inhabitants had come, the northern and central sections of the United States, where the main struggle for industrial democracy occurred, had been relatively egalitarian prior to 1865—in economic returns as well as social and political patterns. By the end of the century, marked inequalities scarred the scene. Big city slums teemed with impoverished families in the midst of unparalleled national affluence. The distinctions between the wealthy and the poor were intensified, not only by spreading income levels but by growing differences in standards of dress, housing, education, culture, and recreation. The sudden vast influx of non-English-speaking immigrants from continental Europe added to class stratification. It is no wonder that the social-psychological climate of the period, following on the heels of the traumatic experience of a convulsive Civil War, was a hurly-burly of protest and conflict, of trying to recapture the past or leap into a utopian future, of reformism and radicalism, of uncertainty and experimentalism, of rapid and frequent shift from one position to another. Following is a brief examination of these environmental factors and a description and analysis of the ideas (and some relevant experiences) bearing on the theme of industrial democracy.

Industrialization

The facts of economic and technological growth can be found in any of the economic histories.[1] The number of manufacturing establishments, for example, rose from 252,000 in 1869 to 512,000 in 1899, or by 103 per cent; the number of factory wage earners, from 2.1 to 5.3 million or by 152 per cent; the value product of manufactures, from $3.4 to $13.0 billion or by 282 per cent; and

---

[1] See particularly U.S., Department of Commerce, *Historical Statistics of the United States, 1789–1945* (Washington, D.C.: Government Printing Office, 1949).

value added by manufactures, from $1.4 to $5.6 billion or by 300 per cent.[2] Persons' index of physical manufacturing production jumped from 8.5 in 1865 to 57.3 in 1898 (1909–1913=100), or by 574 per cent. Since the total population of the country for the comparable dates did not quite double, the advance in manufacturing productivity obviously reflected a great increase in material wealth on a per capita as well as gross basis.

Other indicators of economic development in addition to manufacturing were equally or even more impressive. Miles of railroads operated rose from 35,000 in 1865 to over 245,000 in 1898 or by 600 per cent. Production of bituminous coal mines rose from 12 million net tons in 1865 to 167 million in 1898 or by 1290 per cent; anthracite coal production increased from 12 million net tons to 53 million or by 342 per cent. The annual supply of energy from mineral fuels and water power used is estimated to have risen from 1520 trillion btu's in 1871–1875 to 6690 trillion btu's in 1896–1900 or by 340 per cent. By the end of the century the industrial revolution was in full swing, with vast new industries (steel, electricity, petroleum, street railways, agricultural machinery) and vastly expanded old ones (coal, railroads, garments, meat packing) transforming the face of the land.

Because it was a largely uncontrolled, unregulated laissez faire society, the inevitable problems of social adjustment to exceptionally rapid economic and technological change were aggravated by two forces. One was the fluctuation of the business cycle, with its deep and long depressions in 1873–1879 and 1893–1896. The other, and related, complication was the widening spread in income and wealth and the intensification of class distinctions. Unprecedented fortunes were amassed by Rockefeller, Gould, Whitney, Widener, Vanderbilt, Carnegie, Harriman, and many others immune from significant (if any) income or inher-

[2] Since price levels were appreciably lower in 1899 than in 1869 (the BLS wholesale price index fell from 93.5 to 52.2 [1926=100]), the dollar figures greatly understate the rise in real product.

itance taxes. At the other end of the scale were the slum dwellers (mostly new immigrants) of the new big cities. It is true that the society afforded numerous opportunities for upward class mobility, if not so many as the Horatio Alger myth suggested,[3] and that a sizable middle class of small businessmen and skilled artisans existed. But the growing disparities in economic returns became increasingly glaring to the members of the "gilded age."

Urbanization and Immigration

In 1860 over 25 million Americans out of a total population of 31.4 million lived in rural areas (on farms or places with less than 2500 persons) and only 2.6 million lived in cities with 100,-000 or more inhabitants. By 1900, out of a total population of 76 million, a substantial majority of 45.8 million was still composed of rural inhabitants, but 14.2 million now lived in cities of 100,000 or more. The growth of the large city was a major factor in industrial relations because, with the exception of coal and metal mining, almost all of the significant labor ferment emerged out of large city conditions. The following table illustrates this urban dynamic:

TEN LARGEST CITIES IN 1900	POPULATION		% INCREASE
	1860	1900	
New York	814,000	3,437,000	322
Chicago	109,000	1,699,000	1458
Philadelphia	566,000	1,294,000	129
St. Louis	161,000	575,000	259
Boston	178,000	561,000	215
Baltimore	212,000	509,000	140
Cleveland	43,000	382,000	788
Buffalo	81,000	352,000	335
San Francisco	57,000	343,000	502
Cincinnati	161,000	326,000	102

[3] See Stephan Thernstrom, *Poverty and Progress: Social Mobility in a Nineteenth Century City* (Cambridge: Harvard University Press, 1964).

These and lesser urban centers were not only industrial key-points, but also the chief drawing force of the massive new immigration which furnished so much of the ferment. This, again, is a well-explored subject. Not only was the number of immigrants substantial—14 million between 1861 and 1900—but the composition increasingly was shifting from English to non-English speaking. Whereas new British and Irish immigrants numbered 4.2 million, German and Scandinavian numbered 4.8 million, Italian 927,000, Polish and Russian 841,000, and the remaining 3 million were chiefly from non-English-speaking cultures. Many of the new immigrants had to learn a new language and become acquainted with new ways of living, particularly if they settled down in the big cities. The process of Americanization, however, was slowed down by the very fact of their numbers and their propensity to cluster into urban ghettoes where they could continue to use Old World tongues and customs. Thus, the elements of heterogeneity in American industrial society increased in the period under discussion. This heterogeneity promoted conflicts and complicated adjustment to change, but it also provided a source of vitality, of new ideas and new proposals.

The Socio-Psychological Climate

These elements of economy, technology, urbanization, and culture were combined with unprecedented speed, without any serious effort at regulation, and with a minimal regard for human values. Inevitably the result was dissension and struggle, often of a violent nature. A mere listing of prominent disturbances during the period reveals why American labor relations got the reputation of being the most violent in the Western industrial world: Tompkins Square, the Molly Maguires, the railroad strikes of 1877, Hocking Valley, Haymarket, Homestead, Coal

Creek (Tennessee), Cripple Creek (Colorado), Coeur d'Alene (Idaho), Pullman.

Underlying these conflicts and rationalizing the positions of the opposing parties were a number of intellectual and ideological themes and theses. Perhaps the dominant ideology shaping the socio-psychological climate of the period was that of individualism and free enterprise—the right of individuals to acquire and use wealth in accordance with their abilities and energies and with a minimal interference from the government. Initially bulwarked by the Protestant ethic, the ethos of the American Revolution, and the spirit of the pioneers, this individualistic ideology was strongly reinforced by the Social Darwinism of Herbert Spencer and William Graham Sumner. Individual liberty and the survival of the fittest joined hands. "Rugged individualism" was tempered only by the religious principle of trusteeship—that the man of wealth, who had rightfully obtained his wealth through the exercise of his God-given talents, had the obligation to use it in a humane and charitable manner.

This dominant ideology of laissez faire individualism within a setting of economic capitalism and political democracy was countered by a variety of themes, which were united only in their sentiment for reform or radical change. In general they were expressions of protest against the visible human costs of the unregulated industrial, capitalistic revolution. Some were essentially backward-looking pleas for a return to the status of the independent small producer, artisan, or householder. Some were utopian calls for the establishment of small communistic societies or for a system of small producers' cooperatives, emphasizing the virtues of cooperation and harmony rather than of competition and struggle. There were radical programs ranging from the highly structured planned society of Bellamy and the "scientific socialism" of the Marxists and the Lassalleans to the anarchistic ideas of the followers of the Black International. In between were the numerous brands of the moderate reformers, for the most part accepting the private property, capitalistic system but demanding government intervention and reform of its major abuses. The latter included academic economists like Henry Carter Adams and Richard T. Ely who founded the American Economic Association on an anti–laissez faire platform; clergymen pursuing the "social gospel" like Congregationalist Washington Gladden and Episcopalian Bishop Henry Potter; trade unionists of a conservative nature like Samuel Gompers and Frank K. Foster; the rural populists and their urban allies who were combatting the power of the railroad and other monopolists; and a miscellany of businessmen, politicians, writers, and social workers, including Abram Hewitt, Governor John Peter Altgeld, Henry George, William Dean Howells, and Jane Addams.[4]

The Views of Organized Labor

The principal demands for a system of industrial democracy in this hectic and confusing environment came from the spokesmen of labor rather than from intellectuals. Since the workers more than any other group were the victims of industrial abuses, the search for new forms and rules of industrial government was a major concern of their leaders and organizations. The conditions described above made the search a fitful one. For more than two decades after 1865 labor experimented with a variety of approaches, none of which could claim either a firm base or

[4] Despite the turmoil and conflict, there was a widespread feeling of optimism at the end of the century about the emergent democracy. Typifying this sentiment was an article by Columbia University president Seth Low, "The Trend of the Century," *Atlantic Monthly* (August 1898). The two main influences shaping the nineteenth century, he wrote, were the scientific spirit and the democratic spirit: "the tendency to democracy in industry" seemed "as marked a fixture of our times as the tendency to democracy in the political life of men" (p. 159).

a promising future. By the turn of the century, however, the field had narrowed. One model (job control through collective bargaining) had crystallized in theory and gotten a foothold in practice. A second model (constitutional socialism) was on the threshold of assuming the role of serious competitor. Other models had been found wanting and had fallen by the wayside. I shall examine all three categories by studying the views of representative spokesmen and the organizations which they led as well as by considering events and experiences which reflected their views.

TWO PERIPATETIC SEARCHERS

Labor's experimental and shifting course during the last third of the nineteenth century is well illustrated by the ideas and activities of William E. Sylvis (1828–1869) and George E. McNeill (1837–1906). Although Sylvis' life largely antedated the period with which we are concerned, it was during the last six years, when he served as president of the then powerful Iron Molders' International Union and as a founder and president, for a year, of the National Labor Union, that his thoughts about industrial government were most sharply revealed. Sylvis did not use the term *industrial democracy*, but his speeches and activities clearly reflected his strong concern for this form of industrial practice. His initial solution to problems of workshop government was strong trade union control, especially with respect to the qualifications and numbers of apprentices, hiring through the union, and shop committees to enforce work rules.[5] In forming nationwide associations to combat the union, foundry employers claimed that they had been seriously interfered with in the management of their business by the Iron Molders' Union, whose committees told them how many apprentices they might

[5] Jonathan Grossman, *William Sylvis, Pioneer of American Labor* (New York: Columbia University Press, 1945).

employ, how many molds should be a day's work, the number of hours for a day, and the amount of wages.[6] But Sylvis was not anxious to achieve job control through strikes. As his biographer, Jonathan Grossman, reports, he "urged compromise, conciliation, arbitration, and asked for a joint convention of employer and employee representatives to come to an understanding on such vital questions as shop rules and apprenticeship."[7] He worked for signed agreements. His efforts failed, partly because of internal union dissension over his conciliatory attitude and partly because of the hostile attitude of the employers toward unionism. In 1867 and 1868 depressed conditions in the industry and resistance to wage cuts led to a series of unsuccessful union strikes and a marked diminution in union strength.

The failure of the job control approach to industrial government led Sylvis to turn to an alternative solution which had achieved considerable popularity among skilled craftsmen particularly in time of depression or following strike defeats. The idea of self-governing producers' cooperatives had its practical contemporary genesis in England and France in the 1830's and 1840's. Sylvis seems to have been most influenced by the Rochdale movement, a consumers' cooperative system that extended into production activities rather than a system of workers forming their own producers' enterprise. However, between 1864 and 1868 he actively supported local groups of molders who set up stove foundries in Troy, Albany, and Rochester, New York, as well as in other parts of the country. In 1867 he took the further step of creating an International Union cooperative foundry in Pittsburgh where a serious strike had been in progress. The temporary success of the Troy and other foundries led to a wave of enthusiasm for cooperation among molders. In 1868 at a convention in Toronto, Sylvis urged the Union to "abandon

---

[6] John R. Commons et al., eds., *A Documentary History of American Industrial History*, 2d ed., vol. 9 (New York: Russell & Russell, Publishers, 1958), p. 97.

[7] Grossman, *William Sylvis*, pp. 170–171.

the whole system of strikes and make cooperation the foundation of our organization and the prime object of all our effort."[8] The convention endorsed the idea of cooperation and authorized the establishment of a board of directors to advance union funds to local members sufficient for working capital. Shares in the Pittsburgh foundry were sold to union members throughout the country. But the Pittsburgh venture was a total failure and although union members owned fourteen local cooperative foundries by the end of 1869, the Molders' International abandoned the cooperative approach in 1870.

The model of industrial government which the molders adopted in their cooperatives was based on the principle of shareholding, with the majority of shares owned by the workers. In Sylvis' Pittsburgh project, shares cost only $5 each; no individual could own more than four hundred shares; and non-union members could not purchase stock unless the local group and the International Board of Directors had given approval. The reward to capital was to be 15 per cent of profits, no more than five per cent was to be put in a sinking fund, and the rest was to be distributed to the employees in proportion to wages as "interest on labor." A significant change made by the Toronto Convention of 1868 was to provide for 12 per cent of profits to go to capital, 12 per cent to labor, and the balance as determined by the stockholders. In various of the local cooperatives, 12 per cent of profits went to capital and the rest was divided among the stockholders employed in the foundry.

In pure theory, as Grossman noted, the producers' cooperative was intended to eliminate the profit-maker and to be run on the principles of direct democracy by the owner-producers. Each worker would have a single vote; the management would be selected by the workers; and major policies would be determined by group discussion and decision. All workers would be co-owners so that the employer-employee relationship and the

[8] Ibid., p. 203.

wages system operating within that relationship would be eliminated. Outsiders would have no voice in the government of the
enterprise. The small size of the average foundry—few exceeded
one hundred men—and the small capital required ($15,000 to
$20,000) made this view seem feasible. In practice, however,
the foundry cooperatives were joint-stock companies with majority ownership by the workers. They were often dominated
by a few of the original founders. Their most skillful managers
tended to break away and set up private establishments. They
lacked sufficient capital. "Most superintendents were grossly
incompetent; and in their foundries democracy was confused
with anarchy."[9]

Sylvis' interest in both job-control unionism and cooperation
took him in a third direction as far as industrial government was
concerned—national political action. But he turned to political
action for a variety of reasons of which the improvement of the
worker's position in the workplace was only one. At this time,
as well as later, many labor leaders felt that the basic problems
of labor could not be dealt with at the enterprise level but required governmental action. This belief was explicitly expressed
in the platform of the 1874 Industrial Congress at Rochester,
New York, which stated: " . . . We recognize in the ballot box
the great agency through which our wrongs can be redressed;
and . . . while we fully recognize the power and efficacy of trade
and labor unions, as now organized, in regulating purely trade
matters, yet upon all questions appertaining to the welfare of
the masses as a whole, the influence of these organizations, without closer union, must prove comparatively futile."[10]

In order to strengthen the political effectiveness of labor,
Sylvis joined other prominent labor leaders in forming the National Labor Union (1866–1872). The achievement of an eight-

---

[9] Ibid., p. 211.
[10] Quoted in George E. McNeill, ed., *The Labor Movement: The Problem of
Today* (Boston: A. M. Bridgman & Co., 1887), p. 152.

hour work day through legislation had become one of labor's primary objectives and the National Labor Union gave it top priority, urging "systematic agitation and the establishment of eight-hour leagues" and recommending "to every friend of the movement to vote for no candidate not unequivocally pledged to vote for a law making 'eight hours' a legal day's work." However, the program of the NLU contained several other planks bearing on industrial government.[11] Foremost among these was the endorsement of trade unionism. In the words of the committee trades' unions and strikes at the first annual meeting in 1866: "Recognizing as a fundamental truth that in 'union there is strength,' and believing also that all reforms in the labor movement can only be effected by an intelligent, systematic effort of the industrial classes, and believing also that that effort can at present best be directed through the trades' organizations, your committee would recommend the formation of unions in all localities where the same do not now exist, and the formation of an international organization in every branch of industry as a first and most important duty of the hour. . . ."[12] The committee also suggested a more rigid enforcement of the apprenticeship system, the discontinuance of strikes except as a last resort ("they have been productive of great injury to the laboring classes"), and the appointment by each trades' assembly of an "arbitration committee" to deal with all matters of dispute arising between employees and employers. The convention hailed "with delight the organization of cooperative stores and workshops" and urged their formation in every section of the country and in every branch of business. The principle of equal pay for equal work, as between men and women, was enunciated

[11] The following references to the NLU are taken from John R. Commons et al., eds., *A Documentary History of American Industrial History*, 2nd ed., vol. 9 (New York: Russell & Russell, Publishers, 1958), pp. 115 ff.

[12] Ibid., p. 130.

and a strong plea was made for inclusion in the ranks of organized labor of all workers regardless of race or nationality. The latter was mainly directed at Negro workers.[13]

During its short career, the National Labor Union increasingly shifted its focus from what might be regarded as specific "labor" issues to an attack on the financial interests of the country. Greenbackism, high interest rates, and the banking system drew particular attention. However, shortly before his death, Sylvis led a strong drive for the establishment of a federal department of labor and the gathering of labor and industrial statistics to further the interests of the working class. The National Labor Union also sponsored the formation of a labor reform party and subsequently allied itself with the Marxist-led International Workingmen's Association.

The shifts and turns in thinking and action which characterized the final decade of Sylvis' life were repeated over a much longer period and in even more diversified fashion in the career of George McNeill. After a few years as a shoeworker, McNeill began four decades of involvement in the labor movement as journalist, government statistician, organizer, union official, and politician. The phases of McNeill's thoughts and activities which have particular relevance to this study of industrial government deal with the eight-hour campaign, the Bureau of Labor Statistics, the Knights of Labor, the AFL, and Christian social reform.

McNeill's first solution for labor's plight, under the strong influence of Ira Steward, was the establishment by law of the eight-hour day. With Steward, he became the foremost advocate of eight-hour legislation, serving as president of the Boston Eight-Hour League. These men were strongly opposed to green-

---

[13] See A. C. Cameron, "The Address of the National Labor Congress to the Workingmen of the United States," in Commons et al., *Documentary History*, 9:141ff.

backism and other efforts to solve labor's problems through financial reform. They saw the eight-hour day not simply as a means of easing the burden of work but as a revolutionary force in a democratic society. It meant an increase in pay, more work for the unemployed, more hours for individual and public good. But beyond these gains, the eight-hour movement sought to give "to the laborer under the wage-system, first, the advantages now possessed by the capitalist until the profits upon his labor now obtained by the employer and middle-man shall so diminish and his own increase, that finally the profit upon labor shall cease, and cooperative labor be inaugurated in the place of wage-labor."[14]

McNeill turned to legislation because he believed that most employers were unwilling to enter into contractual relations with their employees. "The only opportunities for the nearest approach to the freedom of contract, is when a powerful labor organization has practically obtained a monopoly of their craft, —that is, that a manufacturer cannot employ help, unless they are members of the union. In this case, the manufacturer and the representatives of the employees meet on equal terms, provided that the organization is strong enough to remain from work for such a length of time as shall so diminish the capital invested in the enterprise as to cause bankruptcy."[15]

A second subject to which McNeill devoted much thought and effort was the establishment of state and federal bureaus of labor statistics. He was one of the lobbyists who succeeded in getting the Massachusetts legislature to establish the first Bureau of Statistics of Labor in 1869, and he was appointed deputy to the chief of the new bureau, serving in that position until 1873. Beginning with the National Labor Union, almost every important labor organization included in its constitution, platform, or some resolution support for the gathering of economic and industrial

[14] McNeill, *The Labor Movement*, p. 482.
[15] Ibid., pp. 479–480.

information which would throw light on the "educational, moral and financial condition" of the "producing masses."[16]

The recognition that the advancement of labor's interest depended upon factual information as well as upon shorter hours was reflected in an important way in the declaration of principles, measures, and methods of the International Labor Union of America. McNeill and Steward helped found it together with a group of Socialist trade unionists in 1878, and McNeill served as president. Although it had only a few thousand members scattered among seventeen states and expired in 1881, the ILU expressed sentiments which related directly to the theme of industrial democracy:

> The safety of society depends upon the equality of rights and opportunities of all its members; and whenever, from any cause, the freedom of a part of the community is endangered, either in their political or economic rights, it behooves the people to devise methods by which the usurpations of the powerful shall be overthrown, and the fullest freedom of the humblest be maintained. The political rights of a people are not more sacred than their economic rights, and to prevent a class from possessing all the material advantages of a progressive civilization is as much an act of tyranny as to prevent them from exercising their right of self-government.
>
> The victory over "divine-right" rulership must be supplemented by a victory over property-right rulers . . . those who control the industries of people can and do control their votes. . . .
>
> The liberty of labor is the hope of the world, and that liberty can only be obtained by the solidarity of laborers upon labor measures. We therefore, in the interests of a common brotherhood, declare:—
>
> 1st. That the wage-system is a despotism, under which the wage-

[16] See third resolution of platform of Rochester Industrial Congress, 1874, cited in McNeill, *The Labor Movement*, p. 152. McNeill attended the Congress as a representative of the Sovereigns of Industry, and served as chairman of the Committee on the Constitution.

worker is forced to sell his labor at such price and such conditions as the employer of labor shall dictate.

2nd. That political liberty cannot long continue under economic bondage. . . .

3rd. That civilization means the diffusion of knowledge and the distribution of wealth; and the present system of labor tends to extremes of culture and ignorance, affluence and penury.

. . .

5th. That as the wealth of the world is distributed through the wage system, its better distribution must come through higher wages, and better opportunities, until wages shall represent the earnings and not the necessities of labor; thus melting profit upon labor out of existence, and making cooperation, or self-employed labor, the natural and logical step from wage slavery to free labor.

. . .

7th. That the first step towards the emancipation of labor is a reduction of the hours of labor, that the added leisure produced by a reduction of the hours of labor will operate upon the natural causes that affect the habits and customs of the people, enlarging wants, stimulating ambition, decreasing idleness, and increasing wages.

. . . the objects shall be to secure the following measures: —The reduction of the hours of labor; higher wages, factory, mine, and workshop inspection; abolition of the contract convict labor and truck system; employers to be held responsible for accidents by neglected machinery; prohibition of child labor; the establishment of labor bureaus.[17]

It was during 1878 that the United States Congress undertook its first major investigation of labor conditions. Three years later the Knights of Labor abandoned its secrecy and began its phenomenal if short rise to leadership in the labor movement. McNeill became a member of the Knights in 1883, the secretary-

[17] Ibid., pp. 161–162.

treasurer of District 30 in Boston in 1884, and Washington representative in 1885. He was a member in 1886 of the Knights' nine-man committee, chaired by Frank K. Foster,[18] that attempted to promote an accommodation between the Knights and the national craft unions, which within a few months formed the American Federation of Labor. When the accommodation move failed and Terence Powderly, Grand Master Workman of the Knights, showed little enthusiasm for the eight-hour drive, McNeill left the Knights and joined the AFL. As a delegate from Massachusetts, he attended AFL conventions annually until 1898 when he attended the British Trade Union Congress meeting as AFL representative. He became a strong friend and supporter of Samuel Gompers.

One other strand of McNeill's labor wanderings is worth noting. In 1872 he helped form the Christian Labor Union in Boston—one of the first formal expressions of the Social Gospel movement in the United States.[19] Throughout his life he held strong views as a Christian Socialist, and in the 1890's he served as warden of the Mission of the Carpenter established by Reverend William D. P. Bliss in Boston. Because other individuals are more significant spokesmen of the views reflected by the Knights, the AFL, and the Social Gospel movement, McNeill's ideas in these sectors will not be treated here.

The diversity of activities and thoughts concerning industrial government portrayed in the careers of Sylvis and McNeill could be found in the lives of numerous labor leaders of the last third of the nineteenth century. What is important for this inquiry is the enormous variety of organizations and programs

---

[18] Foster soon became a leader of the AFL in Massachusetts and cooperated closely with McNeill, whose mantle as labor philosopher he began to assume. See Arthur Mann, *Yankee Reformers in the Urban Age: Social Reform in Boston 1880–1900* (New York: Harper Torchbook, 1966), pp. 188–200.

[19] See Robert C. Reinders, "T. Wharton Collens and the Christian Labor Union," *Labor History*, 8 (Winter 1967), 1:57, and Mann, *Yankee Reformers*, pp. 183–184.

which were competing for the loyalty and support of workers. The three most important were the Knights of Labor, the AFL, and the programs of the radicals.

THE KNIGHTS OF LABOR

The Knights meant many things to many people, and the behavior of Knight units often deviated from Knight principles, but the views expressed by its top leader during its heyday, Terence V. Powderly (1849–1924), and its formal statements of principle effectively convey its basic approach to industrial government. This approach had both a backward-looking and forward-looking dimension. It looked back in the sense that it appealed to all "producing classes" rather than to industrial workers and held up as its ideal the status of the independent artisan or farmer as transformed through the principle of cooperation. It was forward-looking in the sense that it preached the solidarity of skilled and unskilled workers and proposed organizational structures which would facilitate such solidarity. Both of these aspects are expressed in the 1878 preamble to the constitution or declaration of principles, which, as Terence Powderly pointed out, was a direct descendant of the constitutions of the National Labor Union (1866) and the Industrial Brotherhood (1874).[20] The fifteen goals of the Knights called for:

1. Organization throughout productive industry.
2. A fair share of the wealth and more leisure.
3. The establishment of bureaus of labor statistics.
4. The establishment of producers' and consumers' cooperatives.
5. The reserving of public lands for settlers.
6. Removal of laws that are not equal for capital and labor

[20] Terence Powderly, *Thirty Years of Labor: 1859 to 1889* (Columbus, Ohio: Excelsior Publishing, 1890), pp. 242–243.

and adoption of health and safety laws for workers in mining, manufacturing, and building.

7. Laws requiring weekly payment of wages in lawful
money.
8. Mechanics and laborers' lien laws.
9. The abolition of the contract system on public work.
10. The substitution of arbitration for strikes whenever and
wherever employers and employees are willing to meet
on equitable grounds.
11. Prohibition of child labor before age 14.
12. Abolition of contract labor of convicts.
13. Equal pay for equal work for both sexes.
14. The eight-hour day.
15. A national legal tender system.

In his book tracing the evolution of these goals and interpreting their intent, Powderly placed primary emphasis on political
action. "In accepting the preamble of the Industrial Brotherhood, the convention [of the Knights] fully realized that for the
most part the reforms which were asked for in that preamble
must one day come through political agitation and action."[21]
And in fact much of their activity was political, leading to the
establishment of state and federal bureaus of labor statistics and
later to the federal department of labor, to restrictions on Chinese immigration, and to the adoption of the anticontract labor
law. On the other hand the Knights, often despite the opposition
of Powderly and other national leaders, engaged in numerous
strikes and sought wage increases and improvements in employment conditions through collective bargaining. Thus, it is essential to distinguish theory and doctrine from practice.

It is clear that Powderly himself hoped that ultimately the
competitive wage system and private capitalism could be eliminated and replaced by a system of cooperation. This hope was

[21] Ibid., p. 248.

expressed in the 1884 revision of the preamble wherein it was agreed that all Knights would "endeavor to associate our labors; to establish co-operative institutions, such as will tend to supersede the wage system by the introduction of a co-operative industrial system."[22] Powderly did not expect such a reform to come quickly. However, he was both appalled and instructed by the rise of the combinations, trusts, and pools which were crushing "healthy competition." Cooperation of a few should be replaced by cooperation of the many. Despite the failure of many past cooperatives, such as those of the Iron Molders, the Knights set up a cooperative department and provided for a small per capita payment (10 cents per month for male members and 5 cents for women) to help finance cooperative undertakings. As Powderly candidly admitted, most of the cooperatives failed, partly because they were set up with little planning after or during a lost strike (a leading example was the mine at Cannelburg, Indiana), partly because workers lacked managerial ability, and partly because it was difficult to change the psychology of workers reared in a competitive wage system to a cooperative way of producing and distributing goods. Yet he was convinced that the cooperative principle would triumph in the end and would "eventually make every man his own master, —every man his own employer; a system which will give the laborer a fair proportion of the products of his toil."[23]

Also imbedded in the complex and confused mélange of Knight principles was a mild form of socialist thought. In 1884 following several serious strikes on the railroads and in the telegraph industry, the Knights added a new goal to their list: "that the Government shall obtain possession, by purchase, under the right of eminent domain, of all telegraphs, telephones, and railroads." It lobbied seriously but vainly in 1887 for the nationalization of the Western Union telegraph company which had

[22] Ibid., p. 453.
[23] Ibid., p. 464.

recently absorbed its rivals and established a virtual monopoly. By this time it was past its zenith and on the road to rapid decline.

In one important respect the Knights were in advance of their age. As Powderly stressed, until quite recently the belief was widespread that "only the man who was engaged in manual toil could be called a workingman." The Knights sought to broaden this concept to include "the draughtsman, the timekeeper, the clerk, the reporter, or the worst paid, most abused and illy appreciated of all toilers—woman." The only categories excluded were the banker, lawyer, and liquor dealer. For Powderly personally and for a significant segment of the reform movement, excess drinking was viewed as a serious ailment of many workers. He claimed that at least one hundred thousand members took the "Powderly pledge" to abstain from hard liquor.

THE AMERICAN FEDERATION OF LABOR

The national trade or craft unions which constructed the AFL in 1866 were based on a very different set of assumptions from the Knights. Although they used the language of class struggle, their principal objective was to improve the lot of their members within the existing private enterprise, wage-earner system. This meant the development of strong, well-financed, disciplined union organizations, bargaining with employers from a position of strength, seeking maximum control over jobs within a clearly defined job territory, continuously improving the standards and conditions of employment, and raising the status of workers to a position of respect and dignity. The federation leaders regarded the producers' cooperatives as impracticable in the new industrializing economy; they had little faith in the socialist's vision of publicly owned and managed enterprises. They recognized the importance of political action to protect the unorganized, to prevent unfair competition from such difficult-to-control sources as prison labor or cheap contract labor from abroad, and as defenses against hostile courts, but they placed major reliance upon their economic strength within their own industries. Given respect and fair treatment, they were prepared to help stabilize their industries through signed agreements of fixed duration, to use conciliatory methods, and to forego the strike except as a last resort.

Samuel Gompers epitomized this approach. In testifying before the Senate Committee on Education and Labor in August 1883, he listed as two objectives the guarantee of payment to workers as taking precedence over compensation to the capitalist and the achievement of a just and reasonable wage. But he was also concerned about the treatment of the men in the factories—not as slaves but as men. "The machinery is guarded against rust, and, when passing, if one of the arms or wheels or belts is rather lower than the other, the employer will take off his hat and pass beneath it. We do not ask the employer to take off his hat to his employes, but we do say that 'good morning' will not hurt him, more especially when he is spoken to."[24] Gompers at this time was willing to accept arbitration of economic issues, but only under certain conditions, namely that the workers had equal bargaining power with the employers and that employers who could not compete effectively in the product market without using cheap labor should be put out of business. He also suggested three governmental "remedies," the first two of which he was later to repudiate: the passage and enforcement of a national eight-hour law, the right of unions to become incorporated, and the establishment of a national bureau of labor statistics (achieved in 1884).

When Gompers testified before the U.S. Industrial Commission in 1899, the AFL was in the midst of its first great perma-

[24] *Report of the Committee of the Senate upon the Relations between Labor and Capital,* 1 (Washington, D.C.: Government Printing Office, 1885):377.

nent advance, and he could speak with the confidence of a leader whose views had outpaced all competitors. As in his 1883 testimony, he expressed the view that the relationship between employees and their employers was based on the age-old conflict of interest between the possessors of wealth and the producers of wealth, and that the exercise of power was a decisive factor. When power existed on both sides, then the relationship could be based on reason. Thus, he strongly defended the right to strike—much more than in the earlier period, although even then he was anxious to distinguish the good points of strikes.

> Strikes have convinced the employers of the economic advantage of reduced hours of labor; strikes have rid many a trade of the "jerry builder"; of the fraudulent employer who won't pay wages; strikes have enforced lien laws for wages, where laws have been previously unable to secure the payment; strikes have organized employers as well as employees; strikes have made strong and independent men who were for a long period of years cowards; strikes have made a more independent citizenship of men who often voted simply because it pleased the boss; strikes have given men greater lease of life; strikes have resulted in higher wages, better homes, demand for better things. . . . The strike has taken the place of the barbarous weapons of the dirk and bludgeon. Strikes in the modern sense can occur only in civilized countries.[25]

In contrast to his earlier position, he was now opposed to the incorporation of unions and the enforcement of written agreements through the courts. "The terms of a contract between an employer and the employees are generally observed, not because of the written agreement or the contract, but because of the power of the organization."[26] Gompers felt that the employ-

---

[25] *Report of the Industrial Commission on the Relations and Conditions of Capital and Labor, Hearings on April 18, 1899,* 7 (Washington, D.C.: Government Printing Office):608.

[26] Ibid., p. 602.

er had many methods of evading agreements with weak unions and that court proceedings would be more likely to favor the employer rather than the union.

His reliance on government legislation was also tempered by the growth in union power. He approved legislation for women and children and he supported the eight-hour law for public employees, but he felt that for male workers in private industry, union pressure was the best solution. At a time when the rise of the trusts was a major public issue, he believed that legislation of a restrictive nature would prove futile. He had no objection to the trusts in principle. He felt that the unions could cope with them through collective bargaining. He cited the strength of the iron and steel workers' union as an example—an unfortunate choice in view of its disastrous defeat at the hands of the new United States Steel Corporation two years later.

Gompers' attitude toward the wage system of industrial government was thoroughly pragmatic. When asked whether he believed in the wage system, he responded:

> I can not assent to that. I know that we are operating under the wage system. As to what system will ever come to take its place I am not prepared to say. I have given this subject much thought; I have read the works of the most advanced economists, competent economists in all schools of thought—the trade unionist, the socialist, the anarchist, the single taxer, the cooperationist, etc. I am not prepared to say, after having read, and with an honest endeavor to arrive at a conclusion—I am not prepared to say that either of their propositions are logical, scientific, or natural. I know that we are living under the wage system, and so long as that lasts, it is our purpose to secure a continually larger share for labor, for the wealth producers. . . . For the present it is our purpose to secure better conditions and instill a larger amount of manhood and independence into the hearts and minds of the workers, and to broaden their mental sphere and the sphere of the affections.[27]

[27] Ibid., p. 645.

He was very suspicious of the intentions of employers who advocated profit-sharing plans; he thought that colonization schemes of cooperation were unrealistic and a withdrawal from the world.

As to the union-management relationship, he was vigorously opposed to compulsory arbitration on the ground that it might compel a man to work under conditions which were abhorrent to him—that was involuntary servitude or slavery. He favored conciliation for the settlement of disputes and had no objection to voluntary arbitration. He was even willing to accept compulsory arbitration under some conditions provided that it did not involve the compulsory enforcement of the terms of the award, but rather relied on the weight of public judgment and opinion. He was, of course, for higher wages and shorter hours. He approved of the sliding wage scale if there was a standard minimum to assure a "living wage." He opposed overtime work except in case of absolute necessity, because otherwise it would become the rule and wages paid for the longer period would be no higher than for the shorter period. Overtime, he observed, shortens the seasons of employment, makes the workman slovenly, deadens his senses, makes him careless of himself and his fellows. The eight-hour day was essential to counteract the speed and tension of work brought about by the machine. The apprenticeship system which had once been so important to the unions in the shops had declined in importance because of technological change. Requiring workers to buy from company stores was both an infringement on the freedom and mobility of citizens and a source of overcharging. Gompers also insisted that the AFL was opposed to racial discrimination in practice as well as in principle.

Within a few years Gompers was to make a much more positive and explicit statement for the signed agreement system as the constitutional basis for industrial democracy. The words *industrial democracy* had not yet come into his vocabulary. Although written collective bargaining agreements had been gradually growing in importance since the end of the Civil War, and the 1898 bituminous coal agreement was a tremendous achievement, Gompers was testifying at a time when stable and enduring agreement systems were still a rarity.

THE RADICALS

Labor's grievances in the period under discussion led to an extraordinary range of radical doctrines—from the pacific ideas of Christian Socialists to the revolutionary anarchism of the Black International. Most of the doctrines came from abroad, brought by immigrant followers of Marx, Lassalle, Proudhon, Bakunin, Kropotkin, the British Fabians, and other European thinkers. Some were native products such as Laurence Gronland's revision of Marx,[28] Henry George's single tax program, and Edward Bellamy's planned, nationalized society. Most of the originators of radical programs were not manual workers themselves, but their ideas found many receptive ears among workers in this period.

The radicals had only one theme in common, hostility to the prevailing laissez faire capitalist system. By and large, however, radical thought had slight focus on the manner in which industrial enterprise should be governed. Instead, attention was devoted to how society as a whole should be reorganized and to the means for gaining the necessary power to institute the change, i.e., through revolution, political action, or trade union tactics. The main exceptions were the "utopians" like the earlier Fourierites and Bellamy, and these had more a middle-class than a working-class appeal.

[28] Laurence Gronland, *The Cooperative Commonwealth* (Cambridge: Harvard University Press, 1965), which was published originally in 1884, placed strong emphasis on social democracy and envisioned the operation of industry in terms of civil service and town hall government. See particularly chapters 6 and 8.

Nevertheless, certain characteristics of socialist thought about how industrial government should function are revealed in their manifestos, declarations of principle, and other publications. For example, the Pittsburgh manifest (1883) of the anarcho-syndicalist International Working People's Association, which was mainly a vigorous attack on reformers and an unrestrained advocacy of the use of force to achieve the destruction of capitalism, called for, among other things, establishment of a free society based upon cooperative organization of production, equal rights for all without distinction of sex or race, and regulation of all public affairs by free contracts between the autonomous (independent) communes and associations, resting on a federalist basis.[29] In these respects, the revolutionary anarchists shared common ground with the pacifistic communitarians of the 1890's who, like the "utopians" of the 1840's, believed that the establishment of cooperative small colonies would provide an example of the new society.

At the other end of the spectrum was the highly centralized planned system proposed by Edward Bellamy and endorsed by many of the Christian Socialists as well as others. Although the overwhelming tone of Bellamy's conception stressed cooperation and harmony, the elimination of competitive struggle, and full equality of employment and income as well as social rights among all members of the population, the productive system he envisioned was constructed on military principles and framed in military terms.[30] All adults between the ages of 21 and 45 were required to participate in the "industrial army" and three allied corps: the women's army, the professional army, and the

[29] Quoted in John R. Commons et al., *History of Labour in the United States,* 4 vols. (New York: Augustus M. Kelley, Publisher, 1918–1935), 2:295.

[30] This appraisal of Bellamy's system of industrial government is indebted to Sylvia E. Bowman, *The Year 2000: A Critical Biography of Edward Bellamy* (New York: Bookman Associates, 1958), especially chapter 6. Miss Bowman describes the Bellamy system as "industrial democracy" although Bellamy himself did not use the term in his two main works, *Looking Backward* (1888) and *Equity* (1897).

invalid's army. The President of the federal government was to be commander-in-chief of the industrial army, its top disciplinarian, and the enforcer of the law. The department heads on the President's council were called lieutenant-generals. After three years of general service, every member of the industrial army was to be assigned work in part on the basis of his desires but mainly in terms of his abilities and aptitudes as judged by the officials of the Labor Exchange, as well as the needs of the society. The top managerial staffs were to be elected by the citizens over the age of 45 who had served in the particular department or bureau involved. Lower level officials were to be appointed. Pay and conditions of work were to be equalized to the greatest extent possible. Incentives for high achievement were public recognition and election or appointment to some office. Officials could be replaced at any time by a vote of their electing body. Complaints of unfair treatment and other grievances were to be handled through the courts. There would be no need for trade unions. Planning for the economy was to be highly centralized and orders for production and distribution were to be handed down from the top. These and other details suggest a highly regimented system, but Bellamy thought of it as democratic because he believed that human nature would be so changed by the elimination of class inequalities and struggle as to minimize the coercive elements. Popular control over the officialdom was to be preserved by majority rule of the citizens over 45 and the members of the professional army. Members of the industrial army would not have voting privileges until they reached the retirement age, but then they would have complete equality.

Between these extremes of anarcho-syndicalism and Bellamy nationalism, the socialists fell into two main categories: those who stressed the political process and those who preferred the industrial process. These were not sharply demarcated. There were many possible combinations. The orthodox Marxists, like Daniel De Leon who dominated the Socialist Labor party from the early 1890's till his death in 1914, either explicitly or implicitly envisaged three stages requiring very different forms of industrial government. The first was the contemporary capitalistic stage in which trade unionism was to be primarily an educational and tactical instrument to help achieve worker control over the society, although primary reliance was to be placed on political means. After failures in attempts to dominate both the Knights of Labor and the AFL, the Socialist Labor party set up the Socialist Trade and Labor Alliance in late 1895 as its union arm. A party statement at its tenth national convention in 1900 stated the attitude toward trade unionism as follows:

1. We conceive the genuine trade union as a militant labor body, originating from the very nature of the class struggle under capitalism, instituted to resist the degradation and promote the elevation, not only of its own members, but of the whole working class, and destined, therefore, to act an important part in the war for social emancipation.

Since capitalism, with its consequent wage systems, rests upon institutions essentially political, genuine trade unionism, as above defined, not only must fight in the shop every work day the individual exploiters of labor, but must especially, uncompromisingly, at all costs and all hazards, fight the political parties of capitalism on election day. . . .

2. . . . the bogus trade unionism, now known as "trade unionism pure and simple," from which the natural, fundamental purpose of union, namely, the conduct of the class struggle with a constant view to the complete emancipation of the wage working class, is entirely banished, and in which capitalism is accepted as a finality.[31]

The second stage was to be reached when the workers gained control over the political and economic institutions of society—

[31] *Proceedings of the Tenth National Convention of the Socialist Labor Party,* June 2–June 8, 1900 (New York: New York Labor News Co., 1901), pp. 198–199.

a period of centralized planning and direction. The unions then were to serve as an arm of the state in furthering its economic goals. Ultimately, and vaguely, would come the third and final stage of the cooperative commonwealth, no longer requiring the coercive elements of statehood.

Prior to the break of the DeLeonists with the AFL, socialists belonging to the Socialist Labor party, as well as those outside the party, made a strong and almost successful effort to win the AFL to their program. In 1893, Thomas Morgan, the Chicago socialist leader and former machinist, introduced at the AFL Convention an eleven-plank program which won widespread support among AFL unions. Only astute maneuvering by Gompers and his allies prevented adoption of the entire program although all but the tenth item were individually approved. The following items had particular relevance to industrial government:

3. A legal eight-hour workday.

4. Sanitary inspection of workshop, mine, and home.

5. Liability of employers for injury to health, body, or life.

6. The abolition of the contract system in all public work.

7. The abolition of the sweating system.

8. The municipal ownership of street cars and gas and electric plants for public distribution of light, heat, and power.

9. The nationalization of telegraphs, telephones, railroads, and mines.

10. The collective ownership by the people of all means of production and distribution.[32]

To right-wing socialists like Max Hayes of the printers and Victor Berger, the Milwaukee leader, the twin routes to the socialist cooperative commonwealth were independent political action and trade unionism. Pending the achievement of the socialist state through evolutionary means (akin to British Fabian-

---

[32] Item 1 called for compulsory education, Item 2 for direct legislation, and Item 11 for the use of the referendum in legislation.

ism), they were content to extend industrial democracy through wider organization (especially of the unskilled and semiskilled) in industrial unions such as the Brewery Workers and the Mine Workers and through the development of systems of collective bargaining, supplemented by the passage of laws to establish acceptable minimum employment standards. The first two decades of the twentieth century were to be the high point of socialist success in the United States in both the political and economic arenas.

CHAPTER 3

ALTERNATIVE SEARCHES
FOR A NEW MODEL

LABOR LEADERS and socialists were not the only searchers for a viable system of industrial democracy in the new industrial order that was emerging so rapidly and so haphazardly in the post–Civil War decades. Although the typical employer remained wedded to the notion that he had the right to run his enterprise as he saw fit,[1] a number of more sensitive and far-

---

[1] What seems to have been a generally held employer view was presented by a well-known capitalist of the period, Henry W. Sage of Ithaca, New York, at a discussion sponsored by Cornell University on the "Labor Problem" in August 1886. In his brief comments, Sage asserted: "There is no danger here that the men who organize our great enterprises of commerce, manufactures, or transportation will deal unjustly with the laborers who are their instruments and helpers. They have not done so; on the contrary, all the great organizations of capital and able men for such enterprises have been beneficent to labor—increasing vastly its area and uses, and increasing the wages paid for it. They have paid labor its full value to them, and all they can afford to, the proof of which is that nowhere are wages so high as here, nowhere do laborers have so many comforts as here. . . . The world owes no man a living unless he squarely earns it. Let this be remembered. The farmer cannot have corn without plowing and planting, gathering and saving. The remedy for present evils is not in combinations to force from capital already earned, and possessed by somebody, an unjust demand for more wages—that is the freebooter's method; not by co-operative partnerships, not by schemes of social reformers, who assume that they can manage the affairs of all mankind with more wisdom than they have yet acquired, each acting for himself under the pressure of his own interests. The world is not ready yet to accept or even to try the methods of these self-appointed reformers. The remedy

sighted employers recognized that new approaches were needed, not only for humane reasons but because they were more appropriate to industrial society. Similar concerns were held by individuals in other sectors of the nation—political figures like Governor Altgeld of Illinois, academicians like Richard T. Ely and Henry C. Adams, engineers like Frederick W. Taylor, clergymen like Washington Gladden and William D. P. Bliss, social workers like Jane Addams, and novelists like William Dean Howells. This chapter will be devoted to an examination of some of their views.

Three Employer Views: Hewitt, Nelson, Carnegie

Abram S. Hewitt (1822–1903), iron manufacturer, congressman, mayor of New York City, was chairman of the first Congressional committee to focus on "the labor problem" following the national shock of the great railroad strikes of 1877. Unfortunately, he never completed the interpretative report which he started to make on the basis of the thousand pages of testimony. However, in 1878 he delivered a widely discussed speech at a church congress in Cincinnati on "The Mutual Relations of Capital and Labor,"[2] based partly on the public hearings held

---

is in the moral elevation of men to the point where they are willing to do justly, to perform their contracts, to be true to all their obligations; to be industrious, prudent, saving; to practice self-denial when need be while laying foundations for future wealth and comfort; and to be contented and manly in the sphere wherein God has placed them. These qualities in the laborer, and on the part of the employer such breadth of justice, wisdom, and kindness as we may reasonably expect, will best serve to build up the great industrial interests of this country, and will always insure the rights of both by wise and peaceable methods. Until this moral condition is reached, there is but one other remedy by which turbulence and anarchy, such as now exist in portions of our country, can be suppressed. That is in these three words—'*Enforce the laws!*'" From *Scientific American Supplement*, 556 (August 28, 1886):8877.

2 For a discussion of Hewitt's labor views, see Allan Nevins, *Abram S. Hewitt, with Some Account of Peter Cooper* (New York: Harper and Bros., 1935), espe-

by his committee and partly on his personal industrial experiences and observations. In contrast to most employers of his time, Hewitt strongly favored unionism, especially the type of craft union which was soon to form the AFL. He was also a staunch advocate of conciliation and arbitration, as practiced in England, for the resolution of disputes between labor and capital. He thought that conflict between these two classes was inevitable because of the growth and concentration of wealth, and labor's desire for a fair share. Strikes of powerful worker-organizations against powerful employers were ultimately destructive, but they served the purpose of compelling the employer to listen to labor's case. If the evils of contemporary industry were to be eliminated or significantly curtailed, however, the solution lay in the development of a system of "joint ownership," by which he meant worker stock-ownership and profit sharing. Mutual interest rather than either conflict or charity was the key. "Until labor becomes an owner it never will understand the capacity of business to pay."[3] Steadiness and stability of business would emerge from this understanding between labor and capital as well as from closer association of different organizations engaged in the same kinds of business—thus mitigating the evils of the competitive system.

The transition to joint ownership, Hewitt noted, would be facilitated by the fact that labor and capital already practiced "free and open discussion," employers opened their books to arbitration tribunals when the issue of ability to pay was raised, workers were free to "proclaim their grievances and to assert

---

cially pp. 409–419 and 510. This speech was appended to a speech on "The Emancipation of Labor" (urging free trade) which Hewitt delivered in the House of Representatives, April 30, 1884, and which was separately published.

[3] A considerable literature in favor of "industrial partnership" through profit sharing and worker stock-ownership appeared in the 1870's. An interesting example is J. N. Larned, *Talks about Labor* (New York: Appleton, 1876). See also Washington Gladden, *Working People and Their Employers* (Boston: Lockwood, Brooks, & Co., 1876). These works usually were critical of the trade unions.

their rights," and workers accepted the decisions of arbitrators. Hewitt believed that workers needed a good deal more education in order to contribute significantly to the progress of business, but he also believed that the advancement of education in the United States was proceeding at an encouraging rate. If labor saved and invested its money in business enterprises, "in a generation the whole capital invested in industrial undertakings might be transferred to the wage-earning class." Although these thoughts seemed to reflect a view of industrial society composed of small establishments and simple technology, Hewitt was well aware of corporate growth and technological development—unlike many of the reformers in the labor movement of the 1860's and 1870's, he was looking ahead to the future and not back to the past.

In the next two decades the idea of profit sharing impressed a number of employers and others as a possible cure for the ills of industrial government. In 1892 the Association for the Promotion of Profit Sharing was established, with Carroll Wright, the federal commissioner of labor statistics, as president, and the Reverend Nicholas P. Gilman as its intellectual spearhead.

One of the pioneers among the employers and a fluent spokesman for profit sharing was N. O. Nelson (1844–1922), head of a St. Louis manufacturing establishment. Nelson appears to have been greatly disturbed by the economic waste and the emotional frictions resulting from a series of strikes on St. Louis street car lines and other area strikes. Following the great 1886 strike on the Gould Southwest rail lines, which he tried, as member of a three-man committee, to mediate, he introduced a profit-sharing plan for his 500 employees, based on the experience of two French companies—Leclaire and Godin. In 1890 he set up the village of Leclaire, Illinois, across the Mississippi River from his factory, and transferred some of his operations there.

Nelson called his system "industrial democracy" although he, its head and sponsor, was not to be elected by the employees. His explanation was grounded on an interesting, if unconvincing, assumption of Social Darwinism:

> The administration by one permanent head is a necessity, if the best results in manufacturing are to be attained. Such heads, as a rule, will be an evolution of the fittest. They are most frequently drawn from the rank and file, promoted by reasons of adaptability to their station. The relation of master and servant appears historically to be itself an evolution; first, as slave, without rights; then as serfs, with certain personal, but no property, rights; and at the present-time, wage-workers, nominally free, but in reality dependent.[4]

Nelson described profit sharing in both political and economic terms:

> This is what profit sharing or participation essays to create. It is a democracy in which capital represents the constitution, management represents the government, and clerks and workmen the people. Monarchists have never failed to find fatal flaws in democratic structures, and yet democracies have developed the strongest individualism and the greatest security to the rights of all. Industrial democracy is quite as feasible and advantageous. The essential features of profit sharing are to pay customary wages to all employees, including managers; pay interest on capital, and divide the remaining profits rateably upon wages and capital. Proceeding upon the assumption that wages have been adjusted according to the value of the services contributed by each, the same standard is equally accurate as the basis for dividing the profits.[5]

Fourteen years later, in an affidavit submitted to the U.S. Industrial Commission in 1901, Nelson argued that profit sharing as he conceived it was morally right as well as economically

---

[4] N. O. Nelson, "Profit Sharing," *North American Review*, 265 (April 1887): 390.

[5] Nelson, "Debate on Profit Sharing," *Journal of Social Science*, 23 (November 1887):63.

efficient. "That such a joint interest will, in the long run, affect the quality of work seems to me an unavoidable conclusion, and upon this general reason the economic value of the system must rest." Ultimately, he foresaw that the employees would be recognized as the "vital element" in the business association. He had no objection to the employees joining unions, but the basic relationship was one of mutuality of interest and therefore strikes were inconceivable.

In keeping with his beliefs, Nelson in 1895 offered one of his cabinet plants at Leclaire to the employees on easy, deferred terms, with the expectation that he would do the same with the others later. The offer was first rejected and then accepted; the plant was set up as a self-governing workshop. But for reasons which are not entirely clear, the experiment was a failure and the plant reverted to its original status. Despite this setback, Nelson continued in his remaining active years to seek new forms of industrial government. Thus in 1905 he modified his profit-sharing plan by offering customers as well as employees the opportunity of becoming co-owners of the company. Profits beyond 6 per cent interest on capital were henceforth to be distributed in the proportion of 1 per cent to employees on wages and salaries and 1.5 per cent to customers on gross profits on their purchases. Whereas employees were required, after 1888, to take their dividends in stocks, the customers had the option of taking them either in stocks or cash.

The most important industrialist of the late nineteenth century to propound public ideas on how the labor difficulties of the time could be resolved was Andrew Carnegie (1835–1919). A self-made man, who had started work as a "bobbin-boy" at twelve and rose to steel magnate and multimillionaire, Carnegie was an outstanding example of the combination of Social Darwinism and Christian trusteeship (the Social Gospel).[6] A staunch

6 See Andrew Carnegie, *The Gospel of Wealth and Other Timely Essays* (New York: The Century Co., 1901).

individualist, he opposed the ideas of producers' cooperation and profit sharing because they ran counter to human nature. Not all people were equally competent to run industry. Rewards in industry should be based on ability. If workers genuinely wanted to become owners of industry, they could easily purchase stocks. On the other hand, Carnegie endorsed collective organization of workers in large-scale enterprises which were no longer managed by their owners but "by salaried officers, who cannot possibly have any permanent interest in the welfare of the working-man." In these enterprises the historic personal ties between employer and employees had been broken and could only be replaced by direct discussions between representatives of the workers and the managers. Carnegie accepted unionism but preferred organizations of men by establishment, with the representatives, "the natural leaders, the best men," selected from within the establishment. "The right of the working-man to combine and to form trades-unions is no less sacred than the right of the manufacturer to enter into associations and conferences with his fellows, and it must sooner or later be conceded."[7]

He believed that most difficulties could be resolved between management and labor if they held three or four meetings each year to discuss matters of common interest and if wages were paid to the men on the basis of a sliding scale which varied with the price received for the product—an idea utilized in the iron and coal industries since the 1860's. On the assumption that prices were closely related to profits, Carnegie declared that the employer and employees under the sliding scale system would share prosperity and adversity and would thereby develop a mutuality of interest.

He recognized that not all difficulties would be eliminated. To avoid strikes, he advocated the use of voluntary arbitration, in

[7] Ibid., "An Employer's View of the Labor Question," p. 114.

the English tradition, by neutral, competent third parties, drawn preferably from the ranks of retired businessmen or the ex-presidents of trade unions. The arbitrator's award was to be binding on the parties and to take effect as of the date of reference. He expected few cases to go to arbitration because the parties would prefer to settle their own affairs "within the family" than to go to outsiders.

Strikes and lockouts would not be permitted under this system unless one of the parties refused to agree to arbitration. In the event of a strike, Carnegie advised employers not to attempt to operate the establishment with the use of strikebreakers unless some vital public service were involved because this would create bitterness and conflict and would, in any event, require the employment of inferior workmen. He also cautioned against the quick dismissal of worker representatives because of the loyalty which workers attach to their leaders.

Displaying keen insight into the psychology of workers, Carnegie urged managers to devote some part of their attention to searching out the causes of disaffection among their employees and to meet the men more than halfway to allay them. "There is nothing but good for both parties to be derived from labor teaching the representative of capital the dignity of man, as man. The working-man, becoming more and more intelligent, will hereafter demand the treatment due to an equal."[8]

Finally, Carnegie placed stress on the importance of establishing reasonable standards of labor. He noted that many men were still working in 1886 over ten hours per day, and in some industries over twelve. These should be reduced to ten and gradually, by half-hour intervals, to eight. But he strongly opposed the eight-hour movement which called for an immediate two-hour reduction from ten to eight because this was uneconomic. He endorsed a half-holiday on Saturday, a policy which was proving

[8] Ibid., "Results of the Labor Struggle," p. 132.

highly successful in England. Public opinion would support workers when they made reasonable demands; it would oppose them when they were unreasonable or turned to violence. It is worth noting, however, that in 1892 when Henry C. Frick, as the new chairman of the Carnegie Steel Corporation, deliberately set out to break the power of the Amalgamated Association of Iron and Steel Workers at Homestead, Carnegie made no effort to restrain Frick. As so often happened among leading employers of the time, his liberal words were not matched by corresponding actions in his enterprises.

The Engineers

Another segment of industry, the engineers, began to develop the theme that the solution to the labor problem was to be found in a more scientific approach to the wage system—not, as Nelson had suggested, by sharing profits or, as Carnegie had proposed, by linking wages to prices, but by relating wages to costs and productivity. In an address to the American Society of Mechanical Engineers in 1886, entitled significantly "The Engineer as an Economist," Henry Towne (1844–1924), owner-manager of the Yale and Towne Manufacturing Company of Stamford, Connecticut, had called attention to the great and growing importance of shop management and the need for managers to combine the roles of the businessman and the mechanical engineer. He urged the ASME, of which he was then vice president, to set up a special division to concentrate on problems of shop management and shop accounting. An exclusive concern with machines and machine methods was no longer sufficient. About the same time he turned his attention to the wage question which was the source of so much contemporary conflict.

Towne rejected profit sharing because profits were dependent on many factors uninfluenced by workers. Sharing profits, in his view, was little more than an act of charity and not relished by intelligent and self-respecting men. "Certainly the problem we are considering will be best solved if it can be so formulated that the element of gratuity or charity, of giving without tangible consideration, can be eliminated, and that, as presented to the employee, it becomes an invitation from the principal that they should enter into an industrial partnership, wherein each will retain, unimpaired, his existing equitable rights, but will share with the other the benefits, if any are realized, of certain new contributions made by each to the common interest."[9]

Towne's plan, which he introduced in his foundry in 1887, was to make a careful analysis of production costs and to share any gains in efficiency (as reflected in cost reduction) with the fore- man and the workers in the ratio of 50 per cent to the company, 10 per cent to the foreman, and 40 per cent to the workers pro- portioned according to the wages actually earned during the year. The cost gains were to be computed monthly, but to be paid annually. The company guaranteed payment of regular wages earned by each employee, on daywork or piecework, re- gardless of the profit situation.

The plan was embodied in a written contract between the company and its employees. The shop rules of the company were made part of the contract. Only two conditions were attached, but they were important in explaining the company motivations. Participation in the sharing of "gains" was to be forfeited by an employee "in the event of discharge by reason of misconduct or incompetency, or in the event of his combining with others in any way to disturb or affect the relations between the Company and its employees."[10]

In 1891, two years after Towne presented his paper on gain sharing to the ASME, F. A. Halsey challenged both profit shar-

[9] Henry R. Towne, "Gain Sharing," reproduced in American Economic As- sociation, *Economic Studies*, 1 (New York: Macmillan Co., 1896), 2:54.
[10] Ibid., p. 73.

ing and gain sharing on the grounds that the promised rewards were too remote, that they were not based on the direct efforts of the individual employee, and that workers had no way of knowing if the agreement was being carried out unless a worker committee was allowed to inspect the books—a process to which most employers would object and which, in any event, workers were not competent to conduct. Halsey's alternative was a "premium plan" in which the worker received a premium payment for every hour of work saved as measured by previous experience. The premium was appreciably less than the regular hourly pay, but increased with each hour saved. The specific premium rate was to be determined on the basis of "good sense and judgment" in each case, and, once set, was not to be cut. Halsey's conclusion was typical of the engineer's prevailing notion of worker psychology:

> . . . the writer confidently predicts that the more it [the plan] is studied the more perfect will appear its adaptation to the requirements of industrial enterprise and human nature. Surely, a system which increases output, decreases cost, and increases workman's earnings simultaneously, without friction, and by the silent force of its appeal to every man's desire for a larger income, is worthy of attention. . . . No opposition to it, organized or otherwise, is possible, since there is nothing compulsory about it, and nothing tangible to oppose. It is simply an offer to gratify one of the strongest passions of human nature, and the difficulty often found in introducing piece-work cannot occur with this.[11]

Three years later, in 1895, Frederick W. Taylor presented his first notable paper on the subject, entitled "A Piece-Rate System: Being a Step Toward Partial Solution of the Labor Problem." Taylor was just on the threshold of developing his comprehensive system of scientific management (to be discussed in chapter 7). At this stage his principal focus was on three elements: the

[11] Ibid., pp. 84–85.

introduction of a method of rate-fixing through time study of the elementary operations of a job; the use of a differential rate system of piece work in which a high price per piece is given if the work is finished in the shortest possible time and in perfect condition, while a low price is given if it takes a longer time to do the work or if there are imperfections; and payment of men rather than positions when daywork operates.

Taylor challenged the traditional ways of production management without system or method. He challenged the daywork plan of grouping workers into occupational classes and paying them a standard rate of wages for each class. He argued that ordinary piecework encouraged "soldiering" and deceit among workers. He criticized Towne and agreed with Halsey that a proper pay plan must allow "free scope for each man's personal ambition." He also shared Halsey's critique of profit sharing. But he believed that Halsey's incentive was inadequate and, more important, did not involve scientific time study of jobs.

Taylor felt that trade unions, particularly the English unions, had "rendered a great service, not only to their members but to the world, in shortening the hours of labor and in modifying the hardships and improving the conditions of wage-workers."[12] But his system would make unions and strikes unnecessary. He cited his ten years of strike-free experience at Midvale Steel in contrast to the rest of the industry. More than differential rates were involved, however. It was the policy of the company to stimulate the personal ambitions of every employee by keeping records of the men's good and weak points and rewarding achievement by wage increases and promotions. They also were careful to talk to men on their own level, never condescending, and they encouraged men to discuss their problems, whether plant or outside, freely with their bosses.

[12] Ibid., p. 128.

Some Public Views

The problems of labor and industrial relations troubled many socially minded people who were not direct participants in industrial life, but who believed that industrial strife could endanger the welfare of the entire society. For a number of them it became essential to discard the prevailing laissez faire approach, to encourage labor organization as a countervailing force to the corporations, and to involve government in industrial affairs.

HENRY C. ADAMS, ACADEMICIAN

One of the most insightful of these "outsiders" was Professor Henry C. Adams (1851–1921) of the University of Michigan and Cornell University who helped to found the American Economic Association in 1885 on an anti–laissez faire platform. This platform was later set aside to win the cooperation of the more conservative academicians who were still in the majority, but its main theme was not forgotten by the "young Turks" who drafted it: "We regard the state as an agency whose positive assistance is one of the indispensable conditions of human progress. . . . We hold that the conflict of labor and capital has brought into prominence a vast number of social problems, whose solution requires the united efforts, each in its own sphere of the church, of the state, and of science."[13]

In 1886, in response to a series of questions distributed by a St. Louis trade journal, the *Age of Steel*, Adams expressed the views that strikes and lockouts were an inevitable consequence of the wages system, that there could be no permanent solution

[13] Richard T. Ely, *Report of the Organization of the American Economic Association*, 1 (Baltimore: Publications of the American Economic Association, March 1886): 35–36.

of the labor problem as long as the wages system existed, that arbitration was not the solution but it was a useful first step in overthrowing the wages system, that "co-operation" (i.e., producers'-consumers' cooperatives) was not a practical answer, but that the remedy lay in the direction of industrial partnerships (dependent unfortunately on the charity or self-interests of isolated employers) and ultimately industrial federation (a system of legally enforceable rights).[14]

Adams presented a much more sophisticated and original analysis of the labor problem in a Cornell University lecture.[15] In it he observed that labor organizations had set for themselves a "new purpose." The right to combine was no longer denied. Until recently, unions had struggled over wages, hours, and apprentice regulations. But now they were trying to create for themselves, upon the basis of an agreement, "certain rights not recognized in the present organization of industries." As examples he cited the demands of strikers on the Gould railroads for a rule prohibiting a reduction in the wage rate of any worker without agreement of a joint labor-management "arbitration committee"; the requirement that no employee could be discharged "without a just cause" and would be entitled to an investigation if he thought he was unjustly discharged; establishment of the practice that all promotions, such as foremen, be made from the ranks; consultation with the men before any reduction of hours or of men to reduce expenses; and reference to a bipartite committee (three chosen by each side) for binding resolution of any matter between the employees and the company which might arise. Adams felt that the unions probably did not appreciate the full implications of their new claims. But he

14 Adams' responses as well as those of a large number of other academicians, industrialists, and labor leaders were printed in the *Age of Steel* and then published in book form by William E. Barns, *The Labor Problem: Plain Questions and Practical Answers* (New York: Harper and Bros., 1886). For Adams' responses, see pp. 62–63.

15 *Scientific American Supplement*, 555 (August 21, 1886):8861.

thought that the solution of the labor problem lay in a redefinition of property rights, which was in full harmony with the further development of Anglo-Saxon liberty as distinguished from socialism or anarchy.

Adams' presidential address to the American Economic Association in 1896, under the title "Economics and Jurisprudence," contained some further subtle insights and anticipations. His opening paragraph set the tone: "Convinced as I am that much of the confusion in economic theory and much of the discord in industrial life, are alike due to inadequate expression by formal law of fundamental industrial rights, I desire to point out, as well as I may, the character of that confusion and discord, and to suggest the line along which evolution in jurisprudence must proceed in order that harmony in economic theory and peace in the business world may be established."[16]

Adams first explained why the individualism of the eighteenth century, expressed in the doctrines of laissez faire and natural law in the business world, was no longer applicable. He emphasized the great interdependence of society as a result of the industrial revolution and the development of steam transportation. Every industrial quarrel now affected the interests of all. He also noted the changed character of the corporation from what was originally an agency of the state to serve some social or national goal without direct governmental involvement to a private institution amassing industrial power to serve private ends. Finally he developed the thesis that English jurisprudence had been based on the idea of the enforcement of voluntary contracts between parties who were "commercially responsible," that is, "they must be in possession of some property, privilege, or advantage that may be placed in jeopardy as surety for their conduct." But this could not be applied to labor contracts since most workmen had none of these assets. Hence workers were

[16] American Economic Association, *Economic Studies*, 2 (New York: Macmillan Co., 1897), 1:7.

encouraged to be reckless in their demands and employers appealed to force to restrain them.

The solution according to Adams was to enable workers to reacquire a sense of responsibility by gaining a new property right in industry. The new industrial order needed a new conception of industrial liberty, based on the eighteenth-century democratic principles of "independence in matters of thought" and "equality of opportunity in matters of action." For as Adams saw it: "The institution of private property, as defined in the eighteenth century, worked fairly well so long as tools were an appendage to the worker, but it fails to guarantee equality in opportunity now that the worker is an appendage to the machine. The fundamental principle in the theory of Anglo-Saxon liberty is, that the fruits of liberty can be reaped by him alone who has a voice in determining the conditions under which he lives. This is the defense of popular government, and the same argument applies to industrial association."[17]

Adams admitted that he did not yet have the answer to the concept of the new worker property right, but he proposed it as a hypothesis for investigation. "The existence of the property right which attaches itself to a citizen of the industrial world in much the same way that political right attaches itself to citizens of a democratic society, is rendered probable by its necessity. Its discovery is essential if liberty and responsibility are to be restored to the industrial order, and on that account its existence may be assumed as a scientific hypothesis for the direction of industrial analysis."[18] He suggested three major propositions for consideration. The first was that the productive process is essentially social rather than individualistic in character, that the captains of industry depend for their success on the cooperation and association of the great mass of men. Second was the belief that the clarification of the concept of worker property rights

17 Ibid., p. 27.
18 Ibid., pp. 29–30.

would take place through "the evolution of collective bargaining and the formal labor contract." Neither employers nor employees yet fully recognized this development. Through the labor contract, Adams perceived, would come the determination of pay for work performed, an "industrial home" (i.e., job security) for each worker, and a board of arbitration in each industry through whose bylaws and decisions would eventually come "a common law of labor rights." The worker would be "the proprietor of the rights which the board of arbitration defined." Finally, Adams suggested that the theory of property reflected in the common law needed to be restated along two dimensions. On the one hand, it should express the rights of individuals to associate together, i.e., to organize into companies or unions for their mutual benefit. On the other hand, it should express the duties of these industrial units to the public at large, i.e., to regulate monopoly and to assure "just price" and "industrial mobility." These rights, once discovered and expressed, should be incorporated into contracts in the first case and legislative enactment in the second.

The varied discussion at the American Economic Association meeting which followed the address by Adams was both laudatory and critical, depending in large measure on how the speakers felt about unionism. The critics, who were in the majority, stressed union irresponsibility; the supporters, industrial injustice. Professor Franklin H. Giddings of Columbia University, who thought Adams did not go far enough, elaborated on his thesis by suggesting that the law should recognize not only the right of workers to receive payment for work performed (as it did) but also the value of long years of service in case of dismissal. He observed that the most bitter complaint of workers was the liability to dismissal without notice and held that any "faithful employee" should be entitled to a reasonable notice of impending dismissal and that the notice should be proportionate to the length of the faithful service.

WILLIAM D. P. BLISS AND THE SOCIAL GOSPEL

Adams and like-minded academicians, such as Giddings, Richard T. Ely, Simon Patten, John B. Clark, and John R. Commons, were much influenced in their reactions to the problems of labor and industry by a spirit of Social Christianity which has come to be known as the Social Gospel movement. Only a small minority of the clergy actively propounded the Social Gospel, but almost every major Christian denomination had some adherents of the view that the social and economic problems and abuses of the new industrialism could not be left to the individual conscience but required social action. Although they all agreed that change must come peacefully and through evolution, the Social Gospel adherents varied widely in their solutions —from mild reformism, such as prohibiting child labor and banning sweatshops, to radical transformation of society from a laissez faire, private capitalist competitive order to a cooperative socialist commonwealth. The more radical Christians, like their predecessors in England (Charles Kingsley, J. M. Ludlow, Thomas Hughes, and F. D. Maurice), called or considered themselves Christian Socialists.

One of the earliest important proponents of the Social Gospel in America was Reverend Washington Gladden (1836–1918) who spoke frequently from his pulpit on the labor question and wrote a series of books on social problems in the thirty years between the 1870's and the first decade of the 1900's.[19] In the first of these books, Gladden criticized restrictive trade-union practices as monopolistic, rejected both revolutionary and political socialism as immoral, and condemned the small communistic societies like the Shakers, the Mormons, and Oneida

---

[19] In 1912 Gladden was one of twenty-eight sponsors of the *Survey* Group petition to President Taft urging the appointment of a commission to study problems of industrial relations, conditions, and conflicts in the United States.

for depriving men of their individual personalities. On the other hand, he was also hostile to the contemporary capitalist wages system which he saw continuously widening class differences and violating Christian principles of justice. His solution was the gradual adoption of the principles of cooperation, by encouraging workers to save and buy stocks, or to form producers' cooperatives and thereby to join the ranks of the capitalists.[20]

Perhaps the most notable of the Christian Socialists was Reverend William D. P. Bliss (1856–1926), an 1882 Congregationalist seminary graduate who transferred to the Episcopal Church in 1885. Bliss was a close friend of George McNeill, and their paths joined at several points—in the Knights of Labor, where Bliss served as Master Workman of a local assembly, in the Massachusetts Labor party which nominated him for lieutenant-governor in 1887, in the Boston Society of Christian Socialists which he helped to establish in 1889, and in the Mission of the Carpenter which he founded in 1890. Like McNeill, Bliss combined an extraordinary energy with a variety of talents as preacher, organizer, and writer. In addition to the activities listed above, he edited one of the leading monthlies expounding the Social Gospel, *The Dawn: A Magazine of Christian Socialism and Record of Social Progress;* he helped to organize in New York the Church Association for Advancement of the Interests of Labor (CAIL); he cofounded the first Bellamy Nationalist Club in Boston; he established the Fabian Society of Boston and the magazine, *The American Fabian;* and he edited and published, among other works, the impressive compendium, the *Encyclopedia of Social Reform.*

An eclectic of the first order, Bliss supported virtually every reformist idea which circulated in the social whirlpool of the last two decades of the nineteenth century, with the significant exclusion of class struggle and violent revolutionary tactics. He identified himself at one time or another with the ideas of Marx-

[20] Gladden, *Working People and Their Employers.*

ism, Fabianism, Bellamy Nationalism, producers' and consumers' cooperation, trade unionism and collective bargaining, profit sharing, industrial partnership, and protective social legislation. His basic sentiments, however, were probably most clearly reflected in the declaration of principles which the Society of Christian Socialists formulated in 1889, the principles of the Bellamy Club, and in the program of the American Fabians in 1896.

The declaration of principles asserted:

I. We hold that God is the source and guide of all human progress, and we believe that all social, political and industrial relations should be based on the Fatherhood of God and the Brotherhood of Man, in the spirit and according to the teachings of Jesus Christ.
II. We hold that the present commercial and industrial system is not thus based, but rests rather on economic individualism, the results of which are:
(1) That the natural resources of the earth and the mechanical inventions of men are made to accrue disproportionately to the advantage of the few instead of the many.
(2) That production is without general plan, and commercial and industrial crises are thereby precipitated.
(3) That the control of business is rapidly concentrating in the hands of a dangerous plutocracy, and the destinies of the masses of wage-earners are becoming increasingly dependent on the will and resources of a narrowing number of wage-payers.

. . . .

III. We hold that united Christianity must protest against a system so based, and productive of such results and must demand a reconstructed social order which, adopting some method of production and distribution that starts from organized society as a body and seeks to benefit society equitably in every one of its members, shall be based on the Christian principle that "we are members one of another."
IV. While recognizing the present dangerous tendency of business towards combinations and trusts, we yet believe that the economic

circumstances which call them into being, will necessarily result in the development of such a social order, which, with the equally necessary development of individual character, will be at once true Socialism and true Christianity.

V. Our objects, therefore as Christian Socialists, are:

(1) To show that the aim of Socialism is embraced in the aim of Christianity.

(2) To awaken members of Christian churches to the fact that the teachings of Jesus Christ lead directly to some specific form or forms of Socialism. . . .[21]

The principles of the Nationalist Club of Boston, without reference to God or Christianity, expressed the same social and economic attitudes:

> . . . those who seek the welfare of man must endeavor to suppress the system founded on the brute principle of competition and put in its place another based on the nobler principle of association.

> But in striving to apply this nobler and wiser principle to the complex conditions of modern life, we advocate no sudden or ill considered changes; we make no war upon individuals; we do not censure those who have accumulated immense fortunes simply by carrying to a logical end the false principle on which business is now based.

> The combinations, trusts and syndicates of which the people at present complain demonstrate the practicability of our basic principles of association. We merely seek to push this principle a little further and have all industries operated in the interest of all by the nation—the people organized—the organic unity of the whole people. . . .[22]

TWO GOVERNORS—HARTRANFT AND ALTGELD

The active concern of politicians with the problems of labor in the post–Civil War period was aroused nationally by the great

[21] Philo W. Sprague, *Christian Socialism: What and Why* (New York: E. P. Dutton & Co., 1891), pp. 144–145.

[22] Ibid., pp. 145–146.

strikes of the 1870's and particularly by the railroad strikes of 1877. In his annual message to the Pennsylvania general assembly of January 4, 1876, Governor John F. Hartranft warned that "the rights of property must be respected, and no interference with its legitimate use will be tolerated. Every man must be allowed to sell his own labor at his own price, and his working must not be interrupted either by force or intimidation."[23] But he also noted that corporations cannot "unlawfully or oppressively" control production and trade so as to raise or depress the price of labor or the cost of living. And he suggested to the assembly the appointment of a court of arbitration, composed of three or more judges and equal numbers of operators and worker representatives to hear labor disputes so that "at least a full, fair and impartial discussion could be had, and the public enlightened upon the merits of the controversy; and if there was no legal remedy, the force of public opinion would constrain the parties whose claims were arbitrated, to do justice to those who were wronged."[24] In 1877 Governor Hartranft sent Joseph D. Weeks[25] to England to investigate their methods of settling labor disputes and in January 1878 devoted the bulk of his annual message to the state assembly to an analysis of the railroad strike. He recommended again his Arbitration Court Plan of 1876, stating that "it is becoming the settled conviction that nothing can be gained by a war of classes, to compensate for the loss caused

[23] Message of John F. Hartranft to the General Assembly of Pennsylvania, January 4, 1876 (Harrisburg, Pa.: B. F. Meyers, State Printer, 1876), p. 23.

[24] Message of Hartranft to General Assembly, 1876, p. 26.

[25] Joseph D. Weeks was one of the first serious students of American labor relations. In addition to his report on "Industrial Arbitration and Conciliation in England" for Governor Hartranft, he prepared a report on "Arbitration and Conciliation in New York, Pennsylvania, and Ohio" for the Massachusetts Bureau of Labor Statistics in 1880, and in 1886 he published a very insightful monograph entitled *Labor Differences and Their Settlement: A Plea for Arbitration and Conciliation* (New York: The Society for Political Education, 1886), Economic Tracts No. 20, 79 pp. He also prepared a report on strikes and lockouts in 1880 for the Tenth Census of the United States. His views on conciliation and arbitration were very similar to those of Abram Hewitt.

by the disturbance of all industrial relations, and the dangers
threatened to individual independence and free institutions."[26]

Perhaps the most thoughtful assessments of the labor situation by an elected official came from Governor John Peter Altgeld of Illinois. In the critical year of 1886, six years before he
became governor, Altgeld had felt impelled to discuss the government role in labor disputes. His central argument was that,
contrary to the laissez faire proponents, government had the
obligation to intervene in employer-employee relations when
the parties themselves were unable to resolve their disputes
peacefully and when the public interest was seriously affected.
"The duty of the State is not simply to protect life and property,
but also to enable all those agencies that are necessary to the
existence of modern society to perform their functions properly."
Altgeld advocated a system of compulsory and binding arbitration by tripartite boards selected in each case by the parties
(one member by each side and the third member by the first
two members), with the costs to be distributed as in lawsuits
and the public paying the fees of the arbitrators.[27]

Altgeld was a strong advocate of what many decades afterwards Galbraith was to call his theory of countervailing power.
In a speech to railway trainmen in 1895, he stated: "If concentrated capital shall meet with no checking influence, or force,
then republican institutions must come to an end, and we will
have but two classes in this country, an exceedingly wealthy
class on the one hand, and a spiritless, crushed, poverty-stricken
laboring class on the other. The hope of the country depends
upon having a number of forces that will counterbalance or
check each other."[28] He therefore continually urged workers to

[26] Message of John F. Hartranft to the General Assembly of Pennsylvania,
January 2, 1878 (Harrisburg, Pa.: Lane S. Hart, State Printer, 1878), p. 21.

[27] "Protection of Non-combatants or, Arbitration of Strikes." Reprinted from
the Chicago *Evening Mail*, April 26, 1886 in John P. Altgeld, *Live Questions*
(Chicago: Geo. S. Bowen & Son, 1899), pp. 107–116.

[28] Ibid., p. 480.

organize and stand firmly together, for political as well as economic ends, for free institutions as well as decent living standards.

The Federal Government

At the federal level the first known congressional investigation of labor conflict was undertaken by the Select Committee of the House in 1878 and 1879, chaired by Abram Hewitt (whose views have already been examined). Following the widely publicized strikes on the Gould-controlled Southwest railroad and against the Western Union Telegraph Company, the Senate Committee on Education and Labor undertook a similar investigation between 1883 and 1885. Neither of these committees reached any consensus on how to deal with labor conflict, although their hearings elicited numerous suggestions from witnesses representing virtually every interested branch of American life.

On April 22, 1886, President Grover Cleveland sent to Congress the first Presidential message devoted exclusively to labor. In it he expressed his deep concern over the unsatisfactory condition of relations between labor and capital, and he urged the expansion of the recently created Bureau of Labor (1884) to include a three-member Commission of Labor whose functions would be to investigate and conciliate labor disputes and to serve as arbitrator at the request of the conflicting interests. This commission was to have no power to enforce its decisions but, like the railroad commissions in many of the states, it would have, he believed, a "salutary influence" in the settlement of disputes. Cleveland observed that "the establishment by Federal authority of such a bureau would be a just and sensible recognition of the value of labor, and of its right to be represented in the departments of the government."[29]

[29] George F. Parker, ed., *The Writings and Speeches of Grover Cleveland* (New York: Cassell Publishing Co., 1892), p. 334.

In December 1886 in his second annual message to Congress, the President repeated his recommendation for the enlargement of the Labor Bureau and emphasized once more the obligation of the federal government to avert labor controversies, within the limits of constitutional authority, in order to protect the welfare and prosperity of the nation. He urged that "capital should, in recognition of the brotherhood of our citizenship and in a spirit of American fairness, generously accord to labor its just compensation and consideration, and that contented labor is capital's best protection and faithful ally."[30]

Cleveland's main impact on labor relations, however, was not in the private sector, but rather in his advocacy of civil service reform at both the state and national levels. In pressing for civil service reform, he was mainly concerned with improving the efficiency of the public business and putting it on a par with private enterprise. But he also saw it in broader terms. In a letter to resigning commissioner Dorman B. Eaton, he wrote: "I believe in civil service reform and its application in the most practicable form attainable, among other reasons, because it opens the door for the rich and the poor alike to a participation in public place holding. And I hope the time is at hand when all our people will see the advantage of a reliance for such an opportunity upon merit and fitness instead of upon the caprice or selfish interest of those who imprudently stand between the people and the machinery of their government."[31] A few months later, in his first annual message to Congress, he stated: "Civil service reform enforced by law came none too soon to check the progress of demoralization. One of its effects, not enough regarded, is the freedom it brings to the political action of those conservative and sober men who, in fear of the confusion and risk attending an arbitrary and sudden change in all the public offices with a change of party rule, cast their ballots against such

[30] Ibid., p. 337.
[31] Ibid., p. 45.

a change." To what extent labor relations in the private sector was influenced by the rise of the civil service system is difficult to ascertain. Insofar as the latter helped to form a national climate against arbitrary hiring and dismissal procedures, some influence, however intangible, may be said to have been exercised. This speculation is reinforced by a statement of Henry C. Adams in August 1886 that "if men are promoted from the ranks (that is, according to civil service rules), they may be said to have a vested interest in the industry."[32]

In the decade following the year of the "great upheaval," continuing labor strife led to a series of governmental investigations and reports in which the evolving concept of industrial democracy may be traced. The first was the House of Representatives' Select Committee investigations of railroad and other "labor troubles" in Missouri, Arkansas, Texas, and Illinois in 1886 and of labor troubles in the anthracite regions of Pennsylvania in 1887–1888. The central conclusion of the committee was that the inequality in bargaining power between the employer and the individual employee justified the right of workmen to combine "provided the combination be perfectly voluntary and full liberty be left to all other workmen to undertake the work which the parties combining shall refuse, and no obstructions be placed in the way of the employer resorting elsewhere in this country in search of a supply of labor."[33] The committee curiously did not envisage arbitration as an effective device because it required the prior agreement of both sides. However, it stressed the grievances of the workers which involved employer violations of the existing labor contract, such as some employees being asked to work extra hours and others having their work time reduced without notice.

[32] *Scientific American Supplement*, 555 (August 21, 1886):8862.
[33] U.S., Congress, House, Select Committee on Existing Labor Troubles, *Investigation of Labor Troubles in Missouri, Arkansas, Kansas, Texas, and Illinois,* 49th Cong., 2d sess., 1887, H. Rept. 4147, pt. 1: xxiv.

In its anthracite report, two years later, the committee reflected some more sophisticated observations and ideas. It criticized the employers for expressing a willingness to deal with their own employees but not with officials of an outside labor organization to which the employees belonged. It also recommended that the parties establish an impartial tribunal, without state interference, to assure a fair hearing for discharged employees.

The gradual crystallization of thinking about industrial relations and industrial government was further demonstrated in the 1894 report of the United States Strike Commission appointed by President Cleveland to look into the causes and conditions of the Pullman strike. The commission was chaired by one of the nation's most experienced observers of the labor scene, Carroll D. Wright, U.S. commissioner of labor. Although its recommendations pertained solely to the railroad industry (which it explicitly distinguished from the rest of private industry because of its quasi-public character), it made some statements of a general character which are relevant here.[34] First it reflected the widespread public concern over strikes, boycotts, and lockouts, which it referred to as "barbarisms unfit for the intelligence of this age" and "internecine war." But it also noted that "much progress has been made in the more sane direction of conciliation and arbitration" although America still lagged appreciably behind England. "Argument to sustain the justice and necessity of labor unions and unity of action of laborers is superfluous." The growth of corporate power and wealth, the report stated, has been the marvel of the past fifty years. "It will not be surprising if the marvel of the next fifty years be the advancement of labor to a like position of power and responsibility."

The commission then recommended for the railroad industry

[34] The following quotations are taken from The United States Strike Commission, *Report on the Chicago Strike on June-July, 1894* (Washington, D.C.: Government Printing Office, 1894).

the enactment of federal legislation which would establish a permanent U.S. strike commission to investigate and conciliate serious disputes. To the states which had not already acted, it recommended the adoption of some system of conciliation and arbitration, like that of Massachusetts, and the illegalization of employment contracts which required men to agree not to join or remain in a labor organization. To employers at large it urged not only the recognition of labor organizations and the use of conciliation and arbitration when difficulties arose, but also that they keep "in closer touch with labor," because while the interests of the two were not identical, they were reciprocal. Finally, they stated that "if employers will consider employees as thoroughly essential to industrial success as capital and thus take labor into consultation at proper times, much of the severity of strikes can be tempered and their number reduced."

THE UNITED STATES INDUSTRIAL COMMISSION, 1898–1902

The search for a new working conception of industrial government during the last third of the nineteenth century appropriately was climaxed by the joint appointment by the Congress and President McKinley of an eighteen-man commission to investigate the industrial life of the nation. Aided by a large and able technical staff, including John R. Commons, E. Dana Durand, Samuel M. Lindsay, and William Z. Ripley, the commission obtained testimony from nearly seven hundred witnesses—among them an impressive cross-section of American industrial and labor leadership—as well as combing a vast amount of documentary and statistical information. Eighteen fat volumes embodied the testimony and special studies and a nineteenth of more than 1200 pages summarized the chief findings and presented recommendations for legislation. The section on labor in the final report alone ran 232 pages.

This section has a number of features which are especially

pertinent to the subject under discussion. For one thing, it is the first official report to make specific reference to "Democracy in Industry." But more important is the sophisticated tone of many portions of the report—its explicit and extended treatment of the new concept of collective bargaining,[35] its precise definition of and distinction among terms like *conciliation* and *arbitration,* its careful description of disputes over the interpretation of existing contracts and disputes over the terms of future contracts, and its consideration of numerous issues which were to dominate industrial relations during the next two decades.

In discussing democracy in industry, the commission attributed the problem to the growing size of industrial units and the growing inability of the individual worker to control his daily work-life. Expectations that employee stock-ownership and producers' cooperation would provide workers with "effective participation" in the government of the great industries were judged to be "chimerical." The only solution was labor organization and the development of such joint conferences as those between the United Mine Workers and the coal mine operators. If employers refused to deal with the unions, the workers would turn to socialism to achieve "an element of democracy in industrial life." The commission recognized the difficulties in achieving industrial democracy, but it concluded that it would come in time with practice and experience.

> Proficiency and wisdom in self-government are gained by practice. Men who have been accustomed to absolute submission in industry show the same faults when they first take up the burden of self-government as men who have been accustomed to absolute political submission. Only experience with democratic forms and methods can develop the good that is in democracy; but so far as employers take a long look ahead, and act in the interest of the

[35] Like *industrial democracy,* this term was "not often employed in common speech in the United States, but is gradually coming into use among employers and employees in Great Britain." *Report of the U.S. Industrial Commission,* 19 (Washington, D.C.: Government Printing Office, 1901):834.

ultimate welfare of society, it is believed that they will encourage rather than repress the growth of democratic government in their industries. Their guidance may be the means of preventing many mistakes that would otherwise be made, and their friendship will be rewarded with friendship. If they adopt a repressive policy they may perhaps succeed in it; but so long as the tradition of freedom is strong in the minds of the working people they can not destroy the aspiration for a measure of self-government in respect to the most important part of life.[36]

The nub of industrial democracy for the commission was the "system" of collective bargaining—particularly over the terms of a new contract dealing with wages, hours, and other conditions of employment. For collective bargaining to be successful "there must be on each side approximately equal strength, a fairly high degree of intelligence, and a disposition to fairness and to businesslike methods."[37] The advantages of collective bargaining were threefold:

(1) It gives each side a better understanding of conditions in the industry, the positions of each party, and the motives influencing behavior.

(2) It removes many minor misunderstandings and causes of conflict and facilitates their speedy correction.

(3) It promotes cumulatively mutual understanding and mutual respect between employers and employees.

Those who have had the most experience with this practice repeatedly speak in the highest terms of the ability and the moderation which they have found on the part of those whom they had too often in earlier times looked upon as in a sense enemies. The distinction of superiority and inferiority is more and more forgotten, as such democratic methods of adjusting labor questions are developed. Employers and employees meet and bargain as business men do regarding other than labor matters—as equals.[38]

[36] Ibid., p. 805.
[37] Ibid., p. 844.
[38] Ibid., pp. 844–845.

Collective bargaining was primarily a matter of business although its "moral effect" was highly important.

The commission was fully appreciative of the distinction between the negotiating of a contract and the interpretation of its terms in everyday practice. However, it regarded disputes over interpretation as "relatively minor" which could be adjusted by procedure "of a more or less judicial character." Thus it approved the many local, and the few national, procedures of conciliation and binding arbitration which had been established, noting that neutral umpires rarely had to be used because the bipartisan committees usually could resolve any grievances which the employer and employees could not settle by themselves.

On the role of government in regulating or otherwise influencing collective-bargaining systems, the commission took what was then regarded as a moderate position. It called for the following provisions: state laws should protect both the right of workers to organize and the right to work without belonging to a union; Congress should enact a law similar to those in many states protecting trade union labels; laws against blacklisting and the use of private police in labor disputes should also be adopted; strikes should be regarded as legal "except when conducted on a public employment in such a manner as to injure the public safety or health," but boycotts or combinations to injure or control the liberty of an individual should be considered illegal. Arbitration and conciliation laws were found to be effective in regard to conciliation but not arbitration; however, where such laws existed, as in the case of the federal statute pertaining to the railroads and a number of general state laws (going back to 1886 in New York and Massachusetts), the commission felt that strikes and lockouts should be prohibited until conciliation and arbitration had been tried. But neither side should be compelled to abide by an arbitration award, for "it is believed that a full and fair investigation of the facts will, in most cases, bring the parties into substantial agreement, while in other cases the result may be safely left to public opinion."[39] The use of the injunction to enforce labor contracts should be preserved to prevent irreparable loss or wrong, but the commission noted that it had been widely abused and judicial restraints were necessary. Union incorporation had been possible at the federal level since 1886, but not one prominent union had taken advantage of it.

Thus the commission, elaborating on the positions of earlier governmental committees, provided the basis for a legal code of fair labor practice within which collective bargaining could operate freely. In addition, it visualized two other roles for government. One was to enlarge the role of the state bureaus of labor through exchange of statistics and reports and the convening annually of a national conference which would recommend uniform statutes on labor subjects to Congress and to the separate states. The other was the establishment through legislation of certain minimum standards of employment concerning child labor; the maximum hours to be worked by adolescents, women, and men in dangerous occupations; the payment of labor in cash; the regulation of company stores; the prevention of sweatshops; and industrial safety (especially on the railroads).

[39] Ibid., pp. 952–953.

CHAPTER **4**

AT THE CENTURY'S END

THE DIVERSITY of ideas about industrial government and industrial society which flourished in the last third of the nineteenth century was clearly a response to the profound changes occurring throughout American life. The new industrialism magnified class differences and created inter-class problems and tensions which traditional ideas and methods were incapable of resolving.

For the most part the new ideas had little or no grounding in experience. However, the Industrial Commission was able to conclude that producers' cooperation, industrial partnership, and profit sharing were not realistic solutions. They judged that voluntary arbitration was useful but that compulsory, binding arbitration would not be acceptable in the American environs. They decided that only through trade unionism and labor-management agreements, supplemented by a limited amount of protective state legislation for the largely unorganizable, could democracy in industry be achieved.

This final determination by the commission was supported by the most comprehensive survey of labor relations made until that time in the United States. It was a natural sequel to the studies by the state and federal bureaus of labor and the state legislative and Congressional inquiries of the preceding thirty years. Thus it is possible both to assess the new ideas about industrial democracy which prevailed during the period between 1865 and 1898 and to compare the dominant idea (collective bargaining) which had crystallized out of the maelstrom of competition with the practices of industrial life. Such an assessment will be based on the dimensions and standards of industrial democracy delineated in chapter 1. It will then be possible to consider why industrial democracy made the gains attributed to it and why it suffered defeats and failures.

Representation

By 1865 organized labor had achieved only a minimal role in industrial life. It is true that in times of prosperity and rising prices, the unions were able to exercise considerable influence on wages and working conditions in a variety of industries, including house and ship construction, printing, iron making, foundries, mining, railroads, stoves, cigars, and tailoring. But with the onset of a serious downturn in the business cycle—and these downturns came frequently—the unions proved ineffective and often disappeared entirely. This familiar pattern was repeated in the 1870's and 1890's. However, in 1896 Samuel Gompers was able to proclaim with pride to the AFL convention that for the first time American trade unions had survived a major depression with their basic strength intact. Thus the stage was set for the spectacular more-than-quadrupling of union membership, which occurred between 1897 and 1904, and the leap to power of organized labor as a national institution. By the turn of the century, organized labor had achieved a significant membership in bituminous coal mining, the railroad operating services, street railways, building construction in the larger cities, printing and publishing, and some segments of manufacture. Although only about 6 per cent of nonagricultural employees were union members in 1900, and very few of them were in the major mass production industries, government service, trade, or private office work, the idea of collective bargaining as a form of industrial democracy had gained a firm and enduring foothold. The idea worked in practice. Nineteenth-century unionism was, with some conspicuous exceptions, democratic unionism. The majority-rule principle played an important role in union government. But it was not an established principle in determining union representation in the workplace. On occasion employers would agree to recognize a union in an establishment if the majority of employees were members (e.g., the 1891 agreement between the Stove Founders National Defense Association and the Iron Molders' Union), but normally the union established its status by persuading the employer of its desirability or by a showing of strength through a strike. Majority rule played little or no role on the management side.

Participation

The scope of union voice in the decision-making process varied considerably among industries, but there was a common thread among all of them. Wages, hours, and apprenticeship rules were from the outset accepted as appropriate matters of concern. The first written agreements tended to focus on them. As unionism and the agreement system spread, union influence extended to an increasing number of issues. By the 1890's the more highly developed agreements such as those in printing, the railroads, and glass and stove manufacture encompassed such items as discharge and discipline, restriction or regulation of fines, pay for train delays and deadheading, the use of seniority, the hiring of men on the extra list, call-in procedures and pay for lack of work when called in, meal hours, pay for appearances in court at company request, posting of bulletins, safety provisions in the workplace, the right of miners to choose their own doctors, the provision of specific types of equipment, regulations on certain kinds of printing type, a no-strike and no-lockout clause, and grievance and arbitration machinery. Experience under these agreements was to lead to further elaboration of their terms and the addition of new items. But the basic pattern of the later agreements was clearly evident.

Equal Rights and Opportunities

Discrimination was widely practiced throughout the period despite espousals of nondiscrimination by major labor organizations such as the National Labor Union, the Knights of Labor, and the AFL. According to Spero and Harris, the Knights of Labor made the most serious (although far from successful) effort to break down anti-Negro prejudice and at its peak in 1886 claimed some 60,000 Negro members.[1] As a symbol of its attitude, Grand Master Powderly told the General Assembly at Richmond, Virginia, that white members had walked out of a hotel when black members were refused accommodations and a black delegate was selected to introduce Powderly in the presence of Virginia Governor Lee.

The skilled trade unions which comprised the AFL, however, resisted efforts at integration. Since over 97 per cent of the Negro workers were unskilled in 1865, the crafts had much less interest than the Knights in organizing them. But even the skilled Negroes were discriminated against—in some instances by total exclusion, in others by the establishment of separate black and white locals. Apprenticeships were generally restricted to whites. Even when the national union adopted a progressive

[1] Sterling D. Spero and Abram L. Harris, *The Black Worker: The Negro and the Labor Movement* (New York: Columbia University Press, 1931), pp. 41–45. The following discussion is based mainly on this book.

policy, as in the case of the cigarmakers and carpenters, it was often frustrated by the locals. The unions with the largest Negro membership were the United Mine Workers and the Longshoremen against whom unskilled Negroes had often been pitted as strikebreakers.

In 1893 the Federation reaffirmed "as one of the cardinal principles of the labor movement that the working people must unite and organize irrespective of creed, color, sex, nationality or politics." And for a time every candidate for membership was required to take a nondiscrimination oath. In 1895 the AFL Executive Council accepted the International Association of Machinists on a nondiscrimination basis after rejecting an existing union limited to whites. But discrimination was achieved in various informal and formal ways, such as the inclusion of pledges in the union ritual, binding members to propose only whites for membership. In 1900 the Federation recognized its inability to change the discriminatory practices of its national unions by adopting a constitutional amendment that permitted the issuance of separate charters to central labor unions, local unions, or federated labor unions, composed entirely of black workers where such action appeared advisable to the Executive Council.

The attitude of the labor movement, including the Knights, was even more openly and unrestrainedly hostile toward Chinese and other Oriental immigrant workers. This feeling was expressed in successful legislative campaigns to restrict immigration of these groups. The unionists showed relatively little formal discrimination in the nineteenth century toward European immigrants, from whose ranks most of them came, but this was to change later on as huge numbers of immigrants from eastern and southern Europe entered the country.

Women workers were largely scorned by the craft unions (in contrast again to the Knights) and generally excluded from their rolls. Women tended to be bracketed with children as requiring special legislative protection. The Federation, however, did support organizational efforts in predominantly female industries like textiles and women's clothing, employing its first female organizer, Mary Kenny, in 1892. The National Women's Trade Union League, which was formed in 1903, was mainly the product of the settlement social workers, although Samuel Gompers and other labor leaders gave their endorsement and support.[2]

Right of Dissent

Where unionism and collective bargaining prevailed, the right of the individual employee or of groups of employees to express themselves freely in opposition to the views of either the employer or the union leadership seems to have been generally respected. This contrasted sharply with the unorganized establishments where challenges to the employer were not tolerated. But even in the organized situations the dissident voice sometimes encountered difficulties. As an early experience in the cigar industry revealed, where rival unionism prevailed and unions felt insecure, they tended to be less sympathetic to minority dissent. Where they were strong, as in printing, dissent was less interfered with. Where corruption prevailed, as in Chicago construction and teaming at the turn of the century, dissent was not tolerated.

Due Process

For most of the period under review the complaints of individuals or groups of employees were handled informally by

[2] See Allen F. Davis, *Spearheads for Reform: The Social Settlements and the Progressive Movement, 1890–1914* (New York: Oxford University Press, 1967), chapter 7.

the employee with his immediate boss or by a committee of employee representatives and the employer. The development of a formal due process, i.e., a systematic and clearly delineated procedure for the hearing of employee complaints or grievances and a body of industrial substantive law, came out of the ideas and practices associated with arbitration and the written joint agreement. The source of these ideas and practices was British experience. The developing character of due process is reflected in the ambiguities which were attached to the word *arbitration* for a number of years and which were not fully clarified until the last decade of the century. Initially, arbitration seems to have had at least three rather different meanings: (1) joint negotiations of a conciliatory manner, (2) adjudication of disputes by a joint labor-management body beyond the level of the establishment, and (3) referral of disputes to a neutral third party. Moreover, no distinction was made between disputes over the terms of a new agreement and disputes over grievances or the interpretation and application of agreement terms. By the time of the Industrial Commission, however, arbitration was clearly distinguished from collective bargaining, and arbitration of interests (in disputes over new agreements) was distinguished from arbitration of rights (in disputes over the application of agreements).

Due process seems to have emerged out of four different channels—the informal grievance handling of the workshop, which led to customary practices or usages; the more formal and constitutionally oriented disposition of union member complaints and appeals within the union governmental framework, such as the law of the typographical union; the provision of formal grievance procedures, often but not always including arbitration as the final step, in written trade agreements; and off to the side, but nonetheless a matter of widespread knowledge and influence, the development of Civil Service systems and rules for governmental employees especially after the passage of the Pendleton Act of 1883, which provided for hiring and promotion through competitive examinations and relative security of tenure.[3] The 1891 stove industry agreement, which was in its original form solely concerned with the settlement of disputes through the use of arbitration, established a formal procedure through which unresolved disputes were to be taken. Agreements of the Chicago carpenters in 1890, the Massachusetts shoeworkers in the 1880's and 1890's, and the interstate bituminous coal industry in 1897 contained well-developed grievance procedures.

Because lasting agreement systems did not originate until the 1890's, however, and the permanent impartial-umpire role was not established until about 1910 in the garment industry, the idea of substantive due process—of a common law of industry—was primarily the product of the next period. Yet the experience in printing forecast the future.

The development of the idea of discharge only for "just cause" provides the best illustration of both procedural and substantive due process in a number of industries. The beginnings are seen, for example, in an 1870 anthracite coal agreement in which "it is agreed that the Workingmen's Benevolent Association shall not sustain any man who is discharged for incompetency, bad workmanship, bad conduct, or other good cause; and that the operators shall not discharge any man or officer for actions

[3] However, as Paul P. Van Riper has noted in his *History of the United States Civil Service* (Evanston Ill.: Row, Peterson, 1958), the main restriction on dismissal for many years after 1883 was in the area of partisan, political reasons. The "just cause" basis of dismissal was not directly introduced until President McKinley's Executive Order of July 27, 1897. As amended and strengthened on May 29, 1899, it provided that "no removal shall be made from the competitive classified service except for just cause and for reasons given in writing; and the person sought to be removed shall have notice and be furnished a copy of such reasons, and be allowed a reasonable time for personally answering the same in writing" (p. 144).

or duties imposed upon him by the Workingmen's Benevolent Association."[4] The following year it was agreed that all questions of disagreement except wages were to be referred to a district board of arbitration of three men from each side, with power, in case of their disagreement, to select an umpire whose decision was to be final. These early agreements were very short-lived; but after the great 1898 interstate bituminous coal agreement was negotiated, the basis was set for an enduring grievance machinery.

The federal civil service experience is also of relevance here.

Responsibility

The idea of responsibility in labor-management relations assumed particular importance with the negotiation of written agreements, which contained either a fixed term or was of indefinite duration but required a specific number of days' notice before the agreement could be revised or terminated. In the absence of such agreements it was considered fair play for either side to exercise its power to change wages or conditions of work when circumstances seemed favorable to that side, and for the other side to seek a reversal when the power balance shifted. One of the main arguments for the written agreement was that it would stabilize relations and would assure employers of continuity of operations. The written agreement seems to have been taken seriously as an obligation by both sides. Testimony before legislative committees, for example, contains frequent references to the responsible attitude of the parties toward written agreements and few references to agreement violations.

Examples of written agreements (usually in the form of wage

[4] Margaret A. Schaffner, *The Labor Contract from Individual to Collective Bargaining* (Madison: University of Wisconsin Press, 1907), p. 111.

scales or schedules) may be found prior to the Civil War in the printing and shoe industries. A famous sliding scale agreement (tying wages to product price changes) between the Sons of Vulcan and the Iron Manufacturers of Pittsburgh was negotiated in 1865. More comprehensive agreements, covering not only wages but also hours, apprenticeship rules, a variety of working conditions, and a grievance procedure, were adopted for bricklaying and masonry work in Boston and New York by 1886 and in Chicago by 1887. The Iron Molders' Union, which appears to have had some local agreements as early as 1873, negotiated a national agreement in 1891 with the Stove Founders' National Defense Association which included machinery for the peaceful settlement of disputes between members of the two organizations. A similar national agreement in 1899 between the International Association of Machinists and the National Metal Trades Association was short-lived, but local agreements in the metal trades became widespread. Coal mining agreements were reached in anthracite as early as 1870 and in bituminous by 1885, but an enduring agreement system was not established in the latter branch of the industry until 1897 and in the former until 1902. As these and other examples indicate, the concept of a written constitution or code of rules for industrial government and a sense of responsibility for living up to the rules gradually evolved after the Civil War, and by the turn of the century they were hallmarks of industrial democracy through collective bargaining.

Minimum Standards

One of the major objectives of organized labor throughout the study period was to establish certain minimum standards of employment, and particularly with respect to work hours. The eight-hour movement as developed by Ira Steward and George McNeill in the 1850's first endeavored to reach its goal through the enactment of state general eight-hour laws and a federal eight-hour law for government employees. The failure of the legislative approach (in no small measure because of adverse interpretations or constitutional objections by hostile courts) caused the trade unions to substitute direct economic (i.e., strike) action—in 1886 on a general basis and in 1889 and 1891 on a selective industry basis. A few strong unions like the carpenters and the printers were successful; most workers did not gain the basic eight-hour day until long afterwards.

The other areas, in addition to basic work hours, where general minimum standards were sought on a statewide or industry basis were child labor limitations, restrictions on the nighttime hours of women, and safety rules for hazardous trades like mining and transportation. The first two were mainly outside of the collective-bargaining sphere; the latter was attacked through both collective bargaining and legislation. In all cases the achievements were quite limited.

No minimum wage standards were seriously pursued. The unions, in each bargaining situation, insisted on a standard (minimum) rate for a given job and since many of the agreements during the period were marketwide, the standard rate served as a wage floor for competitive producers. However, the idea of a general minimum "living wage" was not widely advocated—even by an organization like the Knights of Labor which enrolled all categories of employees and did not concentrate on the skilled trades as did the AFL.

Information

The willingness of employers to provide workers or their representatives with economic data bearing on wages seems to have been a function of their willingness or need to recognize a union. Employers, like Hewitt, who accepted unionism and advocated arbitration (whether interpreted as collective negotiations or third-party intervention) recognized the necessity for economic information. Likewise the advocates of profit sharing and industrial partnerships adopted this position. But the bulk of employers maintained that their businesses were their private domain, and thus economic information was guarded as zealously as technological secrets.

Personal Dignity

To an increasing degree during the last third of the nineteenth century, organized labor sought not only material gains but employer respect for the human dignity of workers. In the pre–Civil War era this was not a major issue because the relationship between employer and employees was on a small scale and therefore personal basis. The man-to-man relationship became steadily less common as the size of industrial enterprises increased and the managers were no longer the owners or entrepreneurs. Labor became a commodity. The vast influx first of German and Scandinavian immigrants and later Italians and eastern Europeans encouraged this view. Even the more humane and personnel-minded capitalists adopted a paternalistic rather than an equal-citizen approach to their employees. For the trade unionists and the reformers, shorter hours, higher wages, improved working conditions, collective bargaining, all had more than material values; they signified a gain in human dignity as well. In these respects it may be said that labor was trying to regain the standing of the skilled artisan and the self-sufficient producer of the past. The average white worker of the last decade of the century probably had lower status than his counterpart in the first decades.

Some Interpretive Judgments

By the turn of the twentieth century, the single most widely accepted idea of industrial democracy was bilateral collective bargaining between a trade union and an individual employer or group of employers, with the working rules expressed in a written trade agreement, disinterested outsiders playing a very limited role as conciliators or arbitrators when requested by the parties, and government serving primarily as a source of factual information, as the guardian of women and children in certain limited respects, and on occasion as the protector of the public peace and safety. Other models of industrial democracy, such as producers' cooperatives, profit sharing, and industrial partnership, were viewed as ineffectual or impracticable except under very special conditions. The radical model of a socialist commonwealth had a growing support but no practical implementation.[5]

Though the collective-bargaining model was the front-line contender ideologically and practically, it was still very much a minority idea. Clearly the great majority of employers and probably the public at large were not prepared to support it. The dominant model of industrial government was not democratic— it was employer controlled and directed, premised on the principles of laissez faire capitalist enterprise and individual liberty (especially the liberty of the employer to run his enterprise as he saw fit and the liberty of the employee to either accept the terms and conditions of employment offered by the employer or to look elsewhere for a job).

Thus two questions must be raised and considered: Why did the collective-bargaining model finally, after a century of frus-

---

[5] The first socialist mayor was elected in 1898 at Haverhill, Massachusetts. Socialist-dominated unions did not differ significantly from their more conservative counterparts in the AFL except for their support of industrial unionism.

trations, become the dominant idea of industrial democracy? But also why was its scope and its progress so limited?

Part of the answer to the first question is that, for certain categories of employees and under certain industrial conditions, the model of unionism and collective bargaining appeared to work whereas rival models of industrial democracy did not. It had survival power. Despite many attacks, it provided a governmental apparatus which could function more or less successfully over long periods of time, years and decades, and did not depend solely on novelty or the charisma of leaders. It could adapt to the extremely changeable conditions of industrial life, including, by the 1890's, business depressions. It provided benefits to the owners and managers as well as employees. For the latter, it raised wages, improved employment conditions, and gave a personal sense of dignity; for the former, it provided a challenge to govern imaginatively and creatively rather than by arbitrary or dictatorial rule; and in highly competitive markets, it served as a stabilizing force which prevented cut-throat competition.

The collective-bargaining model took hold also because the unions were able to impose it despite employer resistance, in certain industries and under certain conditions. For the most part, success was achieved by tightly organized, skilled craftsmen whose bargaining power was relatively strong in relation to their small, highly competitive employers. In construction, printing, or cigar manufacture, for example, the strike was a powerful weapon since the skilled worker was not easy to replace and the financial reserves of the employer were limited. The union, in addition, could perform some useful services, such as recruiting workers who were often in short supply and keeping unfair competitors in line. In the special case of the railroads, where the employers were large and powerful and competition was not a factor, the establishment of collective bargaining was influenced by the conservative policies of the

unions and the employers' recognition of the public unwillingness to tolerate prolonged and destructive conflicts such as the
strikes of 1877 and the Pullman strike.

To say that the collective-bargaining model appeared workable, however, did not mean that it worked ideally or even well
in practice. In bituminous coal mining, for example, the central
states system was not established on a going basis until 1898,
and in anthracite the comparable stage was not reached until
after 1902. More than thirty years of struggle and experimentation preceded these agreements. In the building construction
industry of several large cities—notably Chicago, New York,
and San Francisco—corruption, gangsterism, and authoritarianism marred relationships between the contractors and some of
the crafts. With respect to railroads, the managers shared sovereignty only with the operating brotherhoods (the shop crafts
were not well organized), and the job territory was the separate
system rather than the entire industry as it later became. Due
process for individual and group complaints was still poorly
developed.

That collective bargaining applied to less than 6 per cent of
the nonfarm labor force in 1900 did not mean that the model
could not work in other sectors of employment, if given a chance.
Its restricted scope was due mainly to the unwillingness of employers to accept any form of industrial government which restricted their freedom to manage as they saw fit. And these
employers had the economic and political power at this time to
enforce this will. The pattern of resistance was set by the big
employers, most notably in the Homestead steel strike of 1892
and the Pullman railroad car strike of 1894. Overtures from the
AFL leadership were spurned. The small employers of the National Metal Trades Association followed suit in 1901 and by
1903 the National Association of Manufacturers had assumed
leadership of the open-shop movement throughout the country.

The negative attitude of the large corporations in the heavily trustified industries, which emerged in the last decade of the nineteenth century, was based on three assumptions: (1) that unions served no useful function to management either as a communications mechanism or as a stabilizing force in the product market, (2) that management had exclusive responsibility for the government of its enterprise, and (3) that the largely immigrant and unskilled work force was not capable of contributing to the rule-making process. These assumptions made industrial democracy in any form impossible. They were soon to be challenged and revised.

THE BURGEONING
OF THE IDEA
OF INDUSTRIAL
DEMOCRACY,
1898–1920

CHAPTER 5

THE COLLECTIVE-BARGAINING
MODEL CRYSTALLIZES

THE TEMPER of the first two decades of the twentieth century was symbolized by the title of Walter E. Weyl's book, *The New Democracy.* The process of economic growth that had characterized the preceding half century continued with the same intensity, but the promoters and managers of this growth no longer could disregard the consequences of their actions on the conditions of life of the workers who made their enterprises possible. The diverse elements of reform which had struggled with slight avail for so many years finally began to have a significant impact—in the political arena, in social welfare action, and in the workplace. The term *industrial democracy,* which was just beginning to come into popular use at the turn of the century, became one of the most widely used terms in the lexicon of individuals and groups concerned with industrial relations. The conflicts in industry were no less frequent nor less bitter and violent than in the earlier period; but generally speaking, the corporate employers recognized that they were much more vulnerable to public criticism, and they sought to improve their public image. This chapter will depict first the main aspects of the growth pattern and the changing character of the political, social, and psychological environment. Then it will trace the further development of the collective-bargaining model of industrial democracy which the Industrial Commission had endorsed.

Industrialization

The National Bureau of Economic Research estimates that real gross national product of the private domestic economy rose from an index of 36.1 in 1899 (1929=100) to 69.1 in 1919 or by 91 per cent. This was less than in the preceding twenty years when the increase had been by 123 per cent, but it was a significant figure considering the continually expanding base.[1] An even more significant indicator of growth was that manufacturing product rose from 27.5 to 61.0 or by 122 per cent. Although the number of factories (excluding some 300,000 small-hand and neighborhood establishments with about 800,000 wage-earners) was practically stationary (up slightly more than 5000 to about 210,000), the average number of wage-earners nearly doubled (from 4.5 million to 8.4 million) and the horsepower used slightly more than doubled, reflecting the growing size of industrial units.[2]

Physical output figures affirmed the growth of the great mass production industries which had become the symbol of American life throughout the world. Between 1898 and 1920, for example, steel ingots and castings increased from 8.9 million long tons to 42.1 million; bituminous coal went from 167 million tons to 569 million; and freight carried one mile by railroads rose from 114 billion tons to 414 billion. Energy from water power and mineral fuels is estimated to have nearly tripled. Although

[1] See John W. Kendrick, *Productivity Trends in the United States* (Princeton, N.J.: Princeton University Press, 1961), Table A-IV, pp. 302–303.

[2] U.S., Department of Commerce, *Historical Statistics of the United States, 1789–1945* (Washington, D.C.: Government Printing Office, 1949), p. 179.

the age of the motor vehicle was just dawning, by 1920 8.1 million autos and 1.1 million trucks were registered.

In one significant respect, the economy behaved diametrically contrary to that of the preceding third of a century. Whereas the Bureau of Labor Statistics wholesale price index fell almost continuously from 116.3 in 1866 to 46.5 in 1896 (1926=100), it rose gradually but steadily to 85.5 in 1916 and then skyrocketed with the World War I inflation to 154.4 in 1920. Professor Paul Douglas' cost of living index rose from 100 in 1897 to 149 in 1916 and then to 286 in 1920. The rising level of prices provided a powerful impetus for labor organization and a major issue in collective bargaining. It also intensified the problems of the poor.

Another significant, although less extreme, contrast with the earlier period was the relative moderation of business cycle fluctuations. The depressions of the 1870's and the 1890's were shattering blows to the economic aspirations of the labor movement. From 1896 to 1920, however, the economy avoided sustained depression. Although Stanley Lebergott[3] has estimated that non-farm employees had unemployment rates of between 8 and 16 per cent in all but two years between 1900 and 1916, and many workers were at or below the poverty line, there was a buoyant atmosphere of economic advance and improvement for the majority.

Urbanization and Immigration

This economic buoyancy was accompanied by a continuing expansion of population and urbanization. Again we are dealing with well-known facts which may be quickly summarized. The population grew from 76 million in 1900 to 106 million in 1920

[3] Stanley Lebergott, *Manpower in Economic Growth* (New York: McGraw-Hill Book Company, 1964), pp. 512, 523.

or by nearly 40 per cent, a larger absolute amount although a smaller percentage than in the preceding two decades. Of the 30 million increase, immigration accounted for about a third since there were almost 15 million immigrants as against about 4.5 million emigrants. The shift in the ethnic composition of the immigrants which began to become visible in the early 1890's sharply accelerated in this period. The Anglo-Saxons declined absolutely as well as relatively; the Italians, Polish, and Russian Jews, and other east and south Europeans came in a multitudinous stream, bringing with them new customs and ideas and new organizational and acculturalization problems.

Cities continued to attract a large proportion of the immigrants as well as many of the natives. Residents of urban places with 2500 or more people increased from some 30 million in 1900 to 54 million in 1920 while rural residents rose only from 46 to 52 million. Moreover, by 1920 almost a quarter of the total population lived in cities of 100,000 or more and the huge city slums and ghettoes became larger. The evidence of poverty in the midst of affluence became more visible.

The Socio-Psychological Climate

What was distinctive of this new period, however, was not its economic or population trends, but its democratizing spirit. Historians have given it a variety of common-sounding labels— the age of reform, the progressive era, progressive democracy, the new democracy, the rise of liberalism, the square deal, the new freedom, etc. All symbolize the shift, which began to take practical effect at the turn of the century, in behalf of human values as against property values. In the political sphere the shift was expressed concretely in the elections and programs of Roosevelt and Wilson as well as in the growth of the Socialist party. In the economic sphere it was reflected in the dramatic expansion of union membership from about 450,000 in 1897 to 2 million in 1904, 2.7 million in 1913, and, with the stimulus of World War I, 5 million in 1920. In the social sphere it was exhibited by the public reaction to the writings of the "muckrakers" and the reformers, by the adoption of workmen's compensation and factory safety laws and maximum hours legislation for women and children, and by the social security movement to reduce and ultimately to eliminate poverty.

There was, in short, a growing consensus that the unrestrained capitalism of the post–Civil War decades required "humanization." But views differed widely both on the types of constraints to be applied and the speed with which they should be introduced. Thus the period was characterized by a large number and variety of conflicts and accommodations in labor relations as in other sectors of society.

The labor conflicts were typified by the steel strikes of 1901 and 1919; the anthracite coal strike of 1902; the ladies' garment strikes in New York of 1910; the dynamiting of the *Los Angeles Times* building in 1910; the IWW strikes at Lawrence, Massachusetts, in 1912 and Patterson, New Jersey, in 1913; the Ludlow (Colorado) Massacre of 1914; and the railroad eight-hour dispute of 1915–1916. The steel strikes, both of which were severe union defeats, signalled the determination of the steel magnates (and most of the other corporate giants) to maintain exclusive control over their industry's work force and conditions. Their response to the reformers was to take such limited forms as accident prevention programs and share-purchase plans for employees. The anthracite strike, a partial union victory which was to serve as the bedrock for a major boost to collective bargaining, was the first occasion in American history involving personal intervention by the President to force employers to reach an accommodation with organized labor. The New York garment strikes were even more triumphant; through an unusual solidarity of immigrant workers (mostly Jews and Italians), the sympathy and support of the general public, and the mediation efforts of prominent third parties (notably Louis Brandeis), a dramatic new system of industrial democracy was introduced. In contrast to coal and garments, the *Los Angeles Times* dispute demonstrated the degree of violence and guerrilla action to which frustrated business unionists might go and the IWW strikes, although attracting more sympathetic public attention to the substandard plight of the textile workers, indicated the futility of job action oriented toward an ultimate overthrow of the capitalistic system rather than to an accommodation process. The Ludlow mining tragedy is an illustration of corporate-political force and repression creating such an intense public revulsion that it compelled one of the nation's most powerful industrial and financial groups to take a new look at its entire employee relations policy and to institute a system of representation and welfarism which was to play a major role in the next two decades. Finally, in the dispute over the basic eight-hour day on the railroads, the growing strength of railroad unionism was compelling the favorable support of the President and the Congress on an important collective-bargaining issue. These conflict situations do not exhaust the entire range of actions and reactions which reflected and influenced the course of thinking about industrial democracy, but they do suggest the diversity of themes which prevailed within the broad mainstream of progressivism during the period.

The socio-psychological climate of the period was also expressed in and shaped by other forms of activity. One more or less contemporaneous with the hearings and reports of the U.S. Industrial Commission was the establishment of the National Civic Federation in 1899 to promote industrial peace and welfare, collective bargaining, and labor contracts. The dynamic organizer of the Federation, Ralph Easley, had close ties with Samuel Gompers, John Mitchell, and other nonradical leaders of the labor movement as well as with prominent businessmen, politicians, and professionals. For nearly a decade the Federation sought to promote a system of industrial democracy based on an accommodation between conservative labor officials and liberal businessmen, but its rhetoric surpassed its performance and its role was greatly diminished by attacks from the socialists and other radical branches of labor and from the ultraconservative businessmen who directed the open-shop programs of the Citizens' Industrial Association, the National Association of Manufacturers, and the American Anti-Boycott Association.

The writings and activities of what might be called *The Survey* group represented another very influential current affecting industrial government from the outside. These were the liberal social workers, academicians, lawyers, journalists, and ministers who supported and contributed to *The Survey* magazine (until 1909 called *Charities and the Commons*), the main organ of middle-class social reform. Studies by Paul Kellogg, John Fitch, John R. Commons, and other *Survey* contributors played a major role in educating the public about industrial conditions. This group had no unified program, and their views varied over a considerable segment of the radical-conservative yardstick; but they shared a common interest in the humanization of industrial society, and they helped spread this interest throughout a broad network of overlapping publications, private organizations, foundations, and public institutions. *The Survey* group was responsible for enlisting twenty-eight of the most prominent reformers of the country to petition President Taft, following the *Los Angeles Times* explosion episode, to set up a national commission on industrial relations. The hearings and reports of this commission, which will be discussed more fully later, were even more exhaustive than those of the Industrial Commission of 1898–1902 in the industrial relations area, and they attracted widespread public attention.

The pendulum swing to the liberal and socialist side was an international phenomenon which seemed to gain momentum until the outbreak of the European war. The war itself was sloganized into a struggle for democracy; and the immediate postwar period was a highpoint for social democractic thinking until a conservative, antiradical reaction set in. One of the more entertaining aspects of the struggle for social change was the debates between spokesmen of rival views. At the most elevated and sophisticated level was the series of rival articles in *Everybody's Magazine* between Catholic humanist Father John A. Ryan and socialist Morris Hillquit. More earthy were the exchanges between Hillquit and Gompers at a hearing of the Industrial Commission and some of the debates between Gompers and labor socialists in the annual conventions of the American Federation of Labor. More in the nature of polemics were the debates at a distance between radical left-wingers, such as DeLeon, Debs, and Haywood, and the conservative leaders of the AFL. At still another level were the Congressional hearings in which Frederick Taylor expounded and defended his ideas about scientific management against the attacks of prolabor Congressmen.

The U.S. Commission on Industrial Relations, 1913–1915

If the idea of industrial democracy in the form of collective bargaining may be said to have gained the initial stage of public acceptability in the hearings and report of the Industrial Commission, then the hearings and reports of the Commission on Industrial Relations a dozen years later represented a more advanced stage of public encouragement. The remarkable expansion of unionism between 1897 and 1902 had been followed by a series of bitter counterattacks from the exponents of traditional management which in turn had produced a number of violent episodes initiated by both labor and management groups. The liberals and reformers were shocked by this turn of events and called for a comprehensive assessment of conditions. As the petition to President Taft for the commission's establishment stated, "we have yet to solve the problems of democracy in its industrial relationships and to solve them along democratic lines."[4] And the final report of the commission, in the section prepared by Research Director Basil M. Manly and supported by the chairman, Frank P. Walsh, and the three labor representatives, reiterated: "The question of industrial relations assigned by Congress to the Commission for investigation is more fundamental and of greater importance to the welfare of the Nation than any other question except the form of our Government. The only hope for the solution of the tremendous problems created by industrial relationship lies in the effective use of our democratic institutions and in the rapid extension of the principles of democracy to industry."[5]

The report went on to note that "in isolated industrial, mining, or agricultural communities, which are owned or controlled by single individuals or corporations, and in which the employees are unorganized, industrial feudalism is the rule rather than the exception."[6] Industrial democracy "has been established in a greater or less degree in certain American industries or for certain classes of employees. But between conditions of industrial democracy and industrial feudalism there are almost infinite gradations marking the stages of evolution which have been reached."[7] "The crux of the whole question of industrial relations is: shall the workers for the protection of their interests be organized and represented collectively by their chosen delegates, even as the stockholders are represented by their Directors and by the various grades of executive officials and bosses?"[8]

[4] *The Survey,* 27 (December 30, 1911), 13:1430–1431.
[5] U.S. Commission on Industrial Relations, *Final Report and Testimony* (Washington, D.C.: Government Printing Office, 1916), 1:17.
[6] Ibid.
[7] Ibid., p. 18.
[8] Ibid., p. 28.

The answer of the commission to this question was unanimously in the affirmative. But when it came to an elaboration of the implications of this answer, the nine members split three ways. The Manly statement held that the best route to industrial democracy was through joint agreements between associations of employers and trade unions "not merely with reference to wages and hours but with reference to unemployment, the recruiting of the trade, and the introduction of machinery and new processes." The method of regulation by agreement, it argued, "is more comprehensive, is more elastic, and more nearly achieves the ideal of fundamental democracy that government should to the greatest possible extent consist of agreements and understandings voluntarily made." The role of the state, through legal enactment, was to prevent employer interference with the right of organization—including prohibiting the discharge of any person because of union membership or employer refusals to confer with authorized employee representatives—and to safeguard children, women, and male employees in public enterprise or in hazardous private enterprise against unfair or substandard conditions and practices.

A separate report was prepared by John R. Commons and Florence J. Harriman to which the three employer representatives assented with two minor reservations. Commons was not at all in disagreement with the desirability of encouraging collective bargaining, but he thought that the central question confronting the commission was industrial violence and that the solution to violence lay along the lines pioneered by Wisconsin in the enactment and administration of workmen's compensation. The core of the Commons Report was a plan for the establishment of federal and state nonpartisan industrial commissions, with advisory councils of employer and labor representatives, to meet the problems of administering labor legislation, mediating labor disputes, and formulating "agreed bills" for new legislation.

Two sets of principles were imbedded in the Commons' Plan. The first consisted of two propositions: that the struggle between capital and labor must be regarded as a permanent feature of American life, and that there are also certain points where the interests of the opposing forces are harmonious or can be made so by appropriate governmental action. The second set of principles was based on "the fundamental distinction between collective bargaining and the individual labor contract." Government should not employ its coercive powers to regulate collective bargaining, since the parties are competent to act for themselves and, moreover, voluntarism is preferable to legal compulsion. In individual bargaining, however, the worker is at a disadvantage with the employer and cannot really bargain at all. Where this is so, and where there is a public interest to be gained, Congress or the state legislatures and the industrial commissions should equalize the bargaining situation by legal enactment.

The employer members of the commission agreed that labor had many legitimate grievances and that it was "thoroughly justified in organizing and in spreading organization in order better to protect itself against exploitation and oppression." But it found the Manly Report manifestly partisan and unfair to employers generally—partly for minimizing abuses by organized labor and partly for failing to take note of changing attitudes and policies of employers. American democratic ideals, they argued, could be attained only through increases in productivity and the elimination of waste.

Despite the differences among the commission members, all supported a number of common principles about industrial government which, twenty years later, were to become embodied in the law of the land. These principles were not given formal expression until American involvement in World War I and the pressures of patriotism and a national emergency brought about a temporary labor-management agreement. Nevertheless, it

seems appropriate to state them here. They were set forth in
a statement of "principles and policies to govern relations between workers and employers in war industries for the duration
of the war" and were formulated by President Wilson's War
Labor Conference Board, which consisted of five employers
designated by the National Industrial Conference Board and
five unionists designated by the American Federation of Labor,
with two distinguished co-chairmen, ex-president William H.
Taft, selected by the employers, and the former Industrial Relations Commission chairman, Frank P. Walsh, selected by the
union people. These principles were designed to guide the new
War Labor Board. The following are most relevant to the topic
under discussion:

1. The right of workers to organize in trade unions and to bargain collectively, through chosen representatives, is recognized
and affirmed. This right shall not be denied, abridged, or interfered with by the employers in any manner whatsoever.

2. The right of employers to organize in associations or groups
and to bargain collectively, through chosen representatives, is
recognized and affirmed. This right shall not be denied, abridged,
or interfered with by the workers in any manner whatsoever.

3. Employers should not discharge workers for membership in
trade unions, nor for legitimate trade-union activities.

4. The workers, in the exercise of their right to organize, shall
not use coercive measures of any kind to induce persons to join
their organizations, nor to induce employers to bargain or deal
therewith.

5. If it shall become necessary to employ women on work ordinarily performed by men, they must be allowed equal pay for
equal work and must not be allotted tasks disproportionate to their
strength.

6. The basic eight-hour day is recognized as applying in all
cases in which existing law requires it. In all other cases the question of hours of labor shall be settled with due regard to govern-

mental necessities and the welfare, health, and proper comfort of the workers.

7. The right of all workers, including common laborers, to a living wage is hereby declared. In fixing wages, minimum rates of pay shall be established which will insure the subsistence of the worker and his family in health and reasonable comfort.[9]

These principles marked a considerable advance in national thinking about industrial government. Obviously, however, they were far from meeting the standards and goals of industrial democracy which its advocates proposed or even what had been achieved in limited sectors of industry. The hearings of the commission provided a forum for expression of such views. In the remainder of this chapter we shall examine the positions of those who envisioned collective bargaining as the main route to industrial democracy. There were more radical conceptions which also were advocated; they will be the theme of the next chapter.

The AFL Concept

The two most effective labor spokesmen for collective bargaining were Samuel Gompers and John Mitchell. Mitchell lost much of his influence after his retirement from the presidency of the United Mine Workers in 1908, while Gompers remained the dominant AFL spokesman until his death in 1924.

During the ten years of his union and national prominence, Mitchell was an eloquent spokesman for industrial democracy through collective bargaining. In his book, *Organized Labor*,[10] he proclaimed: "Trade unionism stands for liberty, equality,

[9] Several portions of the code, such as the statements on existing conditions, maximum production, and the mobilization of labor, related solely to wartime circumstances and are therefore omitted here.

[10] John Mitchell, *Organized Labor* (Philadelphia: American Book and Bible House, 1903). Written with the assistance of Walter E. Weyl.

and fraternity; it stands for the liberty of workingmen to arrange their own lives and to contract jointly for the manner in which they shall be spent in mine or factory."[11] He strongly rejected the paternalistic approach of many employers. "The ideal of trade unionism is not that of a superior class conferring favors upon an inferior one, not one of loyalty on the one side and generosity upon the other, but the ideal of two separate, strong, self-respecting and mutually respecting parties, freely contracting with each other, and with no limitations upon this right of perfect and absolute freedom of contract, save that which a community in its wisdom may determine to be necessary for its own protection."[12]

As he told the Anthracite Coal Strike Commission, the trade agreement was the only effective method by which it is possible to regulate questions arising between employers and employed in large industries, and he compared the relationship to Congress legislating for a nation or "rather, like a coming together of the representatives of two great nations, upon the basis of mutual respect and mutual toleration, for the formulation of a treaty of peace for the government of industry and the prosperity and welfare of the contracting parties."[13]

He noted that various benefit and cooperative schemes, suggested by humane employers, were an acknowledgment of the claim that workingmen should have a voice in the conduct of business, but they were rarely successful, and "where the employer has, as he should have, the complete control of buying, selling, advertising, accepting credits, and making contracts, the effect of extra exertion by the workingman often has but an inappreciable influence upon his share of the profits of the enterprise."[14]

[11] Ibid., p. 417.
[12] Ibid., p. 414.
[13] Ibid., p. 347.
[14] Ibid., pp. 348–349.

Like all the union leaders of the period, Mitchell saw improved wages and shorter hours as essential to industrial liberty. "No man is free who is forced to work unduly long hours and for wages so low that he cannot provide the necessities of life for himself and his family; who must live in a crowded tenement and see his children go to work in the mills, the mines, and the factories before their bodies develop and their minds are trained. To have freedom a man must be free from the harrowing fear of hunger and want. . . ."[15] He was not opposed to the wage system but felt that it would survive only if work conditions constantly improved.

Although Mitchell emphasized that the unions did not desire to usurp the businessman's function, he noted that union representatives must be informed not only about wages in their own and other industries but also the cost of living, the cost of production, the charges for transportation, the state of the market, the price, cost, and quality of competing products, and the character of machinery and processes used. In bargaining sessions he felt free to suggest price increases to the anthracite coal operators so as to make possible wage increases, and he debated the issue of contracting out work with the Illinois coal operators.

In one important respect, Mitchell differed from Gompers. He felt that there was a place for compulsory investigation and compulsory arbitration, especially in settling disputes in public utilities. But like Gompers he opposed union reliance on government as a substitute for collective bargaining.

Samuel Gompers, of course, was *the* outstanding spokesman for free collective bargaining and the trade agreement system as the expression of industrial democracy. By 1899 when he testified before the Industrial Commission, his views had reached maturity. Thus, when he appeared before the Commission on Industrial Relations in 1913 and 1914, there were no fundamental changes. In a rather extraordinary session in which

[15] *American Federationist*, 17 (May 1910), 5:406.

he and Morris Hillquit were permitted to cross-examine each other before the commission, he emphasized his support for the concrete, pragmatic, day-to-day collective bargaining program of the AFL in contrast to the socialists "who paint a beautiful picture of a future, alluring the workmen from the immediate struggles."[16] He rebutted the criticisms of the socialists and the IWW that the AFL was uninterested in the unskilled workers and opposed to industrial unionism; he rejected labor reliance on government, except for special categories of workers (chiefly women and children) and for special issues (such as accident compensation, the workhours of public employees, and the restriction on the use of court injunctions in labor disputes); and he justified his participation in the National Civic Federation as aiding the cause of labor.

In another session, he succinctly described the general purpose of the AFL as follows: ". . . to improve the condition of the working people materially, economically, politically, socially, to secure better industrial conditions for all the workers, better wages, and shorter or normal workdays; better working conditions for safety, for sanitation; better lives for the workers in their homes and in their daily life; to secure for the children safety from exploitation from employers; to give them the opportunity for the development of a fuller life and understanding; and for their better opportunities; and, in a word, to make life the better worth living after all."[17] At another point in this session, Gompers opposed the New Zealand system of compulsory arbitration and the Canadian system of compulsory investigation as means of settling labor conflicts with the following words: "The difference between a freeman and a slave is the right of the freeman to dispose of himself, his personality, his labor, his power to work, as he himself may determine; his own

[16] U.S. Commission on Industrial Relations, *Final Report and Testimony*, 2:1576.
[17] Ibid., 1:719.

wish, his own whim, his own interest, and not be subject either to the dominating will of an employer on the one hand or the Government of the country on the other; or, I ought to have said, probably his own will, backed up by the power of Government."[18]

Gompers showed an increasing concern about maintaining the rather subtle distinction between unionism which was free of government domination or control and a government role which protected the union against unfair treatment by either employers or the courts.

In a pamphlet on the eight-hour day, he stated: "The stipulation of industrial relations by law does not result in industrial freedom—it only restates all industrial problems in terms of political issues. It substitutes a political boss for an industrial employer. . . . Industrial freedom can be achieved only when workers participate in determining their own hours, wages and conditions of work. This is an industrial problem that must be worked out in the industrial field. It becomes a political problem only when the government is connected with the industry or where the industry is especially hazardous."[19]

He saw industrial democracy as a self-limited process functioning within the capitalist system.

> Collective bargaining in industry does not imply that wage earners shall assume control of industry, or responsibility for financial management. It proposes that the employees shall have the right to organize and to deal with the employer through selected representatives as to wages and working conditions.

> Among the matters that properly come within the scope of collective bargaining are wages, hours of labor, conditions and relations of employment, the sanitary conditions of the plant, safety and comfort regulations and such other factors as would add to the

---

[18] Ibid., p. 721.
[19] Samuel Gompers, *Labor and the Employer* (New York: E. P. Dutton & Co., 1920), p. 102.

health, safety and comfort of the employees, resulting in the mutual advantage of both employers and employees. But there is no belief held in the trades unions that its members shall control the plant or usurp the rights of the owners.[20]

These Gompersian remarks accurately reflect the traditional public position of business unionism, but they fail to portray the long-held interest of many unions in not merely influencing but, if possible, controlling the job territory. No practitioner or scholar has expressed this concept more imaginatively than Selig Perlman, who wrote in the late 1920's about the typographical union's "ownership" of the employment opportunities in the printing industry and its code of "rules of occupancy and tenure."[21]

Employer Support for the Collective Bargaining Model

Like labor, the employer group was not united in its views on industrial government. Most employers clearly had no sympathy with ideas about industrial democracy, as indicated by the actions of both the great capitalists (e.g., the practical destruction of collective bargaining in steel by U.S. Steel in 1901 and the resistance to a signed agreement of the anthracite coal operators in 1902) and the small employers (e.g., the open-shop drive and the conversion of the National Association of Manufacturers into an anti-union organization). To put the matter in the baldest possible terms, the typical employer felt that he was entitled to run his business as he saw fit, though recognizing an obligation to be fair and humane. Whatever else he might have seen it as, he certainly did not see industry as an arena for the democratic process.

[20] Ibid., p. 286.
[21] Selig Perlman, A Theory of the Labor Movement (New York: Macmillan Co., 1928), pp. 262ff.

This hostility is clearly expressed in the principles adopted by the National Metal Trades Association in 1901.

We, the Members of the National Metal Trades Association, declare the following to be our principles, which shall govern us in our relation with our employes:

1. *Concerning Employes.*—Since we, as employers, are responsible for the work turned out by our workmen we must have full discretion to designate the men we consider competent to perform the work. While disavowing any intention to interfere with the proper functions of labor organizations, we will not admit of any interference with the management of our business.

2. *Strikes and Lockouts.*—This Association disapproves of strikes and lockouts in the settlement of industrial disputes. This Association will not countenance a lockout, unless all reasonable means of adjustment have failed; neither will the members of this Association deal with striking employes as a body.

3. *Relations of Employes.*—Every workman who elects to work in a shop will be required to work peaceably and harmoniously with all his fellow employes, and to work loyally for the interests of his employer.

4. *Apprentices, Etc.*—The number of apprentices, helpers and handymen to be employed will be determined solely by the employer.

5. *Methods and Wages.*—The responsibility for management, methods and the production of our shops rests upon us, and no restriction upon these matters will be allowed. We will require proper production for proper compensation.

Employes will be paid by the hourly rate, by premium system, piecework, contract or other system, as the employers may elect.

6. *Freedom of Employment.*—It is the privilege of the employe to leave our employ whenever he sees fit and it is the privilege of the employer to discharge any workman when he sees fit.

7. *Concerning Disagreements.*—The above principles being absolutely essential to the successful conduct of our business, we cannot permit the operation of our business thereunder to be in-

terfered with. In case of disagreement concerning matters not covered by the foregoing declaration and not affecting the economic integrity of the industry, we advise our members to meet such of their employes who may be affected by such disagreement and endeavor to adjust the difficulty on a fair and equitable basis.

8. *Equitable Wages.*—In the conduct of our business and in the payment of wages, by whatever system, this Association will not countenance any conditions or any rates of compensation which are not reasonable and just or which will not allow a workman a proper wage in proportion to his efficiency and productiveness.[22]

Nevertheless, the democratic winds were not to be ignored. At least five different categories of employers who attempted, in some fashion or other, to accommodate to the rising democratic spirit of the times are discernible: (1) the employers who supported unionism, collective bargaining, and the trade agreement; (2) the majority of employers in the National Civic Federation, who paid lip service to collective bargaining but were mainly interested in industrial peace, welfare work, and individualism; (3) the advocates of profit sharing; (4) the scientific management people; and (5) the pioneers in employee representation schemes other than unionism. This chapter is concerned with only the first two categories—the other three will be treated in Section III.

Between 1898 and 1915 an increasing number of employers espoused the virtues of collective bargaining; it must be added, however, that the behavior of the corporations with which many of these men were associated often seemed to belie their words. Nevertheless this was a significant index of the changing times. For example, George W. Perkins, a partner in the Morgan firm and a director of numerous major corporations including U.S. Steel and International Harvester, testified before the Commission on Industrial Relations:

[22] Reprinted in U.S., Congress, Senate, *Hearings of Subcommittee of Committee on Education and Labor,* 75th Cong., 1st sess., 1937, pt. 3:1010.

I do not believe that competition is any longer the life of trade. I have long believed that cooperation is the life of trade. I believe this because it is clear that competition, driven to its logical end, gave us the sweatshop, child labor, long hours of labor, insanitary labor conditions, and bred strife and discord between employer and employee. I have long believed that cooperation by the Federal Government, is the only method of eliminating the abuses from which labor has suffered under the competitive method. I believe in cooperation and organization in industry. I believe in this for both labor and capital.[23]

At a later point in his testimony, Perkins stated: "I believe that every man should have the right to so exercise his freedom as to render the most good to the most people. I think collective bargaining comes nearer representing that notion than individual management."[24] But when pressed to explain why neither U.S. Steel nor Harvester dealt with organized labor, Perkins asserted: "I did not mean to say I believed in the organization of labor as it is; I said I thought organized labor had helped labor; but I also said I felt that labor should be required to incorporate and be under Federal regulation and to be of known responsibility in its negotiations, which is not now the case."[25]

The position of Joseph Schaffner, secretary-treasurer of Hart Schaffner & Marx, was a much more genuine affirmation of industrial democracy.

If we did not have an agreement with an organization such as we now have, I would certainly insist upon having our employees represented so that they would have an organization among themselves that would dispense the same kind of justice as we have now dispensed by the arbitration board and the trade board. I think the conditions such as we had before, while we got along for many

[23] U.S. Commission on Industrial Relations, *Final Report and Testimony*, 8:7598–7599.

[24] Ibid., p. 7606.

[25] Ibid., p. 7620.

years, and got along very well—in fact, just a few days before the strike one of my friends came in and congratulated me on the fine business that we had and the achievement we had made, and I told him I was very proud of it, but I was prouder still of the happy and contented condition of our employees. That was just two days before the strike. I thought they were just as happy as they are now. I did not know any different.[26]

Even before Schaffner gained his new perspective on labor relations, the ladies' garment manufacturers of New York had been persuaded by Louis Brandeis and Louis Marshall, a prominent New York lawyer, to work out a system of industrial government based on the trade agreement, collective bargaining, and arbitration.

NCF EMPLOYERS

Like Perkins, many employers belonging to the National Civic Federation did not challenge the right of workers to form unions and to bargain collectively. But their arguments focused on responsibilities rather than rights, on the liberty of the individual rather than the solidarity of the group, on the welfare actions to be provided for the employees rather than the nature of their participation in decision-making. Typical was the following excerpt from a talk by the president of the New York, New Haven, and Hartford Railroad to the Hartford West Side Workingmen's Club:

To those of you who belong to unions I wish to say I believe they have accomplished much good; but they are, nevertheless, not an unmixed blessing to the laboring man. They tend to the discouragement of individual effort and reduce man to a part of a machine. They are a good thing for the drone, the inefficient man, for the walking delegate and the officers, but are unnecessary for the man who has the stuff and courage within himself to carve his own way in the world. . . .

[26] Ibid., 1:575.

Now, having hurt the feelings of some of you by the foregoing, I am going to surprise you by saying that I regard the unions as a condition that has come to stay; that I have no prejudice whatever to properly conducted ones, and express my wish that our men generally would join them, not that I would run a union plant as such, for I would not coerce my men nor consent to discriminations as between those who were and who were not members, but I would wish to have in the unions the conservative influence of many of the good men who are out to counteract the floater, the anarchist, the man who has nothing at stake in the world, who works with his mouth more than his hands.[27]

Few of the employer members of the NCF shared the enthusiasm of Ralph M. Easley, founder and general secretary, and later Executive Committee chairman of the organization. Easley, not an employer himself although a close associate of many, often expressed views similar to those of Gompers with whom he had strong rapport. But he also strongly defended the employer's interest in efficiency. Easley was a supporter of conservative unionism and the trade agreement against both "Parryism" (the vituperative anti-union movement led by David M. Parry, president of the Citizens' Industrial Association of America) on the right, and the equally outspoken, anti-Gompersian socialism of Debs and De Leon on the left. He saw unionism as an "industrial democracy"[28] whose major need was to overcome the apathy of its members through education. Industrial peace and industrial justice were his twin goals. When the New York Interborough Rapid Transit Company reached an agreement with its unionized employees, the *Review* wrote applaudingly:

This largest employer in its line of business in the United States did not reply to these [union] demands with the old-fashioned answers that it would "manage its affairs in its own way"; that it would not brook the "interference of outsiders"; that it would

[27] *Monthly Review,* 1 (July 15, 1904), 5:18.
[28] Ibid., 1 (November 15, 1904), 9:16.

"meet only the men in its employ"; that there was "nothing to confer about"; that there was "nothing to arbitrate." Instead, it accepted, through an enlightened directorate and its president, August Belmont, that method of round-the-table conference whose efficacy in securing industrial peace has been practically demonstrated elsewhere, and whose promotion is the main object of the National Civic Federation.[29]

Easley saw no conflict between collective bargaining and the employer's right to control his business. He looked forward to the time when "national prosperity will be coincident with the uplifting of organized labor, so that its admitted errors may become fewer and its sincere cooperation with capital in increasing productivity more frequent."[30] Easley staked much of this thought and prestige on the continued support of big business leaders. When they turned away from their temporary accommodation with the AFL, Easley's voice quickly faded.

Neutral Third-Party Advocates

Of the influential supporters of collective bargaining outside of the ranks of labor and management, three men merit special attention not only because of the views which they held but also because of the practical consequences of their behavior. They were Louis D. Brandeis, John Williams, and John R. Commons.

LOUIS D. BRANDEIS

Brandeis, the great "attorney for the people," saw the achievement of industrial democracy through the combination and integration of unionism and scientific management. As early as 1904, he told the Boston Typothetae, an employers' association,

29 Ibid., 1 (September 15, 1904), 7:15.
30 Ibid.

that they must fully recognize the right of labor to organize and to be represented by union officers, and he urged the owners or real managers to participate themselves in labor conferences and not act through intermediaries. But he also advised them to resist lawless or arbitrary claims of organized labor at whatever cost. "We gain nothing," he said, "by exchanging the tyranny of capital for the tyranny of labor."[31]

Speaking to the Boston Central Labor Union the following year, Brandeis suggested that they should demand steady employment for the workingman throughout the year and seek to secure all the earnings of a business except what is required to get necessary capital and managing ability. But he also insisted that union representatives understand and be responsive to the conditions of each business, and that elimination of waste and of output restrictions should always be a major union concern. Brandeis was an enthusiastic supporter of the ideas of Frederick Taylor and is believed to have been responsible for the label "scientific management" which helped give Taylorism such widespread publicity. He contended, however, that scientific management could not be imposed by the employer or engineer on the employees, that it could succeed only with the consent and cooperation of the employees. Brandeis put his ideas into practice through his mediatory and arbitration activities in the New York ladies' garment industry. The Protocol of Peace, with its preferential union shop, its grievance arbitration machinery, and its joint board of sanitary control, which he helped construct in 1910, was a milestone (despite its temporary breakdown within a few years) in the development of the present system of industrial democracy.

In his testimony in 1915 to the Commission on Industrial Relations, Brandeis presented one of the most perceptive statements on industrial democracy to be found in the literature. The fundamental cause of the industrial conflict of the period, he

[31] Ibid., 1 (August 15, 1904), 6:10–110.

asserted, was the contrast between "our political liberty and our industrial absolutism." Unrest could never be removed by "mere improvement of the physical and material condition of the workingman."

> We Americans are committed not only to social justice in the sense of avoiding things which bring suffering and harm, like unjust distribution of wealth; but we are committed primarily to democracy. The social justice for which we are striving is an incident of our democracy, not its main end. It is rather the result of democracy—perhaps its finest expression—but it rests upon democracy which implies the rule by the people. And therefore the end for which we must strive is the attainment of rule by the people, and that involves industrial democracy as well as political democracy. That means that the problem of a trade should be no longer the problems of the employer alone. The problems of his business, and it is not the employer's business alone, are the problems of all in it. The union cannot shift upon the employer the responsibility for conditions, nor can the employer insist upon determining, according to his will, the conditions which shall exist. The problems which exist are the problems of the trade; they are the problems of employer and employee.[32]

Brandeis saw collective bargaining—the making of a contract with a union—a great advance, but only a first step. To result in industrial democracy it must "create practically an industrial government—a relation between employer and employee where the problems as they arise from day to day, or from month to month, or from year to year, may come up for consideration and solution as they come up in our political government."[33] This entailed employer understanding of the conditions and facts concerning labor, and union understanding of the problems of business. It meant a willingness of the employer to open his

[32] *U.S. Commission on Industrial Relations, Final Report and Testimony,* 8:7659–7660.
[33] Ibid., p. 7662.

books to union representatives and a willingness on the part of the union to eliminate waste and to increase efficiency. It required both parties to live up to their agreements and to abstain from violence and other unlawful acts.

As to the role of the state and the enactment of legislation to assure industrial democracy, Brandeis took a very flexible position. "We should not regulate anything by law except where an evil exists which the existing forces of unionism or otherwise, labor, are unable to deal with it."[34] Even the provisions for the protection of women and children or for sanitary conditions and safety for all wage earners, which he had strongly espoused, were to be subject to this rule. Thus, the situation might vary from community to community and from trade to trade.

JOHN E. WILLIAMS

Although not so well known by the general public as Brandeis, John E. Williams served as impartial chairman of the arbitration board of the famous Hart Schaffner & Marx system from 1912 till his death in 1919. Among his other achievements, Williams is credited with having saved the system from collapse and with having developed the philosophy and procedures which made it a national model.[35]

Williams' conception of industrial democracy is perhaps best expressed in the preamble to the Hart Schaffner & Marx contract of 1913 and in his testimony before the Commission on Industrial Relations in 1914 and 1915. Three paragraphs of the preamble set forth the respective responsibilities of employer, union, and workers:

> On the part of the employer it is the intention and expectation that this compact of peace will result in the establishment and

[34] Ibid., p. 7672.

[35] This discussion of Williams is based on an unpublished M. A. thesis written under my supervision by Donald Otis Clark, "John Elias Williams (1853–1919) —Labor Peacemaker" (University of Illinois, 1957).

maintenance of a high order of discipline and efficiency by the willing cooperation of union and workers rather than by the old method of surveillance and coercion; that by the exercise of this discipline all stoppages and interruptions of work, and all willful violations of rules will cease; that good standards of workmanship and conduct will be maintained and a proper quantity, quality, and cost of production will be assured; and that out of its operation will issue such cooperation and good will between employers, foremen, union, and workers as will prevent misunderstanding and friction and make for good team work, good business, material advantage, and mutual respect.

On the part of the union it is the intention and expectation that this compact will, with the cooperation of the employer, operate in such a way as to maintain, strengthen, and solidify its organization so that it may be strong enough and efficient enough to cooperate as contemplated in the preceding paragraph; and also that it may be strong enough to command the respect of the employer without being forced to resort to militant or unfriendly measures.

On the part of the workers, it is the intention and expectation that they pass from the status of wage servants, with no claim on the employer save his economic need, to that of self-respecting parties to an agreement which they have had an equal part with him in making; that this statement gives them an assurance of fair and just treatment and protects them against injustice or oppression of those who may have been placed in authority over them; that they will have recourse to a court, in the creation of which their votes were equally potent to that of the employer, in which all grievances may be heard, and all their claims adjudicated; that all changes during the life of the pact shall be subject to the approval of an impartial tribunal and that wages and working conditions shall not fall below the level provided for in the agreement.

Williams held that industrial relations were essentially a struggle over the division of power. Capital, he believed, could respond in two ways: rejecting labor's demands while trying to satisfy the employees by palliative measures, such as voluntary correction of grievances and by welfare work of different kinds; or recognizing the union and dealing through joint agreements, grievance committees, arbitration boards, and the like. Williams was a staunch advocate of the latter course, a course he believed was inevitable in a democratic society.

JOHN R. COMMONS

Commons' views on the role of government in industrial democracy have already been discussed, but his central emphasis was on collective bargaining. He wrote in the *Review of Reviews*, in March 1901, that the highest form of industrial peace could be established only through negotiations between two equally powerful organizations—labor unions and employer associations. The practical model was the trade agreement systems of bituminous coal mining, stove foundries, and longshoring on the Great Lakes. And because these systems reminded him of parliamentary government in England, he called the process "constitutional government in industry." The parties to negotiations in these industries frankly admitted that self-interest was the ruling motive and that agreement was needed to avoid anarchy. The trade agreement usually involved two main issues —wages and methods of managing employees. Each system needed to control a complete competitive field; each needed not only a legislative branch to negotiate the basic rules but also a judicial branch to interpret and an executive branch to enforce them.

Constitutional government, Commons believed, was not always good government, and in support of his argument he depicted union and employer abuses in the Chicago teaming and trucking industry and the New York building trades between 1902 and 1905. The reason, he declared, lay in the fundamental principle that no institution or individual can be trusted with absolute power. "Employers' associations are just as necessary to restrain labor unions, and labor unions to restrain employers' associations as two houses of Congress, a Supreme Court, a president and political parties to restrain social classes. Progress does not come when one association destroys the other, but when one association destroys the excesses of the other."[36]

From his studies in labor history Commons had concluded that union success could come only by abandoning the field of production—i.e., cooperatives and profit sharing—and concentrating on distribution of wealth. It was the employer who assumed the risks of business and who bore the responsibilities of production. A trade union was a combination to get a larger economic return for its members and to protect their economic interests. Unions were necessarily restrictive, even when they provided technical or trade education for apprentices. "If they increase production, it is because they set other forces at work to over-balance their restrictions."[37] As efficiency and restriction are two conflicting principles, they must therefore be brought into a kind of equilibrium "in the same way that similar conflicts are met in the region of politics; namely, a constitutional form of organization representing the interests affected, with mutual veto, and therefore with progressive compromises as conflicts arise."[38]

[36] "The Union Shop," address to the American Economic Association, December 1904, reprinted in John R. Commons, *Labor and Administration* (New York: Macmillan Co., 1923), p. 104.

[37] "Restrictions by Trade Unions," *Outlook* (November 1906), reprinted in Commons, *Labor and Administration*, p. 122.

[38] "Unions and Efficiency," *American Economic Review* (September 1911), reprinted in Commons, *Labor and Administration*, p. 140.

CHAPTER **6**

THE CHALLENGE
FROM THE LEFT

COLLECTIVE BARGAINING as the expression of industrial democracy encountered two main challenges during the first two decades of the present century. One was the negative approach of hostile employers who were determined to preserve their traditional sovereignty despite employee efforts to unionize. After 1902 this approach bore considerable success in checking the momentum of union gains around the turn of the century and, except for the rather unique developments in the needle trades, restrained unionization until U.S. involvement in World War I. Although many of the anti-union employers developed welfare programs, safety and sanitation improvements, and retirement or stock-ownership benefits, their attitude was traditionally authoritarian and paternalistic.

The second challenge to the collective bargaining model came from the left—those who believed that it was not possible to achieve industrial democracy without major changes in the prevailing capitalist order. These leftist views ranged from relatively limited reforms in industrial practice (e.g., the establishment of industrial councils) to varying degrees of constitutional socialism to the violent overthrow of the wage system. It is these views which will be the focus of this chapter, not because any of them achieved much practical or lasting success but because they forced the moderate trade unionists and many of the leading employers to reexamine and liberalize their policies. They also added to the environmental pressures which affected governmental policy, particularly at the federal level. For analytical purposes, I shall treat these leftist views under the following four headings: the Social Democrats, the revolutionary Socialists, the Plumb Plan, and the religious social reformers. The responses of the collective-bargaining proponents will be discussed in a concluding section.

The Social Democrats

When the Socialist party of America was formed in 1901, it included in its ranks such diverse groups as orthodox Marxists, revisionist Marxists, Fabians, Christian Socialists, Bellamyites, and radical Populists. Eugene Debs, the party's charismatic leader, who had begun his career as an industrial unionist, became a staunch advocate of political socialism, saw little hope in working within the American Federation of Labor and, after a brief disillusioning experience with the IWW, tended to play down the industrial side of the socialist program. But there were other prominent socialists who regarded the trade unions as essential to the achievement of industrial democracy–socialist model and who actively worked within the American Federation of Labor in opposition to the Gompers majority. Their principal aim was to get the Federation and its constituent organizations to endorse the socialist plank of government ownership of the means of production and distribution—the equivalent of the Article 10 which the Gompers forces so narrowly defeated in 1893 and which cost Gompers the presidency of the AFL in 1894. For tactical purposes, however, they stressed secondary issues in the AFL meetings, such as condemnation of the National Civic Federation with which Gompers and Mitchell were closely associated, adoption of the principle of industrial as against craft unionism, and support for anti-Gompers candidates for AFL positions. The socialists never came as close to their objective as they did in 1893–1894, but they did win the endorsement of various aspects of their program in a number of important AFL unions,[1] and they amassed nearly a third of the delegate votes in the 1912 AFL national convention.

The leading spokesman for the socialists who stressed close trade-union relations as well as political action was Morris Hillquit, an articulate New York attorney and counsel for the Ladies Garment Workers Union. Hillquit expounded the socialist concept of industrial democracy in numerous books, articles, and speeches. "As democracy means political self-government, so socialism stands for industrial self-government."[2]

Hillquit saw the state taking over the great trustified industries and operating them for the benefit of the public. "These trusts," he wrote, "will be governed neither by a bureaucracy nor a system of mob rule. In its purest form it is a rational democracy which allow its affairs to be administered by appropriate general and local agencies, deriving their powers from the people and exercising them in conformity with their will."[3]

In a debate over socialism with Father John A. Ryan, appear-

---

[1] According to Ira Kipnis, by 1907 national and international unions with some 330,000 members had endorsed the socialist program and by 1912, their peak year, they had the official support of the Brewery Workers, Bakery Workers, Cloth Hat and Cap Workers, Ladies' Garment Workers, Fur Workers, Machinists, Tailors, and Western Federation of Miners as well as strong minorities among the United Mine Workers, the Flint Glass Workers, Painters, and others. Kipnis, *The American Socialist Movement, 1897–1912* (New York: Columbia University Press, 1952), pp. 338–340.

[2] Morris Hillquit, *Socialism Summed Up* (New York: H. K. Fly, 1913), p. 25.

[3] Hillquit, *Socialism in Theory and Practice* (New York: Macmillan Co., 1913), p. 25.

ing in seven consecutive issues of *Everybody's Magazine* in 1913, Hillquit spelled out what he meant in detail:

> Socialism advocates not only collective ownership, but also democratic administration of the industries. In practical application this principle must be interpreted to mean that under a socialist regime the workers in each industry will have a voice in the selection of the managing authorities and in the formulation of the main features of industrial policy, subject to such general laws and regulations as will be necessary to safeguard the interests of the community as a whole. This, of course, does not imply that the workers will elect each shop foreman or factory superintendent, or that the managing authorities will fix in advance a uniform scale of wages or a uniform labour day for each group of employees. It is not at all unlikely that in its practical workings the socialist industrial democracy will be somewhat similar to the forms of our present political democracy. The workers in each industry may periodically select the managing authority with power to make appointments and to fix rules. Such elected board or body may consist of shop representatives, and these would be better judges of the qualifications of the chief manager or executive committee of the industry than the bankers who now control the directorates of the great corporations.[4]

In his famous appearance with Samuel Gompers at the May 1914 hearing of the Commission on Industrial Relations, Hillquit emphasized the political program of the Socialist party and its dual character: first, a gradual socialization of the ownership of industries through the political process, and at the same time advocacy of "every measure calculated to improve the condition of the workers—such, for instance, as better wages, shorter hours, abolition of child labor, state insurance, national insurance [for] workers against old age, sickness, disability, and so

---

[4] U.S. Commission on Industrial Relations, *Final Report and Testimony*, (Washington, D.C.: Government Printing Office, 1916), 1:1467.

on."[5] He asserted that the party "encourages and supports economic organizations and the struggles of the labor movement, of the trade-union movement, in all its forms" but that it did not engage in the economic struggles of the workers except where such struggles assumed a political and general aspect. He cited a resolution adopted by the 1912 convention of the party which urged its members who were eligible for union membership to take an active part in such organizations and to press for organization of the unorganized, especially the immigrant and unskilled laborers, but which also stressed that the party should not intervene in internal union controversies over form of organization or techniques. When pressed by Gompers to account for Debs' participation in the IWW, his attacks on the craft unions, and his urging the Metal Miners and Coal Miners to secede from the AFL, Hillquit disassociated himself and the Socialist party from these actions. He contended that the Socialists wanted to work within and with the AFL although they differed strongly with the Gompers leadership and with some of its attitudes toward industrial unionism and political action. He felt that the future was on the side of the Socialists and that the AFL itself was gradually moving in the correct direction because of the environmental pressures on it.

The Revolutionary Socialists

With the formation of the Socialist party in 1901, the Socialist Labor party, which had been formed in 1876 and for a decade had been under the domination of Daniel De Leon, played a decreasingly important role in American labor relations. Nevertheless, De Leon himself remained a figure of some intellectual significance in radical circles. In terms of contemporary goals,

[5] Hillquit and Ryan, *Socialism: Promise or Menace* (New York: Macmillan Co., 1914), pp. 79–80.

tactics and strategy, as well as in polemical style, De Leon differed considerably from Hillquit, but his normative view of the industrial society of the future was not fundamentally different. Although not explicitly stated, De Leon's conception seemed to consist of worker administration of socialized enterprise on an industrial basis, combined with a parliamentary system in which representation would be on industrial rather than geographical lines.[6]

This view of the future was shared to a degree by the syndicalist leaders of the IWW; the main distinction was that the former greatly deemphasized the role of the state. In a symposium by *The Survey* just before the Commission on Industrial Relations began its hearings, the IWW leader "Big Bill" Haywood wrote: "The Commission on Industrial Relations is a tragic joke, perpetrated by legislative jugglers. . . . There are those of us who believe there can be no solution as long as the distinction between capitalist and worker exists. . . . It rests with the working class to find the solution."[7] Subsequently, in testifying before the commission, Haywood unveiled his vision of a syndicalist-anarchist society in which "each branch of industry would be operated by a group of workers who best know that branch, and among that group of workers if foremen or overseers were necessary they would be selected from among the workers"—independent of the state.[8] IWW short-run objectives and tactics were very different from those of the Socialists. Haywood had no faith in political action. He was totally antagonistic to working within the AFL. His conception of industrial unionism as "one big union" went far beyond the Hillquit version. He opposed the signed agreement system and viewed plant union-management

[6] See, for example, "The Preamble of the I. W. W.," later renamed "Socialist Reconstruction of Society: The Industrial Vote," in Daniel De Leon, *Speeches and Editorials* (New York: Labor News Co., n.d.), vol. 1.

[7] *The Survey* (August 2, 1913), p. 580.

[8] U.S. Commission on Industrial Relations, *Final Report and Testimony*, 11:10586–10587.

relations as no more than a temporizing arrangement until the workers secured control over industry.

Both Vincent St. John, general secretary and treasurer of the IWW, and Joseph J. Ettor, national organizer, also told the commission that their goal was worker control over industry, without government intervention. Contemporary government to them was simply a tool of the capitalist class. They saw little need for government after the overthrow of the capitalist system. Society would be made up largely of self-governing workshops and industries which would cooperate with each other. The fundamental objective of the IWW was to drill and educate the workers so that they could learn how to control industry. Until workers achieved the needed power and training, they would deal with their employers on a pragmatic, fighting basis. Employee-employer cooperation always worked to the disadvantage of the workers. Fixed-time agreements were unacceptable, because they tied the hands of the workers and benefitted the employer. ". . . if the effort to gain better conditions resulted in a strike and this strike resulted in a victory for the workers involved, work would be resumed simply upon the representatives of the employer, the qualified representatives of the employer, saying that they agreed to the terms for which the workers were fighting, and a notice posted in the mill to that extent."[9] Although there would be worker grievance committees to deal with management, they would have to take everything back to the workers for their approval. Full-time union officers and formal structures were to be held to a minimum. Pending the final victory, reliance would be placed on job action (strikes, slow-downs, sabotage, whatever action seemed justified by the circumstances). In brief, the IWW distrusted formal organization of any kind and advocated self-government for all of industrial society in terms of a participative democracy often associated with the village, kibbutz, or small group.

[9] Ibid., 2:1450.

The Plumb Plan

By 1915 the Socialist party had passed its peak and the IWW had experienced samples of the bitter hostility and harassment which in a few years would lead to its virtual destruction. But some aspects of socialist thought continued to attract wide support, particularly after the successful wartime administration of the railroads by the federal government. Next to municipal utilities and, perhaps, the telephone and telegraph industry, the railroads had most generally been regarded as an appropriate subject for federal regulation. Unlike the case of manufacturing, the U.S. Constitution posed no bar. In addition to regulation of rates and other aspects of competition such as the Interstate Commerce Act of 1887 provided, a variety of railway labor laws had been passed for the safety and health of the workers and for the settlement of labor disputes. In 1916, in the face of a threatened national railroad strike, President Wilson recommended and the Congress enacted a basic eight-hour day law (the Adamson Act) for operating employees. In December 1917 the President, by proclamation, directed government possession and operation of the railroads because of the wartime emergency, and the roads were not returned to private ownership until the passage of the Transportation Act of 1920.

During the two years of government operation, railroad unionism made appreciable gains in membership (especially among the shop crafts and other non-ops who had lagged behind the Big Four Brotherhoods), wages and other conditions of employment, and union voice in the government of the industry. As a result of these gains, the railroad unions, which had traditionally been among the more conservative elements in the labor movement, were won over to support of the Plumb Plan, which would have nationalized the railroads and provided for their continued operation after World War I by a tripartite administration. Although the Plumb Plan got little support in Congress, it stirred considerable interest in labor ranks, particularly among railroaders and miners, for whom it was proposed and by whom it was endorsed.

Glenn Plumb, a Streator, Illinois, attorney who represented the railroad unions, was author and chief exponent of the plan to place the railroads in public hands (through the sale of bonds which would enable the government to pay the railway stockholders the value of their investment) and to administer them through a public corporation whose board of directors would consist of an equal number of representatives of the public, the railroad management, and the classified employees. As an incentive to efficiency and economy in the operation of the roads beyond that which he expected from the participation of the unions in the management process, Plumb embodied a savings-sharing plan in his program. Rates were to be set by the Interstate Commerce Commission so as to cover the liquidation of all indebtedness to the former owners as well as all operating and betterment costs. If the actual costs were reduced by the managers below the anticipated level, one-half of the savings would belong to the government and the other half would be distributed as a dividend to managerial and ordinary employees based upon their respective salaries or wages.[10]

Plumb conceived of his plan as a form of industrial democracy to be applied ultimately to all industry, and this conception was adopted by his followers. The Plumb Plan League, which was established by the railroad unions in 1919 to win public and Congressional support, weekly published the *Railroad Democracy*. The lead article in the first issue by Warren S. Stone, grand chief of the Brotherhood of Locomotive Engineers, contained the following:

[10] Plumb's plan and the philosophy underlying it were described in detail in a posthumous volume: Glenn E. Plumb and William G. Roylance, *Industrial Democracy: A Plan for Its Achievement* (New York: B. W. Huebsch, 1923).

Labor offers an opportunity which means for all railroad men the larger life and the higher service that is generally represented by the phrase "industrial democracy." It is an opportunity by which we, the members of the organized railroad employes, and those who believe in the same cause that we do, may blaze a better trail for all labor.

. . . .

It makes the worker a partner of his country, one of the trustees of a great new enterprise of human service and organization. It relieves him for all time from being a mere cog in a machine for grinding out profits for someone else.

. . . .

It makes him the true servant of the public and of the country, which rewards his efficient service with an interest in the dividends of the enterprise. It makes the railroads his not in the property sense, but in an even more vital way—the way of service. They are entrusted to him free of politics, free of bureaucracy, free of the pressure of financial domination, to show what efficiency in a real democracy of workers can be made to mean.

. . . .

We believe that by efficient railroad management passenger rates can be lowered to 1½ cents a mile and freight rates 30 to 40 per cent. And ultimately the railroads will belong to the country debt-free, and labor will be a permanent partner in the greatest cooperative enterprise that the world has seen.[11]

In a subsequent issue, the presidents of the four operating Brotherhoods contended that their proposal was "to operate the railroads democratically, applying the principles to industry for which in international affairs the nation has participated in a world war."[12] They also cited President Wilson's message of May 20, 1919, calling for "the genuine democratization of industry, based upon a full recognition of the right of those who work, in whatever rank, to participate in some organic way in

[11] *Railroad Democracy*, 1 (July 22, 1919), 1:1–2.
[12] Ibid., 1 (August 7, 1919), 3:6.

every decision which directly affects their welfare in the part they are to play in industry."

Throughout their short campaign, the Plumb Plan advocates kept stressing the Wilsonian theme of the democratization of industry. Although they tried to disassociate themselves from the Socialists, their journal printed two approving articles by the leading British guild socialists, D. G. H. Cole and S. G. Hobson, which claimed the Plumb Plan as a form of guild socialism. But the national reaction against anything which resembled socialism had set in and the plan failed to get Congressional approval. The railroads were returned to their private owners and managers on March 1, 1920.

The Religious Reformers

SOCIAL PROTESTANTISM

The Social Gospel movement of the nineteenth century was discussed in chapter 3. It continued to broaden in the first two decades of the twentieth, not merely becoming an expression of the more radical clergy but also strongly influencing the mainstream. The idea of industrial democracy was a major ingredient of this religious social thought.

The central figure in Social Protestantism during the period under discussion was Walter Rauschenbusch whose widely read book, *Christianity and the Social Crisis*,[13] originally appeared in 1907. Later sermons, articles, and books expanded his reputation. Writing in 1952, Frank Grace, a student of the Social Gospel movement, has stated:

After the phenomenal success of this volume he was generally considered the outstanding figure of Social Protestantism. Raus-

[13] See the recent Harper Torchbook edition of Walter Rauschenbusch, *Christianity and Social Crisis* (New York: Harper & Row, Pubs., 1964) with its perceptive introduction by Robert D. Cross.

chenbush spoke for a comparatively small segment of American Protestantism, but it was a vigorous and growing segment. The ideas which he stated more than a generation ago have become, with exceptions, an accepted part of contemporary Protestant thought. They are, by and large, the ideas of the Federal Council of Churches of Christ in America and the ideas of the major denominations comprising the Council.[14]

Like such nineteenth-century Social Gospel leaders as Gladden, Bliss, and Herron, Rauschenbusch rooted his message of social regeneration in the teachings of Jesus and in the principles of social cooperation and justice as opposed to the Social Darwinian principles of competitive struggle and the survival of the fittest. However, he went beyond his predecessors in challenging not only the commercial and industrial interests of the country but also the churches for their failure to understand the problems, aspirations, and methods of the working class. He sensed a growing alienation between the church and labor because so many of the preachers were concentrating on the abuses of labor and reflecting the attitudes of the business and professional classes who "dominate the spiritual atmosphere in the large city churches."[15] He argued that "a Church which believes in political democracy can easily learn to believe in industrial democracy as soon as it comprehends the connection."[16]

In his climactic chapter "What to Do" he asserted that the first step for the true Christian was his personal regeneration on

---

[14] Frank Grace, *The Concept of Property in Modern Christian Thought* (Urbana: University of Illinois Press, 1953), p. 81. The literature on Social Christianity is enormous but I shall not attempt any extensive assessment because it had, in my judgment, relatively little impact on the development of industrial democracy—either as idea or practice. Among the well-known surveys of the subject are Henry F. May, *Protestant Churches in Industrial America* (New York: Harper and Bros., 1949) and Donald Meyer, *The Protestant Search for Political Realism, 1919–1941* (Berkeley and Los Angeles: University of California Press, 1960).

[15] Rauschenbusch, *Christianity and Social Crisis*, p. 329.

[16] Ibid., p. 323.

social issues and that the solution of "the social question" lay with the ordinary Christian man. The pulpit could also make a contribution by more effective preaching on social issues. The clergy had the power to "soften the increasing class hatred of the working class" and "awaken among the wealthy a sense of social compunction and moral uneasiness."[17]

But Rauschenbusch was not content with lofty general principle. He thought that the Church was in a position to "mitigate the social hardships of the working classes by lending force to humane customs," such as the Saturday half-holiday in the summer, seats and rest rooms for department store clerks, less crowding in tenements, more employer consideration of aged workers, and less exploitation of children. Moral conviction was needed before any social legislation would be effective. He strongly endorsed the trade unions despite the fact that "they have often been foolish and tyrannical in their demands, and headstrong and even lawless in their actions."[18] He observed that the unions "have not yet won from their employers nor from public opinion the acknowledged right to be organized, to bargain collectively, and to assist in controlling the discipline of the shops in which they have to work. The law seems to afford them very little backing as yet. It provides penalties for the kind of injuries which workingmen are likely to inflict on their employers, but not for the subtler injuries which employers are likely to inflict on their workingmen." He then concluded that "the labor movement must go on until public opinion and the law have conceded a recognized position to the labor unions, and until the workingmen interested in a given question stand collectively on a footing of equality with the capitalists interested in it."[19]

Rauschenbusch ended his assessment of Christianity and the social crisis with the judgment that the ultimate solution was

[17] Ibid., p. 368.
[18] Ibid., p. 404.
[19] Ibid., pp. 405–406.

Christian socialism or communism in the spirit of the primitive church. But this radical view seems not to have affected his widespread popularity among the progressives of the day, including President Theodore Roosevelt, because he did not affiliate himself with any radical action group and his entire program was couched within the setting of the church. In Rauschenbusch's next major work,[20] he came out for the moderate idea of industrial profit sharing or industrial partnership which had been so strongly advocated in the 1890's by another clergyman, N. P. Gilman. As Grace has noted, Rauschenbusch's primary emphasis was placed on the worker's property right in a job, reminiscent of the earlier insights of Henry C. Adams: "The workingman must be protected in sickness and age by the collective wealth of the community. He must have a recognized property right in the industrial organization. The minimum form of that right is the right to get employment and to stay in his job as long as he does honest and efficient work."[21] Such an idea had a growing receptivity, even in quite conservative circles. Rauschenbusch was no Norman Thomas or A. J. Muste.

It is a rather significant index of their still limited concern that none of the major church organizations participated in the hearings of the Commission on Industrial Relations, although some individual ministers from various parts of the country which had experienced labor conflicts did testify. By the end of World War I, however, there is strong evidence of a powerful awakening, notably in the activities of the Interchurch World Movement (through its Industrial Relations Department) and the Federal Council of Churches of Christ (through its Commission on the Church and Social Service). The former of these overlapping bodies created a wide controversy as a result of its investigation

[20] Rauschenbusch, *Christianizing the Social Order* (New York: Macmillan Co., 1912).

[21] Grace, *Concept of Property in Modern Christian Thought*, p. 350.

and report of the steel strike of 1919.[22] Whatever the merits of the charges of bias, radicalism, and distortion made against the report and its technical authors, its conclusions and recommendations were endorsed by the committee of eminent clergymen. Among these recommendations, the following have particular relevance to the idea of industrial democracy:

> 3. Recognition of right to join regular Craft Unions or any other freely chosen form of labor organization; recognition of right to open conference, either through shop committees or union representatives; recognition of right of collective bargaining.
>
> . . . .
>
> 5. That organized labor:
> (a) Democratize and control the unions, especially in regard to the calling, conduct and settlement of strikes.
> (b) Reorganize unions with a view of sharing in responsibility for production and in control of production processes; to this end:
> 1. Repudiating restriction of production as a doctrine.
> 2. Formulating contracts which can be lived up to.
> 3. Finding a substitute for the closed shop wherever it is a union practice.
> (c) Scrupulously avoid all advocates of violence.
> (d) Accept all possible proffers of publicity and conciliation.
> (e) Promote Americanization in all possible ways and insist upon an American standard of living for all workingmen.
> (f) Prepare more adequate technical information for the public in regard to all conditions bearing upon the calling and the conduct of a strike.
> (g) Seek alliance and council [sic] from the salaried class known as brain workers.

[22] The Commission of Inquiry, The Interchurch World Movement, *Report on the Steel Strike of 1919* (New York: Harcourt, Brace and Howe, 1920). Critical books include: Marshall Olds, *Analysis of the Interchurch World Movement Report on the Steel Strike* (New York: G. P. Putnam's Sons, 1923) and Ernest W. Young, *Comments on the Interchurch Report on the Steel Strike of 1919* (Boston: Richard G. Badger, 1921).

6. That the President's Industrial Conference's plan for standing tribunals of conciliation and publicity be given a fair trial.

7. That minimum wage commissions be established and laws enacted providing for an American standard of living through the labor of the natural bread-winner permitting the mother to keep up a good home and the children to obtain at least a high school education.

8. That the Federal Government investigate the relations of Federal authorities to private corporation "under-cover" men and "labor detective agencies."

9. That the eight-hour day be accepted by labor, capital and the public the immediate goal for the working day and that government provide by law against working days that bring over-fatigue and deprive the individual, his home and his community of that minimum of time which gives him an opportunity to discharge all his obligations as a social being in a democratic society.[23]

The Federal Council of the Churches of Christ also reflected the advance in the mainstream of Protestant social and industrial thought. The 1920 report of the Committee on the War and the Religious Outlook, for example, noted the strong impact of the war on the Christian conscience and the realization that the time had come to cease uttering "pious platitudes" on such problems as industrial reconstruction and to come to grips with concrete issues, despite the risks of controversy as in the case of the Interchurch Movement Report on the Steel Strike.[24] Perhaps its most significant statement was that issued by the commission on the Church and Social Service in May 1919 and entitled "The Church and Social Reconstruction." In a section labeled "Democracy in Industries," it stated:

Controversies over wages and hours never go to the root of the industrial problem. Democracy must be applied to the government

23 The Commission of Inquiry, pp. 249–250.
24 The Federal Council of the Churches of Christ in America, *Report of the Third Quadrennium, 1916–1920:* "The Churches Allied for Common Tasks" (New York: Federal Council, 1921), p. 45.

of industry as well as to the government of the nation, as rapidly and as far as the workers shall become able and willing to accept such responsibility. . . . This may be accomplished by assuring the workers, as rapidly as it can be done with due considerations, a fair share in control, especially in matters where they are directly involved; by opportunity for ownership with corresponding representation; or, by a combination of ownership and control in co-operative production.[25]

The commission went on to stress that as workers obtain more social justice and more participation in industrial decision-making, they had the obligation to cooperate with management and to improve their productive efficiency.

In response to this statement, the Federal Council adopted four resolutions as supplements to the Social Creed of the Churches. These warrant full quotation because they sum up so well the status of church thinking of the time and in the subsequent decades:

1. That the teachings of Jesus are those of essential democracy and express themselves through brotherhood and the cooperation of all groups. We deplore class struggle and declare against all class domination, whether of capital or labor. Sympathizing with labor's desire for a better day and an equitable share in the profits and management of industry, we stand for orderly and progressive social reconstruction instead of revolution by violence.

2. That an ordered and constructive democracy in industry is as necessary as political democracy, and that collective bargaining and the sharing of shop control and management are inevitable steps in its attainment.

3. That the first charge upon industry should be that of a wage sufficient to support an American standard of living. To that end we advocate the guarantee of a minimum wage, the control of unemployment through government labor exchanges, public works, land settlement, social insurance and experimentation in profit sharing and cooperative ownership.

[25] Ibid., p. 110.

4. We recognize that women played no small part in the winning of the war. We believe that they should have full political and economic equality with equal pay for equal work, and a maximum eight-hour day. We declare for the abolition of night work by women, and the abolition of child labor; and for the provision of adequate safeguards to insure the moral as well as the physical health of the mothers and children of the race.[26]

SOCIAL CATHOLICISM

The attitude of the Catholic Church toward the industrial democracy idea in the United States was greatly influenced by the famous papal encyclical of Leo XIII in 1891, *Rerum Novarum,* generally called "On the Condition of the Working Classes."[27] Basically, this was the hierarchy's answer to Marxism and, as Marc Karson has ably demonstrated, it served as the springboard for the effective anti-Socialist movement which the Catholics promoted and encouraged between 1900 and 1918. I am concerned here, however, with the positive elements in the Catholic position bearing on industrial government—and for this I shall turn, after a brief discussion of the papal encyclical, to the American Catholic clergy themselves, most notably Father John A. Ryan.

The first major theme of the encyclical was that private ownership of property is in accord with the law of nature and therefore, contrary to the main tenet of socialism, must be regarded as inviolate. But it also stressed the dignity and worth of every human being and the obligation of employers to respect that human quality. Thus, it followed that the employer must not take unfair advantage of his employees, must give everyone at

[26] Ibid., p. 114.
[27] The text of the encyclical, with a background commentary, is included in Anne Fremantle, ed., *The Papal Encyclicals in Their Historical Context* (New York: G. P. Putnam's Sons, 1956).

least a minimum living wage, and must provide decent conditions of employment. It was an obligation of the government to safeguard the weak among the wage-earners without undermining private property. The government should forestall and prevent strikes from occurring by removing their causes. Workers are entitled to Sunday and holiday rest and to reasonable working hours; children should not be employed in workshops and factories, and women should only be employed in certain occupations compatible with their nature.

Beyond the idea of a living wage, the encyclical expressed the hope that as many workers as possible would become property owners because in this way the classes in society would be brought closer together, the gap between vast wealth and poverty would be reduced, and men would work harder and more willingly. But for most workers, it was recognized that organizations and associations would be required to provide adequate protection against want and hardship. These included mutual aid societies, benevolent foundations, and institutions for the care of children, young people, and the aged. Most important of all were the workers' unions, which like the guilds of earlier days could contribute much to the welfare of workers, employers, and society as a whole. These unions must be organized and governed in keeping with the tenets and laws of the gospel, exhibiting self-restraint, moderation, and a desire for class harmony. Within that context they should be encouraged and supported by the state as well as by the clergy and the laity. One precautionary note: the state should aid and protect them but it should not interfere in their normal processes nor try to dominate them.

Rerum Novarum was far from a resounding endorsement of collective bargaining or industrial democracy, but it gave the American Catholic supporters of unionism a greatly desired official boost. This was clearly reflected in the writings of one of the ablest of the Catholic social thinkers and reformers, John A.

Ryan. In his doctoral dissertation, written under the supervision of Richard Ely at the University of Wisconsin, Ryan in 1906 justified the principle of the living wage on religious and moral as well as economic grounds.[28] He observed that "a formal defense of the necessity and utility of the Labor Union is happily no longer necessary."[29] After a long period of opposition, the economists had finally concluded that unions could improve the economic condition of the worker. Unfortunately, the most underpaid workers were the least skilled and, despite the example of miners and garment workers to the contrary, the unskilled were the most difficult to unionize. It was therefore essential for the state to assure a minimum living wage by appropriate direct and indirect legislation. The direct method was a minimum wage law; the indirect methods included limiting the workday to eight hours, fixing the minimum work age at sixteen, providing inexpensive housing for worker purchase, and establishing a system of old age pensions. It is interesting to note that in his 1920 version of A Living Wage, Ryan recorded that whereas in 1905 he could find only two economists who had discussed the feasibility of enforcing a living wage by law, and both of them were in the negative, "today the great majority of American economists are of the contrary opinion."[30]

In an exciting literary debate with Morris Hillquit in 1913 over the merits and demerits of socialism, John Ryan indicated additional views on how the prevailing ills of American industrial society could be alleviated. The three main defects which he perceived were: insufficient remuneration of the majority of wage-earners, excessive incomes obtained by a small minority

---

[28] John A. Ryan, A Living Wage: Its Ethical and Economic Aspects (New York: Macmillan Co., 1906; 1912). After going through several printings, this book was published in an abridged and revised edition in 1920. See pp. 32–34 of the 1912 edition for a comment on the role of the encyclical in the history of Catholic thought on the living wage.

[29] Ibid., pp. 291ff.

[30] Ryan, A Living Wage, p. 171.

of capitalists, and the narrow distribution of capital ownership. The remedy for the first of these defects lay in a legal minimum wage supplemented by legislative insurance programs against sickness, accident, unemployment, and old age and provision for decent housing. Also needed were a better adjustment between the supply of and demand for labor, improvements in the conditions of female labor, reduced hours of work, a rational provision for the adjustment of industrial disputes, and a universal system of industrial education. The ends sought by these forms of legislation would be greatly promoted "by an indefinite increase in the extent and power of labor organizations."[31]

The remedy for excessive incomes and profits was the abolition of special privilege and unregulated monopoly, public ownership or regulation of the public utilities—railroads, telegraphs, street railways, and municipal utilities—and a more equitable system of taxation.

His most fundamental reform related to the narrow distribution of capital ownership. It was essential, in his view, to broaden worker ownership interests through copartnership and cooperative societies. This would take time but such has been the history of all enduring improvements. The responsible direction of industry could not remain in the hands of a small number of very powerful persons.

The views which Ryan expressed in 1913 were almost literally reiterated in the postwar reconstruction statement by the Administrative Committee of the National Catholic War Council.[32] The committee, composed of four leading bishops, expressed disappointment that of the major employer organizations, only the Chamber of Commerce had issued a reconstruction state-

[31] Hillquit and Ryan, *Socialism: Promise or Menace,* pp. 40ff.

[32] Administrative Committee of the National Catholic War Council, *Social Reconstruction: A General Review of the Problems and Survey of Remedies,* Reconstruction Pamphlets, 1 (January 1919). An interesting historical treatment of industrial democracy from a Catholic viewpoint is Joseph Husslein, S.J., *Democratic Industry* (New York: P. J. Kenedy and Sons, 1920).

ment, and it was largely negative and defensive in character. They did not expect radical changes to occur in the United States, but they did hope that in the peacetime period both the United States Employment Service and the National War Labor Board would continue to function because of the excellent work they had done during the war, that wartime wages should not be reduced, and that both a legal minimum wage and social insurance would be legislated. In a section entitled "Labor Participation in Industrial Management," they endorsed the position of an English group of Quaker employers calling for greater representation by labor (through shop committees working wherever possible with the trade union) in the "industrial" part of business management—the control of processes and machinery, nature of product, engagement and dismissal of employees, hours of work, rates of pay, bonuses, etc., welfare work, shop discipline, and relations with trade unions. They supported vocational training and the abolition of child labor under the age of sixteen. Finally, they urged, as ultimate and fundamental reforms, Ryan's points about cooperation and copartnership, increased incomes for labor, and the abolition and control of monopolies.

In a concluding paragraph, they applauded Pope Leo XIII's statement that "society can be healed in no other way than by a return to Christian life and Christian institutions." What was needed most of all was a new spirit:

> The laborer must come to realize that he owes his employer and society an honest day's work in return for a fair wage, and that conditions cannot be substantially improved until he roots out the desire to get a maximum of return for a minimum of service. The capitalist must likewise get a new viewpoint. He needs to learn the long-forgotten truth that wealth is stewardship, that profit-making is not the basic justification of business enterprise, and that there are such things as fair profits, fair interest and fair prices. Above and before all, he must cultivate and strengthen within his

mind the truth which many of his class have begun to grasp for the first time during the present war; namely, that the laborer is a human being, not merely an instrument of production; and that the laborer's right to a decent livelihood is the first moral charge upon industry. The employer has a right to get a reasonable living out of his business, but he has no right to interest on his investment until his employees have obtained at least living wages. This is the human and Christian, in contrast to the purely commercial and pagan, ethics of industry.[33]

The Response of the AFL

The rising tide of liberal and radical thought about industrial government was reflected in, reinforced, and expanded by the evolving views and actions of the AFL leadership. The most significant aspect of this evolution was in the political and governmental areas. The favorable intervention of President Roosevelt in the anthracite coal dispute of 1902 and the report of the Anthracite Strike Commission indicated the benefits which might accrue to the labor movement if it could achieve a friendly relationship in the White House. The continuing hostility of the courts, as evidenced by the disapproval of federal and state legislation on constitutional grounds as well as by the widening use of the injunction in labor disputes and the application of the Sherman Anti-Trust Act to labor, provided a spur to political action from the opposite direction. In 1906 labor's Bill of Grievances, adopted by the AFL Executive Council and the presidents of all the affiliated national unions, called for Congress to enact a series of laws, providing among other things for restrictions on court injunctions, an effective eight-hour day for employees engaged in work for the government, and the rescinding of President Roosevelt's ban on the right of federal employees

[33] National Catholic War Council, *Social Reconstruction,* p. 24.

to petition Congress. From 1906 until the election of Woodrow Wilson in 1912, AFL political action was intensified to the point of reversing a long-practiced policy of remaining neutral in Presidential elections and explicitly endorsing the Wilson candidacy.

The fruits of the new political policy (clearly a significant step beyond the traditional "reward your friends, punish your enemies" approach) were to be enjoyed throughout the two Wilson terms. They ranged from the establishment of a Department of Labor, with a former union official as the first secretary, the passage of the Clayton Act, which ostensibly exempted trade unions from antitrust actions,[34] and adoption of liberating legislation for seamen and postal employees, to easy access by AFL leaders to the White House and a voice of considerable influence in the formulation of prewar and wartime labor policies. By November 1917 labor representatives had been given places on "most of the important national, state, and local boards that had to do with industrial reorganization for war."[35] Although not all members of the Wilson administration were labor sympathizers, the labor movement had never before had such a close relationship with an American government. This relationship was symbolized by President Wilson's appearance before the AFL Annual Convention in 1917 as the first President to address such a labor meeting.

The mounting enthusiasm for industrial democracy was also reflected in the AFL's policies on postwar reconstruction, although in comparison with most of the preceding statements

[34] The report of the Executive Council in 1918 continued to quote the language of this act that "The labor of a human being is not a commodity or article of commerce" and to conclude that "it follows that since labor is not a commodity, workers are human beings contributing to production certain personal abilities and skill, and therefore have the right to participate in control of industry." *Report of Proceedings of the Thirty-eighth Annual Convention of the American Federation of Labor* (Washington, D.C., 1918), p. 83.

[35] Gordon S. Watkins, *Labor Problems and Labor Administration in the United States during the World War* (Urbana: University of Illinois Press, 1920), p. 27.

the AFL position under Gompers' leadership was conservative. The Federation issued a Reconstruction Program in 1918 in which it noted that the World War "has awakened more fully the consciousness that the principles of democracy should regulate the relationship of men in all their activities." Under the first main heading of "Democracy in Industry," the statement read: "It is, therefore, essential that the workers should have a voice in determining the laws within industry and commerce which affect them, equivalent to the voice which they have as citizens in determining the legislative enactments which shall govern them." To protect the right of workers to organize into trade unions, Congress was asked to enact legislation "which make it a criminal offense for any employer to interfere with or hamper the exercise of this right or to interfere with the legitimate activities of trade-unions."

Nevertheless, it should be emphasized that the AFL continued to stress economic rather than political means to achieve industrial democracy, especially with respect to higher wages, shorter hours of work, and equal pay for women. As in the past, the legislative program called for a child labor law (for children under sixteen), the right of public employees to organize and engage in collective bargaining, improvements in workmen's compensation for industrial accidents and diseases, and the prohibition of private employment agencies. The Federation also stated that public and semipublic utilities should be owned, operated, or regulated by the government in the interest of the public, although nationalization of the railroads was not specifically endorsed. At the same time, it reasserted its traditional objection to a separate Labor party and its support of a nonpartisan political policy. Its continued concern with the courts was shown in a proposal that if a court declared a law unconstitutional, the Congress or state legislature should have the power to reenact the law and make it binding. It was not until 1919 that the Federation backed public ownership of the railroads by endorsing the Plumb Plan.

The Confrontation

The climactic events of the Progressive Period for industrial democracy came in the final months of 1919.[36] On September 3, as AFL efforts to gain recognition from U.S. Steel were approaching a total breakdown, President Wilson convened a conference of labor, management, and public representatives to meet on October 6 for the purpose of working out a peacetime program of industrial cooperation. The 59 delegates who were designated included 19 labor representatives (15 of whom were AFL and 4 of the operating railroad Brotherhoods), 15 representatives of a variety of business, financial, and farm organizations, and 25 so-called public representatives (many of whom were prominent businessmen such as Elbert H. Gary—head of U.S. Steel, John D. Rockefeller, Jr., and Bernard M. Baruch). On September 22, just two weeks before the conference convened, the great steel strike began and it was under this dark cloud that the fruitless conference was conducted until the frustrated labor delegation and then the management groups withdrew on October 22. The crucial issue was the union contention that employees should have the right to be represented by spokesmen "of their own choosing" while the employers, in fact led by Gary, insisted that worker representatives should be employees of the company involved and not outside union officials. The unwillingness of the employers as a whole (there were some dissenters) to accept a long-established principle of collective bargaining signalized that the country's major industrialists and businessmen had decided to take a firm stand against

[36] One of the most useful contemporary sources on the postwar period, particularly because of its documentary appendices, is W. Jett Lauck and Claude S. Watts, *The Industrial Code* (New York: Funk and Wagnalls Co., 1922).

trade unionism and the collective bargaining model of industrial democracy. The collapse of the steel strike on January 7, 1920, was a confirmation of this decision.

In the course of the conference each of the three groups introduced a program for a postwar policy. The public group's approach was to be later elaborated and will therefore not be treated at this point. The labor proposal was mainly a restatement of the AFL reconstruction program with the following significant additions: that in each industry there should be established by agreement between organized workers and associated employers a national joint conference board to consider "all subjects affecting the progress and well-being of the trade, to promote efficiency of production . . . and to protect life and limb, as well as safeguard and promote the rights of all concerned within the industry." The federal government should encourage and promote the formation of such national conference boards, the Department of Labor should provide them with information and advice, and the boards should be urged to consider any proposed legislation affecting industry and advise the government whenever industrial legislation was needed.

The employer group submitted a program originally prepared by the National Industrial Conference Board. It emphasized the importance of productive efficiency and of cooperation between employer and employee to achieve such efficiency. While in effect adopting the principles of a living wage and of equal pay for women and of upholding the right of association, the statement asserted the importance of protecting freedom of contract for each individual, defended the open shop (although agreeing that employers and employees might voluntarily enter into a closed union shop or closed non-union shop), and pronounced that "no employer should be required to deal with men or groups of men who are not his employees or chosen by and from among them." With the recent Boston police strike clearly in mind, the employers opposed the right of public employees to strike or to join a private organization which might oblige them to strike or to assist them morally and financially if they did.

In the face of the mounting industrial strife throughout the country, President Wilson decided to make a second effort at achieving a workable consensus and he convened another conference on December 1, 1919. This conference included fifteen "public" representatives who came from various walks of life including business, the professions, and the universities. None had been at the previous conference. The conference group first put together a preliminary report, dated December 19, on dispute settlement procedures regarding which it solicited criticisms and suggestions. It reconvened on January 12, 1920, for hearings, consultations, and discussions and then issued a 50-page final report on March 6, 1920.

The report was thoughtful and perceptive. It noted that the causes of industrial unrest were many and that, for the most part, they were not the result of the war although accentuated by it.

> It can not be denied that unrest to-day is characterized more than ever before by purposes and desires which go beyond the mere demand for higher wages and shorter hours. Aspirations inherent in this form of restlessness are to a greater extent psychological and intangible. They are not for that reason any less significant. They reveal a desire on the part of workers to exert a larger and more organic influence upon the processes of industrial life. This impulse is not to be discouraged but made helpful and cooperative. With comprehending and sympathetic appreciation, it can be converted into a force working for a better spirit and understanding between capital and labor, and for more effective cooperation.[37]

The report endorsed the principle of an organized relationship between employer and employee and suggested that the start-

[37] Ibid., p. 328.

ing point was the local plant where mutual understanding had to be established. "The strategic place to begin battle with misunderstanding is within the industrial plant itself. Primarily the settlement must come from the bottom, not from the top."[38] The managers needed to know their men at least as intimately as they know materials, and the employees needed to have a knowledge of the industry, its processes and policies.

The form of joint relationship is not, the report stated, a field for legislation because it may vary in every plant. Employee representation could occur under union agreements in organized shops, within a non-union framework of shop committees and works councils, and in mixed situations. Some industries, such as clothing and printing, had extended the principles of employee representation beyond the plant; these were fruitful experiments in industrial organization.

The conference frankly noted the dispute over representation in collective bargaining which had disrupted the preceding conference, and it took a position not only in favor of collective bargaining but also for unrestricted selection of representatives by employees (by secret ballot election if necessary).

The major recommendation of the report was for the establishment of a tripartite nine-member National Industrial Board and regional Adjustment Conferences and Boards of Inquiry whose responsibility would be to settle labor disputes over wages, hours, and working conditions which could not be settled by the parties or by existing machinery. Disputes voluntarily submitted by both parties would be referred to an Adjustment Conference of nine persons—four representing the parties, four selected from standing employer and labor panels of the appropriate region, and a regional chairman, appointed by the President as public representative for a three-year term. The

[38] Ibid., p. 329.

disputing parties would be required to agree that if the conference failed to settle the dispute by a unanimous vote, it would then be referred to the National board or an umpire selected by the board for a binding decision. If the parties were unwilling to submit their dispute to a regional Adjustment Conference, the regional chairman might set up a regional Board of Inquiry, which would conduct a fact-finding procedure (with the power of subpoena) and make a public report within thirty days of the establishment of the board. Modifications in these procedures were provided for public utilities and public agencies.

In addition to this recommendation for a national system of dispute settlement, the President's conference also made comments and recommendations on a wide variety of substantive issues. The relevant sections may be summarized briefly as follows:

1. On collective bargaining, the report emphasized the importance of adhering to the standards or terms of the agreement, without strike or lockout, during its life. This did not bind the employer to provide work or to keep open his plant for economic reasons, nor did it preclude employee resignations. Breach of the standards, however, was unjustifiable. Enforcement of the agreement was vital but legal enforcement did not seem realistic —"for the present at least, enforcement must rest substantially on good faith."

2. Studies of work hours and fatigue indicated the desirability of not more than forty-eight work hours per week, the restriction of overtime to temporary emergencies, and one day's rest in seven. Further studies by industry and the government were suggested.

3. Special provisions were needed to keep the hours of women within reason, to prohibit night employment in factories and workshops, and to exclude certain trades entirely. Women doing equal quality and quantity of work should receive the same pay

as men and should have equal opportunity for training, advancement, and representation.

4. Children under sixteen should be prohibited from industrial labor and schooling should be compulsory until sixteen.

5. Wages should not sink below a living level but employees should also not restrict production. There should be more studies of methods of wage payment, especially in relation to incentives to production.

6. Neither profit sharing nor gain sharing was a panacea, but if properly carried out, they might better industrial relations. More experiments were encouraged.

7. The proper extension of the insurance principle to problems of health and old age needed more study and public discussion.

8. Inflation and the high cost of living had to be dealt with through credit restriction by the banks, increased production, and by economy in consumption. Government statistics on living costs should be further developed.

9. The low salaries and poor conditions of many public employees, notably teachers and protection employees, were recognized. However, the use of the strike was not a legitimate method for public employees. Policemen and firemen should not have the right to affiliate with organizations which hold to the right to strike and the propriety of the affiliation of other classes of public employees was an issue on which the Conference could not agree. This made it all the more important that society recognize its special obligation to compensate public employees fairly and to insure prompt consideration of grievances. In case of labor disputes of public employees the Conference proposed fact-finding with recommendations but not arbitration.

10. The seriousness of unemployment was stressed. Efforts to regularize seasonal unemployment in garments and coal mining was approved. So was the undertaking of large public works programs. The Conference recommended the establishment of

a system of public exchanges similar to the wartime system which had lapsed, but with more decentralization of responsibility.

In concluding, the report stated that its recommendations would not only contribute to the elimination of the causes of industrial strife but that "they will make for the introduction, in American industry, of those democratic principles which constitute the most precious heritage of the American citizen."[39]

Despite the caliber of the conference members and support from some prominent congressmen (including the Senate Committee on Education and Labor), the time for favorable government action on even the moderate conference report had passed. Partly because of his preoccupation with the League of Nations, partly because of poor health, and partly because he was nearing the end of his term of office, Wilson was no longer in a position to exercise leadership. Moreover, the mood of the country had changed. The antiradical drive, spurred by the unprecedented number of workers on strike and by fears generated by the Communist revolution in Russia, was in full swing. The IWW was virtually destroyed as an organization; the domestic Communists were driven underground. The Plumb Plan of the railroad Brotherhoods was swept into oblivion, although the unions did make an important gain in the Transportation Act of 1920 which set up the Railroad Labor Board and perpetuated the adjustment board system developed during the war for the settlement of disputes. Even the conservative unions of the AFL were placed in jeopardy. The depression which began in the second half of 1920 rang the curtain down on the Progressive Period.

[39] Ibid., p. 379.

CHAPTER 7

THE SCORE IN 1920

COMPARED WITH ITS STATUS at the end of the nineteenth century, industrial democracy appeared to have made impressive gains by 1920, notwithstanding the failure of President Wilson's postwar conferences and the union defeats in steel, with the Boston police, and in other industries. At the start of the century the term *industrial democracy* was just beginning to be used and collective bargaining as its expression was only on the threshold of national acceptability. By 1920 industrial democracy was a household term and, in one form or another, every important interest group paid at least lip service to it. The idea of employee representation and collective bargaining, although not necessarily through trade unionism, was no longer an issue per se, as President Wilson's second conference group pointed out.

The war had accelerated this development. The rise in union membership from under 500,000 in 1897 to over 5 million in 1920 was probably greater by some 2 million than if the war had not occurred. The international climate generated by the war to make the world safe for democracy unquestionably made Americans more conscious than they might otherwise have been of industrial as well as political democracy. Yet the basic trend of the century's first two decades was firmly established long before the nation became involved in the war. It was inherent in the spirit of the Progressive Period, in the "square deal" of Theodore Roosevelt and the "new freedom" of Woodrow Wilson. It was evidenced in the union boom between 1897–1904, the activities of the National Civic Federation, Roosevelt's intervention in the anthracite coal strike of 1902, the report of the U.S. Industrial Commission, the political gains of the Socialist party, the appeal of the IWW to the unskilled workers, the Protocol of Peace in the New York ladies' garment industry and the Hart Schaffner & Marx agreement of the Chicago men's clothing industry, the labor laws of Wilson's first administration, the hearings and reports of the U.S. Commission on Industrial Relations, and the dramatic shift in the labor policy of the Rockefeller interests— to cite only some of the major examples prior to 1917. There were indeed negative factors also—the hostility and successful resistance of U.S. Steel and other major manufacturers to unionism, the open-shop campaigns of 1901–1908, the corruption in a number of labor unions, especially in the building trades of Chicago and New York, and the violence exemplified by the McNamara case.

However, Walter Lippmann, just beginning in 1914 his remarkable career as observer of the American scene, summarized the crystallizing status of industrial democracy with deep insight:

> Now men don't agitate for democracy because it is a fine theory. They come to desire it because they have to, because absolutism does not work out any longer to civilized ends. Employers are not wise enough to govern their men with unlimited power, and not generous enough to be trusted with autocracy. That is the plain fact of the situation: the essential reason why private industry has got to prepare itself for democratic control.
>
> I don't pretend for one moment that labor unions are farseeing, intelligent, or wise in their tactics. I have never seen a political democracy that aroused uncritical enthusiasm. It seems to me

simply the effort to build up unions is as much the work of pioneers, as the extension of civilization into the wilderness. The unions are the first feeble effort to conquer the industrial jungle for democratic life. They may not succeed, but if they don't their failure will be a tragedy for civilization, a loss of cooperative effort, a balking of energy, and the fixing in American life of a class structure.[1]

Thus far the discussion has dealt with the idea of industrial democracy in general, overall terms. Adequate analysis requires a systematic consideration of the nine dimensions that comprise the model of industrial democracy on which this study is based.

Representation

The extension of employee organization was the clearest index of the more democratic sharing of industrial sovereignty. At the peak of the period in 1920, about 19 per cent of nonfarm employees were union members compared to 10 per cent in 1910 and about 6 per cent in 1900. If we add to the 5 million unionists in 1920 close to 1 million workers newly covered by employee representation plans and work shop committees (a subject to be discussed in detail in the next section), then the 1920 figure becomes nearly 23 per cent. In short, some form of representative system had come to a large segment of manual workers in the United States engaged in mining, transportation, large city construction, and manufacturing. For the first three categories, it was a process of extension, i.e., the anthracite miners were added to the central states bituminous miners, the seamen and the non-operating railroad workers to the operating Brotherhoods, and the construction workers to other cities as well as to existing groups within previously unionized cities. In manufac-

[1] Walter Lippmann, *Drift and Mastery* (Englewood Cliffs, N.J.: Prentice-Hall, 1961 reprint), pp. 59–60.

turing the most dramatic breakthrough came in an area which no less an authority than John R. Commons had contended in 1905 was virtually unorganizable—the needle trades of the large eastern cities and Chicago. But other important manufacturing groups also achieved at least a measure of representation, mainly because of governmental and wartime pressures—for example, in steel (outside of U.S. Steel), in electrical products (e.g., General Electric and Westinghouse), in oil refining, and in rubber. Even government and private white-collar employees were obtaining representation rights on a small scale, notably postal workers (after the 1912 Congress revoked the so-called gag rule which President Roosevelt had imposed in 1902 on public employee groups seeking to lobby in Congress), theatrical performers, and musicians.

The critical issue regarding representation in this period (although it was decades old) was whether employees could choose representatives who were not company employees, that is, outside union officials. This issue was raised mainly by employers who wished to exclude unions from their plants and who were basically opposed to collective bargaining. It was the rock on which President Wilson's postwar conference foundered. Although the Commission on Industrial Relations had recommended legislation to prohibit employer interference with employee organizational efforts and although the War Labor Board adopted and enforced this policy, once the board ceased functioning, there was nothing to prevent such interferences and they were reinstituted in many quarters with the acquiescence of the courts.

The role of government as a third-party factor in industrial relations was characterized by a shift in emphasis from the state to the federal level. State interest did not diminish—the concern with arbitration and conciliation laws was replaced by much more effective legislation on workmen's compensation and industrial safety. But the enhanced federal interest was reflected in the establishment of the Department of Labor, the vast extension of Bureau of Labor Statistics fact-finding and reporting, the activities of the Conciliation Service, and most of all, although only temporarily, in the wartime program of intervention and control.

The principle of majority rule as the basis for the selection of employee representatives got its start late in the period. There is no mention of the principle in the reports of either the Industrial Commission or the Commission on Industrial Relations, nor does it appear as one of the guiding principles and policies formulated by the War Labor Conference Board. But as the wartime administration began to implement the principle that both workers and employers had the right to organize and to bargain collectively *through chosen representatives,* it seemed logical and natural to invoke the democratic idea of majority rule. In the first month of its existence, July 1918, the National War Labor Board issued awards providing for secret-ballot elections to elect department committees at plants of the General Electric and Bethlehem Steel companies and in October 1918, the board's joint chairmen approved a plan for the election of shop committees. The plan called for the selection of one committeeman for each one hundred employees in each department or section of the shop, for the nomination of candidates, for the holding of secret-ballot elections inside the shop or in a public building, and other arrangements.[2] Since the board refused to impose unionism on an employer or to compel him to deal with nonemployee representatives if he had not previously done so, these elections were not designed to determine whether a particular organization or which of two competing organizations should have bargaining rights. The Shipbuilding Labor Adjustment

[2] U.S., Department of Labor, *National War Labor Board* BLS Bulletin no. 287, pp. 60ff.

Board followed a similar policy when in October 1918 it ordered the election by secret ballot of shop committees in all Atlantic, Gulf, and Great Lakes yards.[3]

Participation

The basic outline of worker participation in industrial government under the collective-bargaining system had been clearly delineated in the 1890's and, generally speaking, this was not altered. Nevertheless new ground was broken in specific cases. The most dramatic development occurred in the garment industry. The famous Protocol of Peace, which was negotiated with the aid of the notable lawyers Louis Brandeis and Louis Marshall for the New York cloak and suit industry in September 1910, had a number of pioneering innovations.[4] The first of these was the preferential union shop which Brandeis devised as a compromise between the traditional union demand for the closed shop and the employer insistence on the open shop. A second was the establishment of the tripartite standing board of arbitration, which will be discussed in the section on due process. A third was the tripartite Board of Sanitary Control which had a marked impact upon the disgraceful health and safety conditions in the industry. In addition, the employees, through the union, for the first time began to have a voice in shaping the very nature of the clothing market by negotiating rules pertaining to subcontracting and tenement work as well as the "inside" shops. The Protocol broke down in 1915, was revived for two

[3] The same procedure was ordered or recommended by other wartime agencies, including the U.S. Railroad Administration, the U.S. Fuel Administration, and the Presidential Mediation Commission investigating and seeking a settlement of disputes in the copper, oil, and packing industries.

[4] Among the numerous works on the Protocol, the contemporary analysis by the employers' counsel, Julius Henry Cohen, is especially insightful—*Law and Order in Industry* (New York: Macmillan Co., 1916).

years, and then broke down again. But it served as an example for the clothing industry throughout the country and was widely imitated in whole or in part.

The scope of worker participation in industrial government was also significantly advanced in the railroad industry. This occurred through the so-called concerted movements which began in 1902 when representatives of the conductors' union made a joint bargaining demand on all the western railroads instead of negotiating with individual roads. From this movement by a single union against a regional group of employers, there was a gradual progression until in 1915 all four railroad Brotherhoods initiated a combined demand for the basic eight-hour day from all the railroads of the country, the outcome of which was the passage by Congress of the Adamson Act to avoid a national railroad strike. This widening of the unit of industrial government to a regional or national multiemployer basis was not new. Unions in construction, stove manufacture, printing, coal mining, longshore, and other industries had previously taken similar steps in order to "take wages out of competition."[5] The railroad development had the unique quality that it facilitated government operation of the roads during the war, encouraged union support for the Plumb Plan, and deepened the need for governmental participation in the affairs of the industry.

The extension of union participation in garments, railroads, mining, and other industries on a bilateral collective bargaining basis was accompanied by a strengthening of unilateral job control in segments of printing, construction, and a few other centers of maximum union power.

In the unionized sectors of the printing industry, for example, the International Typographical Union exercised unilateral con-

[5] See George E. Barnett, "National and District Systems of Collective Bargaining in the United States," *Quarterly Journal of Economics*, 26 (May 1912): 425–443. Another valuable early review of collective bargaining is Margaret A. Schaffner, *The Labor Contract from Individual to Collective Bargaining* (Madison: University of Wisconsin Press, 1907).

trol over much of shop life, including hiring, apprenticeship, discharge and discipline, the distribution of overtime, the employment of substitutes to fill temporary vacancies, and the exclusion of non-unionists from the composing-room floor during work hours. This control was achieved partly through the requirement that the foreman representing management be a union member and subject to union discipline; and partly through the union's ability to establish certain national "laws" which were not negotiable or arbitrable, e.g., the basic work week, the union shop, apprenticeship, the reproduction of previously used type, and the priority principle. (The Pressmen's Union, in contrast, did not insist on unilateral national rules.) Employers, of course, retained many important functions relating to the production process as well as total control over finance and sales. They determined the location of the enterprise, the products to be manufactured, the volume of output, the equipment to be used, and the supervisory staff. They bargained over wages and employment conditions which were not covered by the union's national laws. And in some places, they shared a voice in the areas presumably preempted by the "laws."

Nonetheless, as Selig Perlman wrote in the late 1920's: "it appears that, in the printing industry, the industrial constitution is not a joint instrument administered by joint or impartial agencies, but rather a document drawn up by one party, accepted by the other, and thereafter to a large extent administered and interpreted by the party which enacted it. As regards a large part of the sphere which has been called industrial relations, the employer has practically abdicated. This state of affairs goes back to a policy of practical 'job syndicalism' long pursued by the union in its dealing with the employers."[6]

The situation in the main unionized sectors of the building construction industry was similar. The contractors conducted

[6] Selig Perlman, A Theory of Labor Movement (New York: Macmillan Co., 1928), p. 264.

the "business" side of construction without union interference—bidding for work, arranging financial details, determining (with the cooperation of architects and of clients) the nature of the structures and the means of creating them. But the hiring process was done through the union business agents; the foremen were required to be union members and were therefore subject to union discipline; and the terms and conditions of employment were largely imposed on the employers, including even limitations on certain kinds of equipment and materials.

Equal Rights and Opportunities

All of the public reports of governmental bodies concerned with labor and many statements by union, management, and other private groups enunciated the doctrine of equal pay for women doing the same quality and quantity work as men. But until World War I few women performed the same kind of manual labor as men and thus the equal-pay principle meant little in practice. During the war, circumstances changed as many women took over previously male jobs; as a result, the War Labor Board issued a considerable number of awards implementing the equal-pay principle. After the armistice, the board continued to support the principle, and when an effort was made in some cities to discharge women street railway conductors in the interest of returning men, the board held such efforts to be unfair. The demise of the board eliminated this important protective mechanism for women workers. Despite the growing equality of women in American public life, as evidenced by the Nineteenth Amendment, women continued to be treated as a minority group in industry.

Throughout the period there was a major movement of Negroes from the South into northern industry. Much of this movement was actively fostered by industry; some of it was the result of the natural attraction of available jobs and high pay. The union response to black labor was generally hostile, in part because of racial prejudice and in part because the black workers were often recruited as strikebreakers and scabs. With some exceptions, such as in mining, teaming, and on the docks, the advances in industrial democracy were not shared by the Negro. This was a matter of concern to the radicals and to some of the religious groups, such as the Federal Council of the Churches of Christ, whose reconstruction statement applauded the "splendid service of the colored soldiers in the war," called for their full recognition "as Americans and fellows," and asserted among other things, that they should be given "equal economic and professional opportunities" including equal wages for equal work. But in general these views carried little weight. It is significant that the Commission on Industrial Relations which ranged so widely made no mention of the problem of Negro workers.

A third group which often failed to get equal rights in industry consisted of the non-English-speaking foreign-born, and particularly those who had not yet become citizens. Discrimination took several forms. One stemmed from the fact that the foremen and higher levels of management were from older (usually Anglo-Saxon, Teutonic, and Irish) stock and looked down on the ethnic groups from Eastern and Southern Europe. Another emerged from within the labor movement, which had become increasingly concerned about the flood of new immigrants as a competitive menace to union standards. The Knights of Labor had been a leader in the post–Civil War period in opposing Oriental immigration and contract labor from Europe. The AFL, which shared these concerns, became an increasingly strong and outspoken proponent of general immigration laws, which were finally adopted in 1921 and 1924. Some of the craft unions even adopted rules excluding noncitizens from membership. In many respects, it might be concluded that for the foreigner, the 1900–

1920 period afforded less industrial democracy than the preceding forty years.[7]

Right of Dissent

Throughout the period there were frequent complaints that individual workers or groups were unable to speak their minds freely. On the one side were the complaints against autocratic management and the use of state, local, and private police to suppress free speech and organization efforts. These are illustrated by Paul V. Kellogg's observations in the famous Pittsburgh Survey about the fear of steel workers to assemble and express their grievances against their employers[8] and by the Manly Report of the U.S. Commission on Industrial Relations which condemned the activities of the Pennsylvania State Constabulary and other state police forces and which charged that "on numerous occasions in every part of the country, the police of cities and towns have either arbitrarily or under the cloak of a traffic ordinance, interfered with or prohibited public speaking, both in the open and in halls, by persons connected with organizations of which the police or those from whom they received their orders did not approve."[9] Bad as these and related practices (e.g., the use of spies, provocateurs, and armed guards) were, the most brutal repression of free speech by workers occurred after 1917 when local sheriffs, vigilante groups, and federal authorities launched anti-red drives against the IWW and later anarchists and Communists under criminal syndicalist and anarchist statutes.

[7] The general character of this development, although not much detail, is admirably portrayed in Oscar Handlin, *The American People in the Twentieth Century* (Boston: Beacon Press, 1963 paperback edition) especially chapter 4.

[8] See introduction to John A. Fitch, *The Steel Workers* (New York: Russell Sage Foundation, 1911), p. vi.

[9] U.S. Commission on Industrial Relations, *Final Report and Testimony* (Washington, D.C.: Government Printing Office, 1916), p. 98.

The other side of the complaint picture consisted of charges that union members and other workers were often prevented from speaking their minds or otherwise influencing union policies by despotic and corrupt union bosses. The most patent examples were those in the building trades of Chicago and New York where state investigations led to the conviction and imprisonment of several union leaders for corrupt practices. No one questioned that the convention floor of the AFL offered full opportunity for the expression of dissenting views by Socialists and others. But in some of the national unions and at the local level, constraints were reported. Sometimes the reason was that there was too much freedom. The typographical union, with its unique two-party system and its tradition of debate, reflected a concern over "the custom of maligning and slandering our officers," and an international union law was adopted about 1911 that prohibited impugning the motives of officers. In regard to the United Mine Workers, a strong example of democratic procedure prior to World War I, Illinois leader John Walker complained that he was twice counted out of the presidency in 1916 and 1918. In general, however, it seems safe to conclude that the majority of unions had not yet become so centrally dominated as to pose a serious problem for dissenters.

Due Process

Advances in the development of a fair and effective "judicial" process for workers with grievances or complaints must be considered one of the major achievements of the period. Grievance procedures including the provision for third-party arbitrators had emerged in a number of industries and localities during the 1890's. In the next two decades experience in dealing with grievances arising over the provisions of signed agreements increased appreciably, and the practice of committing agreements to paper was extended to many more industries and enterprises. In terms of national importance, the rise of "constitutional government" and "due process" in the coal mining and railroad industries warrants primary emphasis; the most interesting innovations were introduced in the men's and women's clothing industries; and some of the oldest systems, notably printing, developed a rich body of industrial common law. To these separate developments the War Labor Board added its general support and influence.

The grievance machinery in bituminous mining took initial form after the signing of the central states agreement of 1898 and the southwestern coal fields agreement of 1900; in anthracite the main impetus came from the award of the Anthracite Strike Commission of 1903. Arthur Suffern, a leading student of coal labor-relations, traced the gradual evolution of the grievance machinery as well as of the substantive rules emerging from the grievance process. He noted the varying experiments with arbitration, the concerns over such matters as precedent in case decisions, and the substitution of formal rules for informal customs. His conclusion in 1926 was that these constitutional developments had gone about as far as in any American industry.[10]

In the railroad industry, the role of the government was a decisive factor. The Federal Railroad Administration in 1918 established three "boards of adjustment" to settle disputes arising over the interpretation and application of collective bargaining agreements, including matters of discipline and other individual grievances. One board dealt with the grievances of the operating employees, another with those of the shop crafts, and the third with the grievances of the remaining union categories like clerks, telegraphers, and maintenance-of-way employees. Each adjustment board was bipartite, consisting of either four or six representatives each from the unions and com-

[10] Arthur E. Suffern, *The Coal Miners' Struggle for Industrial Status* (New York: Macmillan Co., 1926), p. 308.

panies. In case of a deadlock the cases were referred to the director general for final decision. This board system not only served as an additional step in the existing grievance procedures but also contributed to the standardization of working rules throughout the nation.

The most impressive new developments in grievance handling appeared in the clothing industry. The New York Protocol's procedure initially provided for the appointment by the union and the employers' association of "chief clerks" and "deputies" who were authorized to visit shops in order to investigate and settle complaints. If they could not agree, the dispute went to a bipartisan board of grievances. If the latter became deadlocked, the dispute was referred to a board of arbitration, composed of one representative from each side plus an impartial chairman. The arbitration board was not only to serve as the final and binding authority but also to make general policies regarding the interpretation of the agreement. After initial successes, the grievance machinery began to founder and was modified in 1914. If the clerks from the two sides were unable to agree, they would, together with a third impartial person, constitute a "committee on immediate action" to decide all matters except those involving "protocol law." This innovation established the basis for what ultimately became the institution of the impartial chairman. The protocol system, however, collapsed in 1915 in a dispute over the meaning of *discharge* and it was not until 1933 that the impartial chairmanship was permanently revived—with growing responsibility and authority. Concurrently the system of shop chairmen and chairladies was developed by the union, thus strengthening the procedure at the job level. In Hart Schaffner & Marx a similar type of due process evolved without a breakdown, and it had been extended to the entire Chicago men's clothing market by 1919.

The spread of formal grievance machinery and particularly the advent of permanent grievance arbitration not only regularized the process of hearing and settling employee complaints, but also provided the basis for a greatly enlarged industrial jurisprudence. Every enterprise, whether unionized or not, obviously must develop customary practices and rules. Union agreements, particularly when put in writing, tend to make these practices and rules explicit; they become in effect a constitution or code of law. With frequent and regular arbitration, and especially with the intervention of prominent lawyers, as in the garment trades after 1910, the idea of an industrial common law took a further step. Broad general principles, such as those comprising a labor agreement, were translated into more specific rules.

The War Labor Board reinforced these developments by encouraging and directing the establishment of grievance procedures, particularly in plants with new employee-representation systems—a subject to be discussed in the next section.

Responsibility

The principle of the sanctity of agreements was well established by the turn of the century wherever formal agreement systems had developed. As the U.S. Industrial Commission observed: "Where the system of collective bargaining and arbitration has become established for a considerable length of time, both parties recognize what a disadvantage to themselves and to the trade generally would result from a complete breakup of the system because of refusal to carry out agreements or the decisions of arbitrators. It is where the system of collective bargaining itself is but little developed and works more or less intermittently that the decisions of arbitrators are apt to be violated."[11] The commission noted that in a few cases refusals to

[11] U.S. Industrial Commission, *Report of 1901*, 17: LXXXIX.

carry out the decrees of the arbitration committee would subject the offender to a fine or possible suspension of membership.

In 1926 Arthur Suffern reported on the coal mining industry:

> One of the chief inducements which the miners held out to the operators to make a contract was the assurance of continuity of operation for a definite period. This principle has never been deviated from since 1898, as applied to the interstate agreements. . . . This principle also applies to district and subdistrict contracts, but the union has not been so successful in its enforcement. These agreements have been guaranteed by the international union, local stoppages have been condemned, and the union has joined with the operators in recommending by definite clauses in the interstate contract that effective means of enforcement be applied.[12]

Similarly, in testimony before the Commission on Industrial Relations in 1914, leaders of both the typographical union and the printers league stressed the adherence of both sides to the agreement as well as to the awards of arbitration boards. Two unauthorized strikes in 1903–1904 led the International in 1904 to adopt a rule requiring the Executive Council to "immediately disown" all such strikes and "to guarantee protection to all members who remain at, accept, or return to work in offices affected by an illegal strike."[13]

In some of the more recently unionized industries, such as ladies' garments, violations of agreements (usually at the shop level) occurred frequently and were the source of conflict.

As Louis Brandeis stated in an arbitration award in 1915, one of the four main purposes of the Protocol was to "create, through the strengthening of the Employers' Association on the one hand, and of the Union on the other, bodies which should be able to enforce compliance with the terms of the agreement

[12] Suffern, *Coal Miners' Struggle*, pp. 314–315.

[13] Cited in George E. Barnett, *The Printers: A Study in American Trade Unionism* (Cambridge: American Economic Association, 1909), p. 333.

which was made."[14] The inability of the parties to attain this internal strength was a major factor in the breakdown of the Protocol. Thus the idea of responsibility as an element of industrial democracy was well understood although it was often not carried out in practice.

Minimum Standards

The idea of minimum standards of labor had been developed in the nineteenth century mainly in behalf of children and women and, for these groups, it continued to serve as a major motivating force among reformers. Greatly influenced by the famous Brandeis brief, the Supreme Court decision in *Muller* v. *Oregon,* upholding the constitutionality of a state ten-hour law for women, sparked the enactment of similar laws in numerous states after 1908. Minimum-wage laws for women followed in rapid order. Almost all of the states also adopted some minimum employment age for children, although Congressional actions in this direction were frustrated by adverse Supreme Court decisions.

There was similar progress in the industrial-safety area, largely as a result of a series of major catastrophes, such as the Cherry Mine explosion in 1909 and the Triangle Shirt Waist fire of 1911. Reformers and trade unionists jointly pressed for more effective factory inspection laws, workmen's compensation legislation, and accident prevention programs.

A third major theme which crystallized in the period was the minimum "living wage" and, as a corollary to it, the American standard of living. Conservative trade unionists as well as labor radicals had, of course, fought for higher wages and shorter hours for decades, and the idea of the union scale or the standard

[14] Contained in Cohen, *Law and Order in Industry,* Appendix C: "Decision of Board of Arbitration, January 21, 1915," p. 260.

rate implied the living wage idea. But neither the AFL leaders nor most of the academic economists (for very different reasons) were willing to support the proposition that society had an obligation to assure all workers a living wage—through legislation when the private employer failed to do so. The living wage theme had been admirably developed in England by the Webbs in the late 1890's. It was eloquently espoused in the United States by John Ryan in 1906 on the basis of Catholic doctrine, as expressed in Leo XIII's famous encyclical; it was supported empirically by radical economists.[15] It was given national status, at least temporarily, when adopted as a fundamental wartime policy by the War Labor Conference Board.

Information

The collective-bargaining process inevitably necessitates the opening of channels of communication between employers and employees and the providing of economic information bearing on wages and other terms of employment. The growth of collective bargaining meant therefore much wider access to data, as experience in the mining and garment industries indicated. So, too, the hearings of the Industrial Commission and the Commission on Industrial Relations revealed much about industrial economic and institutional practice which had not been generally known. The most powerful force in expanding information for employees, however, was the war and the administrative machinery established by the government to assure needed production for the country and its allies.

Another important source of information was the new Department of Labor, with its enlarged resources and facilities. Its predecessor, the Bureau of Labor in the Department of Com-

[15] See, for example, Scott Nearing, *Financing the Wage-Earner's Family* (New York: Huebsch, 1913).

merce, had begun in the first decade of the century to develop continuing statistical series of prices and wages in addition to the earlier special studies and reports. The statistical bank was now substantially expanded and put to increased use in industry.

Personal Dignity

Perhaps the most important single development for industrial democracy during the first two decades of this century was the shift in the view of industry from labor as a market commodity, as a factor in production, to labor as a human resource. The prime symbol of this shift was the language of Section 6 of the Clayton Anti-Trust Act:[16] ". . . the labor of a human being is not a commodity or article of commerce." Supreme Court decisions soon stripped this act of the Magna Charta role which the AFL leaders initially ascribed to it. Nonetheless, it signified the end of the labor-commodity theory. In the years which followed, public statement after statement reiterated the theme of the human quality of labor and the need to treat labor in a different way from other elements in production. The principles of industrial relations adopted by the United States Chamber of Commerce in April 1919, general as they were, began with the declaration: "Industrial enterprise, as a source of livelihood for both employer and employee, should be so conducted that due consideration is given to the situation of all persons dependent upon it."[17] And the statement of the employer group to the first Industrial Conference assembled by President Wilson in October 1919 noted that: "The industrial organization as a productive agency is an association of management, capital, and labor voluntarily established for economic production through co-

[16] Passed in 1914.
[17] Reprinted in W. Jett Lauck and Claude S. Watts, *The Industrial Code* (New York: Funk and Wagnalls Co., 1922), p. 506.

operative effort."[18] The full implementation of these recognitions of human dignity in labor was a long way from realization. But the direction of the signpost was clear.

Some Interpretive Observations

The "new democracy," as Walter E. Weyl wrote of his time, was an insurgent spirit emerging out of the widespread discontent with tradition, particularly as it applied to the nation's industrial institutions.[19] The technological revolution of the previous half century, the rise of the trusts, the massive immigration from eastern and central Europe, the closing of the frontier, and the rapid urbanization process—these and other factors had created an assortment of complex problems which generated calls for change in almost every aspect of American life. The nation had paid a heavy price in human terms for industrial advance. Class and income differences had widened. Poverty had become more degrading in the midst of affluence. Mechanization had multiplied accidents and disease. Suffering from economic depression was more intense and widespread. Industrial conflict and violence had mounted.

The reform movement was the nation's expression of revolt against these costs of industrialization. It was the social conscience in action. It was an effort to reconstitute industry in human terms, to place human values above property values. That industrial democracy became one of the period's most popular themes was a natural outgrowth of such a movement.

World War I had a similar and reinforcing impact. Although the historian might explain its outbreak in terms of international power politics, numerous people throughout the world, includ-

[18] Ibid., p. 497.

[19] Walter E. Weyl, *The New Democracy* (New York: Macmillan Co., 1912), p. 5.

ing the United States, saw it as a struggle against autocracy. It was the war to make the world safe for democracy. It was the common man's struggle for social justice. Moreover the terrible human sacrifice of the war evoked a widespread belief that new political and social orders were needed to prevent a repetition. Industrial democracy was linked to political democracy as the solution.

That industrial democracy made a giant advance between the turn of the century and the end of the war thus seems incontrovertible. But it was a checkered advance, with setbacks in many places, and imperfections where it was strongest. Even at its peak, there were serious losses. To account for the gains and failures, it is necessary to weigh and balance the determinant factors.

First of all, for industrial democracy to take hold and survive, as I have earlier suggested, there must be a "will" among the participants to make it work. Such a will was widely evidenced among manual workers, more so than in any previous time in American history. It was reflected in union membership, in participation in strikes, in the rise of political radicalism. The negative effects of corrupt leadership and worker apathy were comparatively minor. On the employer side, however, the idea of industrial democracy was far from general acceptability. The large number of relatively small employers who had participated in the open shop drives of 1901–1908 continued to be hostile to unionism. Among the giant industrial and financial interests, there were some like John D. Rockefeller, who under pressure came to recognize the need for a more democratic approach to industrial relations, but most, like Judge Gary and his U.S. Steel associates, were either firmly determined to maintain their traditional autocratic power or were skeptical and waiting to be convinced.

Industrial democracy also requires a body of literate and competent employees who not only have the will but the ability as well to make it work effectively. The fact that in many industries a substantial proportion of the employees were immigrants from non-English-speaking countries without a democratic tradition undoubtedly complicated and slowed down the process. Hence the relatively early success in printing and among the operating railroad employees as contrasted to the difficulties in the mass production industries. On the other hand, one senses a yearning for a democratic way of life among the newcomers which appears to have contributed appreciably to offsetting the handicaps of language and culture. The developments in coal mining after 1898 and in garment manufacture after 1910 are significant illustrations.

The socio-psychological climate was, it is clear, positively correlated with industrial democracy, except in the South and in the rural areas. Reformism was particularly strong in the large eastern and midwestern cities, and while not all reformers were enthusiastic supporters of unions and collective bargaining, they tended to be committed to democratic thinking.

The political process moved in the same direction. It would be a mistake to assume that the administrations of Roosevelt and Wilson gave all-out support to unionism and the union concept of industrial democracy. But their progressive character had an overall reinforcing effect. The contrast between the executive and legislative branches of government and the courts in this respect was striking. It was especially striking at the federal level where, for the first time, major favorable political actions in behalf of industrial democracy were taken.

Economic factors operated in opposite directions but on balance were also favorable. The rising price level gave an added incentive to workers to join unions and a strong bargaining issue for the unions. Employment levels were, on the whole, high; after the recovery from the 1893–1895 depression, there was no major business decline until 1920. The growth of the economy continued to be rapid so that more benefits were attainable. On the other hand, the concentration of capital—symbolized by the formation in 1901 of the first billion-dollar firm (U.S. Steel) in American history—posed an increasingly powerful barrier to employee organization and the sharing of industrial sovereignty.

A DECADE OF WELFARE CAPITALISM— THE TWENTIES

CHAPTER 8

THE CORPORATE
ALTERNATIVE

THE EMPLOYER RESPONSE to the collective-bargaining model of industrial democracy took two forms—purely negative opposition and the formulation of a substitute model. The latter is the subject of this section. Although it will be necessary to return to the end of the preceding century to trace the evolution of this substitute, it was in the decade after World War I that the corporate version of welfare capitalism captured the spotlight and pushed the trade-union model back into the wings.

It is customary to describe the 1920's in terms of the Harding slogan—back to normalcy. This is, however, a highly misleading description from the standpoint of industrial relations. Neither the process nor its environment can be characterized as a "return." Let us look at the environment first and then examine the corporate view.

Industrialization

Industrialism continued apace in the twenties after the recovery from the deep but short depression of late 1920 to mid-1922. The real Gross National Product, as estimated by the Department of

Commerce, increased by about 42 per cent between 1920 and 1929.[1] The Federal Reserve Board index of physical output in all manufacturing increased over 48 per cent.[2] Of particular importance were the advances in the motor-vehicle industry because of its far-reaching impact on the entire economy. Motor-vehicle registrations rose from 9.2 million in 1920 to 26.5 million in 1929 as the annual production of cars and trucks rose from 1.9 million in the former year to 4.6 million in the latter. Motor-fuel usage went from 3.4 billion gallons to 15.1 billion.[3] Steel, textiles, rubber, petroleum, and road building were all directly affected.

Although the automobile was the star economic performer of the twenties, other industries also assumed new major roles— most notably electrical products which ranged from a wide variety of household durables to industrial machinery. Electric energy produced by utilities and industrial establishments more than doubled during the decade.[4] Household refrigerators went from a production level of about 5000 in 1921 to 890,000 in 1929.[5] Radio apparatus and equipment was valued at about $18 million in 1920 and $388 million in 1929.[6]

These massive advances in industrial output were accompanied by a virtual standstill in manufacturing employment. Lebergott estimates that the number of factory employees was the same in 1929 as in 1920—about 10,702,000.[7] The number of man-hours worked actually fell by about 7 per cent. Thus output per man-hour rose very sharply (63 per cent), reflecting the technological changes and the huge product demands. The

[1] John W. Kendrick, *Productivity Trends in the United States* (Princeton, N.J.: Princeton University Press, 1961), p. 299.

[2] U.S., Department of Commerce, *Historical Statistics of the United States, 1789–1945,* (Washington, D.C.: Government Printing Office, 1949), p. 180.

[3] Ibid., p. 223.

[4] Ibid., p. 156.

[5] Ibid., p. 186.

[6] Ibid., p. 181.

[7] Stanley Lebergott, *Manpower in Economic Growth* (New York: McGraw-Hill Book Company, 1964), p. 514.

significance of this efficiency increase may be more fully appreciated by noting that despite a substantial increase in gross product, output per man-hour rose only 17 per cent between 1900 and 1909 and only 14 per cent between 1910 and 1919.[8]

Since the labor force (over age fourteen) increased by about 7 million during the twenties, the stability in manufacturing employment might indicate a serious national unemployment problem—all the more since employment in the key industries of mining and transport and utilities declined by 8 and 9 per cent respectively. But after the recovery in 1922, unemployment averaged only about 3.3 per cent of the civilian labor force in the rest of the decade because of a 76 per cent jump in contract construction employment and sizable gains in trade, finance, service, and civilian government. The ratio of unemployment to nonfarm employees was unfortunately more serious—5.5—so that industry had an ample labor supply and labor was generally not in a strategic bargaining position.[9]

Because of the latter conditions, industrial workers did not achieve any great economic gains from the national prosperity. It is true that after about 24 years of rising living costs, workers were the beneficiaries of depressed farm prices. The Bureau of Labor Statistics consumer price index fell from the postwar peak of 199.7 (1914=100) to 166.9 in 1922 and stood at 170.9 in 1928 and 1929. But industrial money earnings were practically stationary, and real earnings for the employed rose only because of the decline in prices.

Urbanization

Industrialization went hand in hand with continued urbanization. Although the flood of European immigrants was sharply

---

[8] Kendrick, *Productivity Trends*, p. 465.
[9] These employment and unemployment figures are from Lebergott.

reduced by the restrictive immigration laws of 1921 and 1924, the internal migration from the farms to the cities and from the South to the North continued. Of the 17 million additional inhabitants in the nation, only 2.3 million were rural—in places with under 2500 people. By 1930 the 69 million urban residents represented 56 per cent of the total population of 123 million. More important, the number of cities with 100,000 or more people rose from 68 to 93 and their population from 27 million to 36 million.

While the cities of the north and central regions slowly absorbed and "Americanized" the immigrants, the migration of southern rural Negroes into these regions grew from a net of about 700,000 between 1910 and 1920 to almost 1.3 million between 1920 and 1930. Many of these migrants found jobs in industry—invariably at the lowest skill and pay levels.

The Socio-Psychological Climate

There is a widely accepted historical thesis that the United States regularly passes through alternating phases of reform and conservatism and that the period of the twenties was a conservative phase following twenty years of progressivism. The conservatism of the twenties is demonstrated by the national political triumphs and programs of business-minded Republicanism— the Harding, Coolidge, and Hoover administrations—by the vigorous open-shop drive or so-called American Plan and the setbacks which the unions suffered, by the Red Scare and the anti-radical drives, by the continuing anti-union decisions of the Supreme Court, and by the pronouncements from Main Street to Wall Street that business was the business of America and that the age of boom and bust was over.

But the period was far from conservative in certain other

respects—in the rebellion of women against Victorian manners, dress, and behavior, in the discussions and attitudes about sex and religion, in the exuberant nature of the mass media and especially advertising, in the enthusiasm over sports and the movies, and in the speculative frenzies in real estate and stocks. From the perspective of industrial relations the climate of the twenties involved some important socio-psychological changes, although the great mass of small employers undoubtedly continued to view their world in traditional terms. However, the large corporations, which gave the period its distinctive coloration, adopted a very different orientation as a result of the pressures which they had experienced in the previous period. The single most important change was in the recognition that employee relations required top-level consideration and could not be left to the discretion of the shop supervisors. The personnel function became organized and centralized. Specialists in personnel work were placed in positions of responsibility. *Human relations* and even *industrial democracy* became respectable terms in the corporate lexicon.

The new lexicon did not, however, include *trade unionism,* except in the case of a few companies. Instead the view was that industry could work out its own system of welfare capitalism, which in varying degrees and combinations entailed aspects of welfare work, scientific management, personnel relations, and employee representation. This subject will be treated in detail later in this chapter.

By and large the trade unions fared badly in this period, partly because of employer resistance, partly because of a generally unsympathetic public, and partly because of internal weaknesses. Irving Bernstein has aptly termed it "The Lean Years." Union membership, which totalled over 5 million (including Canadian members) in 1920, fell to 3.4 million by 1929, about the same level in relation to the nonfarm population as in the first decade of the century.[10] The main casualties were the mass-production groups organized during World War I which evaporated as government wartime programs ended, as the business interests launched an anti-union drive in the name of Americanism and individual liberty surpassing in intensity and scope the 1901–1908 campaigns, and as the 1920–1922 depression temporarily wiped out several million jobs. But serious losses were also sustained among long-established union organizations for a number of different reasons. In coal mining the failure of the United Mine Workers, the largest union in the nation, to organize the southern mines and the fruitless effort to maintain uncompetitive standards in the unionized mines led to a serious deterioration in the latter half of the decade. The ladies' garment workers union was almost destroyed by a fierce internecine struggle for control between the socialist majority and a communist faction. The railroad shop unions were set back by the loss of the great national shopcraft strike of 1922. The brewery workers were badly hurt by Prohibition.

The only major unions to hold their own or to advance were the building trades (which benefitted from the construction boom), the railroad operating Brotherhoods, the printing unions, the men's clothing workers, and the musicians. They concentrated most of their resources on their own job territories and, especially after the failure of the La Follette third-party political movement, made no effort to reverse the general trend. The result was a pronounced decline in national AFL momentum. The characteristics of the AFL accommodation to welfare capitalism will be treated in the next chapter.

As to the role of government in industrial affairs, the dominant

---

[10] According to Leo Troy's computations, derived from the work of Leo Wolman, the ratio of union members to the nonfarm population was 11 per cent in 1929 and 10.2 in 1910. The ratio to the civilian labor force was 6.8 per cent in 1929 and 5.9 in 1910. See "Trade Union Membership, 1897–1962," *Review of Economics and Statistics*, 47 (February 1965), 1:94.

sentiment was expressed by Herbert Hoover in the concluding speech of his 1928 Presidential campaign:

> When the war closed, the most vital of all issues both in our own country and throughout the world was whether Governments should continue their wartime ownership and operation of many instrumentalities of production and distribution. We were challenged with a peace-time choice between the American system of rugged individualism and a European philosophy of diametrically opposed doctrines—doctrines of paternalism and state socialism. The acceptance of these ideas would have meant the destruction of self-government through centralization of government. It would have meant the undermining of the individual initiative and enterprise through which our people have grown to unparalleled greatness.
>
> . . . .
>
> By adherence to the principles of decentralized self-government, ordered liberty, equal opportunity and freedom to the individual our American experiment in human welfare has yielded a degree of well-being unparalleled in all the world. It has come nearer to the abolition of poverty, to the abolition of fear of want, than humanity has ever reached before. Progress of the past seven years is the proof of it.[11]

Actually rugged individualism was preached more than it was practiced in the twenties. And even the vocabulary was changing as Reinhard Bendix has shown.[12] Bendix traced the shifts in ideology of industrial managers after World War I as compared with earlier years. "Instead of the struggle for survival, they emphasized cooperation; instead of regarding success as self-explanatory, they began to consider the duties of managers; and instead of exhorting workers to emulate their employers and

[11] Reprinted in J. Rogers Hollingsworth and Bell I. Wiley, eds., *American Democracy: A Documentary Record*, vol. 2: 1865–1961 (New York: Thomas Y. Crowell Co., 1962), pp. 236, 239.

[12] Reinhard Bendix, *Work and Authority in Industry* (New York: Harper & Row, Pubs., 1963 paperback edition).

achieve success, they emphasized the modest rewards and inherent satisfactions of good work."[13] And again, "The celebration
of individual character and effort has in some measure been
superseded by a belief in individual adaptability just as the
image of the struggle for survival and the pursuit of self-interest
has been superseded by the image of cooperative teamwork."[14]
To Bendix the major cause of this change was the growing size
and bureaucratization of industrial organizations in the process
of industrialization and economic development. The emergence
of the disciplines of scientific management and industrial psychology were contributory factors.

Industrial Democracy in the Corporate Vein

The corporate model contained varying degrees of four different
elements of industrial relations, each of which can be traced
back some decades prior to the 1920's.

WELFARE WORK

The oldest of these elements was welfare work, which may
claim Robert Owen, the English textile manufacturer and humanitarian of the 1820's and 1830's, as one of its sources. The
model textile towns of Waltham and Lowell, Massachusetts, in
the 1830's and 40's, which were designed to attract, protect, and
reassure the farm girls of New England, were another early example. So too was the company town of Pullman, Illinois, before
its eclipse in the disastrous Pullman strike of 1894.

Clarence J. Hicks, one of the pioneer advocates of welfare
capitalism and a key influence in the reformulation of Rockefeller employee policy, describes in his autobiography his be-

13 Ibid., p. 285.
14 Ibid., p. 339.

ginnings in industrial welfare work in the 1890's as railroad secretary for the YMCA and the problems which he encountered in persuading the magnates of the railroad industry to support decent overnight facilities for their employees.[15] In 1911 Hicks joined the staff of International Harvester to apply the lessons he had learned from his YMCA experience to a large manufacturing enterprise. He found Harvester to be, together with the National Cash Register Company, one of the pioneers in welfare work. About Harvester, he wrote:

> This company was the first great corporation in America to assume responsibility for industrial accidents, far in advance of any state or federal legislation on workmen's compensation. It also assumed a place of leadership in industrial hygiene in a day when most manufacturing plants were far from sanitary; a medical department was early established, which also supervised working conditions. It was among the first of industrial companies to inaugurate a pension plan applicable to all employees, with an accumulating reserve fund to assure solvency. The organization of an employees' benefit association was encouraged to enable employees to secure protection during sickness at the joint expense of employees and the company.[16]

But as Hicks acknowledged, "Welfare work did not stand the proper test of being good business. Most employees resented such dispensations as paternalistic—and still do."[17] The secretary of the Welfare Department of the National Civic Federation, which strongly supported welfare work, also warned:

> The spirit of welfare work must not be that of condescension, nor have the appearance of thrusting benefits upon subordinates, nor rob the worker of self-respect. But any effort at welfare work may be regarded as more or less paternalistic. A resort to direct pa-

[15] Clarence J. Hicks, *My Life in Industrial Relations* (New York: Harper and Bros., 1941).

[16] Ibid., pp. 42–43.

[17] Ibid., p. 43.

ternalism, however, is necessary or desirable only for recent immigrants who in their native lands have been accustomed to the guardianship of superior authority. Going to the other extreme, in the so-called democratic idea, is also to be avoided. When their confidence has been gained, employees will generally prefer to entrust the direction of welfare work to the employer.[18]

By the 1920's many of the major corporations were providing their employees with a host of services, including recreational facilities, cafeterias and club rooms, reading rooms and Americanization programs, and numerous fringe benefits.

SCIENTIFIC MANAGEMENT

The second of the four strands of welfare capitalism was scientific management as promulgated by Frederick Taylor and popularized by his disciples and admirers. There is no evidence that the pioneers of scientific management originally thought that they were promoting the cause of industrial democracy. But after union leaders mounted criticisms of scientific management as authoritarian, Frederick Taylor and his close associates developed a democratic rationale which is of considerable interest. This position was most clearly stated by Taylor on November 11, 1914, in an interview with Professor Robert Hoxie, the chairman of an investigating committee for the Commission on Industrial Relations:

1. Scientific management is based upon the fundamental assumption of harmony of interests between employers and workers, and seeks to establish complete and harmonious cooperation between them.
2. Scientific management attempts to substitute, in the relations between employers and workers, the government of fact and law for the rule of force and opinion. It substitutes exact knowledge

[18] *Monthly Review*, 1 (August 15, 1904), 6:5–6.

for guesswork, and seeks to establish a code of natural laws equally binding upon employers and workmen.

3. Scientific management thus seeks to substitute in the shop discipline natural law in place of a code of discipline based upon the caprice and arbitrary power of men. No such democracy has ever existed in industry before. Every protest of every workman must be handled by those on the management side and the right or wrong of the complaint must be settled, not by the opinion either of the management or the workmen but by the great code of laws which has been developed and which must satisfy both sides.[19]

Taylor emphasized to Hoxie his belief that scientific management democratizes industry and that people, in general, did not have a broad enough idea about it.[20]

Hoxie regarded Taylor's conception of democracy as Utopian —a noble idea, as old at least as St. Simon, but not capable of realization until the science of psychology made great advances, industry became much more stable and regular, and the industrial scientist was very different from the general run of time study men and task setters. His investigation revealed two general classes of managers favoring scientific management. One adopted the assumption of class conflict and regarded industrial democracy as folly. The other was enthusiastic about industrial democracy, would readily consent to giving workers a voice in all sorts of matters (even letting them decide standards of work and rates of pay), and would never act on any matter directly touching the workers' interests without consulting with them, individually or as a group, *but* they insisted on reserving the right to veto "where the workers were governed by improper motives, too much influenced by trade unionists or manifestly wrong."[21]

[19] Robert F. Hoxie, *Scientific Management and Labor* (New York: D. Appleton and Co., 1915), pp. 140–141.

[20] Hoxie, "Scientific Management and Labor Welfare," *Journal of Political Economy*, 24 (November 1916), 9:837.

[21] Hoxie, *Scientific Management and Labor*, p. 102.

During the 1920's industrial engineers assumed a role of growing importance in large-scale enterprises, and many of the ideas of scientific management were adopted, including over-refined wage incentive systems like the Bedaux plan. None of the companies, however, adopted Taylorism as a total system.

PERSONNEL RELATIONS

The idea of a specialized personnel function was a natural outgrowth of welfare work, which required a corps of staff employees, and of scientific management, which stressed functional differentiation and specialization. As companies grew in size, it was neither efficient nor rational to leave the employment function solely in the hands of shop management and in the decade before World War I, many large employers appointed employment or personnel managers to coordinate the tasks of recruitment, assignment, and training. During the wartime boom, the competition for labor became intense and the costs of labor turnover attracted national attention. The employment manager assumed mounting importance as a result.

Although many of the personnel departments were eliminated during the postwar depression, there was a strong revival following economic recovery. This development was encouraged by the emergence of the discipline of industrial psychology under the leadership of scholars like Hugo Munsterberg of Harvard, Walter D. Scott of Northwestern, and Walter V. Bingham of Carnegie Institute of Technology shortly before World War I, by the effective use of intelligence tests during the war, and by studies of employee attitudes, job satisfaction, and morale by psychological consulting firms like Houser Associates and the Psychological Corporation. The expanding programs of the University of Pennsylvania's Wharton School, the Harvard Business School, and others gave a further boost to personnel work and research, as illustrated by the famous project of Western Electric at Hawthorne, Illinois.

Leading illustrations of new personnel programs were the "sociological department" developed by Henry Ford at his Dearborn plant and the labor department established at Hart Schaffner & Marx under the direction of Professor Earl D. Howard. A 1928 study made by the National Industrial Conference Board found that of 4500 plants with over 4 million workers, 34 per cent of the firms with 250 workers or more had personnel departments in contrast to only 3 per cent of those with less than 250 workers.[22]

EMPLOYEE REPRESENTATION

The fourth and most important element of the welfare capitalist model of industrial democracy was the introduction of shop committees, work councils, and employee representation plans. Again it is necessary to turn to pre-1920 history for an explanation of the emergence of this strand.

Employee representation plans had European (especially German) ancestors in the nineteenth century, but they seem to have originated in the United States around the turn of the twentieth century out of indigenous conditions and experimentation. They took a variety of forms. One of the first, most comprehensive, and longest-lived was that of Boston's Filene Department Store, whose owners organized the Filene Cooperative Association about 1898, giving the employees responsibility for management of the lunch room and the relief and entertainment funds. Soon thereafter, the Association was given the right to make or change any store rule (except business policies) by vote, subject to the owners' right of veto, which

[22] *Industrial Relations in Small Plants* (New York: National Industrial Conference Board, 1929), p. 20.

in turn could be overridden by a two-thirds vote of the Association. In 1901 an arbitration board of elected employee representatives was established to settle grievances over wages, discharge, and working conditions.[23]

A second prominent type of employee representation plan was adopted in 1911 and 1912 by the Philadelphia Rapid Transit Company and the Milwaukee Electric Railway. Thomas E. Mitten, the executive responsible for the plan, told the U.S. Commission on Industrial Relations that he was willing to sign a union contract if the union got a two-thirds vote of the men and if they accepted his cooperation program. The program provided for (1) a joint committee system made up of elected worker representatives and superintendents from each division, and (2) a fund based on 22 per cent of gross passenger receipts from which wages and other forms of compensation would be paid. The ballot fell slightly short of the two-thirds requirement, however, and the plan operated on a non-union basis.[24]

John Leitch, one of the pioneer "industrial consultants," achieved impressive success at the trouble-ridden Packard Piano Company in 1913, and during the ensuing decade ardently promoted an employee representation system superficially patterned on the federal government, which he labeled "Industrial Democracy."[25] The basic structure, which varied among different companies, provided for a House of Representatives elected by the workers, a Senate elected by the foremen, and a cabinet made up of top management officials. To become a "law" a measure had to be adopted by both "Houses" and approved by the cabinet.

The Rockefeller employee representation plan for the Colora-

[23] Mary La Dame, *The Filene Store: A Study of Employees' Relation to Management in a Retail Store* (New York: Russell Sage Foundation, 1930).

[24] U.S. Commission on Industrial Relations, *Final Report and Testimony*, (Washington, D.C.: Government Printing Office, 1916), 3:2734–2735.

[25] See John Leitch, *Man to Man, the Story of Industrial Democracy* (New York: Forbes, 1919).

do Fuel and Iron Company, with its bipartite joint conference and committee structure and a grievance procedure that included outside impartial arbitration, came closest to a collective bargaining model. This plan added a new dimension to the movement because of the widespread public protest against the brutality to which the striking miners had been subjected in 1914, the admission to the Industrial Relations Commission that the absentee financier had been ignorant of the company's labor policies, and the extensive publicity given to the plan as a democratic alternative to unionism and collective bargaining.

Alarmed by the unfavorable reactions of the public and unhappy over the violence of the conflict, John D. Rockefeller, Jr. engaged W. L. Mackenzie King, Canadian labor relations expert and later the longtime prime minister of his country, to develop a representation scheme which would allay employee unrest and promote harmonious relations. He also hired Clarence Hicks from International Harvester to help introduce the plan in Colorado and later to extend it to various branches of the Standard Oil Company.

The expansion of employee representation was hastened by the National War Labor Board on a theoretical basis very different from the foregoing. The guiding policies promulgated by the War Labor Conference Board, which recommended establishment of the NWLB, had a pronounced pro-union flavor, in keeping with Wilsonian labor policy and the greatly enhanced position of the union movement under wartime conditions. But the board was not prepared to impose unionism on previously unorganized firms. Experience in Britain with the Whitley Councils suggested an alternative solution.

With the acquiescence of its union members, the NWLB deliberately fostered a significant number of employee representation plans in non-union establishments on the expectation that these plans would subsequently lead to unionization. The board's theory proved erroneous, for most of these plans were eliminated shortly after the armistice by the employers. Yet the ideas which they reflected soon spread to hundreds of other enterprises. The National Industrial Conference Board, which made counts of the number of representation plans among its members, reported 225 in 1919, 725 in 1922, and 814 in 1924. The number of workers covered by these plans increased from 391,000 to 1,117,000. Among the major firms which adopted some form of representation system, apart from those mentioned above, were such prominent names as General Electric, Bethlehem Steel, Goodyear Tire and Rubber, Endicott Johnson, International Harvester, Pennsylvania Railroad, Dennison Manufacturing, Proctor and Gamble, Commonwealth Edison, Youngstown Sheet and Tool, Westinghouse Electric, and Armour.

The representation plans of the 1920's were the subject of a great deal of contemporary study, analysis, and debate. Books, articles, pamphlets, and speeches reached flood dimensions. The subject was of concern to the professional scholar as well as to the practitioner and the general public. The American Academy of Political and Social Science devoted an entire issue to "industrial stability" of which Part One dealt with the trend to industrial democracy, Part Two with employee representation, and Part Three with collective bargaining.[26] The Academy of Political Science in New York City sponsored a conference on "constructive experiments in industrial cooperation between employers and employees."[27] A series of case studies was published by John R. Commons and his associates in 1921 and later by the Russell Sage Foundation.[28] Industrial leaders and con-

[26] American Academy of Political and Social Science, *The Annals*, 90, (July 1920). The next issue, 91, (September 1920), dealt with "Labor, Management and Production." Relevant articles also appeared in other issues.

[27] Academy of Political Science, *Proceedings*, 9 (January 1922):4 (New York: Columbia University).

[28] John R. Commons, *Industrial Government* (New York: Macmillan Co., 1921). The Foundation volumes included studies by Ben M. Selekman on the

sultants wrote personal accounts of their experiences relating to employee representation. Unions, business associations, the American Economic Association, and the Taylor Society of Professional Engineers all held conferences or seminars on it. The Social Science Research Council suggested new avenues of scholarly investigation. The central question was whether the representation schemes were simply "company unions" and tools of management, subject to management domination and control, as the unionists declared, or whether they were a genuine new approach to industrial democracy, particularly when considered in relation to the other benefits and programs of welfare capitalism.

The Rockefeller position, as expressed in a statement of labor policy by the Standard Oil Company in 1922, affirmed the democratic character of the management approach and called it "a square deal for all concerned—the employees, the management, the stockholders and the public."[29] The policy contained the following seventeen points:

1. No discrimination by the company or its employees against any employee on account of membership or nonmembership in any church, society, fraternity or union.

2. Collective dealing as to all matters of mutual interest, made effective through the industrial representation plan.

3. Paying at least the prevailing scale of wages for similar work in the community.

4. The eight-hour day, or its equivalent.

5. One day's rest in seven, preferably on Sunday, or the equivalent of such period.

6. Sanitary and healthful working conditions.

Minnequa Steel Works of the Colorado Fuel and Iron Company (1924), the Dutchess Bleachery (1924), and (with Mary van Kleeck) the mining operations of the Colorado Fuel and Iron Company (1924) as well as Mary La Dame's study of The Filene Store (1930) and Louis Bloch's study of labor agreements in coal mining (1931).

[29] Cited in Hicks, *My Life in Industrial Relations*, p. 55.

7. Just treatment assured each employee, with opportunity for submission of all grievances for adjustment through the industrial representation plan.

8. Continuous effort to eliminate accidents through effective safeguards and active cooperation of employees and committees, under expert supervision.

9. Payment of disability benefits in case of accidents incurred while at work.

10. Health supervision by a competent medical staff.

11. Payment of sickness benefits after one year's service.

12. Opportunity for special training to qualify employee for better work, with standard system of keeping record of service performed.

13. Promotion according to ability demonstrated and length of service.

14. One week's annual vacation with pay—for both wage earners and salaried employees—after one year's service, extended to two weeks after five years' service.

15. Partnership through stock ownership made easily possible for the thrifty employee after one year's service, through a stock acquisition plan, the company adding to the amount invested by the employee.

16. Assurance of a generous annuity at the age of sixty-five, guaranteed for life after twenty years of service, with special consideration for those who became disabled before that period.

17. Death benefits or insurance, for dependents of employees of one year or more of service.

In his retrospective defense of the Rockefeller policy, Clarence Hicks argued that it was never intended to be an anti-union device; nor was it thought of as a form of collective bargaining.

> The truth of the matter is that, as originally expounded and recommended, employee representation was not thought of as an agency for collective bargaining but as a fair and practical means of giving

workers a contact with their management and a needed voice in the determination of matters vitally affecting their interests, including wages, hours, and working conditions. Recognizing the fundamental need of a two-way communication between employees and management, it was proposed as a means of securing elemental justice for employees and of assuring to management that the views and interests of its employees would be taken into account in the formulation and development of its labor policies. Although the employee representation plans were not without a certain amount of power and ability to bring pressure upon the employer, this was not a major consideration, nor was the degree of bargaining power a measure of the benefits of such plans to the employees. . . in many places employee representation has proved and is proving entirely acceptable to both management and employees, both union and nonunion, and through it many groups of workers have been able to bring about improvements in their wages, hours and working conditions which would not have been secured otherwise, and which compare most favorably with those obtained in other industries through the efforts of organized labor.[30]

According to Hicks, the underlying principles of employee representation, which distinguished it from collective bargaining, were as follows:

1. The voluntary recognition by the employer that a system of employee representation satisfactory to the employees was necessary to assure fair treatment on wages, hours, and working conditions.
2. Emphasis upon a mutuality of economic interests between employees and employers.
3. Provision for continuing contact and collective dealing between employee representatives and management, starting at the foreman level, with right of appeal to top management.

[30] Ibid., pp. 87–88.

4. Recognition of the right of minorities to deal with management personally or through representatives.

5. Acceptance of the shop, plant, or department as the basic unit of collective relations rather than separate craft groups, the company as a whole, or the industry.

Hicks reaffirmed a statement which he had made in a 1928 speech that the "voluntary surrender of a portion of the autocratic rights of the employer . . . is the most significant development in American industrial relations during the past twenty years."[31]

For some, perhaps many, of the employers who instituted employee-representation plans there seems little doubt that they did not share Hicks' enthusiasm for collective dealing and that the plans were largely a facade or sophisticated device to forestall genuine collective bargaining. This view is supported by the vigor and extent of the open-shop (meaning anti-union) drive between 1919 and 1922 and of the continuing open-shop movements during the whole decade.[32] On the other hand, a number of thoughtful, socially conscious leaders of industry and business had become increasingly sensitive to the democratizing forces of the twentieth century and were genuinely searching for new institutional solutions—solutions based on different premises than those underlying trade unionism and collective bargaining.

As Edward A. Filene expressed it: "I believe that industrial democracy, under which employees will have an adequate voice in the policies of industry and an adequate stake in the profits of industry, is inevitable. I believe this, not because industrial democracy is theoretically right, although I do believe it is the-

[31] Ibid., p. 91.
[32] See Allen M. Wakstein, *The Open-Shop Movement, 1919–1933* (Urbana: University of Illinois Ph.D. thesis, typescript, 1961).

oretically right, but because we have committed ourselves to political democracy, because we have given to the masses of employees who far outnumber the employers a political vote with which they can get anything and everything they find themselves unable to get by industrial methods."[33]

Cyrus S. Ching, long-time director of industrial relations for U.S. Rubber and later director of the Federal Mediation and Conciliation Service, also made a favorable evaluation of the representation plans although his retrospective view was rather different from Mary Parker Follett's contemporary one.[34] Ching felt that the plans "provided a stepping-stone to the collective bargaining stage of labor relations" and were "in no small way" responsible for the labor peace of the twenties. He concluded that there was no substitute in advancing the best interests of both workers and employers for "a democratically and intelligently run union, operating apart from the cloak of management." Nonetheless "our captains of industry may have buried their heads in the sands [in the 1920's] to the signs of economic collapse, but many of them gave a great deal of thought to labor-management relations, and actually, for the first time on any sizable scale, began doing something to improve those relations."

The Evaluation of Outsiders

The leaders of the AFL had endorsed the employee representation plan when it was set up under the auspices of the War Labor Board, but this endorsement soon changed to intense antagonism when the open-shop campaign got underway.

At its 1919 convention, the Federation condemned all "com-

[33] Edward A. Filene, *The Way Out* (New York: Doubleday, Page, 1925), p. 170.
[34] Cyrus S. Ching, *Review and Reflection* (New York: Forbes, 1953), especially chapter 3.

pany unions" as a "delusion and snare."[35] Ching relates that in 1920, shortly before Herbert Hoover was appointed secretary of commerce, he urged a group of leading industrialists to establish "liaison" with Samuel Gompers (whom Hoover had gotten to know well during the war) and the AFL in order to overcome this hostility. The idea was summarily rejected.[36] From the labor standpoint, the employee representation plan became a "company union" pure and simple—unless it functioned on the basis of unionism. The friends of the unions in the professions and the academic world took a similar view. For example, Otto S. Beyer, the originator of the famous Baltimore & Ohio Railroad labor-management cooperation plan, told a meeting of the Taylor Society in 1926 that employee representation or company union plans "either have been brought into being by management or exist by sufferance of management . . . without independent leadership and without the assurance that organizations will safeguard for them their share of the gains of cooperation, company union employees can have no confidence in the company union type of organization."[37]

Professor Paul Douglas of the University of Chicago, who was one of the first to make a comparison of shop committees and trade unions in 1920, distinguished between the shop committees in practice and their potentiality in theory.[38] In practice he found them to be an instrument of the open-shop movement, with six serious defects:

1. In many cases the employers control or influence the election of committeemen.

[35] *Report of Proceedings of Thirty-ninth Annual Convention of American Federation of Labor* (Washington, D.C., 1919), pp. 302–303. Hereafter cited as *AFL Annual Convention Proceedings.*

[36] Ching, *Review and Reflection,* p. 28.

[37] Otto S. Beyer, Jr., "The Technique of Cooperation," *Bulletin of the Taylor Society,* 11 (February 1926), 1:7.

[38] "Shop Committees: Substitute for, or Supplement to, Trades-Unions?" *Journal of Political Economy,* 29 (February 1921), 2:89–107.

2. The function of many shop committees is limited to non-vital matters.

3. Frequently the control in the joint committee is held by the employer.

4. In many cases the decision of the joint committee is not final but must be approved by the executive before taking effect.

5. The qualifications for voting and holding office are such as to debar a large number of employees.

6. Shop committeemen are frequently prevented from pleading the cases of the workmen very strongly because of their fear of being discharged or discriminated against.

Even in a model situation, Douglas saw serious flaws:

1. Because it was limited to a single shop or company, it could not protect the fair employer from being undermined by unfair competition.

2. Since in the typical case the representatives of the employees had to be employees themselves, the workers were deprived of expert outside advice in presenting their case and in negotiations.

3. It did not provide a mechanism through which essential labor laws could be obtained.

4. Except in a very large plant, the system could not afford the protection against sickness and unemployment which a national union could provide.

5. It deprived the employees of bargaining power which the national union could offer.

6. Since employers were everywhere united in associations and chambers of commerce, why should not employees have similar rights and benefits?

Thus Douglas did not see the employee representation plans as a lasting substitute for unions. But he did believe that the two systems could be combined in a highly beneficial manner which only the miners, garment workers, and printers had been able to achieve. The union would be responsible for the collective-bargaining function. The shop committee would fulfill five supplemental functions:

1. It would furnish the mechanism for applying and interpreting the terms of the labor agreement and would facilitate the settlement of grievances.
2. Workers and employers would be able to meet on a common ground and understand each other.
3. The workers' interest in production could be enlisted to a much greater extent and would contribute to efficiency.
4. It would train the worker in the real problems of industry and would acquaint him with the actual conditions of affairs.
5. It would lay the basis for a more effective organization of the workers, with the plant as the unit of organization rather than the present heterogeneous local composed of workers from different plants—i.e., industrial unionism rather than craft unionism.

Earl Miller, who wrote a monograph on the subject, reached conclusions very similar to Douglas', although he did not share Douglas' view about the possibility of combining the two systems. It is interesting to note that he felt obliged to counter an argument of some writers that the non-union council plans achieved "real democratic industrial management" while collective bargaining through unionism did not.[39] On the contrary, he observed, the two systems dealt with the same problems in much the same manner, but the unions "exercised a more authoritative voice." "Moreover, the total accomplishments of non-union councils have been insignificant in comparison to the accomplishments of the unions." On the other hand, Miller found that the atmosphere in the non-union situations was much more harmonious and constructive than in the union situations

[39] Earl Miller, *Workmen's Representation in Industrial Government* (Urbana: University of Illinois Press, 1922), p. 158.

(in large measure because employers were generally so hostile to unionism).[40] He also reported that in a very large proportion of the non-union council plants, working conditions, hours, and wages were as good as, or better than, in similar plants with unions.[41] But he recognized the argument of the unionists that these results were achieved in good part because of the employer's desire to keep the unions out. Overall he saw the two movements as antagonistic and although he did not expect the non-union council to destroy unionism, he did predict that it would "check materially the growth of unions."[42]

Carroll E. French, who made a survey similar to Miller's and who agreed with him on the "inherent conflict" of the two systems ("The truth is that the trade union and the shop committees are diametrically opposed in principle"[43]), reached conclusions more favorable to the latter. In his view, the shop committee made four distinctive contributions to better local plant relations which "arise from the peculiar advantages of the shop committee itself and can be traced to no other source."[44]

1. The improvement in discipline.

2. The prompt uncovering of grievances and their speedy adjustment.

3. The mutual education of management and men through the system of regular collective dealings in the joint committees.

4. The share in the management of living and working activities allowed to employees through their joint committees.

French accepted the validity of some of the union criticisms— that the shop committee had gained ground largely from the motive of the employer to head off trade union organization; that

[40] Ibid., p. 171.
[41] Ibid., p. 169.
[42] Ibid., p. 177.
[43] Carroll E. French, *The Shop Committee in the United States* (Baltimore: Johns Hopkins Press, Ph.D. thesis, 1923), p. 12.
[44] Ibid., p. 76.

the emphasis of the shop committee upon the individual plant as the unit of industrial relations weakened collective bargaining, especially in "sweated" industries; that the shop committee was inferior in economic power, although not as weak as the unions alleged; and that the shop committee did not guarantee the employee true representation, because it excluded outside expert counsel in negotiations. But he believed that the unions had overstated their case, that there were plenty of bad examples in the union movement which should also not be regarded as typical, that the advance in the shop committee system was as much a result of free worker choice as of management hostility to unions, and that the unions could learn some valuable lessons from the shop committees. These lessons were:

1. Workers were interested in local plant conditions above all and the union insistence on national or regional agreements was insufficient to meet this interest.

2. Organization by craft or trade was not consistent with modern industrial organization, weakened union bargaining power, and encouraged jurisdictional disputes.

3. The unions had failed to develop adequate machinery to handle the many questions of purely plant or shop interest.

4. By emphasizing wages and working rules, unions had neglected the important worker interests in welfare, unemployment, insurance, profit sharing, and production.

5. A fundamental weakness was the failure of the majority of trade unions to provide permanent, local machinery for the adjustment of grievances as they arise in matters of discharge and promotion.

6. Above all, there was no provision for normal association between employees and employer in the individual plant to encourage a progressive development in mutual amity.

French suggested, like Douglas, that "a far-sighted trade union leadership would set about devising the best means of coordinating the shop committee with the union organization and, if necessary, making fundamental adjustments in the constitution of the trade union movement."[45] And he concluded with a remarkably prescient paragraph:

> The shop committee sets forces at work whose ultimate consequences cannot be foreseen. Certainly, employees who have experienced representation through shop committees will never be satisfied with less. The chances are rather that they will desire more. It is inevitable that the workers, through their shop committees, will be led on, step by step, to an increasing participation in industry, to a fuller share in the responsibilities of production, and ultimately to some form of a national organization covering the whole industry. It is not likely that the shop committee will permanently deprive itself of a broader association. It will naturally extend itself over the industry. The trade union stands ready to profit by this inevitable development, unless it alienates itself from the beginning by an unreasoning and short-sighted policy of uncompromising hostility.

W. Jett Lauck, after an extensive study of employee representation in the mid-twenties, concluded that "very few plans hold out any real basis of constructive hope or action" for industrial democracy because employers lacked a sincere desire for genuine democracy in industry.[46] Except for a limited form of collective bargaining, he found none of the elements which he thought essential to industrial democracy, such as employee participation in profits or cooperative gains, employee acquisition of stock on a collective basis with representation on boards of directors, and proper principles of wage-determination, i.e., guarantee of an established ratio of labor and management costs or a cost-reduction-sharing plan. Nevertheless, Lauck identified five plans

---

45 Ibid., p. 101.

46 W. Jett Lauck, *Political and Industrial Democracy: 1776–1926* (New York: Funk & Wagnalls Co., 1926), pp. 279ff. The remainder of this discussion draws especially from chapter 7.

which he regarded as "torchbearers of industrial democracy" be-
cause they met the preceding conditions in varying degrees.
These were the plans of William S. Filene Sons of Boston, the
Dutchess Bleacheries of Wappingers Falls, New York, the Dennison Manufacturing Company of Massachusetts, the A. Nash
Company of Cincinnati, and the Philadelphia Rapid Transit
Company. He also saw promise in two other experiments—
the Baltimore & Ohio Railroad Plan and the small industrial
partnership arrangement of the Columbia Conserve Company.
On the other hand, he rejected as either paternalistic or authoritarian the plans introduced by John Leitch under the label of
industrial democracy. Although not all of the plans which he
cited involved labor unions, Lauck felt that enduring industrial
democracy could not be achieved unless it was based on unionism and collective bargaining. At the same time, he urged the
abandonment of militant tactics, class consciousness, and class
dictation on both sides and the development of cooperation
under the fundamental principles of political and industrial
democracy.

Mary Parker Follett, a pioneer in the study of organizational
behavior, who was close to many of the business and industrial
leaders of her day, saw much more potential in the employee
representation plan. She contrasted the method of compromise
of conflicting interests as reflected in collective bargaining with
what she regarded more favorably as the method of organizational integration or functional unity reflected in employee representation. Mary Follett was not opposed to contemporary
collective bargaining since without it, she believed, minimum
standards of employment would deteriorate. But she foresaw
the ultimate abandonment of bargaining as an obsolete way of
running industry. As to the employee representation movement,
she wrote in 1926: ". . . though the employee representation
movement began partly as a concession, partly to make things
go more smoothly, partly to counter trade unions, today it is

considered by many men as an asset, as an essential part of sound organization. But it needs a certain type of manager to make it an asset. . . . The primary thing he has to learn about his dealings with labour is not how to 'treat' with labour, but how to use labour's ability, yes even labour's aspirations . . . as an asset to the enterprise."[47]

The strength of the employee representation challenge to collective bargaining, despite the many criticisms lodged against it, was perhaps most clearly evidenced in the appraisal of the prominent economist, academician, and arbitrator William Leiserson. At the start of the decade, Leiserson had clearly stated that the shop committee plan was simply an employer device to avoid unionism.[48] As his biographer observed, "Leiserson opposed so-called 'company unions' and various union simulation such as 'employee representation plans,' since these were unilaterally granted and under the controlling thumb of management. They served only as precursors to genuine unions or as methods of adjusting immigrants into industry."[49] Nevertheless, in 1922 Leiserson noted that political democracy in England had originally been *handed down* to the people, and the same evolution might take place in industry. "History will not permit us to assume that there is but one road to democracy."[50] He then concluded: "The employers promulgate their own constitutions in the form of employee representation plans because there is insistent demand for representation in industry. If these plans fail to establish real constitutional government they will not survive in competition with an effective trade unionism. If they do

[47] H. C. Metcalf and L. Urwick, eds., *Dynamic Administration: The Collected Papers of Mary Parker Follett* (New York: Harper and Bros., 1942), pp. 178–179.

[48] American Academy of Political and Social Science, *The Annals*, 91 (September 1920): 2.

[49] J. Michael Eisner, *William Morris Leiserson: A Biography* (Madison: University of Wisconsin Press, 1967), p. 40.

[50] William Leiserson, "Constitutional Government in American Industries," *American Economic Review*, 12 (Supplement, 1922): 78.

survive it will be because these plans, although promulgated in the first instance by employers, also develop into a real constitution for industry similar to trade agreements."

By 1928, when he lectured at Harvard University on personnel management, Leiserson described the total system of welfare capitalism in even more positive terms. Whereas prior to World War I, the corporate leadership defined executive control in terms of finance, manufacturing, and sales, after the war a fourth major category was added—the supervision of personnel or employment management. Personnel management not only led to centralized control of the movement of personnel and the establishment of proper working conditions, but also provided workers with something like a bill of rights, including both representative and judicial machinery. The personnel specialists became serious contenders with union leaders for the leadership of labor. The extension by management of insurance against the risks of industrial life—first, accidents, then diseases, illness, disability, old age and death, and most recently unemployment —was a significant development. The personnel managers also brought about a merit system in private industry, removing from the foreman and superintendent the exclusive powers over hiring, discipline, and discharge and, as in the public sector with civil service laws, eliminating a good deal of favoritism and graft. The new high-wage policy, practiced for the first time by Henry Ford on a large scale, was another move ahead. So too was a changing employer attitude toward hours and leisure for employees, such as the eight-hour day and the Saturday half-holiday. But the most significant contribution of personnel management was the development of employee representation machinery. On this Leiserson wrote: "Whatever the motives of the management may be, when it inaugurates employee representation it is handing the employees a constitution for the government of industry. It may not be much of a constitution. It may give the wage earners little power, few rights, and the management may think that employee representation is different from unionism because it does not provide for the right to strike. But that is quite immaterial. The management has started a movement in the direction of democracy in industry which is bound to grow."[51]

In 1928 the Social Science Research Council sponsored a survey of research in the field of industrial relations—what was being done and what was needed. The report contained the following paragraph which well summed up the situation at the end of the postwar decade: "It is evident that the central problem in this field today is the fact that while unionism was practically the only form of collective dealing two decades ago, since that time there has been a rapid spread of other forms of group representation. A real challenge has been offered, and in the minds of many people, the issue between the two is chiefly a matter of which has the most to offer the employees, the industry and society as a whole."[52]

[51] Leiserson, *Wertheim Lectures on Industrial Relations* (Cambridge: Harvard University Press, 1929), p. 156.

[52] Herman Feldman, *A Survey of Research in the Field of Industrial Relations*—A Preliminary Report to the Advisory Committee on Industrial Relations of the Social Science Research Council, mimeographed (New York: Office of the Council, June 8, 1928), p. 119.

CHAPTER **9**

ORGANIZED LABOR'S
RESPONSES TO
WELFARE CAPITALISM

LABOR'S MILITANT DRIVE for industrial democracy reached a peak in the first half of 1919 and then suffered a series of rebuffs and setbacks during the next three years. The failure of the Wilson conferences, the defeat of the steel and other strikes, Congressional rejection of the Plumb Plan and proposals for a labor code, the success of the open-shop drive and of employee representation, and the 1920–1922 depression—these and other developments compelled the adoption of a significantly different approach. This new approach had two facets: (1) accommodation with management through an emphasis on cooperation to advance productivity and eliminate waste, inefficiency, and restrictionism; in return for (2) union recognition by management and management willingness to give labor a share in productivity gains through a high-wage policy.

The first indicators of the shift appeared in late 1919 and early 1920. In a December 1919 statement of aims signed by the leaders of 110 international unions, the AFL called for "cooperation between the scientists of industry and the representatives of organized workers" to "promote further the production of an adequate supply of the world's needs for use and higher standards of life."[1] In an issue of *The Annals* entitled "Labor, Management and Production" (which was suggested by this statement), Morris L. Cooke, an outstanding industrial engineer and a leading liberal follower of Frederick Taylor, observed that "almost for the first time the recognized spokesmen of organized labor in this country take an unequivocal stand for production as being in the interest of the wage earners. There is no other single development possible in industry which by comparison would be as important."[2] Cooke, of course, had in mind the fierce opposition which the AFL had raised against Taylor's ideas and against efforts to utilize motion and time study in government arsenals in the prewar period.

The Annals issue contained an introductory statement by Samuel Gompers as well as brief articles by Matthew Woll, president of the Photo-Engravers Union, and John P. Frey, editor of the International Molders' journal. Together with Gompers' successor, William Green, they were to be the leading proponents of the new approach during the twenties. Gompers asserted that the labor movement "cannot and will not sacrifice anything of its militancy" and that it would stand firm against the breakdown of worker standards and for a proper consideration of workers. He foresaw, however, a strengthening of the bonds between the engineers and the workers in "the substitution in industry of the ideal of production for use—for service—and not for profit alone."

Woll noted that in the 1918 AFL Convention, labor had called for worker committees in all large shops to meet regularly with shop management to confer over matters of production. How-

[1] Quoted in American Academy of Political and Social Science, *The Annals,* 91 (September 1920):vii.
[2] Ibid., p. viii.

ever, "while the workers do not disapprove of efficiency in workmanship or efficiency in production, they are opposed to the so-called efficiency systems which gauge the worker's usefulness as a productive unit by mechanical rules and devices which do not embrace the safeguarding of the life, health and welfare of the workers."[3] Woll stressed the intimate relation between health and output and the need to reduce working hours (to an eight-hour day) so as to improve health and increase output. He then enunciated the doctrine of high wages as a key to high productivity and the setting of minimum wage standards in every trade through collective bargaining. The main drawback to attaining maximum productivity, he argued, was mutual mistrust between employers and employees. This mistrust can be eliminated only "when employers deal with workers as human beings; when they recognize that the day of autocracy in industry has passed and that the day for the applied principles of democracy in industry is here; when they will as freely concede to the workers the collective rights exercised by themselves, viz., the right of organization, the right of representatives of their own choosing, the right of negotiating and enforcing collective agreements and the right to an impelling voice in all phases of industry which vitally affect and reflect upon their status and relation as workers."[4] Woll concluded by urging the voluntary establishment of national conference boards composed of equal numbers of employer and worker representatives to consider all subjects affecting the progress and well-being of the trade, including productive efficiency, safety, and the rights of all concerned within the industry.

Frey's article added little to the foregoing except to explain why labor had been so critical in the past of so-called "scientific management." His final comment: "Control of industry by management, without cooperation and consultation with labor, is as

3 Ibid., p. 10.
4 Ibid., p. 12.

impractical today as would be the effort of group government for the people without their consent."[5]

These mainstream views of organized labor may be contrasted with two minority voices calling for fundamental changes in American management. R. L. Cornick, a worker representative from a U.S. arsenal, insisted on "labor's right to share in the control of industry by representation in proportion to its basic interest."[6] He wanted labor in a position of equality with capital, with worker representation in management and deciding jointly with the managers not only personnel matters such as employment, promotion, demotion, and discharge, but also matters of finance, distribution, and production methods. Cornick recognized the workers' lack of technical training, but believed that this would be speedily rectified: "The realization of their lack of technical knowledge and special training will spur them to take up special lines of study on their own account. This genuine industrial education is one of the most valuable features, and, when combined with the economic incentive which a partnership involves, places the worker in a position where it is to his advantage to stop waste in material and energy, as well as releases latent resources of human energy and ingenuousness."[7]

John II. Walker, coal miner and president of the Illinois State Federation of Labor, went a step further. He advocated the elimination of the system of private profit and, in a vein reflective of the nineteenth-century socialists, the establishment of a cooperative society at all levels of production, distribution, and consumption.

Early in 1920 Samuel Gompers was asked by business journalist Samuel Crowther to "step into the shoes of an employer" and explain how he would deal with his employees.[8] Gompers

[5] Ibid., p. 145.
[6] Ibid., p. 36.
[7] Ibid., p. 38.
[8] Samuel Gompers, "What I Should Do if I Were an Employer," *American Federationist*, 27 (April 1920), 4:351–360.

reiterated his customary support of collective bargaining as a business arrangement in which employer and employees were all associates in the same enterprise "but approaching from somewhat different standpoints." However, he went considerably beyond the wage contract. "I should, without doubt, consult frequently with the union heads and I should put before them my financial transactions not, however, with the notion that whatever I have done is the best under the circumstances but with the view of obtaining their cooperation to see if the one best way cannot be achieved. . . . In order to obtain increased operating efficiency I should call in the union heads just as I should call in an industrial engineer, but even more frequently and on a more intimate basis." Gompers strongly endorsed technological change, provided the job needs of the workers are recognized and the workers share in the greater profits. He felt that the parties had a particular joint interest in developing a "proper system of planning which will insure a full year's work" because seasonal work was the "curse of American industry." He urged a war upon waste.

Gompers saw the fixing of work standards and quality as "peculiarly a matter for the workers in the plant" and favored elected union committees to handle them. Scientific industrial instruction should be given only in cooperation with the workers and their committees. Hiring and firing should be left to the employment manager acting in consultation with the union. He was opposed to the English-type general works committee but favored union cooperative committees for specific objects. "The matter of committees is not particularly complicated if we regard them not as a substitute for management but as an aid thereto, and assign to each definite and not merely roving functions." Where an industry as a whole was concerned, he believed that it was to the interest of both employer and employees to establish general minimum standards so that none would gain at the expense of others by undercutting such standards.

The changing circumstances in which the AFL found itself were reflected quite explicitly in the report of the Executive Council to the 1923 convention at Portland, Oregon. The report opened with a declaration that the close of the war "marked the opening of the period of intelligent demand and living need for industrial democracy." It was a turning point in human relations. Trade unionism now had a larger message and a larger function in society than "mere organization of groups for the advancement of group interests, however vital that function may yet remain."[9]

But then the report revealed the new orientation. It strongly attacked "the threat of state invasion of industrial life" as illustrated by the Esch-Cummins Act for the railroads, the Kansas Court of Industrial Relations, and the Colorado Commission Act. It defied the radical wing of the labor movement which urged political reform—"even at the cost of being branded as reactionary by those who do but little save propound formulas based upon utopian thought." It acknowledged the competence of the industrialists and their basic responsibility for industrial development, notwithstanding the abuses which had accompanied their ambitious drive.

The solution for the industrial ills of the time was for industry to organize itself properly, "to govern itself, to impose upon itself tasks and rules and to bring order into its own house." There was no need for industrial conflict—such conflict was simply the birth pangs of an industrial order. "The true role of industrial groups, however, is to come together, to legislate in peace, to find the way forward in collaboration, to give of their best for the satisfaction of human needs. There must come to industry the orderly functioning that we have been able to develop in our political life. We must find the way to the development of an industrial franchise comparable to our political franchise. There must be developed a sense of responsibility and

9 *AFL Forty-third Annual Convention Proceedings* (October 1923), p. 31.

justice and orderliness. Labor stands ready for participation in this tremendous development."[10]

The following year, Gompers' final one, the Executive Council reiterated to the convention its Portland declaration. It emphasized labor's commitment to industrial democracy and the necessity for management to eliminate autocracy, thereby permitting "a development of human freedom and a right adjustment of human relations" as well "an approach to the solution of important problems of production."[11] The report warned industry that it must solve its own problems or risk the alternative of state intrusion which must inevitably lead to bureaucracy and breakdown. "Democracy cannot come into industry through the state."

While claiming progress against the industrial autocrats, the Executive Council revealed its concern over the obstacles to industrial democracy.

> Too frequently Labor is still compelled to fight for the simplest rights. It is compelled to fight for the very ABC's of industrial freedom—for the right to organize, the right to cease work, the right to speak through its chosen representatives, the right to fair conditions under which to work, the right to keep its childhood away from the mill and factory.

> We still have our barbarous "open shop" movement, our autocratic injunction judges, our stop-watch employers, our blind and reckless managements, and we still have production methods inspired by the investor for the investor without regard either to the worker or the consumer.

In December 1925 the new president of the AFL, William Green, delivered the main address at a joint meeting of the Taylor Society and the Management Division of the American Society of Mechanical Engineers—a talk which Mary Parker

---

[10] Ibid., p. 32.
[11] *AFL Forty-fourth Annual Convention Proceedings* (October 1924), p. 31.

Follett hailed as "one of the most significant utterances of the century in regard to industrial relations."[12]

In this talk Green paid tribute to the vital role of management (as distinct from capital) in controlling and directing the forces of production and called attention to the changing attitudes of labor and management of the time.

> Many of our older concepts are giving way to the newer and more progressive point of view. . . . Management is understanding more and more that economies in production can be brought about through the cooperation of labor and the establishment of high standards rather than through the autocratic control and exploitation of labor. Labor is understanding more and more that high wages and tolerable conditions of employment can be brought about through excellency in service, the promotion of efficiency and the elimination of waste. It is becoming more clearly understood that high wages and a high standard of efficiency in industry are correlated and the industry that is best managed, most economically controlled, where workmanship of the highest order under satisfactory conditions is maintained, is the industry that can pay the highest wages.[13]

From this point until 1932 the AFL regularly endorsed scientific management and labor-management cooperation on production and efficiency. In 1929 the AFL hired an engineer, Geoffrey Brown, as management consultant, and the following year *The Federationist* published "Labor's Principles of Scientific Management" which fully endorsed Taylorism when merged with unionism.[14]

The trade unionists hoped that this new approach would enable them to persuade the major industrialists to integrate col-

[12] H. C. Metcalf and L. Urwick, eds., *Dynamic Administration: The Collected Papers of Mary Parker Follett* (New York: Harper and Bros., 1942), pp. 177–178.

[13] "Labor's Ideals Concerning Management," *Bulletin of the Taylor Society,* 10 (December 1925), 6:245.

[14] Milton Nadworny, *Scientific Management and the Unions* (Cambridge: Harvard University Press, 1955), p. 138.

lective bargaining with employee representation. They were disappointed. Along this line specific proposals were made to Henry Ford and other Detroit automobile manufacturers, but these were quickly repulsed.

The response of employers was, however, far from uniform. In three important industries, as well as some lesser ones, significant developments in union-management cooperation occurred. The three were the railroad industry, the men's clothing industry, and the printing industry.

Cooperation on the Railroads

Governmental operation of the railroads during World War I and the campaign of the railroad unions after the war on behalf of the Plumb Plan had engendered considerable hostility between the employers and the labor organizations. As far as the shopcraft employees were concerned, this hostility reached a peak in the national shopcraft strike of 1922. Although the unions lost the strike and their bargaining position in many systems, there was one favorable aftermath for them—the establishment of the widely heralded Baltimore & Ohio Plan in 1923. In 1928 William Green singled out this plan (which was also adopted by five other railroads) as the outstanding example of union-management cooperation in the country and a major reason for a new spirit of partnership in the industry.

The B & O Plan was basically the idea of Otto S. Beyer, Jr., a professional engineer with considerable railroad and ordnance experience and a close observer of the administration of the railroads from his graduate school days in 1907 through the wartime administration and the postwar readjustment period. In 1919 Beyer strongly attacked the inefficiencies of the industry and urged three possible courses of action: nationalization, representation and participation of workers in management under private ownership, and cooperation between public bodies and the railroads.[15] The plan had actually been proposed prior to the strike and preliminary conferences had been held between union leaders and Daniel Willard, president of the B & O, but the strike prevented an earlier arrangement.

The agreement on the plan noted that it was intended to help stabilization of employment, thereby improving employee morale which in turn would enhance efficiency and quality of work. "The welfare of the Baltimore and Ohio Railroad and its employees is dependent on the service which the railroad renders the public. Improvements in this service and economy in operating and maintenance expenses are greatly promoted by willing cooperation between the railroad management and the voluntary organization of its employees. When the groups responsible for better service and greater efficiency share fairly in the benefits which follow their joint efforts, improvements in the conduct of the railroad are greatly encouraged."[16] In brief, the plan provided for local shop committees of supervisors and workers to meet bi-weekly to discuss shop operations, output, equipment, schedules, scrap, etc.; for meetings every three months of the general shop managers and the Executive Board of the system federation of craft unions to act on the recommendations of the shop committees and to explore other forms of cooperation; and to share the benefits of cooperation through collective bargaining.

President W. H. Johnston of the International Association of Machinists indicated to the seventeenth convention of the union the five principles on which he believed the B & O Plan rested.

[15] American Academy of Political and Social Science, "Railway Efficiency and Labor," *The Annals,* 86 (November 1919): 227ff.

[16] Cited by Otto S. Beyer, Jr. in "The Technique of Cooperation," *Taylor Society Bulletin,* 11 (February 1926), 1:18.

1. Management acceptance of unions as a necessary part of industrial administration whose presence is considered desirable and helpful.

2. Enlargement of the scope of collective bargaining to include constructive as well as protective functions. "Where we now enjoy recognition and have agreements with management, our task is simply to negotiate wage rates, working rules and prevent injustice to our members. This is our protective function. If, however, we want to lay claim to the argument, as the theory of industrial democracy stipulates, that industry can afford better wages and working conditions when its workers share in the management of it, then we must be prepared to assume definite responsibility for better industrial performance."

3. Agreement between unions and management to cooperate for public service. "If as a result of cooperation railroads are not going to run better than they were before, then the workers' argument for more democracy in industry comes to naught."

4. Sharing the gains of cooperation: steadier and more employment, better employment, greater yearly income, and better wage rates for the workers.

5. Establishment of joint machinery of cooperation, in addition to the regular grievance machinery, to deal with shop policy and operation, such as job analysis, scheduling and routing of work, building up shop forces, hiring new men, developing new lines of work, stabilizing employment, providing better tools and equipment, etc.[17]

In 1928 Otto Beyer looked back at five years of experience with labor-management cooperation and concluded that there was "no agency or administrative arrangement more effective for improving industrial relations along fundamental lines than joint cooperative committees composed of union and management representatives which both subscribe definitely to the

[17] Reprinted in David J. Saposs, *Readings in Trade Unionism* (New York: George H. Doran Co., 1926), pp. 59–64.

principles of cooperation." [18] The results were a great improvement in efficiency, in employment conditions, and in morale.

The B & O Plan was not extended to the operating Brotherhoods. The Brotherhoods and the railroads, however, moved toward a more harmonious and mature collective-bargaining system within a governmental framework that was unique to the country. When the railroads were returned to their private owners in 1920, Congress provided for the continuation of a government role in the industry's labor relations by establishing a tripartite Railroad Labor Board (with three representatives each from labor, management, and the public) to hear any dispute over wages, rules, or working conditions. It also authorized the establishment of bipartite Adjustment Boards (similar to those set up during the wartime period) by voluntary agreement of the carriers and the unions to settle grievances over existing agreements or rules. Failure of an Adjustment Board to resolve an issue might lead to a referral of the issue to the Railroad Labor Board. Except for publicity, the Labor Board had no means of enforcing its decisions.

The Railroad Labor Board had a fitful and largely unsuccessful history although several of its decisions on working rules had a long-term impact on the industry.[19] Its wage decisions were generally unpopular; many of its awards were ignored; it was unable to prevent or settle the great shopcraft strike; and the Adjustment Board system was not implemented on a national scale. In 1926 the labor section of the Transportation Act of 1920 was abolished and replaced by the Railway Labor Act.

The most significant fact about the new act was that it was an "agreed bill" negotiated by the representatives of the railroad executives and the labor organizations. The new Board of Med-

[18] Otto S. Beyer, Jr., *Wertheim Lectures on Industrial Relations* (Cambridge: Harvard University Press, 1929), p. 20.

[19] For a definitive history of the board, see Henry D. Wolf, *The Railroad Labor Board* (Chicago: University of Chicago Press, 1927).

iation (composed of five members appointed by the President) was, like the prewar agency under the Newlands Act, empowered to mediate disputes and, if unsuccessful, to recommend voluntary arbitration. If neither of these courses resolved the dispute and a strike was threatened, the board was obligated to notify the President, who could then appoint an Emergency Board to investigate and make a report. Strikes and lockouts were forbidden until thirty days after the submission of the Emergency Board report to the President. The Railway Labor Act also directed the creation of national, regional, or local adjustment boards by agreements of the parties. It did not, however, provide any means for implementing this directive and again the results were unsatisfactory.

The experience of the railroad industry in the 1920's was unique because of the traditional public concern with railroad conflicts. It was a period of trial and error in which the unions, employers, and government officials sought to work out an acceptable accommodation between the three main interests involved. The B & O Plan and the 1926 Railway Labor Act reflected two different courses to that end.

The New Unionism in the Men's Clothing Industry

Welfare capitalism had little import in the clothing industry with its thousands of small, highly competitive, and (for the most part) poorly managed firms. The future of industrial democracy depended on the feasibility of establishing an effective collective-bargaining system. Although John R. Commons, early in the century, had concluded that the temperament of the Jewish garment worker made enduring unionism unlikely, the astonishing emergence of the Protocol of Peace in the New York ladies' garment market after 1910 seemed to disprove this judgment. But the Protocol system broke down in 1915, and despite the fact that collective bargaining was soon reinstituted, relations between the International Ladies Garment Workers Union and the employers remained troubled. In the decade after 1918 the Cleveland garment manufacturers and the ILGWU achieved a promising relationship under an agreement which provided machinery for shop grievance handling, a board of referees with binding authority to settle unresolved disputes and to set wage scales, control of contracting and subcontracting shops, a joint committee to establish production standards in each shop, a forty-week employment guarantee or one-half the minimum wage, and an unemployment insurance fund paid for wholly by the employers. Unfortunately, in the mid-twenties conflict between the moderate Socialists and the Communists for control in New York City almost destroyed the national union and made a shamble of its collective-bargaining systems.

The outcome in the men's clothing industry, especially in Chicago but also in other important markets like New York and Rochester, was much more favorable, partly because of differences in the structure of the industry but mainly because of the gifted leadership of Sidney Hillman in working out accommodations with employers and in preventing ideological differences from splitting the union.[20] As indicated in an earlier chapter, the starting and focal point was the Hart Schaffner & Marx system which evolved out of the agreement of 1911 and which developed shop grievance machinery and the impartial-chairman idea to a new level of significance. Hillman was not the only important figure in this process. For the company, Earl Howard, who left the academic community to become a notable pioneering "labor manager," received farsighted and imaginative support from chief owner Joseph Schaffner and the company attorney

[20] This story is well told in a sympathetic biography by Matthew Josephson, *Sidney Hillman: Statesman of American Labor* (New York: Doubleday and Company, 1952).

Carl Meyer. And standing between them as a source of strength and creativity was the first of the nation's great permanent umpires, John E. Williams.

From Hart Schaffner & Marx, the Amalgamated Clothing Workers (unaffiliated wtih the AFL because it had split from the United Garment Workers) gradually extended the new system to the entire Chicago clothing market and to other major markets as well. The skilled use of economic pressures combined with maximum exploitation of government support during the war in the program to supply army clothing led to the growth of the Amalgamated into one of the nation's largest unions.

During the twenties the Amalgamated suffered early losses because of the termination of wartime clothing orders, resistance from some of the employer groups (especially in New York), and the general depression of 1920–1922. But in contrast to the experience in the industries dominated by the huge corporations, the union survived the challenge and then proceeded to create its own system of industrial welfarism which gave it national prominence. It was no accident that Arthur "Golden Rule" Nash, after six years of successful operation of his Cincinnati plant on a non-union basis, decided to urge his employees to join the Amalgamated.

Although Hillman and his colleagues, as well as many of the rank-and-file, were socialists, the union adopted a highly pragmatic program based on accommodation with the realities of the capitalist society in which they lived and in tune with the dominant technological and economic themes of the period. However, instead of being a follower of the mainstream, Hillman was an innovator of the first order. Not only did the union improve its collective-bargaining system on a marketwide scale, but it introduced new techniques and policies to deal with the difficult problems of the complex clothing industry. To cope with seasonal and later cyclical unemployment, the Joint Board in Chicago first set up an employment exchange in 1919 and then in 1922 got the employers to agree to the establishment of an unemployment-insurance system, based on a 1.5 per cent worker contribution and a 3 per cent employer contribution. To standardize labor costs, the piece-rate system was revised and group production standards were introduced. When intense competition made technological changes essential, the union worked out a severance pay plan for displaced employees.

Impressed by the idea of the Brotherhood of Locomotive Engineers to set up labor banks, the Amalgamated followed suit and established their own banks in Chicago and New York. While the banks of the Engineers and other unions proved disastrous failures, the Amalgamated banks flourished. They were used not only to encourage worker savings but as a source of small loans to workers, for relief in times of strikes, and for aid to garment companies which were in financial difficulty.

Cooperation with employers to improve productive efficiency and to avoid bankruptcy and the resultant loss of jobs became a continuing union function. As the General Executive Board reported to the 1926 Amalgamated Clothing Workers convention, describing how the 1924 wage negotiations led to a survey of the industry "with a view to discovering all possible sources of saving and means of increasing employment:"

> Prolonged conferences were had with individual firms in which labor costs, overhead, sales methods, shop organization were all discussed and analyzed. The union made suggestions and took under consideration proposals from the employers. The technically trained deputies of the union worked with the management in devising more economical methods of production; whole new shops, with this effective cooperation of the union, were quickly organized and put into operation without friction and high expense of promotion. . . . Through them [these activities] the Amalgamated was assuming in practice, as well as in theory, a large share in the actual management and responsibility of the industry.[21]

[21] Seventh Biennial Amalgamated Clothing Workers Convention (1926), *Proceedings*, p. 13.

The secretary-treasurer of the Amalgamated summed up the new situation in his report to the 1924 convention. "Our work today is entirely different from what it used to be. . . . Our big struggles in the past were for the right to organize, for a voice in the industry, for representation in industrial conferences. That we now have. . . . Our constructive work today is of a more advanced character . . . that has placed upon us new responsibilities and brought us new opportunities."[22]

The Crafts in Printing and Construction

Old-line craft unions like the printers and construction trades— the backbone of the AFL—suffered some initial setbacks in the early twenties but made a strong recovery as the decade progressed.[23] The governmental process had become firmly set in most of the major centers of these industries prior to the war and the ideas of welfare capitalism do not seem to have had a significant impact.

Contemporary writers on the building trades were impressed, however, not by the bargaining process but by the growing importance of the business agents, their personal alliances with local political machines (regardless of party), and their short-run economic views. One critic wrote:

> They [the unions] rest heavily upon local politicians for support. They have not used their economic advantage to establish constitutional rights and guarantees in their industry and at the same time have failed to grasp the meaning of the economic situation. Slumps have been something to worry about when they would occur, non-union workers have been left to their fate in accor-

[22] Sixth Biennial Amalgamated Clothing Workers Convention (1924), *Proceedings*, p. 225.

[23] One major exception was San Francisco where twenty years of union domination was broken by an "American Plan" attack.

dance with an unenlightened selfishness, and changing technique has been important only as it affected jurisdictional questions. The chief policy has been so-called non-partisan politics—non-partisan because some cities are run by Republican machines and others by Democratic.[24]

A more profound analysis was provided by William Haber. Haber agreed that bargaining power was so unevenly distributed that genuine collective bargaining was the exception. In the open-shop cities, like San Francisco, the employers called the tune. In most of the large cities, the unions dominated mainly because the contractors were unwilling to sacrifice any of their individual interests and "to accept the obligations and self-discipline of group organization which inevitably accompany association membership."[25] In some cases there was collusion against the public. Haber felt that in order to eliminate restrictionism and to promote labor-management cooperation for the good of the industry, the collective-bargaining process had to be materially improved and the subject matter of collective agreements had to be significantly enlarged. He portrayed the situation in the following terms:

> Unions look upon their rules as a part of their industrial constitution, embodied in a trade agreement, and while they concede that the more flexible terms of the agreement may be changed, they feel that the rules should be modified only after conclusive proof of necessity. Since rules seek to protect the members of the union against sudden changes in working conditions which might endanger the tenure of their job or the skill of their trade, any effort to abolish or change them is stubbornly opposed. It is this fundamentalist attitude on the question which often makes working rules an obstacle to changes in methods of production and to

[24] Louis Stanley, in *American Labor Dynamics: In the Light of Postwar Developments*, ed. J.B.S. Hardman (New York: Harcourt, Brace, 1928), p. 204.

[25] William Haber, *Industrial Relations in the Building Industry* (Cambridge: Harvard University Press, 1930), p. 513.

the introduction of labor-saving devices. This is the reason why to the employer they appear vicious. Employers desire that rules shall remain flexible and changeable with industrial conditions—a part of the statute law of industry, and not of the industrial constitution as the unions would have it.[26]

Haber saw the building unions as playing largely the role of the policeman or vigilante committee, on the lookout for violators of the standards agreed upon. He noted many problem areas which merited joint cooperation of unions and employer organizations—industrial education, poor and inadequate training, accidents, wasteful practices, cost reduction, and irregular employment. He found little evidence of such cooperation, notwithstanding some postwar efforts sparked by national figures like Herbert Hoover as secretary of commerce and Franklin D. Roosevelt, to attack the problems of the industry on a national scale.[27]

The relationships in the printing industry were different in numerous respects from those in the building industry, but they also reflected the longtime bargaining power of the unions and their determination to assume, through union rules, one-sided control over employment conditions. As in construction, the printing unions suffered some losses from the open-shop American Plan movement, especially in the book and job printing industry, and there were some experiments in non-union employee representation in Baltimore and Boston.[28] However, their basic prewar position remained intact. The International Typographical Union continued to assert that certain ITU "laws" were not bargainable or arbitrable although they were willing to listen to employer objections. Such laws covered, for example, the

[26] Ibid., pp. 512–513.
[27] Ibid., chapter 16.
[28] See Emily C. Brown, *Book and Job Printing in Chicago* (Chicago: University of Chicago Press, 1931).

length of the work week (as of 1915 it was six days, as of 1925, five days), apprenticeships, the reproduction of previously used matter, priority or seniority in the decrease or increase of employment and the hiring of substitutes, and union membership by foremen.

Writing in the second half of the twenties, Selig Perlman selected the ITU as the prime example of the authentic organic unionism of the country, with its elaborate code of rules controlling the job, a "complete law of the job." "Studying the rules of the printers' union, we get a picture of a carefully worked out labor dictatorship, not, however, a dictatorship in the Russian style, but in a style all its own, since it is content to leave the employer in the unchallenged position [sic] of his property and business, and brings under a union dictatorship the employment opportunities only."[29]
The union achieved a complete control over the job by insisting that the foreman—a union member—should have full responsibility for hiring, firing, and otherwise dealing with employees in the shop, and that the foreman in turn should be subject to union discipline if he violated union rules. The union itself—in contrast to many of the building trades—was run on a highly democratic basis, with a unique two-party system for the election of officers and an extensive judicial machinery for membership appeals and grievances.

Other AFL Units

Between union weakness or nonexistence in the large mass production industries and union dominance in important sectors of building and printing, there were a considerable number

[29] Selig Perlman, *A Theory of the Labor Movement* (New York: Macmillan Co., 1928), p. 263.

and types of relationships built around the bilateral collective-bargaining model of industrial democracy. In the street railway industry, for example, local transit companies and the Amalgamated Association of Street Railway Employees developed harmonious working arrangements through collective bargaining which included the binding arbitration of disputes not only over grievances but also over the terms of new agreements. The Electrical Workers Union achieved comparable relations with a variety of public utilities. And national systems of bargaining of a highly sophisticated nature evolved out of earlier experiences in the pottery and glass industries.

In the hosiery industry, following a major conflict in 1921, there was an impressive development from a decentralized system of "more or less undisciplined shop control" to a system of uniform shop rules for the entire Philadelphia area (then the center of the industry) to the signing of a national agreement in 1929 under which unresolved disputes were to be referred from the shop through the national officials of the union and the manufacturers' association to a national impartial chairman. The latter's decisions applying to one area were binding on all other areas. "The gradual accumulation of settlements of individual shop, grievance questions by means of the various types of machinery just described came eventually to have the force of shop custom in the industry."[30]

On the other hand, as noted earlier, collective-bargaining systems in coal mining and ladies' garments deteriorated. For a variety of reasons, the same process occurred in other previously well-established systems, including several branches of textiles like the silk ribbon weaving industry, carpetmaking, and upholstery. In short, industrial government during the 1920's simultaneously went through many different stages—some advancing toward industrial democracy, others retreating from it.

[30] Gladys L. Palmer, *Union Tactics and Economic Change* (Philadelphia: University of Pennsylvania Press, 1932), p. 84.

The Plight of the Radicals

Whereas the first two decades of the century were years of promise for the radicals in and close to the labor movement, the decade of the twenties was one of disarray and frustration. The antiradical campaigns of World War I and the postwar years had resulted in the virtual destruction of the IWW. The war had created divisions among the main body of socialists, and after the successful seizure of control by the Communists in Russia, the American radicals fell into two main groups: the supporters of the Socialist party and the supporters of the Workers or Communist party. Much of the energy and resources of the radicals turned to internecine warfare, particularly on the part of the Communists who attempted, with minimal success, to take over various progressive, labor, and socialist political organizations and trade unions.

As Draper and others have demonstrated, the Communist party was almost totally dominated by policies formulated in the Soviet Union.[31] After a few years of underground life, the Communists, on dictation from Moscow, decided to establish a legal, publicly identifiable party and embarked on a program of dual unionism to rival or displace the AFL. Ideologically, they contributed nothing new. Class struggle and industrial unionism were their key slogans; class collaboration and labor fakirism were the epithets which they hurled at their opponents both in the conservative trade union ranks and in the socialist fold.

Although Eugene Debs, while still in prison for his antiwar speeches, received over 915,000 votes in the 1920 Presidential race—the largest vote ever received by a Socialist candidate—the Socialist party fell into rapid decline. It supported Senator

---

[31] See, for example, Theodore Draper, *The Roots of American Communism* (New York: Viking Press, 1957) and *American Communism and Soviet Russia* (New York: Viking Press, 1960).

Robert La Follette in his 1924 campaign for the Presidency but made a poor showing in most of the state and local elections. Despite the emergence of Norman Thomas as a forceful and dynamic successor to the charismatic Debs, the Socialists could poll only 267,000 votes in the 1928 Presidential election. Nor did the Socialists have much success in union affairs, especially after their ruinous conflict with the Communists in the New York ladies' garment industry.[32]

The main role played by the Socialists in American life during the twenties was that of critic of the dominant business society and this function was carried on most effectively by the League for Industrial Democracy—an organization modeled after the British Fabian Society—which Harry W. Laidler and Thomas led.

In a symposium sponsored by the League, the chief criticisms were expounded by a number of prominent Socialists as well as by some non-Socialist progressives and by some Communists.[33] The first and major criticism, expressed by a number of speakers, was that the prosperity of the twenties was very inadequately shared by the workers, that there was no evidence that the working man was really better off than in the prewar years, and that he was faced with as many and as serious hardships as ever before. Abraham Epstein argued that the failure of the trade union movement to provide workers with adequate protections against the basic insecurities of industry—those of sickness, unemployment, orphanage and widowhood, invalidity, and old age—and the adoption by employers of many welfare activities, however inadequate, were largely responsible for the decline in the labor movement. Epstein was particularly critical of the AFL refusal

---

[32] The story of the Socialists is well told in David A. Shannon, *The Socialist Party of America* (New York: Macmillan Co., 1955).

[33] Harry W. Laidler and Norman Thomas, eds., *Prosperity?* (New York: Vanguard Press, 1927).

to fight for state benefits, except for workmen's compensation. James Maurer strongly attacked the "false prosperity" which he saw resting on the new "installment loan" frenzy; he predicted a crash since the country had gotten to the limit of credit on the installment plan. Joseph Schlossberg, secretary-treasurer of the Amalgamated Clothing Workers, saw the problems of the labor movement not only in the open-shop drive and company unionism but especially in the failure to break the fetters of craft unionism, to develop industrial unionism, to create realistic idealism among workers through labor education, to eliminate the slot-machine slogans of a living wage or a saving wage, and to support an independent labor party.

On the other hand, Morris Hillquit, while accepting most of the preceding criticisms, felt that the weakness of the socialist movement was due to a long list of factors, including the youth of the country, the absence of hereditary and crystallized classes, the heterogeneous character of its population, the greater opportunity for individual advancement, the constant flux of economic life, the rapidity of industrial development, and most of all the comparative prosperity of the American workers. To Communist Scott Nearing, the crux of the problem was the indisputable power of a unified business class and the need to organize and train a professional revolutionary class.

Most of the foregoing comments were restated in greater detail in a volume of essays edited by J. B. S. Hardman, journalist and educational director for the Amalgamated Clothing Workers, and a socialist of the Hillman variety. Hardman summed up the labor situation from a socialist perspective in the following terms: "The discussion of these issues indicates that the labor movement is, on the whole, lacking in social vision. There is trade-union capitalism, of course; and the 'social wage policy' of adapting wages to increased production. But one proposal is an evasion of these issues, while the other has so far had no influence on policy. Labor in most industries is still drifting, and is itself unaware of the whys and wherefores of the 'luck' which has brought substantial increases in real wages."[34]

The socialist view of industrial democracy was simply outlined in two short League for Industrial Democracy pamphlets, one entitled *Roads to Freedom* by Harry Laidler[35] and the other entitled *What Is Industrial Democracy?* by Norman Thomas.[36] Laidler contrasted the socialist alternative to capitalism with its numerous rivals—communism, anarchism and syndicalism, guild socialism, consumers cooperation, and the single tax. He stressed eight dimensions of the socialist approach:

1. The ultimate transfer to municipal, state, or federal ownership of large-scale industries, beginning with those of a public character, such as banking, insurance, mining, transportation, communication, and the trusts, and extending to others as rapidly as feasible.

2. Support of voluntary cooperation among both consumers and producers, including farmers' cooperatives, self-governing workshops, and other forms of producers' associations. Private ownership would be permitted among farmers and handicraftsmen, experimental new industries might be started as private enterprises. Free-lance writers, artists, etc. would continue to function.

3. The aim of socialism is not to superimpose upon the people any particular industrial mechanism, but to abolish the system of exploitation of man by man, to eliminate industrial waste, to secure equality of opportunity and the maximum of social welfare, and to develop the personality of the mass of the people.

[34] Hardman, *American Labor Dynamics*, p. 172.

[35] Harry Laidler, *Roads to Freedom*, League for Industrial Democracy pamphlet, 3rd ed., no. 10 (1927).

[36] Norman Thomas, *What Is Industrial Democracy?* League for Industrial Democracy Pamphlet, no. 12 (1925).

4. In publicly owned industries, an effort would be made to eliminate bureaucratic and autocratic control and to give adequate representation in industrial control to all the concerned elements—workers, technicians and administrators, and the general public.

5. No commitment to any one form of compensation. While the money incentive would continue to be used as needed to promote efficiency, the greatest possible encouragement would be given to other incentives—social prestige, creative desire, to pay one's way in life, to develop one's potentialities, to serve one's fellow men, and to be part of a great enterprise.

6. Maintenance of a democratic state which would give adequate room for the expression of minority opinion, and should not interfere with the freedom of the individual to order his own life, except where the exercise of that right interferes with the equal rights of others.

7. No interference with either the family or with religious beliefs.

8. A gradual transition to socialization of industry, with some method of compensation for industries transferred, the funds to be raised mainly by graduated income, inheritance, land value, and other forms of taxation.

As illustration of how democratic control under public ownership could be established in a particular industry, Laidler referred to the contemporary proposal of the Nationalization Research Committee of the United Mine Workers. This provided for national ownership of the mines, with control vested in a Federal Interstate Commission of Mines, composed of eleven members, five chosen by professional and industrial organizations and six by the President, and with a cabinet officer serving as head. Administration would be carried on by a National Mining Council, regional councils, and mine committees, with three different kinds of members— (1) the financial, technical, and managerial administrative heads of industry, (2) the miners, and (3) consumers of coal, consumers in allied industries, and the community. Wages would be determined through collective bargaining between mine representatives appointed by the directors of the industry and representatives of the United Mine Workers Union. Like the Plumb Plan, which it resembled, this mine plan had no practical consequences.

The pamphlet by Norman Thomas was in close harmony with Laidler's, but it dealt more specifically with contemporary programs to democratize industry as well as theoretical systems. Thomas defined "industrial democracy" as the application to industrial life of Lincoln's concept of government of the people, by the people and for the people. He also quoted with approval the remark of one public speaker that under the capitalist system the boss selects the worker while under industrial democracy the workers will elect the boss. Thomas noted, however, that any sweeping generalization is bound to be defective and leaves unsolved such questions as: How will the workers elect the bosses? How will coordination between different industries be obtained? How under a simple system of electing the bosses in productive enterprises will the needs of men as producers be related to their needs as consumers?

Although extremely sympathetic to trade unionism, Thomas did not believe that even the most advanced form of collective bargaining, such as practiced by the needle trades or in the Baltimore & Ohio Railroad shops, was adequate. Labor banking and labor ownership of industry through stock purchase seemed futile. The Plumb Plan and the miners nationalization plan were promising, but the former had died with its creator and the latter had been shelved by UMW president John Lewis. Moreover the unions had failed to carry democracy within their own ranks anywhere near to perfection. Race prejudice, autocracy, and bureaucracy in union government, violence and corruption in factional strife, and narrow craft forms of organization were all evils which the unions had to cure themselves.

As to employer efforts to establish relationships which they called "industrial democracy," Thomas was generally negative. But he saw a ray of hope in those employee representation plans which were not meant as a substitute for trade unionism and which did not entail such coercive methods as industrial espionage and armed guards. The works councils had three values: (1) they were an admission that manual workers were capable of assuming a responsible and efficient part in the management of their own industry, (2) they were a good training ground for workers in production and management, should they ever be able to take control from absentee owners, and (3) by breaking down craft barriers, they encourage cooperative action by labor.

Thomas also considered and then rejected the arguments that men were not able, by their very nature, to achieve industrial democracy. He cast aside the notion that men will work only for profits. He agreed that men were unequal in ability and character, but he did not regard this as a reason for not establishing a democratic system. Nor did democracy require all men to be passionately interested in the problems of government and administration. It primarily requires:

1. That ordinary people be given legal and peaceable machinery of control in their own interests over the experts and specialists who must necessarily direct administration.

2. That those workers who were capable of, and interested in, more direct participation in management should get the chance without having to become an owner.

He had no illusion about the difficulties involved in reeducating society to a "fellowship of free men" nor about choosing men for responsible administrative posts on a democratic basis (he suggested that all candidates for such positions must meet certain tests of knowledge and ability).

He concluded with three guiding principles:

1. Industrial democracy must be efficient; it must provide a basis for existence.

2. It must be a living growth, not a mechanical creation.

3. It must be based on great and truly revolutionary conceptions of human freedom and fellowship.

CHAPTER 10

AT THE CROSSROADS

$\mathbf{F}$ROM A UNION STANDPOINT the twenties were indeed, as Irving Bernstein has characterized them, "lean years," although some unions—notably the building trades, the printers, the operating railroad Brotherhoods, and the men's clothing workers—were able to surmount the hurdles which frustrated the labor movement as a whole. From the standpoint of industrial democracy, taking into account the humanizing effects of welfare capitalism in many of the large corporations, a more positive conclusion seems justified. The industrial democracy trend, on balance, held its own and may have advanced. It would be naive to ignore the elements of corporate policy which concentrated on anti-unionism and which rejected the ideas of collective bargaining. Many of the employee-representation plans were transparent facades. But as a number of the keenest and most dispassionate observers of the decade stated: Regardless of their motivation, the sponsors of employee representation, personnel management, and human relations had set in motion forces which inevitably entailed the democratization of industry. The only question was whether these forces would ultimately redound to the favor of the trade unions and the collective-bargaining model or whether a company-oriented system of representation and integration would triumph. This question

259

was to be definitively resolved in the next decade. In this chapter attention will be directed to an assessment of the various dimensions of industrial democracy along the lines undertaken for prior periods.

Representation

The extent to which industrial sovereignty is shared may be estimated in various ways. One is to determine the magnitude and spread of the membership of organizations speaking on behalf of workers. Another is to analyze the coverage of labor-management agreements. For the period of the twenties, the former seems preferable. Although the practice of the written agreement was spreading, it was far from universal in collective-bargaining situations. Furthermore statistics on agreements were still quite limited.

As noted previously, union membership declined appreciably from a peak of 4.9 million in 1920 to 3.2 million in 1930 (excluding Canadian members).[1] But the number of workers covered by employee representation plans (including a small number of unionized shops) rose from about 400,000 in 1919 to 1.5 million in 1928.[2] Thus the total workers under some form of organized collective system of industrial government was only slightly below the postwar high.

The industrial distribution of covered workers was perhaps more significant in terms of the long-run trend. The employee-representation movement brought a measure of representation

---

[1] Leo Troy, "Trade Union Membership, 1897–1962," *Review of Economics and Statistics* (February 1965).

[2] Derived from surveys made by the National Industrial Conference Board. These surveys were more limited than the union member surveys and therefore probably understate worker coverage in both absolute and relative terms. See *Collective Bargaining through Employee Representation* (New York: National Industrial Conference Board, 1933).

rights to workers in industries which had had little experience with this type of relationship before World War I. This fact applied particularly to the mass of unskilled and semiskilled workers in oil refining, iron and steel, electrical products, and rubber products. Since these industries stood out as the symbols of the new industrial America, their representation policy was bound to be widely noted and imitated. The major exceptions were U.S. Steel and the auto companies. On the other hand, the union setbacks in bituminous coal mining, ladies' garments, the railroad shops, the brewery industry, and textiles, although they were severe, were only partial. The idea of industrial democracy remained a visible force in these industries, and it was reasonable to expect that in time a restoration might occur. It might then be argued that the sharing of industrial sovereignty was more widespread than it had been even though the employee-representation model was more limited than the collective-bargaining model because the corporate managers retained more power and control in the former.

As noted in chapter 7, the idea that union or other employee-organization representation should be determined by majority vote of the employees involved may be said to have taken root during World War I, particularly in the decisions of the War Labor Board ordering shop elections by secret ballot among unorganized employees to enable them to have some type of representative system in dealing with the employer. But it should be emphasized that neither the War Labor Board nor the other government agencies which sponsored similar elections conceived of the election device as a technique for determining whether employees wanted one organization rather than another or none at all.

A step in the latter direction was taken in the postwar period by some employers who conducted plant elections to ascertain whether or not their employees wished an employee-representation plan. But the most important development with regard to the ultimate establishment of the majority rule principle occurred in the railroad industry.[3]

Shortly after the railroads were returned to private operation in 1920, the Railway Labor Board issued a set of principles to guide the parties in their negotiations for new agreements. These principles affirmed the right of employees to organize without interference and to act through representatives of their own choice, whether employees of a particular carrier or otherwise. Principle 15 further provided: "The majority of any craft or class of employees shall have the right to determine what organization shall represent members of such craft or class. Such organization shall have the right to make an agreement which shall apply to all employees in such craft or class. No such agreement shall infringe, however, upon the right of employees not members of the organization representing the majority to present grievances either in person or by representatives of their own choice."

The Pennsylvania Railroad Company refused to accept the board's authority in this matter, rejected the claims of the six federated shop crafts that they represented the majority of employees, and proceeded to establish an employee-representation plan. Legal actions were instituted by both the company and the board, and later by the unions, leading to two U.S. Supreme Court decisions. The Court upheld the right of the board to issue Principle 15, but it also held that the decisions of the board were unenforceable except through public opinion. The company was thus able to defy the board and the unions lacked sufficient strength to overthrow the employee-representation scheme. The Railway Labor Act of 1926 was silent on the question of majority rule.

On the employer side, the decade witnessed the continuing separation of the ownership of the large corporations from the

[3] The following account is based on Harry D. Wolf, *The Railroad Labor Board* (Chicago: University of Chicago Press, 1927), chapter 13.

policy-making and administrative responsibility. It was of this period that Berle and Means wrote their classic work, *The Modern Corporation and Private Property*, demonstrating that the managements had achieved control from within, independent of any significant ownership rights.[4] Nominally big industry had shifted from control by a single individual or family, through ownership, to control by the holders of a majority of the stock. In fact, even this majority principle was normally subject to easy manipulation by a small number of top executives, or by outside financial interests. These individuals in turn determined the selection of the managerial representatives.

Participation

For the most part union participation in industrial decision-making did not change significantly from the level achieved during the wartime and immediate postwar period. In 1920 Samuel Gompers had stated:

> Collective bargaining in industry does not imply that wage earners shall assume control of industry, or responsibility for financial management. It proposes that the employees shall have the right to organize and to deal with the employer through selected representatives as to wages and working conditions.

> Among the matters that properly come within the scope of collective bargaining are wages, hours of labor, conditions and relations of employment, the sanitary conditions of the plant, safety and comfort of the employees, resulting in the mutual advantage of both employers and employees. But there is no belief held in the trades unions that its members shall control the plant or usurp the rights of the owners.[5]

[4] Adolph A. Berle, Jr., and G. C. Means, *The Modern Corporation and Private Property* (New York: Macmillan Co., 1932).

[5] Samuel Gompers, *Labor and the Employer* (New York: E. P. Dutton & Co., 1920), p. 286.

Although accurately reflecting the traditional public position of business unionism, this statement failed to convey the full scope and depth of union participation. Long before 1920, unions had demonstrated their interest in not merely influencing but, if possible, controlling the job aspects of industrial life. The one-sided controls established in the printing and construction industries have already been described in chapter 7.

In contrast to these examples of union control of job conditions, the typical union-management relationship of the period involved bilateral determination of wages, hours, and employment conditions. Outstanding examples were coal mining and railroad operation.[6] In these industries strong unions and large industrial combines, or associations, achieved an approximate balance of power during the first two decades of the century, and the union's impact on the management function widened. A student of the coal mining industry in the mid-1920's wrote: "A survey of the aspects of the process of coal production which are usually regarded as solely under the control of management, but in connection with which it is found the miners have a voice, leaves one with the impression that those who are establishing principles of industrial relations affecting these matters are in the vanguard of a new industrial order."[7] Thus it was noted that the miners shared in the formulation and execution of rules about the condition of equipment, such as the standardization of coal screens and the repair and delivery of coal cars; the furnishing of supplies of a particular quality and quantity; the order in which work was to be performed; the determination of whether a workplace was deficient or unsafe; the methods of weighing and recording the coal mined for compensation purposes; the distribution of available work; hiring, assignment,

[6] The bituminous sector deteriorated after 1926 but anthracite maintained its stability. Less prominent but even earlier examples were the industries engaged in the production of glass bottles, flint glass, pottery, stoves, and street railways.

[7] Arthur E. Suffern, *The Coal Miners' Struggle for Industrial Status* (New York: Macmillan Co., 1926), pp. 357–358.

dismissal, and discipline of employees; and conditions affecting health, safety, and welfare.

Some of the coal agreements written shortly after the turn of the century included management-rights provisions which affirmed managerial rights to direct employees and to operate the mines, but which also—either explicitly or by implication—subjected these rights to challenge if they were applied arbitrarily or beyond certain limits. The manager's right to hire and discharge employees was clearly recognized, for example, but hiring on a discriminatory basis because of creed, color, nationality, or union membership was prohibited; and discharge was permitted only for just cause. Managers had the right to install labor-saving equipment, but the employees involved had to be given other jobs. Custom was also recognized as an important factor in relation to the management process, and changes in customary practice were accepted only if agreements or laws specifically provided for such change.

Railroad relations were basically like those in mining in terms of participation and control. The Railway Labor Board's "sixteen principles" of 1920 included the statements that responsibility for safe, efficient, and economical operation belonged to management, but employees should have the right "to be consulted prior to a decision of management, adversely affecting their wages or working conditions." Although not formally accepted by the parties, the principle of prior consultation became an important feature of collective relations.

One of the most dramatic and far-reaching advances in union participation came in the men's clothing industry. As early as 1920 William Leiserson, then impartial arbitrator in the Rochester clothing market, wrote that the effect of the bargaining system was "to develop in the wage earners a sense of ownership in the industry."[8] He quoted them as saying, in effect, to the em-

[8] American Academy of Political and Social Science, *The Annals*, 90 (July 1920):26.

ployers: "We are not your equal in talking with you individually. You know all about markets. You know all about business. You have lawyers. You have employment experts and time-study men. We have none of those people but we have organized a union and we can get the same kind of experts now, and we want our experts to deal with your experts and then we will deal on equal terms and get somewhere."[9]

In 1928 the Amalgamated reported in its *Documentary History* (pp. 12–13):

> In substance, our organization has been assuming a larger share of the functions of management. Vague terms, like union control, have under our arrangements with many manufacturers been translated into stern reality. Already many of the functions of supervision and management have, in spots, been taken over by the union. The savings that have been effected by this procedure have gone to raise the standards and income of our members and to increase the business of unionized firms. At the same time, to a large extent as a result of these methods, the union has become more indispensable to the industry than it has ever been.

For the most part, the participation of workers in decision-making in employee-representation plants was not as extensive as in the strongly unionized industries. More often than not, the employee representatives were given the opportunity only to express their views, while the final decision remained with management. Nonetheless studies of the operations of the representation plans revealed that the workers' representatives were exposed, often for the first time, to a collective discussion of a wide range of issues, including wages, hours, and employment conditions, grievances and complaints, problems of production and waste, and activities having to do with both in-plant and out-of-plant life. Carroll French concluded from his investigation that "the workers, through their shop committees, will be led on,

9 Ibid., p. 25.

step by step, to an increasing participation in industry, to a fuller share in the responsibilities of production, and ultimately to some form of a national organization covering the whole industry."[10] French, indeed, saw the shop committee and the trade union as complementary, with the former contributing mainly to the internal life of the enterprise and the latter affecting the competitive market situation.

Just as there were a small number of outstanding examples of union participation, so it is possible to identify a small number of employee representation plans in which employee participation went very far. W. Jett Lauck applied a number of "fundamental" tests of industrial democracy (as he defined it) to some 800 employee representation plans, including (1) participation in profits through mutual cooperation rather than employer gift, (2) employee stock ownership leading to employee control of business, (3) employee representation on boards of directors, and (4) customer and, especially, employee provision of new capital.[11] Twelve companies met the first test, including Philadelphia Rapid Transit, Filene, Colorado Fuel and Iron, Dennison, Dutchess Bleacheries, Nash, Ford, Bank of Italy, Boston Consolidated Gas, and Columbia Conserve, plus the various B & O type plans on the railroads. Only five companies met his second test—Philadelphia Rapid Transit, Dennison, Bank of Italy, Nash, and Columbia Conserve. Eight companies met the third test, five of which were through voluntary action of the owners and three through stock purchases. They were Filene, Dutchess Bleacheries, Boston Consolidated Gas, Louisville Rail-

[10] Carroll E. French, *The Shop Committee in the United States* (Baltimore: Johns Hopkins Press, Ph.D. thesis, 1923), p. 105.

[11] His other tests were the existence of a truly independent labor organization (i.e., a trade union), a living wage and acceptable employment conditions, and mutual agreement between employers and employees on cooperative machinery to effect business economies, increase productive efficiency, and expand the volume of business. See W. Jett Lauck, *Political and Industrial Democracy: 1776–1926* (New York: Funk and Wagnalls Co., 1926), especially chapters 3 and 6.

way, Columbia Conserve, Philadelphia Rapid Transit, Dennison, and Nash. Only one plan—Philadelphia Rapid Transit—met his final test. Lauck's tests of industrial democracy go considerably further than the criteria suggested in chapter 1 of this study. The fact that several enterprises met these participative tests illustrates the fact that not all employee-representation schemes were facades or watered-down substitutes for collective bargaining.

Equal Rights and Opportunities

The problem of equal rights in industry existed mainly in respect to three groups—women, Negroes, and foreigners. World War I capped the century-long drive of women for political and industrial equality with the adoption of the Nineteenth Amendment by the Congress in 1919 and the states in 1920 and by the War Labor Board's equal-pay policy. It immediately generated a different conflict—between those professional and business women who wanted to abolish all legal distinctions based on sex, including women's protective labor legislation, and the trade unionists, male and female, as well as other groups, who wanted to continue and improve such legislation.[12] Only about 250,000 women were union members in the mid-twenties (mainly in industries which experienced union difficulties, i.e., the garment and textiles industries) so that, apart from voluntary decisions by humanitarian employers, protection for the standards of female industrial workers lay in legislative enactment. The major railroad unions and many of the craft organizations actually excluded women from membership. The twenties brought little improvement either in the breakdown of union

[12] Robert W. Smuts, *Women and Work in America* (New York: Columbia University Press, 1959), p. 107.

barriers or in the enactment of laws. In theory women workers were on a par with men; in practice women usually occupied the lower paying jobs in industry and exercised little influence over the terms and conditions of employment. The bulk of women workers were employed in education, nursing and social work, libraries, offices, and stores—all of which categories were largely outside the orbit of employee organization, whether union or employee-representation plan.

The position of the Negro worker also failed to improve despite pious pronouncements by church and Socialist groups during and immediately after the war. Between 1916 and 1920 there had been a huge migration of southern Negro workers to northern industries. As noted in chapter 7, they were met with hostility by white union as well as non-union labor, partly out of fear that they would undercut wage standards and partly out of racial prejudice. Bitter race riots stemming from these feelings occurred in East St. Louis in 1917 and in Chicago in 1919. The organization of black workers was the subject of considerable discussion at the AFL's 1920 and 1921 conventions because of "white member only" clauses in the constitutions of three railroad unions.[13] The Federation Executive Council refused to face up to the issue and reaffirmed the policy adopted in 1900 that it could not abridge the autonomy of its affiliated international unions by forcing them to accept Negro members but that it would establish federal labor locals for Negroes whenever the internationals excluded them. This policy was a dismal failure. In 1928 under 3200 Negroes were members of all-Negro federal locals directly affiliated to the AFL, and about 3000 of these were sleeping-car porters who had been organized by the Brotherhood of Sleeping Car Porters, not by the Federation. The Negro membership in the internationals was estimated at about

---

[13] The relation of the AFL to the Negro worker is effectively discussed in Sterling D. Spero and Abram L. Harris, *The Black Worker: The Negro and the Labor Movement* (New York: Columbia University Press, 1931).

41,000 out of a total membership of almost 3.5 million. Four of the AFL unions—the Maintenance of Way Employees, the Hodcarriers, the Longshoremen, and the Miners—represented 25,000 of the 41,000 Negro unionists. Most of the craft unions either barred Negroes outright by constitutional provision or in their ritual or admitted them in separate all-Negro locals.

The most significant Negro labor development in the twenties was the organization of the Brotherhood of Sleeping Car Porters in 1925 by A. Philip Randolph. The Pullman Company had previously established an elaborate employee-representation and personnel program to prevent unionization and it strenuously opposed the new organization. By 1929 the union had lost most of its momentum and membership because of this company opposition; nevertheless it held on as an organization, laying the basis for future development. The AFL gave the Brotherhood its "moral support." It did not accept an affiliation request because of a jurisdictional claim by the Hotel and Restaurant Workers, but it did agree to direct affiliation of a number of the Brotherhood's locals as federal labor unions.

There is little evidence on how Negro workers fared under the employee-representation plans, but since they were almost exclusively employed in the lowest paying, unskilled jobs, it is doubtful that they had much of a voice in such plans. Spero and Harris, who were studying Negro worker status in the late twenties, concluded that the Negro had achieved most favorable conditions in governmentally controlled employment. "The hope of distinctive minorities, like the Negro, which are prone to become the tools in the industrial struggle first of one side and then of the other, rests to no small extent upon industrial stabilization. Few Negro railway men would deny that they were better off under federal control than ever before or since. There is little question that Negroes in government enterprises like the postal service or in other branches of the public services, despite all sorts of discrimination and inequality in assignments and promotions, are better off than in competitive industry."[14]

The twenties was the period in which the radicals made their first conscious efforts to draw Negroes into their organizations on a large scale. Socialists from the beginning had espoused equality of Negroes with whites on the basis of class doctrine. But they rarely moved beyond the resolution stage. The 1917 East St. Louis riot appears to have had a shock impact on Debs and his followers. Nonetheless, although Randolph and some other prominent leaders became Socialists, few of the Negro workers followed suit. The same limited results were achieved by the Communists for whom propaganda and organization among the Negro masses were instruments of international Communist ideology and strategy.

The difficulties of the alien worker (especially the non-English-speaking) in the United States during the twenties were largely related to the antiradical hysteria of the early years of the decade. Numerous radical aliens were deported and many others found themselves in a web of suspicion.[15] But they also encountered resistance from some labor groups. Since the beginning of the century the AFL had been an increasingly vocal advocate of restrictions on immigration because of concerns about an excessive labor supply, unfair competition, unemployment, and the use of immigrants as strikebreakers. The immigration laws of 1921 and 1924 effectively restrained the influx. A small number of AFL crafts excluded noncitizens from membership and, under union urging, some states restricted licenses to engage in certain occupations, like barbering and plumbing. But most of the new immigrants were anxious to assimilate into their new homeland as rapidly as possible and avidly participated in

[14] Ibid., p. 468.
[15] See, for example, Oscar Handlin, *The American People in the Twentieth Century* (Boston: Beacon Press, 1963 paperback), chapter 6.

the many Americanization programs which many large companies and some unions (notably those catering to the unskilled and semiskilled), as well as the public schools and other public and private agencies, sponsored. William Leiserson, who made an extensive study of this subject in the early twenties,[16] found that the unions which readily admitted immigrant workers, such as the miners and clothing workers, served as an Americanization agency through the process of normal union functioning. He discovered that the employee-representation plans which, with rare exceptions, gave the new immigrants full voting and representation rights served the same end. The initial inability of many of these workers to speak or read English caused problems (one reason why some unions established separate language locals with meetings conducted in the foreign language and with publications written in multiple or separate languages). Leiserson, however, concluded: "After a period of years, when he has learned the language and the methods of the American industries in which he is employed, when he has familiarized himself with the social agencies of American life that function in behalf of the wage earner, the immigrant, in most cases, has substantially improved his economic position, and is able to command the same treatment and consideration that native-born wage earners get."[17]

It must be added nevertheless that the ability of the immigrant worker to obtain equal rights in industry was further handicapped by the religious bigotry which prevailed throughout the decade. This bigotry was exemplified by the growth of the Ku Klux Klan in northern states, the political reaction to Al Smith's Catholicism, and the anti-Semitism of Henry Ford. No visible progress appears to have been made in industry on this score.

[16] William Leiserson, *Adjusting Immigrant and Industry* (New York: Harper and Bros., 1924).
[17] Ibid., p. 333.

Right of Dissent

Industrial democracy affords individuals and groups the right to express views which are contrary to the views and policies of those in positions of authority, either in the management or union hierarchy. The development of personnel departments and employee representation programs in non-union enterprises gave workers opportunities not previously enjoyed to speak more freely and particularly to resist arbitrary actions on the part of their supervisors. It is doubtful that most non-union workers felt sufficiently secure to challenge the top management, but within the shop, the foreman was no longer quite as unchallengeable as he had been. Both the personnel department and the employee representatives emerged as countervailing forces to the supervisor. A negative factor, whose full dimensions were not to be revealed until the investigations of the U.S. Senate Subcommittee on Violations of Free Speech and Rights of Labor in 1936 and 1937, was the extensive and growing use of labor spies. The chief purpose of such spies was to uncover, in the corporate view, labor "agitators," "radicals," and "troublemakers." That the existence of company spies had a generally discouraging effect on discussion within the plant seems incontrovertible.

Both the unions and their opponents in industry had strongly emphasized individual liberty—the unions contending that without strong organizations, workers could not stand up to management, while the employers accused the unions of seeking the closed and union shop so that they could control the workers. There was an element of truth in both positions. As Selig Perlman perceptively put it: "All unions sooner or later stress 'shop rights,' which, to the workingman at the bench, are identical with 'liberty' itself—since, thanks to them, he has no need to kowtow to foreman or boss, as the price of holding his job. . . . Frequently workingmen are willing to resign themselves to 'boss control' in their union for the sake of this liberty in the shop. In other words, they are willing to sacrifice their 'political' liberty in the union so long as they may have 'economic' liberty on the job."[18] A few unions and companies were more successful than most in bridging the gap between individual liberty and economic security. The Typographical Union is the classic example with its unique two-party system and its tradition of debate, though throughout the period there seemed to be a considerable concern over "the custom of maligning and slandering our officers," and an international law that prohibited impugning the motives of officers was adopted about 1911.

As long as the unions were reasonably free from external attacks or from corrupt internal influences, they tended to maintain a democratic climate. But when their existence was threatened or their integrity undermined, they became authoritarian. Economic difficulties contributed noticeably to bossism under John Lewis in the mine workers' union; collusion and corruption to business agent domination in many of the construction locals; and ideological conflict to concentration of power in the ladies' garment workers union.

Corrupt and dictatorial union leadership had been attacked long before the 1920's, but the problems of union bureaucracy, oligarchy, and the concentration of power did not receive much serious attention from sympathetic students of unionism until the postwar period. Some of these problems were given intensive and perceptive study by Sylvia Kopald in her investigation of a series of insurgent or "outlaw" strikes which took place in the coal, railroad, and printing industries.[19] Kopald saw the underlying problem as a consequence of the normal growth of organization with roots stemming back to the earliest days of

[18] Selig Perlman, *A Theory of the Labor Movement* (New York: Macmillan Co., 1928), p. 275.
[19] Sylvia Kopald, *Rebellion in Labor Unions* (New York: Boni and Liveright, 1924).

unionism but intensified by increased industrialization, tech-nological advances, economic concentration, and wartime needs. "How does the problem of democracy vs. oligarchy arise in an organization that stands in the fore of the democratic struggle? How does an organization that is fighting in the name of indus-trial democracy, that is fighting consciously or unconsciously for a new, more democratic economic order, that is fighting through and for the very essence of the democratic mass, the working class; how does such an organization come to face a conflict be-tween its leaders and its rank and file?"[20] She partially answered these questions by observing further: "Not only do the unions face the general problem of all political democracy—the prob-lem of adjusting the desire for democratic functioning with the need for getting things done—but because of their very make-up, they face it in sharper and more poignant form than almost any other democratic organization."[21] In short, to get things done, to perform its functions efficiently and effectively, an or-ganization must delegate powers to its leaders. The larger the organization, the more likely power will be centralized. The greater the centralization of power, the more likely that profes-sional leaders will emerge and the rank and file will lose interest in the routine politics of the organization. Leadership becomes stable and lasting, political "machines" are developed, and there is a strong tendency for those in power to "steam roller" the opposition and to balk protest. Dissent becomes less and less acceptable and frequently is repressed on "constitutional" grounds or "in the best interests" of the organization. She found the same process going on throughout the industrialized world.

Kopald concluded that the nature of large organizations strongly favored the leaders. They controlled the union treasury; they controlled the union propaganda machinery; they con-trolled the conventions; in between conventions and elections

[20] Ibid., pp. 8–9.
[21] Ibid., p. 9.

they interpreted and guarded the constitution to their own advantage; and they were viewed by outsiders as the legitimate spokesmen for the organization.

Due Process

The most widespread advance toward industrial democracy in the twenties came in the area of due process for employee complaints. In this respect the employee-representation plans contributed almost as much (and in the same manner) as the unionized situations. Due process developed in three ways: the adoption of formal procedures, starting at the level of the worker and the foreman; the introduction, in a number of important industries, of impartial and binding arbitration as the final stage of the grievance procedure; and the clarification of substantive due process, such as the meaning of discharge for cause.

Formal grievance machinery had been developed in a number of industries before the war. In most of these cases, the procedure was concerned with stages beyond the workplace, since typically the agreements were negotiated between the union and an association of employers covering a local or regional market. The grievances were usually treated informally at the job or shop level—generally by shop representatives or local business agents—and if unresolved were then referred to local joint committees. Occasionally local arbitration by a neutral third party was also provided. But more often the complaints could be appealed to higher levels in the industry, such as a board of conciliation or arbitration made up of representatives from the two sides, with a neutral outsider as a final arbiter. In sections of printing and a few other industries, the union's appeals machinery was the basic procedure.

The coal industry, after the turn of the century, provided an outstanding example of a fully developed formal bilateral grievance procedure.[22] Although there were variations among coal fields, the Illinois agreement is fairly typical. It specified an eight-step procedure, starting with the employee and foreman or mine manager, and moving as needed to the miners' pit committee and the foreman or manager, the union subdistrict president and the mine superintendent, a union Executive Board member and a field man of the coal operators association, a group meeting of operator and miner Executive Board members, a special commission of one or two representatives from each side, the joint meeting of the Executive Boards of the two sides, and finally to arbitration (if both sides agreed) of a three-man neutral board. In lieu of arbitration, either side could resort to economic action. The optional character of arbitration troubled the employers, however, and they pressed for an advance mandatory agreement to use arbitration instead of strikes. By 1914 the parties had agreed to designate three arbitrators as a standing commission, though cases to be submitted required the consent of the joint Executive Board.

The most impressive developments in grievance handling appeared in the clothing industry, especially in men's clothing after the Protocol of Peace machinery in the New York ladies' garment industry broke down. The Hart Schaffner & Marx agreement was the pacesetter; but it was soon duplicated in the entire Chicago market as well as in New York, Rochester, Baltimore, and other major centers of men's clothing manufacture. What was particularly significant in the period from around 1915 to the end of the twenties was the concurrent development of a strong network of shop chairmen and chairladies to deal directly with management and the evolution of the impartial chairman system from the insightful experimentation of John Williams to the highly developed and sure-footed approach of William Leiserson.

[22] This discussion is based on Arthur E. Suffern, *The Coal Miners' Struggle for Industrial Status* (New York: Macmillan Co., 1926), chapter 9.

The spread of formal grievance machinery and particularly the advent of permanent grievance arbitration not only regularized the process of hearing and settling employee complaints, but also provided the basis for a greatly enlarged industrial jurisprudence. Every enterprise, whether unionized or not, obviously must develop customary practices and rules. Union agreements, particularly when put in writing, tend to make these practices and rules explicit; they become in effect a constitution or code of law. With frequent and regular arbitration, and especially with the intervention of prominent lawyers, as in the garment trades after 1910, the idea of an industrial common law took a further step. Broad general principles, such as those comprising a labor agreement, were translated into more specific rules.

The development of the concept of discharge for cause perhaps provides a key example. A study of arbitration awards in the Rochester clothing market between 1919 and 1922 reveals how the industrial law of discharge grew.[23] The agreement left the power to discharge and suspend employees with the employer subject to "justice and due regard for the rights of the workers." It was understood by the parties that discharge could be made at will during a two weeks' probationary period, but thereafter discharge had to be based on "just cause," which was left undefined. On a case by case determination, the arbitrator gradually developed the meaning of "just cause"—poor quality of production, provided the employee had been given at least two weeks' fair trial on the new work; deliberate restriction of output by the worker; refusal to obey reasonable orders of a foreman, etc. In some industries, like sections of the coal industry, the use of precedent was rejected outright or restricted to the life of the agreement, but in most of those utilizing arbitration, precedent inevitably found an important place. The

[23] John R. Commons and E. W. Morehouse, "Legal and Economic Job Analysis," *Yale Law Journal*, 37 (December 1927), 2:139–178.

Rockefeller and other privately installed employee-representation plans, as well as those sponsored by the War Labor Board, also often provided for arbitration as the final step, though this step was rarely used. Many of the employee-representation plans of the 1920's left the final decision to the president or the board of the company. Otherwise the chief difference from the unionized procedures was the limitation of the process to the enterprise and the exclusion of outside representatives. Despite these differences, the employee-representation plan marked a profound change from the non-unionized situation where the shop was ruled autocratically, or benevolently, at the discretion of the foremen and the company heads.

The elaboration of due process by Congressional action was limited to the railroad industry, the labor relations of which had been the subject of special governmental attention since 1888. Following successful experience with bipartite adjustment boards under government auspices during the war, the Transportation Act of 1920 and the Railway Labor Act of 1926 had extended the adjustment board idea to peacetime, including provision for various forms of arbitration. No adjustment boards were actually established under the former act and experience with the boards under the latter act was so poor that amendment was required in 1934.

Responsibility

Did the management and worker groups and representatives become more "responsible" in their interactions with each other? Where written agreements were in effect, adherence to them was apparently strong, but this had been generally true in preceding decades. Kopald's study of insurgent or "outlaw" strikes in the mining, railroad, and printing industries referred several times to the argument of the union leaders that the union must live up to its contract with the employers or be destroyed. Wild-cat strikes were broken by the union leadership itself on this and other grounds. Sometimes, as Kopald indicated, the reason was a specious excuse to destroy rank and file opposition. But the argument of responsibility was taken seriously as an inherent element of the collective-bargaining model. In 1926, for example, Arthur Suffern noted of the coal mining industry:

> One of the chief inducements which the miners held out to the operators to make a contract was the assurance of continuity of operation for a definite period. This principle has never been deviated from since 1898, as applied to the interstate agreements. . . . This principle also applies to district and subdistrict contracts, but the union has not been so successful in its enforcement. These agreements have been guaranteed by the international union, local stoppages have been condemned, and the union has joined with the operators in recommending by definite clauses in the interstate contract that effective means of enforcement be applied.[24]

A new dimension of responsibility was added with the AFL advocacy of union-management cooperation, as for example in the B & O Plan. Not only did unions now underwrite the sanctity of contracts, but they also accepted a responsibility for eliminating waste and inefficiency and for furthering the economic position of an enterprise or industry. As William Green told the Taylor Society:

> While labor is not responsible and has no voice in the selection or employment of management it is vitally and directly interested in the quality and character of management. Labor realizes that the success of management means the success of labor. For that reason labor is willing to make its contribution to assist management and to bring about the right solution of problems dealt with by management. Some of these problems are regularization

[24] Suffern, *Coal Miners' Struggle*, pp. 314–315.

of employment, fluctuation in prices, standardization of output, healthful and sanitary conditions of employment and the ever-pressing problem of unemployment.[25]

In the employee-representation systems, the responsibility of both management and worker representatives to achieve a harmonious relationship based on mutuality of interest was given frequent stress. Indeed the supporters of employee representation often cited enhanced responsibility as a major justification for the program.

Minimum Standards

During the twenties considerable progress was made in raising employment standards, especially in the employee-representation plan sectors, but also in some unionized industries and in some non-union sections of industry. U.S. Steel, for example, though unorganized, finally eliminated the twelve-hour shift in 1923 and adopted the eight-hour shift. Henry Ford, another staunch opponent of worker organization, was a leading proponent of the high-wage, mass-purchasing power philosophy which gained favor in some employer circles in the 1920's.[26] The unionized men's clothing industry pioneered in such areas as work standards, unemployment benefits, and severance pay. The mass-production industries, in their espousal of welfare capitalism, concentrated on safety, sanitation, and certain fringe benefits like pensions and employee stock purchase. Wage levels in the large-scale enterprises were higher than in many union establishments.

[25] "Labor's Ideals Concerning Management," *Bulletin of the Taylor Society,* 10 (December 1925), 6:244–245.
[26] Edward A. Filene strongly endorsed this aspect of "Fordism" despite his rejection of Ford's authoritarian philosophy. See Filene, *The Way Out* (New York: Doubleday, Page and Co., 1925.)

In the legislative area, however, the decade was one of set-backs rather than progress. The U.S. Supreme Court was the main instrument of retrogression. State minimum-wage laws for women had appeared to be firmly established in 1917 after the Court, by a split decision (one justice did not vote), let stand an affirmative verdict of the Oregon Supreme Court on the Oregon statute. But in 1923 the Court struck down, on constitutional grounds, a similar law for the District of Columbia.[27] By 1930, as a result of this and subsequent state court decisions, three of the seventeen laws originally enacted had been repealed, five had been held unconstitutional, and the others were of little practical effect.[28] Laws regulating the labor of children were upheld as long as they were confined to the separate states, but when Congress attempted to discourage child labor in factories first (1916) through the regulation of interstate commerce and later (1919) through the exercise of the taxing power, the Supreme Court in 1918 and 1922 invalidated both statutes.[29] Congress therefore adopted a Constitutional Amendment in 1924, but this was ratified by only six states prior to 1933. The situation was about the same with respect to women's hours and health and safety standards—some progress at the state level but little or none at the federal.

As far as adult male workers in private industry were concerned, the attitude of the AFL remained very hostile to governmental intervention with respect to wages and hours. The Federation continued to fight hard, and with some success, for state laws on workmen's compensation and various safety issues. It opposed all other social security efforts until the Great Depression.

[27] *Adkins* v. *Children's Hospital*, 261 U.S. 525, 43 Sup. Ct. 394 (1923).

[28] John R. Commons and John B. Andrews, *Principles of Labor Legislation*, 4th rev. ed. (New York: Harper and Bros., 1936), p. 56.

[29] *Hammer* v. *Dagenhart*, 247 U.S. 251, 38 Sup. Ct. 529 (1918) and *Bailey* v. *Drexel Furniture Company*, 259 U.S. 20, 42 Sup. Ct. 449 (1922).

Information

Despite the gains in participation and due process achieved by employees under the employee-representation plans, the availability of economic information to them does not appear to have increased significantly during the twenties. Miller in 1921 found only six of one hundred companies with employee-representation plans which reported that they permitted the employees to verify their statements regarding the profits of the company.[30] He quoted a letter from a prominent trade unionist on this point:

> The reason why we oppose all of these plans is that the workers in the plant cannot secure the knowledge necessary to enable them to hold their own successfully in discussing their claims with the management. The workmen in a plant are not familiar with trade reports, with Dunns, with Bradstreets, with counsellor reports, with the tendency of the money market, with internal and external competition, with conditions obtaining within the same industry in other cities and states. Without such knowledge, they are not possessed of the information necessary to discuss successfully wages, etc. with their employers. It is only a trade union movement which elects men to devote their entire time to studying these questions, which is able to supply the workers with the information they require.[31]

Employers often complained about the ignorance of workers regarding business matters, but secrecy rather than information appeared to be their general practice. Only when an employer found himself in dire straits was he likely to "open the books" to union officials or to issue a detailed statement to his employees.

[30] Earl Miller, *Workmen's Representation in Industrial Government* (Urbana: University of Illinois Press, 1922), p. 103.
[31] Ibid., p. 167.

Occasionally in an arbitration proceeding over wages, an employer's plea of inability to pay would lead to a similar revelation. Even in the strongly unionized industries, information was limited because only a few unions—notably the Amalgamated Clothing Workers, the Brotherhood of Electrical Workers, the typographical union, and the pressmen—had effective research departments.

Personal Dignity

It must be concluded, however, that the twenties reflected a further advance in the treatment of workers as adult, mature human beings. Although there continued to be a paternalistic quality in many of the employee-representation plans, and especially in industries where large numbers of new immigrants, women, and Negroes were employed, the age of the paternalist was coming to an end just as the last third of the nineteenth century witnessed the ending of the master-servant period. This fact was stressed either explicitly or implicitly in the whole voluminous literature on industrial democracy, and while practice often deviated from language, the new institutional forms in the larger industries contributed to the process. The further separation of management from ownership in the larger enterprises had the same effect.

Assessing the Causal Factors

As in earlier periods the evolution of industrial democracy contained elements of progress, stability, and retrogression. The progress came mainly in the areas of participation, due process, responsibility, and personal dignity; the areas of majority rule, equal rights, and information remained largely unchanged; and some measure of retrogression could be detected in the right of dissent and minimum standards. Employee representation was probably embodied in a wider cross-section of industry than in any prior period, except during and immediately after World War I, but its depth was reduced because of the union setbacks in several major industries. To what combination of factors should this mixed moving picture be attributed?

Certainly one of the primary forces was the new state of mind of many of the leaders of big business reacting to the previous two decades of reformer criticism, the public distaste for industrial violence, and the worldwide democratic spirit which the great war engendered. In Selig Perlman's terminology, the American capitalists demonstrated politically and economically that they had a tremendous "will to power" and a determination to preserve their basic social system. But they also demonstrated a considerable flexibility of thought and organization which was embodied in the model of "welfare capitalism."

In these respects they were much more effective than their labor counterparts who failed to recognize sufficiently the need for new organizational forms to cope with the changing character of industrial enterprise. Labor organizations were by no means stagnant; their proposals for labor-management cooperation, the experiments in labor banking, their willingness to work with the industrial engineers of the Taylor Society, even the political support which they gave to the La Follette third-party movement reflected something other than standpattism. But they were unable to maintain the wartime gains in mass production because neither the union structure nor the appeals to the rank and file of workers were sufficient for the task.

The environment in which management and labor organizations interacted obviously reinforced the moves of the former and hindered the moves of the latter. After twenty years of reformism, the business interests were once again in the national political saddle. The courts, particularly the U.S. Supreme Court, provided a powerful bulwark for these interests in their interpretation of the Constitution and of statutory law. Except for the farmers, the large and growing middle-class community had never had it so good—in economic terms, in the broadening horizons and excitements afforded by the auto, the radio, and the motion picture, and in the sense of national pride with the standing of the United States as the world's greatest power.

The industrial work force itself was probably more satisfied with its status than it had ever been before, although certain segments, such as the miners and textile workers, experienced serious economic difficulties. Rising *real* income as well as generally favorable employment opportunities, combined with the humanizing tendencies of welfare capitalism, promoted worker morale. For the first time in American history, the unions were unable to enlarge their membership in a period of prosperity. The sharp reduction in immigration reduced competitive menaces from the outside for the native work force; the Americanization of the recent immigrants gave many of them a sense of acceptance and progress in their new homeland.

The sources of progress in participation, due process, responsibility, and individual dignity are to be found mainly in the welfare capitalist model of industrial democracy. The retrogressive elements in the right of dissent and in legislative minimum standards are to be found elsewhere. For the latter, the role of the U.S. Supreme Court must be given prime credit, the Court majority assuming a more conservative posture than many of the leaders of big business. On the right of dissent, internal union factors must be held accountable. Because the union leaders were generally on the defensive, they tended to be less tolerant of member opposition than if they felt more secure in their positions. At the same time the bureaucratization of the larger unions was proceeding quite naturally or organically. In a bureaucratized system, one would expect less opportunity for dissent unless the bureaucracy itself explicitly made provision for the formal channeling of such dissent. Only a few unions had the imagination and disposition to provide such channels.

INDUSTRIAL DEMOCRACY IN ECLIPSE— THE GREAT DEPRESSION

BETWEEN OCTOBER 1929, when the stock market crash signaled the end of the prosperity era, and March 1933, when Franklin Roosevelt introduced his New Deal, the idea of industrial democracy was progressively subordinated to the concern for economic survival.

How to advance democratic ideas seemed of little moment when masses of people lacked jobs and the bare essentials of living. As the depression deepened, both the employers and the trade unionists proved helpless to turn the tide. For a time it was possible to take ameliorative actions by reducing the length of the workweek, by cutting costs, and by providing loans and other benefits to relieve the impact of reduced incomes. But neither the welfare-capitalist model nor the collective-bargaining model could solve the fundamental problem of unemployment. With most of their members out of work or on part-time, even the strongest of the unions became centers of despair and ineffectuality. Union standards were either ignored or undermined. The employee-representation plans served as a mechanism for helping management gradually contract operations and then, for the most part, dissolved into inaction. The

287

leaders of industry and business proved as helpless as the trade union leaders. Governments—local, state, and national—were equally ineffective. For the most part they concentrated on relief and make-work projects.

In the midst of the general deterioration in industrial conditions and industrial relations, a few actions were taken, however, which had long-run effects on the evolution of industrial democracy. These may be summarized briefly as follows:

1. The American Federation of Labor abandoned its long tradition of voluntarism and began to turn to the national government for assistance in achieving a number of basic economic goals. In 1932, for example, the Federation for the first time and with great reluctance on the part of some leaders endorsed the principle of compulsory state unemployment compensation. In the same year the AFL reversed another of its key policies (opposition to general hours laws for adult male workers in private industry) and instructed its Executive Council to press for legislation to secure the six-hour day and the five-day week so as to reduce unemployment. In early 1933 a wide array of Federation leaders testified in Congress on behalf of the Black-Connery thirty-hour bill, although they continued to oppose a minimum-wage law.

2. The Supreme Court in 1930 upheld the constitutionality of the Railway Labor Act which, in Section 2, prohibited either employers or unions from interfering with the right of the other party to organize or designate representatives.[1] In this case, the company had set up a company union and the district court had ordered its dissolution on a suit by the interested railway Brotherhood. This was the first successful legal attack on the employee-representation model.

3. Congress, in the Norris-LaGuardia Act of 1932 which was

---

[1] *Brotherhood of Railway and Steamship Clerks* v. *Texas and New Orleans Railway Company,* 281 U.S. 548 (1930).

important mainly for its curbs on the issuance of court injunctions in labor disputes, for the first time enunciated a general public policy (in contrast to the special legislation for the railway industry) in favor of the worker's "full freedom of association, self-organization, and designation of representatives of his own choosing to negotiate the terms and conditions of his employment" and affirming that the worker "shall be free from the interference, restraint, or coercion of employers of labor, or their agents, in the designation of such representatives or in self-organization . . . ." Although the act made no provision for machinery to enforce this policy, it clearly set the stage for the New Deal legislation which was soon to follow. Moreover, it specifically held that "yellow-dog contracts" (in which the employee on accepting employment agreed not to join a union) were unenforceable in court.

4. But perhaps most important of all was the loss of public confidence in business leadership. In the first two decades of the century there was a notable, if partial, shift in power and responsibility to the leaders of the federal government. The twenties had seen a reversal of this trend and a reassertion of business and industrial power on a more sophisticated basis. The Great Depression set the stage for another major swing in national leadership, with consequences of unprecedented importance for industrial democracy.

SECTION **V**

GOVERNMENT ASSUMES A MAJOR ROLE, 1933-1945

CHAPTER **11**

THE NEW DEAL

A Decade of Economic Depression

The central economic fact of the 1930's was that the American industrial system stopped growing. The country had not experienced a prolonged depression since 1893–1896 and 1873–1879. The apparent prosperity of the twenties had persuaded many influential people, including some prominent economists, that the age of "booms and busts" was over. Now came the worst depression of all, a depression which seemed to defy both traditional remedies and new experiments. Despite the psychological boost which the New Deal gave to the masses of people and the profound structural changes which it engendered, the depression was not conquered until the nation became deeply embroiled in World War II. It was significant that economists began to talk about the maturation of the economic system and demographers began to predict an early peaking of the American population.

The economic and demographic statistics depicted the dreary character of the scene. The unemployment rate, which stood at 3.2 per cent in 1929, climbed to an incredible 24.9 per cent in 1933, gradually declined to 14.3 per cent in 1937, rose again to 19.0 per cent the following year, and was still at the 14.6 per cent level in 1940. Not till 1942, the year of total American involvement in the war, was the relatively respectable figure of 4.7 per cent reached.[1]

The gross national product (1913=100) which had reached an index level of 163.4 in 1929 declined to 117.7 in 1933 and did not reach or exceed the earlier peak until 1937. In 1939 it stood at 175.8 and in 1940 at 191.7, mainly because of emergency war orders from Europe.[2] The Federal Reserve Board index of production for manufacturing (1935–1939=100) fell from 110 in 1929 to 57 in 1932, gradually ascended to 113 in 1937, fell back to 87 in 1938 and stood at 109 in 1939. The numbers employed in manufacturing were 10.6 million in 1929, 10.1 million in 1939, and well below 10 million in every intervening year except 1937.[3] Contract construction workers were 2.3 million in 1929 and 1.9 million a decade later; transportation workers numbered 3 million and 2.2 million in the respective years; miners were 1 million and 870,000 respectively; and communication workers were 539,000 and 424,000. The only major sector which increased employment appreciably was the federal government, and it went from 827,000 in 1929 to 3.3 million in 1939, partly because of the expansion of the bureaucracy but mainly because of the emergency work assistance programs which were established to take families off relief.

Prices declined sharply from 1929 to 1933, rose gradually until 1937 and then fell off slightly till 1939. The BLS wholesale price index (1957–1959=100) went from 52.1 to 35.6 to 47.2 to 42.2. The BLS consumers price index went from 59.7 to 45.1 to 50.0 to 48.4. The average hourly earnings of production workers

---

[1] U.S., Department of Commerce, Bureau of the Census, *Long Term Economic Growth, 1860–1965: A Statistical Compendium. ES4–No. 1* (Washington, D.C.: Government Printing Office), p. 191.

[2] Ibid., p. 248.

[3] Ibid., p. 238.

in manufacturing fell from 56.6 cents in 1929 to 44.2 cents in 1933 and then rose to 63.3 in 1939; but average weekly earnings which were $25.03 in 1929 and $16.73 in 1933 rose only to $24.05 in 1937 and stood at $23.86 in 1939.

Population statistics told the same general story. The total population continued to rise but the increase between 1930 and 1940 (8.9 million) was the smallest absolute increase in any decade since the 1860's, and the percentage increase (7.2) was by far the smallest in the history of the nation. The birth rate per 1000 population fell to a low of 18.7 in 1935 and immigration, both in absolute amount (528,000 for the decade) and in rate per 1000 population (0.4%), was the lowest in a century.[4] Even the urbanization process came to a standstill. The urban-rural population distribution was virtually unchanged between 1930 and 1940.

Socio-Psychological Climate and Institutional Change

If the economic, technological, and demographic aspects of American life reflected stagnation or decline, the attitudinal and institutional aspects reflected profound change. From the time of the stock market crash to Franklin Roosevelt's inauguration, the mood of the nation got progressively more despondent. Why violence and revolution did not sweep the land remains a historical mystery. I once asked this question of Frances Perkins, who served as Roosevelt's labor secretary in both the state of New York and in Washington, but she could not provide an explanation although she had given serious thought to the matter. However, with Roosevelt in the White House and the first phase of the New Deal launched in the famous "Hundred Days," the

[4] *Statistical Abstract of the United States*, 1967, p. 95.

national mood changed profoundly. And despite numerous failures and frustrations, the mood after 1933 remained basically hopeful. Roosevelt's landslide reelection in 1936 and his unprecedented third term in 1940 were evidence of the national willingness (notwithstanding fierce conservative opposition) to remold national institutions and policies to end the depression.

From the standpoint of industrial democracy, the following elements warrant brief treatment:

1. The loss of business prestige.
2. The ascendancy of the federal government.
3. A new concern for the "underdog."
4. The resurgence of left-of-center ideologies.

BUSINESS PRESTIGE AT LOW EBB

Throughout the decade the stock of business organizations and spokesmen remained very low. The negative impact of the depression upon business prestige was perhaps even greater because the standing of business had risen so high during the twenties. It was aggravated by the intense opposition which many of the large corporations and particularly the business associations, such as the National Association of Manufacturers and the U.S. Chamber of Commerce, expressed toward almost all of the reform measures on behalf of workers introduced by the Roosevelt administration. Instead of seeking an accommodation, apart from such programs as the National Industrial Recovery Act which they could dominate, many of the key business leaders (with some important exceptions to be noted in the next chapter) took uncompromising positions against change. The Liberty League challenged the constitutionality of virtually every liberal New Deal measure. Roosevelt was attacked in language of intense bitterness as a traitor to his class. Worker efforts to unionize were met by the revival and extension of company unions and refusals to recognize the new unions of the mass-production industries.

ASCENDANCY OF THE FEDERAL GOVERNMENT

While the star of business faded, that of the federal government grew brighter than it had ever been, far exceeding the intensity of the Theodore Roosevelt and the Wilson Administration days. The reasons for the reversal of role are clear. Business leadership was unacceptable. The trade union leaders, with a few minor exceptions, had been ineffectual since 1920 and had shown no capacity for leadership during the early depression years. The cities and states had proved incapable of meeting the depression challenge because of the limitations of their resources and, more important, because the problem was truly national in scope. Thus, if chaos was to be avoided—and by 1933 the country was very close to chaos—the federal leadership had to assume the primary role. In Franklin Roosevelt a charismatic leader appeared who was willing and able to play the role.

In its first Hundred Days, the New Deal adopted more reform legislation than under both Theodore Roosevelt and Woodrow Wilson, although most of the key labor measures actually came later in the first term and during the early part of the second term. The American constitutional structure—economic as well as political—was dramatically transformed if not actually revolutionized. This transformation was climaxed by the 1937 Supreme Court decisions in which the power of the federal government to regulate interstate commerce was broadened to encompass the key manufacturing sector. Although important events were occurring in many sections of the country and the government's new programs obviously depended upon effective implementation throughout the land, Washington had become the center of national decision-making to a degree matched only in times of major war.

The New Deal, despite its very different origins, was in many ways the offspring of the Progressive period, and as in the earlier period its leaders had the reformers' social conscience—a concern for the "underdog." Neither Roosevelt nor Perkins had much liking for most of the conservative, skilled-craft leaders of the AFL, and the political alliance between Roosevelt and John L. Lewis, the powerful head of the United Mine Workers, the founder of the Committee for Industrial Organization, and a life-long Republican, lasted only until about 1938. But the New Deal's social concern was focused on the underprivileged third of the nation who lacked job security, decent housing, and adequate incomes. These underprivileged included the mass of unskilled and semi-skilled manual workers, the sharecroppers and depressed independent family farmers, the unsuccessful small businessmen, and a variety of special "minority" groups—the aged and handicapped, child workers, the Negro underclass, and many recent immigrants in the big city slums. Roosevelt's political genius lay in his ability to grasp the yearnings of these people despite his personal aristocratic heritage and background and to gain their undeviating loyalty.

Perhaps the single most significant change in public attitudes about the "underdog" was the realization that economic misfortune was a public responsibility and not a sign of personal defect of character. This point was incisively made in Clinch Calkin's book entitled, ironically, *Some Folks Won't Work*.[5] For the first time in American history, it became public policy to treat the unemployed and economically deprived as citizens to whom society had economic and social obligations because of right and justice rather than as objects of charity.

[5] Clinch Calkin, *Some Folks Won't Work* (New York: Harcourt, Brace, 1930).

The New Deal itself was nonideological or, what comes to the same thing, a pragmatic and opportunistic amalgam of many ideologies. During the twenties dissenting groups and individuals, especially of the extreme left, had been subjected to public scorn, hostility, and repression. The Sacco and Vanzetti case was a symbol of this sentiment. In the thirties the near collapse of the capitalist, free enterprise system opened the door to an effusion of radical thought and activity—socialism, communism, technocracy, the Townsend Plan for the aged, Upton Sinclair's EPIC (End Poverty in California), Huey Long's Share-Our-Wealth program, Father Coughlin's National Union for Social Justice, and numerous variants and subdivisions.

The ferment produced by this mélange of ideas was unprecedented. Social change was in the air. People expected change and were receptive to new thoughts, however fuzzy or impractical. From the standpoint of industrial relations, which regained the centrality of attention that it enjoyed between 1912 and 1920, the atmosphere was particularly propitious for innovation.

UNIONISM, EMPLOYEE REPRESENTATION, AND THE LAW

The labor relations history of the 1930's has been told many times, and all that is required here is a brief summary of the relevant events. Even before Roosevelt took office, a few of the major unions like the United Mine Workers and the International Ladies Garment Workers Union had begun to rebuild their organizations. Once the New Deal got underway and the employment situation improved, these unions made spectacular organizing drives. The UMW membership reportedly rose from 298,000 in 1933 to 529,000 in July 1934; the ILGWU rose from less than 50,000 in early 1933 to 200,000 by the spring of

1934. Not all of the old unions recovered so rapidly but almost all of them rebounded vigorously. At the same time the spirit of organization spread in a manner reminiscent of the 1885–1886 upsurge of the Knights of Labor among the previously unorganized, especially unskilled and semi-skilled factory workers. By the end of 1934 the total union membership (3.6 million) exceeded the levels of the twenties after 1923. A major factor in this resurgence was the adoption of Section 7a of the National Industrial Recovery Act affirming the right of workers to organize into unions of their own choice. A popular, if not wholly accurate, union appeal was: "President Roosevelt wants you to organize!"

This initial impetus was temporarily checked by two factors. One was the decision of numerous employers, especially large ones, to revive or to institute "company unions." The other was the split in the labor movement over union structure—whether the newly organized factory workers should be obliged to respect the traditional craft jurisdictions or should be free to establish industrial unions in the manner of the miners and the clothing workers. In this entangled situation, the Roosevelt Administration, which was beset with a host of policy and administrative problems, had difficulty in providing the necessary leadership. Not till the passage of the National Labor Relations Act in July 1935 was a firm policy enunciated. Meantime the coverage of the company unions rose from 1.25 million workers in 1932 to 2.5 million in 1935, a faster rate than that of the trade unions.

Between 1935 and 1937, however, the mainstream became clearly defined. The internal struggle within the labor movement was resolved by the formation of the CIO which, under the leadership of Lewis and Hillman, made mass-production industrial unionism a powerful reality. The split in the ranks of labor had a strong stimulating effect on both sides and by 1939 the AFL had more than offset its membership losses resulting from the expulsion of the CIO unions. Its membership of 4 million was at least a million more than the CIO's. The second struggle—between the labor movement and the employee-representation system—was resolved by the decision in April 1937 of the Supreme Court upholding the constitutionality of the NLRA and thereby destroying most employee organizations which were instituted or controlled or influenced by the employers.

These changes did not come about without considerable conflict and pain. Whereas work stoppages had fallen well below the one thousand mark in the 1920's and early thirties, they rose to 1695 in 1933, to over 2000 in 1935 and 1936, and to a new peak of 4740 in 1937 before falling back to 2613 in 1939. Many of the strikes were violent, causing numerous injuries and some deaths. Property damage was common. The sitdown strike became a common technique, arousing widespread public concern and debate, until the courts ruled it illegal.

Thus by the end of the decade, the faltering and hapless labor movement of the twenties had been transformed into a powerful and aggressive, although bifurcated, national institution. According to the estimates of Leo Wolman and Leo Troy, the closest students of the subject, union membership in 1939 was 6,555,500 compared to 3,442,600 in 1929 and to 5,047,800 in 1920, the previous peak.[6] Between 1930 and 1940, the proportion of union membership to employment in manufacturing had risen from 9 to 34 per cent; in transportation, communications, and public utilities from 23 to 48 per cent; in building from 54 to 65 per cent; in mining, quarrying, and oil from 21 to 72 per cent; in services from 3 to 7 per cent; and in public service from 8 to 10 per cent.[7]

[6] Leo Troy, "Trade Union Membership, 1897–1962," *Review of Economics and Statistics* (February 1965), p. 93.

[7] Leo Wolman, "Concentration of Union Membership," in *Proceedings of Fifth Annual Meeting of the Industrial Relations Research Association* (Madison, Wisc.: IRRA, 1952).

New Deal Legislation

The New Deal introduced a new stage in the evolution of American industrial democracy chiefly because of its far-reaching redefinition of the proper role of government. The collective-bargaining model remained the nucleus, but a number of supplements were added to it which made a profound difference in its quality and performance. The chief characteristics of the new model were as follows:

1. Primary reliance was to be placed on the ability of employers and unions to govern themselves through collective bargaining. Employees were not obliged to form or belong to unions, but their right to do so was positively affirmed and they were encouraged to do so.

2. If the parties in an enterprise or industry could agree on the structure and procedure of the bargaining process, they would be free to develop their own system with a minimum of constraints. If, on the other hand, they disagreed, the government would establish the basic structure and rules of procedure. This meant that an agency of government would determine all questions of employee representation, the nature of the appropriate bargaining unit, and a code of unfair practices on the part of employers.

3. If the bargaining system, once established, failed to function harmoniously, the government would step in as peacemaker and endeavor to promote an agreement by mediation and conciliation. If the peacemaking mission failed, the parties would be free to exert maximum economic pressure through the strike and lockout except where the public interest seemed to be in serious jeopardy. In the latter event, the government would be expected to use whatever powers it could muster to bring about a termination of the conflict.

4. Although the government was not to be concerned with

the substantive rules and conditions of employment about which the parties were to bargain, it had the responsibility of establishing certain national minimum standards in the interest of the general welfare. These applied mainly to child labor, the minimum hourly wage, the basic workweek beyond which premium overtime compensation was to be paid, industrial homework, income provision in periods of unemployment, and old age pension.

Three statutes constituted the basic legislative framework for the new model—the National Labor Relations Act, the Social Security Act, and the Fair Labor Standards Act. A number of more limited laws rounded out the framework. These laws warrant a brief statement although they are treated in considerable detail in numerous text books and monographic studies.

NLRA

The first major segment of the legislative framework was the National Labor Relations Act, popularly known as the Wagner Act of July 1935. As Bernstein and others have shown,[8] the principles of the Wagner Act and much of its crucial language can be traced back to a chain of prior legislation, most particularly the Railway Labor Act of 1926 and its amendments of 1934, the Norris-LaGuardia Act of 1932, the Bankruptcy Act of March 3, 1933, Section 7a of the National Industrial Recovery Act of June 1933, and Public Resolution 44, implementing NIRA, of June 1934. Equally important was the experience under the railway legislation and, particularly, under the NIRA. The frustrations of the National Labor Board which Senator Robert Wagner

[8] See, for example, Irving Bernstein, *The New Deal Collective Bargaining Policy* (Berkeley and Los Angeles: University of California Press, 1950); Lewis L. Lorwin and Arthur Wubnig, *Labor Relations Boards: The Regulation of Collective Bargaining under the National Industrial Recovery Act* (Washington, D.C.: Brookings Institution, 1935); Milton Derber and Edwin Young, eds., *Labor and the New Deal* (Madison: University of Wisconsin Press, 1957).

chaired, the controversy over proportional representation versus majority rule which the Auto Labor Board stirred up, and the decisions of the first National Labor Relations Board based upon Public Resolution 44 and challenged by the Liberty League—these contributed significantly to the principles of the Wagner Act which shaped the new industrial democracy.

Embedded in the act, implemented and elaborated by the second National Labor Relations Board, and confirmed and modified by the U.S. Supreme Court were three basic ideas:

1. The legal right of employees "to self-organization, to form, join, or assist labor organizations, to bargain collectively through representatives of their own choosing, and to engage in con-certed activities, for the purpose of collective bargaining or other mutual aid or protection" (Section 7). The parallel right of refraining from such activities was also specified except where the closed or union shop was agreed to by employers and unions.

2. Majority rule as the basis for determining an exclusive bar-gaining agent. In the words of Section 9a, "Representatives des-ignated or selected for the purposes of collective bargaining by the majority of the employees in a unit appropriate for such purposes, shall be the exclusive representatives of all the em-ployees in such unit for the purposes of collective bargaining in respect to rates of pay, wages, hours of employment, or other conditions of employment."

3. The prohibition, under legal sanction, of unfair labor prac-tices by employers. These practices fell under five headings which may be summarized as interference with the exercise of the rights specified in Section 7; domination over, interference with, or assistance to any employee organization; discharge or discrimination in hiring or conditions of employment to encour-age or discourage membership in a labor organization; discrim-ination because an employee filed charges or gave testimony under the act; and refusal to bargain in good faith (Section 8).

The first of these three provisions ended the long debate over whether employees could be prevented from choosing outside representatives. The third provision established a code of industrial behavior long sought by the unions to sever the employer's control over employee organization for bargaining purposes and thereby destroyed the employee-representation system. In return for these two gains, the unions gave up an old and cherished freedom: the determination of the bargaining unit became a government responsibility. In addition, the idea of an exclusive bargaining agent, which was derived primarily from the AFL's life-long concept of exclusive jurisdiction and its fear and abhorrence of dual unionism, was conditioned by the principle of majority rule as determined either in a secret ballot or in check of signed membership cards.

SOCIAL SECURITY

The second main legislative foundation-block was the Social Security Act of August 1935. This act provided for federal old-age benefits, state unemployment compensation, and a variety of benefits and security provisions for dependent and crippled children, economically deprived mothers, and the blind. It also supported vocational rehabilitation and the public health service. The focus of this law was economic security outside of the enterprise (i.e., when the employment relation ended) rather than within it. But it was conceived of as an integral part of the industrial system, supplementing and inevitably influencing many decisions about employment and income distribution within the enterprise.

WAGES AND HOURS

The Fair Labor Standards Act of 1938 was the third of the major laws shaping the new industrial-democracy model. It bore directly on the plant relationship. Like the Wagner Act, the provisions of this law had antecedents in the National Industrial Recovery Act. The NIRA called upon employer and labor representatives in each industry to formulate codes of fair competition specifying maximum hours of labor, minimum rates of pay, and the abolition of child labor under sixteen. The FLSA, or wage and hour law, dealt with the same topics but on a national rather than industry basis. It set a floor on hourly wage rates starting at 25 cents and gradually rising to 40 cents after seven years, with a provision that the federal administrator might set industry rates above 25 cents but not above 40 cents on the recommendation of industry committees. It set the standard work week at forty-four hours to be reduced after two years to forty, but in contrast to most of the NRA codes and more in keeping with union agreements, it permitted overtime work provided the worker was compensated at the rate of time and a half. It abolished child labor under sixteen and regulated industrial home work.

Once again the new legislation represented both an extension of historic practice and some important innovations. The minimum-wage and maximum-hour provisions were extensions of past principles for female workers, but their application to male workers reflected a reversal of the voluntaristic policy which had underlain the AFL opposition, until 1932, to governmental regulation of wages or hours for the mass of men. The provision for overtime premium pay was a new legal policy although actively applied by the War Labor Board of World War I; the child-labor provision was a substitute for the first federal child-labor law of 1916, which the Supreme Court had declared unconstitutional, and an extension of the many state laws on the subject.

OTHER LAWS

Of the other laws enacted in the 1930's which affected industrial government, reference need be made only to the Davis-Bacon Act of 1931 and the Walsh-Healey Public Contracts Act of 1936. The former (not a New Deal measure) set a basic eight-hour day, with premium pay for overtime, on contract work in the construction of public buildings and other undertakings; it also required the payment of not less than "prevailing wages" as determined by the secretary of labor. The other law provided for the setting of minimum wages and maximum hours, and banned child labor and prison labor on all federal contracts for $10,000 or more. Like the Davis-Bacon Act and unlike the Fair Labor Standards Act, it imposed the time and a half premium rate for work after eight hours per day as well as after forty per week.

The Views of New Deal Leaders on Industrial Democracy

The New Deal laws were concrete evidence of the evolving conception of industrial democracy. But it is instructive to consider the views which New Deal leaders expressed in conjunction with these laws as well as in other statements to grasp the underlying philosophy. There were significant variations among these leaders. However, we may take President Roosevelt, Secretary Perkins, Senator Wagner, and Senator Robert La Follette as representative. In addition, and for more explicit detail, it will be desirable to refer also to some decisions of the National Labor Relations Board and of the U.S. Supreme Court.

FRANKLIN ROOSEVELT

In her informal biography of Roosevelt, Frances Perkins has written that the President did not take part in developing the National Labor Relations Act and was hardly consulted about it. "It did not particularly appeal to him when it was described to him."[9] On the other hand, "He always regarded the Social

[9] Frances Perkins, *The Roosevelt I Knew* (New York: Viking Press, 1946), p. 239.

Security Act as the cornerstone of his administration and, I think, took greater satisfaction from it than from anything else he achieved on the domestic front."[10] These observations reflect two aspects of Roosevelt's early thought about industrial democracy. As assistant secretary of the Navy under Wilson and as president of the American Construction Council in the 1920's, he had absorbed considerable knowledge of the construction industry and generally sympathized with that industry's view of self-regulating labor relations. On the other hand as a liberal product of the Progressive era, he felt a deep and enduring sympathy for the poor, underprivileged, underpaid, and overworked. His feelings in these respects were strongly reinforced by Eleanor Roosevelt and Frances Perkins.

Thus in his first Presidential campaign, Roosevelt stated: "I believe that we are at the threshold of a fundamental change in our economic thought. I believe that in the future we are going to think less about the producer and more about the consumer. . . . It is well within the inventive capacity of man, who has built up this great social and economic machine capable of satisfying the wants of all, to insure that all who are willing and able to work receive from it at least the necessities of life."[11] In asking Congress to adopt the National Industrial Recovery Act, he stated: "My first request is that the Congress provide for the machinery necessary for a great cooperative movement throughout all industry in order to obtain wide reemployment, to shorten the working week, to pay a decent wage for the shorter week and to prevent unfair competition and disastrous overproduction."[12] He saw the NRA as operating on the principle of "self-

[10] Ibid., p. 301.

[11] Franklin D. Roosevelt, *Looking Forward* (New York: John Day Company, 1933), p. 49.

[12] Roosevelt, "A Recommendation to the Congress to Enact the National Industrial Recovery Act," May 18, 1933, in Samuel I. Rosenman, ed., *The Public Papers and Addresses of Franklin D. Roosevelt* (New York: Random House, 1938), 2:202. Cited hereafter as Rosenman.

government in industry." Shortly after the adoption of the first code, he reminded his audience:

> Last Autumn, on several occasions, I expressed my faith that we can make possible by democratic self-discipline in industry, general increases in wages and shortening of hours sufficient to enable industry to pay its own workers enough to let those workers buy and use the things that their labor produces. This can be done only if we permit and encourage cooperative action in industry, because it is obvious that without united action a few selfish men in each competitive group will pay starvation wages and insist on long hours of work. Others in that group must either follow suit or close up shop.[13]

And in his annual message to Congress on January 3, 1934, he stated: "Under the authority of this Congress, we have brought the component parts of each industry together around a common table, just as we have brought problems affecting labor to a common meeting ground. Though the machinery, hurriedly devised, may need readjustment from time to time, nevertheless I think you will agree with me that we have created a permanent feature of our modernized industrial structure and that it will continue under the supervision but not the arbitrary dictation of Government itself."[14]

Shortly afterwards, in speaking to the representatives of some 600 industries that had accepted the codes, he observed: "You have set up representative government in industry. You are carrying it on without violation of the constitutional or the parliamentary system to which the United States has been accustomed."[15]

The President was not opposed to unionism, but he was not

---

[13] Roosevelt, "The Simple Purposes and the Solid Foundations of Our Recovery Program," July 24, 1933, in Rosenman, 2:298–299.

[14] Roosevelt in Rosenman, 3:10.

[15] Roosevelt, "A Survey of the Purposes, Accomplishments and Failings of N.R.A.," March 5, 1934, in Rosenman, 3:126.

initially inclined to impose union organization on workers or to compel employers to abandon their employee-representation programs. Although he readily issued Executive Order 6580 on February 1, 1934, empowering the National Labor Board to effectuate Section 7a of the NIRA by conducting elections and awarding representation rights to the majority union, he went along with the idea of proportional representation and pluralism in the automobile dispute settlement of March 1934, notwithstanding the intense opposition of the union leaders. Despite the strong urging of Senator Wagner and other union sympathizers, he did not press for the passage of what became the National Labor Relations Act until late in May 1935.

Once the Wagner Act was passed, however, Roosevelt became increasingly favorable to it and to the idea of establishing a national system of collective bargaining through government encouragement and support. The increasing hostility of major sections of the business community to New Deal reform legislation and the personal attacks launched against him as the 1936 election approached unquestionably drove him closer to his union supporters. Nonetheless, he continued to see the role of government not as pro-labor and anti-employer but as a "high court of conciliation" fostering "just and peaceable labor relations in industry" when the parties reached the conflict stage.

As he said in September 1935:

> . . . A changing civilization has raised new problems with respect to the relationship between the employer and the employed. It is now beyond partisan controversy that it is a fundamental individual right of a worker to associate himself with other workers and to bargain collectively with his employer. New laws, in themselves, do not bring a millennium; new laws do not pretend to prevent labor disputes, nor do they cover all industry and all labor. But they do constitute an important step toward the achievement of just and peaceable labor relations in industry. This right of the

Federal Government is well established. Every President of the United States in this generation has been faced by the fact that when labor relations are strained to the breaking point there remains but one high court of conciliation—the Government of the United States.[16]

During his second term of office Roosevelt staunchly defended the principles of the Wagner Act, now recognizing the primacy of its role in his program; and it was not simply a coincidence that the cases which finally determined the constitutionality of the New Deal approach to an enhanced part for government in the nation's economic life were Wagner Act cases. But his vision regularly transcended his relationship with the union leadership and focused on the great mass of the workers. Thus he affirmed the right of federal employees to organize for the purpose of presenting their views on pay, hours, and other conditions of employment, but he contended that "the process of collective bargaining, as usually understood, cannot be transplanted into the public service," and he emphatically opposed public strikes and other militant tactics.[17] In the Little Steel Strike of 1937, he did not hesitate to criticize John L. Lewis as well as the steel managers when they refused to accept the government's conciliatory efforts.

His major legislative proposal in the second term relating to labor was the Fair Labor Standards Act, and this he pushed with fervor and vigor. In a message to Congress urging such a bill, he wrote: "A self-supporting and self-respecting democracy can plead no justification for the existence of child labor, no economic reason for chiseling workers' wages or stretching workers' hours." When the bill was blocked in the House rules committee after passing the Senate, he convened a special ses-

[16] Roosevelt in Rosenman, 4:409.
[17] Roosevelt in Rosenman, 6:326.

sion of Congress to which he again urged passage of wage and hour legislation: "I believe that the country as a whole recognizes the need for immediate Congressional action if we are to maintain wage income and the purchasing power of the nation against recessive factors in the general industrial situation. The exploitation of child labor and the undercutting of wages and the stretching of the poorest paid workers in periods of business recession have a serious effect on buying power. In the interest of the national economy such adjustments as must be made should not be made at the expense of those least able to bear them . . . ."[18]

On the third anniversary of the signing of the Social Security Act, Roosevelt praised the law and called for an expansion of its coverage. He revealed his view of the role of government in this area: "Because it has become increasingly difficult for individuals to build their own security single-handed, Government must now step in and help them lay the foundation stones, just as Government in the past has helped lay the foundation of business and industry. We must face the fact that in this country we have a rich man's security and a poor man's security and that the Government owes equal obligations to both. National security is not a half and half matter; it is all or none."[19]

At a climactic moment in his third campaign for the Presidency, in a speech to the Teamsters Union, Roosevelt summed up the accomplishments and spirit of the labor program of the New Deal:

> Much of this progress has been due, I like to think, to the one thing that this Administration from the very beginning has insisted upon: The assurance to labor of the untrammeled right, not privilege, but right to organize and bargain collectively with its employers. That principle has now become firmly imbedded in

[18] *New York Times,* November 16, 1937, p. 14.
[19] Roosevelt in Rosenman, 7:479.

the law of the land; it must remain as the foundation of industrial relations for all time.

. . . .

With that foundation, the last seven years have seen a series of laws enacted to give labor a fairer share of the good life to which free men and women in a free nation are entitled as a matter of right. Fair minimum wages are being established for workers in industry; decent maximum hours and days of labor have been set, to bring about the objective of an American standard of living and recreation; child labor has been outlawed in practically all factories; a system of employment exchanges has been created; machinery has been set up and strengthened and successfully used in almost every case for the mediation of labor disputes. Over them all has been created a shelter of social security, a foundation upon which we are trying to build protection from the hazards of old age and unemployment. . . .[20]

FRANCES PERKINS

A major influence on President Roosevelt's labor ideology and the New Deal labor program was Secretary of Labor Frances Perkins. She had been Industrial Commissioner of New York under Roosevelt and Al Smith and was a specialist in the problems of factory safety, women in industry, workmen's compensation, and other welfare areas. Mrs. Perkins wrote in her Roosevelt biography that when asked to go to Washington as the first woman cabinet member and the first non-unionist labor secretary, she proposed a broad program which met Roosevelt's hearty endorsement. "In broad terms, I proposed immediate federal aid to the states for direct unemployment relief, an extensive program of public works, a study and an approach to the establishment by federal law of minimum wages, maximum hours, true unemployment and old-age insurance, abolition of

[20] Roosevelt in Rosenman, 9:407.

child labor, and the creation of a federal employment service."[21] She told Roosevelt that "to launch such a program we must think out, frame, and develop labor and social legislation, which then might be considered unconstitutional."[22] In short, Mrs. Perkins was a staunch supporter of the social welfare state and saw the need to reform the Constitution to achieve it.

In the annual report of the Labor Department for the 1933–1934 fiscal year, the secretary outlined what she thought was the beginning of a government labor policy. It contained six elements:

1. That the Government ought to do everything in its power to establish minimum basic standards for labor below which competition should not be permitted to force standards of health, wages, or hours;

2. That the Government ought to make such arrangements and use its influence to bring about arrangements which will make possible peaceful settlements of controversies and relieve labor of the necessity of resorting to strikes in order to secure equitable conditions and the right to be heard;

3. That the ideal of Government should be through legislation and through cooperation between employers and workers to make every job the best that the human mind can devise as to physical conditions, human relations, and wages;

4. That Government should encourage such organization and development of wage earners as will give status and stability to labor as a recognized important group of citizens having a contribution to make to economic and political thought and to the cultural life of the community;

5. That Government ought to arrange that labor play its part in the study and development of any economic policies for the future of the United States; and

6. That the Government should encourage mutuality between labor and employers in the improvement of production and in the

[21] Perkins, *The Roosevelt I Knew*, p. 152.
[22] Ibid.

development in both groups of a philosophy of self-government in the public interest. If labor's rights are defined by law and by government, then certain obligations will, of course, be expected of wage earners, and it is for the public interest that those obligations should be defined by labor itself and that such discipline as is necessary should be self-imposed and not imposed from without. . . .[23]

In a book, entitled *People at Work*, published in 1934, Mrs. Perkins elaborated her conception of industrial and governmental relationships in a democratic society. "A stable and healthy industrial life cannot be built unless a sound and cooperative relationship exists between those who manage our basic industries and those who labor in them."[24] She saw the NIRA as an attempt at such cooperation. "Instead of government acting by fiat, there is to be self-government under a partnership which it shares with industry and labor. And in this partnership the government provides supervision and sanctions for the reasonable rules of self-regulated industry."[25] She stressed that this partnership, if industrial recovery is to be achieved "in line with the traditional principles of American democracy," must be characterized by "a new and heavier sense of public responsibility" and by self-discipline.

The concept of a code of socially acceptable minimum standards and conditions was given special stress. To give wage-earners and their families a decent standard of life, the minimum wage should be fixed on a weekly rather than an hourly basis. And she looked forward to the time when it could be put on an annual earnings basis. Every worker had a right to a job and, moreover, to a job which provided him with a high standard of living and "a fair chance for a good life." It was not enough for

[23] U.S., Department of Labor, *Twenty-second Annual Report of the Secretary of Labor*, for the fiscal year ended June 30, 1934 (Washington, D.C.: Government Printing Office, 1935), pp. 5, 12.

[24] Perkins, *People at Work* (New York: John Day Company, 1934), p. 164.

[25] Ibid.

a work place to be safe, sanitary, and healthful; it should be "comfortable." It was essential to exclude boys and girls under sixteen from industrial work and to make an honorable provision for old age. Unemployment insurance to tide workers over slump periods was essential to reduce "the waste and damage to industrial and economic security and personal self-respect, which characterizes our present disorderly method of handling the unemployed."

She strongly endorsed labor's right to organize, bargain collectively, and strike—on both moral and democratic grounds. "The prevention of conflict, always likely in badly conceived or selfishly conducted human relations of any sort, rests in this case as in all others upon regular equalized mutual practices to insure justice, fairness and mutual respect and consideration. These are people—in the image of God—under moral obligations, as well as material needs—not merely 'bosses and hands.'" Moreover a democracy requires that wage-earners be well represented in the great civic groups which formulate public opinion. "It is just beginning to be realized that the cultural and political life of America needs the enrichment of the wage-earners' unique experience and wisdom."

Finally, she developed her ideas about the proper role of government. As long as government only supervised industry as a policeman, there was little hope for permanent results.

An intelligent educative relationship between government and industry, one which naturally presupposes understanding and integrity on both sides, can result from the cooperative or conference method of industrial regulation. To one who believes that really good industrial conditions are the hope for a machine civilization, nothing is more heartening than to watch conference methods and education replacing police methods. This cooperative method of regulating industry, to be valid and trustworthy, must of course include full representation of the workers and their interests. Participation in conferences helps the workers comprehend the needs of various industries for safe practice, for sanitary precautions, and for practical programs of hours and wages, so that presently the whole range of industrial efficiency and human welfare can be put on a participating basis, and brought to the council table.

. . . .

An important duty of a Government Department, segregated for the purpose of emphasizing the interests and needs of labor in our civic life would seem to be to make itself into a sort of bureau of standards for the purely human factors in industry. The Bureau of Standards at Washington serves a valuable purpose with reference to material and machines. Labor Departments should serve a similar purpose for establishing high standard practices for environment and opportunities for the men and women in industry. Having set up such minimum standards, to see that they are really adopted becomes a matter for education, persuasion, direction and enforcement by legislation, for at least the minimum which must be required by law in the public interest.[26]

Secretary Perkins' concern for the establishment of national minimum standards of employment and welfare was far greater than her interest in labor relations legislation. As indicated previously, she consistently supported the rights of workers to organize and to bargain collectively, but she was not a policy initiator in this area. Her testimony before Congressional committees, the annual reports of the Labor Department, and various other writings suggest that she was pleased with certain aspects of the policy which evolved between 1933 and 1935 and was disappointed in others. The idea of conducting elections to determine majority representation rights appealed to her as "democratic in character" and "a dignified basis for representation." She saw collective bargaining as a significant mechanism for employer-worker cooperation and for raising employment conditions above the minimum standards imposed by govern-

[26] Ibid., pp. 284–285.

ment. However, she often felt impelled to emphasize the responsibilities which accompanied the benefits of labor relations legislation.

Thus she told the 1941 AFL Annual Convention:

> This statutory protection gives to trade unionism an enormous prestige and a great responsibility. It places labor also in the same exposed position as any other great American private association charged with public responsibilities—responsibilities for the welfare and improvement of the conditions of the members of the union, certainly; responsibilities for the welfare and improvement in the circumstances of all working people; responsibilities for cooperation in the development and prosperity of modern industry; responsibilities to the whole people of the United States for sound, intelligent economic, social, political, and moral practices, and for the selection of leaders and officers who can be trusted not only by their members, but by the whole people of the United States; also responsibilities to avoid excesses of action and to regard the rights of others, whether in agreement or not, with consideration.[27]

When the Wagner Act was being considered, she urged labor leaders to draw up a code of ethical behavior rather than to have it imposed upon them as in the case of the employer's unfair labor practices.[28]

ROBERT F. WAGNER

The chief architect of the labor relations segment of the New Deal labor program was Senator Robert F. Wagner of New York. Wagner was one of the chief authors of the NIRA with its Section 7a and the voluntary code system. He served for six months as chairman of the National Labor Board which tried vainly to implement the NRA labor provisions. Out of the frustrations and

[27] *AFL Sixty-first Annual Convention Proceedings* (October 1941), p. 329.
[28] Perkins, *The Roosevelt I Knew*, p. 239.

lessons of the NRA experiences, he and his aides gradually formulated the principles and language of the National Labor Relations Act. Throughout the thirties he was organized labor's strongest and most important ally in the Congress.

In his initial statement on the NIRA, Wagner noted that "the bill marks a far-reaching departure from the philosophy that the Government should remain a silent spectator while the people of the United States, without plan and without organization, vainly attempt to achieve their social and economic ideals."[29] Section 7a was not "a mere afterthought or appendage," he testified in March 1934. It was one of the three mainsprings of cooperation among industry, labor, and government. In the NIRA, Congress "projected into economic affairs the essence of true democracy, by outlining a system of checks and balances between industry and labor, crowned by governmental supervision and advice."[30]

After encountering the intense resistance of numerous employers to Section 7a and watching the multiplication of company unions as a barrier to the trade union movement, Wagner became convinced that the critical issue was the need to impose upon employers the duty to bargain with legitimate worker organizations. He therefore launched a powerful attack in the Senate and in articles and speeches outside of Congress upon company unionism and other employer interferences with labor organization.

> The company union, as I have defined it, runs antithetical to the very core of the New Deal philosophy. Business men are being allowed to pool their information and experiences in vast trade associations in order to make a concerted drive against the evil features of modern industrialism. They have been permitted to

[29] U.S., Congress, Senate, Committee on Finance, *National Industrial Recovery: Report on S. 1712 and H.R. 5755*, 73rd Cong., 1st sess., 22 May 1933, p. 3.
[30] U.S., Congress, Senate, Committee on Education and Labor, *To Create a National Labor Board: Report on S. 2926*, 73rd Cong., 2d sess., 1933, pp. 7–8.

recognize the values of unity and the destructive tendencies of discrete activities, and to act accordingly. If employes are denied similar privileges they not only are unable to uphold their end of the labor bargain; in addition they cannot cope with any problems that transcend the boundaries of a single business.[31]

He defended the unfair labor practice section of the Wagner Act by noting that Section 7a of the NIRA had virtually collapsed because a relatively small number of unfair employers had discriminated against and discharged employees exercising their fundamental rights, had set up "a masquerade type of union" which was really the creature of the employer, and had defied the government "with brazen impudence."[32]

Of equal importance to Wagner was the principle of majority rule for selecting employee representatives. He noted that this principle had been used by the War Labor Board in 1918, that it had been applied by the Railway Labor Board under the Transportation Act of 1920 and had been specifically embodied in the 1934 amendments to the Railway Labor Act of 1926, that President Roosevelt had issued an Executive Order in February 1934 authorizing the National Labor Board to hold elections for the purpose of determining majority representation, and that Public Resolution 44 of June 1934 contained a similar provision. "The rule is sanctioned by our governmental practices, by business procedure and by the whole philosophy of democratic institutions."[33] To Wagner the reasons for majority rule were very simple. If the employer dealt with employees as individuals, the inequality of bargaining power was so great that "lib-

[31] Robert F. Wagner, "Company Unions: A Vast Industrial Issue," *New York Times Magazine,* March 11, 1934, p. 1.

[32] U.S., Congress, Senate, *Congressional Record,* 74th Cong., 1st sess., 1935, 79, pt. 6:6183–6184.

[33] U.S., Congress, Senate, Senate Committee on Education and Labor, *Report on S. 1958* (1935); reproduced in National Labor Relations Board, *Statutes and Congressional Reports Pertaining to the National Labor Relations Board* (Washington, D.C.: Government Printing Office, 1945), pp. 13–14.

erty of contract becomes a fiction." In any large plant so-called individual treatment meant despotic rule by management alone. Dealing with various minority groups gave the unscrupulous employer an opportunity to play one group against another and to foment discord and rivalry among workers. Majority rule was the only viable alternative.

Wagner repeatedly expressed his case in terms of democracy. In May 1935 he began a speech to the Senate: ". . . the national labor relations bill does not break with our traditions. It is the next step in the logical unfolding of man's eternal quest for freedom. . . ." And he ended with the conclusion that "democracy in industry must be based upon the same principles as democracy in government. Majority rule, with all its imperfections, is the best protection of workers' rights, just as it is the surest guaranty of political liberty that mankind has yet discovered."[34]

In April 1937, after the Supreme Court upheld the constitutionality of the Wagner Act, he said: "The principles of my proposal were surprisingly simple. They were founded upon the accepted facts that we must have democracy in industry as well as in government; that democracy in industry means fair participation by those who work in the decisions vitally affecting their lives and livelihood; and that the workers in our great mass production industries can enjoy this participation only if allowed to organize and bargain collectively through representatives of their own choosing."[35]

A month later, he told the National Democratic Club Forum:

The development of a partnership between industry and labor in the solution of national problems is the indispensable complement to political democracy. And that leads us to this all-important truth: there can no more be democratic self-government in industry without workers participating therein, than there could be democratic government in politics without workers having the

[34] *Congressional Record,* 74th Cong., 1st sess., 1935, 79, pt. 7:7565–7570.
[35] *New York Times,* April 13, 1937, p. 20.

right to vote. . . . The right to bargain collectively is at the bottom of social justice for the worker, as well as the sensible conduct of business affairs. The denial or observance of this right means the difference between despotism and democracy.[36]

Finally in a letter to the New York *Herald-Tribune,* on November 19, 1939, he asserted: "To increasing millions of wage earners the act is bringing increasing enjoyment in their daily working lives of freedom of expression, of the press, of assembly and of ballot. To increasing millions of wage earners it is guaranteeing a voice and a place in our industrial system which has been too long neglected or denied."[37]

ROBERT LA FOLLETTE, JR.

The last of the New Deal spokesmen to be discussed here is Senator Robert La Follette, Jr., son of the great Wisconsin Progressive governor and senator. The La Follette subcommittee, which spent almost two years investigating violations by employers and others of workers' rights of free speech and assembly and interference with efforts at organization and collective bargaining, laid bare a record that shocked national opinion, shamed many of industry's top leaders, and prevented the opponents of the Wagner Act from revising or weakening its provisions despite considerable public unhappiness over the sitdown strikes and other forms of industrial aggression and conflict.

In proposing a bill based on his committee's inquiry, La Follette said that it would destroy four types of the most flagrantly oppressive practices exercised in the field of labor relations: labor espionage, strikebreaking, private police systems, and the use of industrial munitions.

The bill is another forward step in Federal labor legislation designed to promote the peaceful settlement of industrial disputes

[36] *New York Times,* May 9, 1937, p. 12.
[37] Wagner, "Should Congress Curb the Powers of the National Labor Relations Board?" *Congressional Digest,* 19 (March 1940), 3:89–90.

through collective bargaining. The four types of antilabor practices prohibited by the bill spring from an unyielding hostility both to freedom of association for employees and to the principle of collective bargaining. To make these practices illegal is in a sense to add the capstone to the legislation buttressing the national labor policy. The bill will stand with the Wagner Act and the Walsh-Healey Act as a guidepost to liberty and industrial freedom. It will continue the construction of a framework of labor relationship in which collective bargaining may flourish and bring about the accomplishment in industry of a peace which will be not the death-like peace of oppression, but the peace of freedom in a society of free men.[38]

The specific La Follette proposal was never adopted, but its objectives were secured by the decisions of the National Labor Relations Board. The capitulation of the Ford Motor Company to the NLRB in 1941 signaled the end of an era in labor relations although individual firms, especially in rural areas, continued efforts to evade the Wagner Act principles.

NLRB AND SUPREME COURT DECISIONS

The New Deal's reformulation of American labor policy was translated into detailed concreteness by the administrative acts and awards of the NLB, the first NLRB, and the Wagner Act NLRB, and by a body of Supreme Court decisions reviewing employer appeals from some of these awards. Between 1933 and 1940 a national system of industrial jurisprudence began to emerge which was to give industrial democracy in the United States a unique legal character. The full dimensions of this system were not to become clear until after 1940 and particularly after World War II, and they will therefore not be discussed in detail until Section VI. Nevertheless, a summary of some of the

[38] U.S., Cong., Senate, Subcommittee of the Committee on Education and Labor, *Oppressive Labor Practices Act: Report on S. 1960,* 76th Cong. 1st sess., 25 May 1939, p. 7.

main early principles may be desirable at this point. They fall under four headings:

1. *Representation.* The central issues were "union recognition," the right of employees to select as representatives others than fellow-workers, the holding of elections or membership-card checks, majority rule, and exclusive representation. On each of these issues, decisions of the National Labor Board and the first National Labor Relations Board supplied the basis for NLRB decisions under the Wagner Act. In one of its first major tests, over a recognition strike, the National Labor Board developed its "Reading Formula" which provided for an immediate return to work of all employees on strike, reinstatement of strikers without discrimination, and a secret election to determine representatives for collective bargaining.[39]

In another early case, *Berkeley Woolen Mills,* the NLB interpreted the words "representatives of their own choosing" as meaning that employees had the right to choose anyone they wished as their representative and were not limited in their choice to fellow employees. When several companies defied the board over the election process, the board asked and got the President to issue an Executive Order empowering the conduct of elections and the utilization of the majority rule principle.

On majority rule, a split developed between the board and NRA administrators who favored proportional representation. The *Denver Tramway* case was a firm statement of the board for majority rule. But shortly afterwards the board was given a death blow when the President sided with the opposing view in the auto industry dispute. This setback to majority rule, however, was only a short one. In a landmark case, *Houde Engineering,* the first NLRB affirmed majority rule as the touchstone of

[39] The decisions referred to here and below are published in *Decisions of the National Labor Board* and *Decisions of the National Labor Relations Board* (Washington, D.C.: Government Printing Office, 1933–1935).

collective bargaining and the basis for the idea of exclusive bargaining status. At the same time, it made clear that majority rule did not preclude any employee or group of employees from presenting grievances or conferring with the employer, nor did the rule compel employees to join the majority union, that being a matter of union-management negotiation.

2. *The Appropriate Unit.* Majority rule entails the concept of a unit of employees who will determine by voting or signed cards the representation agent. As Francis Biddle, chairman of the first NLRB, told a Senate Committee, "the major problem connected with the majority rule is not the rule itself, but its application. The important question is to what unit the majority rule applies."[40] This question remains an open one to the present day as industrial processes and corporate and union structures change. The Railway Labor Act specified a "craft or class" basis for determining units. The NLRB was given more discretion and immediately got entangled in the dispute between the AFL craft unions and the CIO industrial unions. During the thirties, the board resolved the issue on the basis of its famous "Globe Doctrine," which held that where the considerations over rival units were evenly balanced, the deciding factor should be the decision of the employees in the craft group. Differences of opinion within the board continued.[41] In 1939, for example, a board majority decided in the *American Can* case to limit the Globe Doctrine when a craft group wanted to gain a severance from an industrial unit with an established collective bargaining history. The single plant versus multiplant unit also posed problems in a relatively small number of cases. Still another unit problem was whether supervisors should be included in the

40 U.S., Congress, Senate, Committee on Education and Labor, *National Labor Relations Board: Report on S. 1958, Part I,* 74th Cong., 1st sess. 11–14 March 1935, p. 82.

41 See Harry A. Millis and Emily C. Brown, *From the Wagner Act to Taft-Hartley* (Chicago: University of Chicago Press, 1950), pp. 140–141.

same unit as nonsupervisory employees. In general, the board excluded supervisors except in those industries like maritime and printing where supervisors had been traditionally included.

3. *Unfair Practices.* The importance of preventing employer interference with the rights of workers to organize and to bargain had been appreciated for decades. In the *Budd* case the NLB made it clear that employer sponsorship and control of a company union was a form of forbidden activity. In the *Caldwell* case the first NLRB ruled that an employer could not compel his workers to bargain individually rather than collectively. The second NLRB found numerous types of employer interference ranging from the blatant use of discharge and refusal to hire union activists to the use of spies and company police for coercive purposes.[42] The *Jones and Laughlin Steel* case was a leading example in which the Board ordered the reinstatement and payment for lost wages of discharged men and the posting of notices throughout the works that the company would cease discriminatory tactics. The *Remington Rand* case involved the use of professional spies and strikebreakers, instigation of violence, mass discrimination, and the promotion of back-to-work movements to break a lawful strike. Discharge and discrimination were involved in almost two-thirds of the board's complaint cases. The company union movement which had reached sizeable proportions by 1935 was broken by a series of board orders, upheld in the courts, for the employers to disestablish such organizations. Not all employee-representation plans were employer dominated, and complex questions often arose when an "independent union" emerged following the disestablishment of a company union. The most subtle unfair practice issue was the allegation of refusal to bargain in good faith. This will be discussed in a later section.

[42] This subject is authoritatively treated in Ibid., especially chapters 4 and 6.

The issue of employer freedom of speech was also raised during the board's first five years but did not become critical until later. In the early years the board simply held that the employer had to maintain strict neutrality in employee organizational periods. Any indication of employer preference was treated as an interference with employee rights. By 1939, however, despite a number of favorable court decisions, the question of the employer's constitutional rights was raised with such vigor that reexamination of the issue seemed necessary. This began with a Supreme Court decision in the *Virginia Electric and Power* case of 1941 in which certain employer statements were held not to be coercive. The new policy held that an employer could express preferences but he was forbidden to exert any pressure on employees either in conduct or words.

4. *Collective Bargaining*. The final category of legal principles shaping the new industrial democracy related to the meaning of collective bargaining. In one of the earliest relevant cases, *Connecticut Coke*, the NLB declared that "true collective bargaining involves more than the holding of conferences and the exchange of pleasantries. It is not limited to the settlement of specific grievances. Wages, hours, and conditions of employment may properly be subject to negotiation and collective bargaining. While the law does not compel the parties to reach agreement, they must approach negotiations with an open mind and make a reasonable effort to reach a common ground of agreement."

In the *Houde* decision, the first NLRB elaborated the bargaining concept. The employer was obligated to negotiate in good faith, to match employee proposals, if unacceptable, with counter-proposals, and to make every effort to reach an agreement. Collective bargaining was simply a means to an end—an agreement. The purpose of such agreement was to stabilize, for a fixed period, the terms of employment for the protection of both employer and employees. In the *National Aniline* case, the board noted that while an oral agreement was not necessarily invalid, the nature of the provisions was such as to make an agreement impractical of enforcement and a source of disputes if it were not reduced to writing.

In its first annual report in 1935, the National Mediation Board, administering the Railway Labor Act, stated that one of the three basic rules for the railroad industry was the establishment of written rules and regulations mutually agreed upon and equally binding on both employer and employees. The second NLRB soon adopted a similar policy. The board emphasized that the employer was not obliged to sign any agreement proposed by the employees or agree to employee demands when genuine accord was impossible, but once an understanding was reached, it must be recorded if the employee representatives so requested. This principle was finally accepted by the Supreme Court in the *H. J. Heinz* case of 1941.

It is interesting to note in conclusion that many of the key board officials viewed their work as contributing to the development of industrial democracy. Francis Biddle, chairman of the first NLRB, in arguing in behalf of the Wagner Act in April 1935, observed that there were two theories of capital-labor relations. One was the class-warfare theory, the other the partnership theory. A partnership was the result of agreement and presupposed equality of bargaining. Most employers, he alleged, wanted neither alternative because they preferred to make improvements from the top down—the old gesture of charity. "But free men hate charity as much as they cherish independence. So that collective bargaining has come to mean industrial freedom to American workmen." And he concluded: ". . . I am convinced that there are today in our country employers who have some vision of the new industrial democracy that is bound to come, that is growing, here at our feet, inexorably; who will, perhaps, be leaders side by side with the leaders of labor."[43]

William Leiserson, who became a member of the NLRB in 1939 after serving as chairman of the National Mediation Board, had long been concerned with the industrial democracy theme. Earlier he had viewed it primarily in terms of a bipartite process —industrial self-government. Now he saw it as "three-handed," although he continued to emphasize the desirability of bipartite agreement. He wrote in 1940 that the nation had "barely arrived at the point where the country is ready to accept the principle of collective bargaining as a basis for labor relations." Everybody had much to learn because labor relations is not merely or primarily an economic problem, but is primarily a psychological problem, "a problem of human minds." Employers had in mind "pleading" by workers, not bargaining with equals. Workers had in mind striking and collective combat instead of collective bargaining. These minds had to be changed by a slow and laborious process of education, of learning to work together.[44]

For Leiserson, the establishment of collective bargaining "probably is the most important need in achieving democracy in American industry." But he also saw a simultaneous need for "control by union members over their own management and leadership." His concept of industrial democracy was thus two-pronged:

1. The fight for employee participation in determination of labor conditions.

2. The eternal vigilance of employees in securing efficient management of union business and protection against corrupt or blundering officialdom.[45]

[43] Francis Biddle, "Should the Wagner Collective Bargaining Proposal Be Adopted?" *Congressional Digest*, 14 (April 1935), 4:123–124.

[44] William M. Leiserson, "Improvement of Employer-Employee Relations," *The Conference Board Management Record*, 2 (August 1940), 2:90ff.

[45] Leiserson, "Industrial Self-Government," in *The Advance*, 26 (May 1940), 4:4.

Both of these facets were to occupy major roles in the evolution of industrial democracy in its next major phase.

THE TVA CASE

The rise of unionism among mass-production and other private-sector employees inevitably sparked interest among public employees. Unions were not new to the public service— at the federal level some postal employees and shipyard workers, for example, had been organized for many decades, and at the local level there had been organization movements among teachers, firemen, policemen, and sanitation workers as well as building craftsmen and maintenance employees. Now these and other groups of public employees developed a revitalized interest in union organization. In the mid-thirties both the AFL and the CIO established separate national organizations for the federal service and for employees of state and local governments.[46] For the most part, however, these efforts made little headway. Public employees were specifically excluded from the coverage of the Wagner Act and comparable state acts. The right of public employees to strike was universally denied by public officials and court decisions. Their right to bargain collectively was widely questioned. The comments of President Roosevelt in a letter to the president of the National Federation of Federal Employees were generally representative of official thought:

> All government employees should realize that the process of collective bargaining, as usually understood, cannot be transplanted into the public service . . . The very nature and purposes of government make it impossible for administrative officials to represent fully or to bind the employer in mutual discussions with government employee organizations. The employer is the whole people,

[46] The best account of these developments is Sterling D. Spero, *Government as Employer* (New York: Remsen Press, 1948). There was also a strong organizational movement among unemployed workers on relief projects.

who speak by means of laws enacted by their representatives in Congress. . . . Particularly, I want to emphasize my conviction that militant tactics have no place in the functions of any organization of Government employees. . . .[47]

Nevertheless, in a few sectors of public service, collective bargaining leading to signed agreements was adopted with considerable success. Examples at the federal level were the Railway Mail Service, the Government Printing Office, the Alaska Railway, and the Inland Waterways. Beyond these in scope and philosophy was the system which developed at the Tennessee Valley Authority—a great pioneering enterprise in so many ways.

The TVA case has received considerable attention in the literature of labor relations.[48] Only a brief statement will be given here to illustrate the advanced view of industrial democracy on which it was constructed. On August 28, 1935, after almost two years of discussion between managers and labor representatives, the Authority's Board of Directors issued a declaration of principles on employee relations. It approved the right of employees to organize (or to refrain from organizing) and to engage in collective bargaining through representatives of their own choice. It accepted the majority-rule principle for determining representation. It promised to support as favorable labor standards and employment conditions as feasible. All rules, regulations, and understandings were to be published for the information and guidance of all concerned. However, the first signed contract for manual workers (with the AFL Trades and

---

[47] Franklin D. Roosevelt, "The President Endorses Resolution of Federation of Federal Employees against Strikes in Federal Service," August 16, 1937, in Rosenman, *The Public Papers and Addresses of Franklin D. Roosevelt*, 6:325–326.

[48] See, for example, "Labor-Management Relations in TVA," Report of the Joint Committee on Labor-Management Relations, U.S. *Senate Report No. 372*, 81st Cong., 1st sess., 1949, and Robert S. Avery, *Experiment in Management: Personnel Decentralization in the Tennessee Valley Authority* (Knoxville: University of Tennessee Press, 1954).

Labor Council) did not materialize until August 6, 1940, reflecting the gradual maturation of the relationship. Two years later a parallel relationship began to develop with the TVA Council of Office, Technical, and Service Employees Unions, also affiliated with the AFL, and with two independent Associations of Professional Chemists, Chemical Engineers, and Engineers.

The TVA relationships did not stop with collective bargaining and grievance handling. The 1940 agreement provided for joint cooperative committees to eliminate waste, conserve materials, improve workmanship, promote education and training, correct conditions making for grievances and misunderstanding, safeguard health, prevent hazards to life and property, better employment conditions, and strengthen morale. An elaborate system of central and local cooperative committees evolved and operated with considerable success. The result was an unusually harmonious system of industrial government.

As a joint Congressional committee concluded in 1949:

> There is nothing in the labor policies of TVA that smacks of paternalism. The Authority is out to receive value for every dollar it spends. It believes in and constantly strives for economical and efficient operation of all the activities in which TVA is engaged. TVA believes that by treating its employees as human beings, honestly and aboveboard, by having the employees express themselves and take part in the joint cooperative committees, by letting its employees join unions if they so desire, by giving the individual some recognition, the individual worker will realize that he is not just another cog in a heartless, impersonal machine.[49]

To longtime TVA chairman David E. Lilienthal, the labor-management system, like the rest of the TVA program, was strong evidence of "democracy on the march."[50] To a later stu-

[49] Ibid., pp. 60–61.
[50] David E. Lilienthal, *TVA: Democracy on the March* (New York: Harper and Bros., 1944), especially pp. 90–97.

dent of the entire personnel program, the TVA story "is a significant experiment" in the application of "democracy to public administration."[51]

[51] Harry L. Case, *Personnel Policy in a Public Agency: The TVA Experience* (New York: Harper and Bros., 1955), p. 117.

CHAPTER 12

LABOR, MANAGEMENT, AND OTHERS

New Modes of Union Thought

Although the most profound change in the industrial democracy model during the 1930's resulted from new governmental views and policies, fundamental shifts also occurred in union thinking about the structure of the labor movement, the appropriate role of government, and the nature of collective bargaining. The first three years of the depression had thrown the AFL and its main affiliates into a state of near paralysis, but they had also marked a new turning point in Federation willingness to seek government aid to attain major goals. Advocacy of and support for a governmental unemployment insurance system, for legislative protection of organizing and bargaining rights, and for a thirty-hour week law illustrated the break with the traditional policy of "voluntarism."

Hallowed views, however, are not easily abandoned. Nor are ideas which affect positions of power and prestige. Although labor was more than ready for a change by the time of the New Deal, its leadership divided on important elements of the change for a number of years. For example, the issue of industrial versus craft unionism, which precipitated the formation of the CIO, combined considerations of ideology, power, and personalities.

Thus despite virtual unanimity of labor support for the Wagner Act, NLRB decisions about appropriate bargaining units drew heated critical reactions from one side or the other. The idea of a national minimum wage for men, ultimately embodied in the Fair Labor Standards Act, was resisted for years by old-line AFL leaders (in contrast to the CIO leaders) and was accepted with reluctance. Nonetheless, by the end of the decade the AFL had undergone an appreciable counter-reformation and the differences between it and the CIO as far as industrial democracy was concerned were comparatively minor.

Many voices spoke for labor on industrial democracy during the New Deal period. For the AFL traditionalists, the most representative spokesmen were the Executive Council of the Federation; president William Green, who was an authentic heir of Gompersian thought; and Matthew Woll, of the Photo-Engravers Union, who defended the interests of the crafts and business unionism with considerable eloquence. For the CIO John L. Lewis was by all odds the dominant figure although Sidney Hillman, Charles Howard, Philip Murray, and others were also highly articulate. Straddling both groups was the dynamic new president of the International Ladies Garment Workers Union, David Dubinsky, while George M. Harrison, president of the Railway Clerks, bridged the AFL and the railroad Brotherhoods. On the left were the revitalized Marxist organizations—the Socialists and the Communists with all their splinter groups and factions—masters of the oral and written language but mainly pouring old wine into new bottles.

THE AFL AND THE RECOVERY PROGRAM

During the initial phase of the New Deal, the AFL leadership had two main goals. One was to revive and expand union membership without employer interference. The other was to exercise a voice in the recovery program insofar as wages, hours, and employment conditions were concerned. Ideologically the only new feature of their approach was the recognition that they needed to act within a broad governmental framework and that they could not function in the context of free markets. The NRA appealed to them in part because of Section 7a, but also because the NRA codes were supposed to be formulated through the mutual agreement of employers and union officials. The syndicalist nature of the code program was not far removed from the industry council idea of the AFL post–World War I reconstruction proposals.

Where the unions were able to rebound quickly, as in coal and garments, the code system worked well and spurred collective bargaining throughout the respective industries. Where, however, the unions were weak or nonexistent, as was the case in most of mass production, the employers dominated the codes, with the government having to safeguard labor's interests. The AFL Executive Council expressed its sentiments and concerns on the recovery program in October 1933. The nub of the issue was the rights of representation and participation.

> The age-long struggle for human justice has centered around some phase of the right to representation for those affected by decisions. Politically, this principle was first proposed so that citizens might have a voice in taxation levied upon their money and properties. . . . With the changes going on in production and in the organization of our economic life, the high degree of interdependence in economic welfare and relationships has centralized decisions that involve working conditions, incomes or the distributions of the returns from joint work. Decisions on these points mean justice or injustice in those things which constitute the foundations of living. . . . Even though the worker has merged with groups associated together for carrying on a great production enterprise, his sense of justice is outraged if he has no voice in making decisions about his work. . . . Representation is either direct or through organized channels. To secure this fundamental right is the primary purpose of the labor movement.

. . . Labor maintains, therefore, that if the Recovery Act is to achieve its purpose—jobs for the unemployed and increased buying power—representatives of wage-earners must have a voice in every stage of code making. . . . The American Federation of Labor declares that labor representation in the drafting of code proposals, in every stage of code hearing before the National Recovery Administration and in the enforcement and administrative agencies provided by the code, is essential to achieving the purposes of the National Recovery Act and to meeting the requirement of human justice.[1]

The following year the Executive Council reiterated the importance of participation. "The worker," it asserted, "must no longer be a mere part of the industrial equipment of the country, but an active and effective participant in the major economic developments." The problems of industries were no longer just the concern of the employers. Responsibility must be shared. Moreover it must be done on a voluntary, not a compulsory, basis. Democracy required "joint employer and employee responsibility and joint employer and employee control."[2]

The inability of the Federation to achieve the participation which it desired in the code program reinforced the importance of strengthening labor organization and getting government assistance in breaking down employer resistance. Hence the Federation threw all the force it could muster behind the implementation of Section 7a and later behind the passage of the Wagner Act. In the process, it altered some traditional values. These changes are reflected in the numerous speeches and writings of William Green, who lacked the leadership qualities of both his predecessor and his successor as AFL president, but who effectively voiced the sentiments of business unionism. It is interesting to note parenthetically that Green was allied mainly with the craft unionists of the AFL although he himself came out of the industrial United Mine Workers.

[1] American Federation of Labor, *Report of the Executive Council*, 1933, p. 54.
[2] Ibid., 1934, p. 102.

In testifying in favor of one of Senator Wagner's early bills, Green observed that "since the power of government has been definitely increased it is of the utmost importance that labor have that status that will provide equality in bargaining." The power of Congress to enact such bills was clear, he contended. The whole "purpose and tendency" of the bills "are to preserve industrial democracy," which in turn was essential to the preservation of a republican form of government.[3]

He also vigorously espoused the idea of majority rule as the basic principle for determining representation. "Collective bargaining can obviously succeed only when majority rule is made effective, just as government can succeed only under majority rule."[4] This was a new theme for the traditional unionists who had often, in the past, achieved recognition by "selling" management on the idea of collective bargaining rather than pursuing the longer route of enlisting a majority of the workers and then exerting economic pressure. Its adoption is attributable not only to the government's new stance in labor relations but also to the concern over the strong revival of company unionism and the talk in some government circles of proportional representation.

The other main change was described in a Green speech to the September 1937 convention of the International Typographical Union when he described the AFL's "social justice program."

There was a time when the A.F. of L. did not look with favor upon the enactment of unemployment insurance legislation and old age pension legislation. It was the opinion of the majority, I might say,

[3] U.S., Congress, Senate, Committee on Education and Labor, *To Create a National Labor Board: Report on S. 2926*, 73rd Cong., 2d sess., March 1934, pt. 1:68, 109–110.

[4] U.S., Congress, Senate, Committee on Education and Labor, *National Labor Relations Board: Report on S. 1958*, 74th Cong., 1st sess., March 1935, p. 119. The same view was expressed earlier in an editorial in the *American Federationist*, 41 (May 1934), 5:465–466.

of the A.F. of L. that there was danger in such a program, because they feared that it subjected the individual employe to the domination and control of governmental bureaus and governmental agencies, and they contended vigorously that the working man sacrificed his independence and his economic freedom when he became subject to legislation of this character. . . . But gradually that state of mind changed. The objection to social justice legislation which involved the enactment of unemployment insurance laws, old age pensions and sick benefits was overcome. And today I am happy to say that the A.F. of L. has placed its great economic and industrial influence behind a constructive, practical social justice legislative program, and we are fighting today for the enactment of adequate unemployment insurance legislation, old age pension legislation, health insurance legislation and child labor legislation.[5]

Despite these alterations, the AFL model of industrial democracy was fundamentally unchanged. Writing in *The Annals* of March 1936, Green emphasized the importance to labor of having employment rest on a contractual basis. Such a contract required an equality of bargaining power. Once collective bargaining is established, workers acquire a new status in industry —as an integral part of the organization, not as commodities purchased at the lowest market price. At first the concern is primarily with terms and conditions of employment. With maturity collective bargaining contributes methods and machinery for dealing with work problems and improving productive efficiency. Joint decision-making leads to mutual responsibility and reliance on the presentation of facts. The worker, however, wants most of all security—security of income during and after his working life, protection against unjust dismissal, seniority rights, and social security.

He stressed the sanctity of contracts as an indispensable part

---

[5] International Typographical Union, *Proceedings of the Eightieth Session* (September 12–19, 1936), p. 85.

of the system. When a union official advocated sympathetic strikes in 1934, Green asserted that although strikes are a necessary union tool, they must not be used to abrogate agreements.[6] In an editorial for the *American Federationist* three years later, he challenged employers who were reluctant to sign collective-bargaining agreements.

> It seems curious that the proposal to extend what is generally accepted as good business practice to a new group should cause so much resistance. Signed contracts in business relations represent mutual agreement upon specific terms of performance, so that misunderstanding may be avoided and difficulties averted that would lead to dissatisfaction. Business relations should rest upon confidence which is possible only with mutual understanding. Reducing understanding to writing with the signatures of the persons concerned or their agents as guarantees of fulfillment is a practical business practice out of which ethical standards will grow.[7]

For Green, as for Gompers, industrial democracy posed no challenge to the principles of private ownership, private initiative, or the right to manage property. It meant cooperation between management and labor through contractual relations, the recognition that employees were partners in production who could make a valuable contribution to the enterprise if treated in a just and responsible fashion.

In a book entitled *Labor and Democracy*,[8] Green summed up the principles which were essential to the survival of democracy:

1. The right of representation for labor in the work place.
2. The definition of employer-employee or work relations in a work contract stipulating terms and conditions of work and

---

[6] International Ladies Garment Workers Union, "American Labor Faces the Future" (New York: ILGWU, August 1934), p. 6.

[7] *American Federalist*, 44 (August 1937), 8:810.

[8] Willaim Green, *Labor and Democracy* (Princeton, N.J.: Princeton University Press, 1939).

machinery for adjusting differences arising under the contract.

3. Labor representation on all governmental control or policy-making agencies.

4. Economic and personal justice.

5. Union-management cooperation on a voluntary basis.

Matthew Woll's numerous writings, even more than Green's, reflected the uneasy shift in AFL "old guard" thinking under the pressures of the depression, the New Deal, and the CIO. For Woll the ideal government role in labor relations was minimal. Labor should rely on economic rather than political action to achieve its goals, although some nonpartisan political activity had been necessary, historically, to protect labor's interests.[9] During the NRA period, he concluded that government was needed to restrain industry from interfering with the workers' right to organize and bargain collectively, but it should not determine the nature or process of organization.[10] He warned that if industry refused to accept labor as a partner, labor would have no alternative than to turn to government for the control and regulation of industry.[11] When the Wagner Act was passed, he commented: "It would be idle to say that labor is not delighted that this much discussed measure is finally the law of the land. . . . Speaking for myself, I do not hesitate to say that it would have been far better, not only for organized labor but for all our democratic institutions, if similar results could have been obtained through frank and open discussion between the accredited representatives of management and the accredited representatives of labor."[12]

Instead of a government-controls system which he feared

[9] See, for example, "The Policies of American Labor," in *American Labor and the Nation*, ed. Spencer Miller, Jr. (Chicago: University of Chicago Press, 1933).

[10] Matthew Woll, *Labor, Industry and Government* (New York: Appleton-Century, 1935), pp. 87–88.

[11] Ibid., pp. 224–229.

[12] Woll, "Labor Had Better Watch Out—or It Will Lose Everything," *Liberty*, 13 (February 8, 1936), 6:6.

would lead to political dictatorship or socialism, Woll proposed the establishment of an industrial congress composed of equal numbers of representatives of management and labor which would formulate, on an industry by industry basis, basic rules of procedure and plans of operation that would eventually lead to the construction of a national economic scheme. Social and economic planning was desirable if it were done by the parties themselves without government interference. Presumably the interests of the general public would be safeguarded by restraint and responsibility of the employer and labor groups. Like the NRA, there was a syndicalist quality in this conception which went back to post–World War I days and which would be revived by much more liberal union leaders during World War II.

JOHN L. LEWIS AND THE CIO

While the traditionalists of the AFL changed with reluctance, the founders of the CIO reformulated the industrial democracy model with vigor and enthusiasm. Although he ran the United Mine Workers in a highly autocratic manner and had been a staunch Republican in the twenties, John L. Lewis was the spearhead and national symbol of the new CIO approach. As head of the foremost industrial union in the country, Lewis shared neither the ideological or political objections of the craft unionists to applying the principles of industrial unionism to the unorganized mass-production industries. Nor were his views on governmental intervention in industry akin to those of most business unionists. Except for railroads and communications, no privately owned industry had received such close governmental attention as coal mining, because of its importance for the heating of homes and offices as well as the fueling of numerous industries.

Since the mid-twenties coal had been a sick industry, and

Lewis was therefore one of the first labor leaders to welcome the NIRA. He was also one of the strongest critics of the National Recovery Administration when labor aspirations and expectations began to be disappointed. In 1934, in an article in *The Annals,* he called for a comprehensive "mandatory" industrial Bill of Rights if the NRA could not protect labor's rights. This would include:

1. Complete copartnership between capital and labor, by providing that code authorities, or code administrative agencies, should be composed of an equal number of representatives of employers and employees, with an impartial chairman with the right to vote in the event of a tie, to be appointed by the government.

2. A maximum working day of six hours and a maximum thirty-hour work week for all codes.

3. Minimum rates of pay for all codes sufficient to enable an unskilled worker to support his family in health and modest comfort and to provide reasonable savings against the contingencies of life.

4. Equal pay for women performing the same work as men.

5. The levying of assessments upon industries under the codes sufficient to yield funds for unemployment insurance payments and old-age and disability pensions.[13]

When NIRA was declared unconstitutional, Lewis was able to get Congress to pass the Guffey Coal Act, which went beyond the codes by giving union representatives a voice in the setting of coal prices. Lewis called the act, which in turn was invalidated by the Supreme Court, as "the achievement of a dream on the part of men of the mines."[14]

Lewis' major contribution to industrial democracy, however,

[13] American Academy of Political and Social Science, "Labor and the National Recovery Act," *The Annals,* 172 (March 1934):62–63.

[14] United Mine Workers of America, *Proceedings of the Thirty-fourth Constitutional Convention* (January-February 1936), p. 9.

was his determination to extend unionization to the major manufacturing industries, particularly steel but also textile, lumber,
rubber, auto, and the rest. In a national radio address launching
a major CIO organizing drive, Lewis declared in his renowned
oratorical style:

> Organized labor in America accepts the challenge of the omni-
> present overlords of steel to fight for the prize of economic free-
> dom and industrial democracy. The issue involves the security of
> every man or woman who works for a living by hand or by brain.
> The issue cuts across every major economic, social and political
> problem now pressing with incalculable weight upon the 130 mil-
> lions of people of this nation. It is an issue of whether the working
> population of this country shall have a voice in determining their
> destiny or whether they shall serve as indentured servants for a
> financial and economic dictatorship which would shamelessly ex-
> ploit our natural resources and debase the soul and destroy the
> pride of a free people.[15]

Lewis' conception of industrial democracy did not entail any
radical change in the general economic or political system. It
meant collective bargaining and fair industrial relationships. It
meant the increase and broadening of mass purchasing power.
It meant a minimum income assuring a level of healthy and decent living, but it also provided that skilled workers should receive higher wages in accordance with skill and training. It
meant maximum hours and decent working conditions. It required legislative enactments to make the principles of industrial democracy realistic.[16]

In contrast to the traditionalists, however, he was convinced
that labor's political strength was needed "so that industrial
planning under Federal auspices may be made possible." Mod-

---

[15] John L. Lewis, "The Battle for Industrial Democracy," in *Vital Speeches of
the Day*, 2 (July 15, 1936), 21:678.

[16] John L. Lewis, "Industrial Democracy," Publication No. 9 (Washington,
D.C.: Committee for Industrial Organization, January 1937), p. 12.

ern industries had to be coordinated by the government to insure maximum productivity instead of restriction and monopoly.
"The main emphasis must not be placed upon high prices and
profits but upon low profits and low prices per unit of output
and upon a constantly increasing mass income and a constant
reduction in hours of work, together with complete reemployment of workers of all classifications who are able and willing to
work."[17]

Although he was intolerant of critics within his own organization, during the thirties Lewis was an eloquent and effective
spokesman for civil rights and freedoms in industry and in national life generally. In his appearance before the La Follette
Committee, he strongly attacked industrial spying, the use of
professional strikebreakers, and other interferences with workers' rights to assemble, speak freely, and strike. "We live in a
democracy. Its essence is freedom of association and the freedom of speech. These rights are meaningless if they cannot be
put into practice by the people who live under our Constitution.
Freedom of association in an industrial society is the right to
organize in trade-unions; freedom of speech is the right to make
just and reasonable demands for better living and working conditions through organization."[18]

Because of its comprehensive character, industrial unionism
tended to break down barriers among workers, not only as between occupations and skill levels but also as between different
religious, national, and racial groups. While practice often failed
to come up to theory, the CIO made much more headway
against race discrimination than its AFL rival. In 1936 the

[17] U.S., Congress, Testimony before U.S. Senate and House of Representatives,
Joint Hearings, Committee on Education and Labor of the Senate and Committee on Labor of the House, *Fair Labor Standards Act of 1937: Report on S. 2475
and H.R. 7200*, 75th Cong., 1st sess., 7–15 June 1937, pt. 2:275–286.

[18] U.S., Congress, Senate, Subcommittee of the Committee on Education and
Labor, *Oppressive Labor Practices Act: Report on S. 1970*, 76th Cong., 1st sess.,
May-June 1939, p. 101.

United Mine Workers called upon the AFL to eliminate Jim Crow locals and all discriminating clauses in union constitutions.[19] The CIO urged Negro workers to enroll in their unions on an equal basis with whites and Lewis, among others, emphasized his belief in equality of opportunity for Negroes.[20]

UNION CONCERNS WITH PRODUCTION PROBLEMS

The major preoccupation of unionists in the 1930's was with achieving or reestablishing organizational rights and collective bargaining. Once recognition was gained, attention was largely directed to developing effective grievance procedures and to safeguarding job rights through seniority and other devices. For most unions the improvement of productivity was a managerial responsibility. Nonetheless some of the concern about production problems which had emerged in the previous decade was revived in a few unions. The garment unions were leaders in this regard. They were among the first to participate in the NRA codes and to reassert that "self-rule in industry" was a two-party process. In May 1935 Jacob Potofsky, assistant general president of the Amalgamated Clothing Workers, told the Bureau of Personnel Administration that once collective bargaining had been reestablished, the garment unions had been able to broaden their approach.

> The old "we want a raise" attitude of the unions has been supplemented by a realization that the welfare of the worker depends also on the welfare of the industry. The union's great problem has been one of education. The members have had to be trained to accept the principle of competitive labor cost as a controlling element in the battle for higher wages. While labor is not primarily concerned

[19] United Mine Workers of America, *Proceedings of the Thirty-fourth Constitutional Convention* (January-February 1936), pp. 218–219.

[20] Congress of Industrial Organization, "Equal Opportunity," Publication No. 46 (April 1940), pp. 14–15.

with total labor cost, efficiency, overhead, etc., as a rule, the union has realized that it must consider these factors if it is to accept its fair share of responsibility. So from the beginning we have been shop-company- and industry-conscious, and we have considered any significant problem confronting the employer as of significance to labor as well. In conformity with this attitude, the unions have assisted employers to reduce cost, without reducing wages, of course, by pointing out wastes in management, inefficient production methods and by reducing overhead.[21]

One of the most significant statements by a top union official on the relationship between labor and production was a book written jointly by Philip Murray, Lewis' right-hand man and vice president of the CIO and the United Mine Workers as well as head of the Steel Workers Organizing Committee, and Morris L. Cooke, a prominent consulting engineer and supporter of scientific management. The book was entitled, significantly, *Organized Labor and Production: Next Steps in Industrial Democracy*.[22] Its central theme was the integration of unionism and scientific management, a theme advocated by Louis Brandeis and Robert Valentine thirty years earlier. But the scope was not merely the workshop, enterprise, or industry—it was the total economy. The goal was a full-employment economy based on collective bargaining and a code of civil rights for employees, on the one hand, and on scientific control of industrial operations on the other.

Murray and Cooke believed that the concept of pure and simple collective bargaining was becoming obsolete and that the objectives of unions were being extended to "industrial stabilization" ventures, social legislation, and increased political activity. This required a greatly increased participation of union

[21] Jacob Potofsky, "Collective Bargaining in the Clothing Industry," in *Collective Bargaining* (New York: Bureau of Personnel Administration, 1935), pp. 3–4.

[22] Philip Murray and Morris L. Cooke, *Organized Labor and Production* (New York: Harper and Bros., 1940).

representatives in matters of plant and business management as well as in industry economics. It called for the giving of information about the business to the employees so that they and their experts could take part in analyzing and dealing with the problems of the industry and of management. It even contemplated the seating of one or more union officials on company boards of directors.

Beyond this, the authors envisioned, at the national level, extensive cooperation among government, management, and labor in order to achieve an uninterrupted flow of production and income. Government could no longer leave the economic process to chance or unregulated market forces. Business and labor organizations could no longer limit their objectives and activities to class interests.

Published on the eve of World War II, the ideas in this book were soon to be translated into a concrete proposal for wartime America—a proposal which will be discussed in the next chapter.

The Radicals

Although the Great Depression provided an unusually favorable climate for radical thought, especially in contrast to the repressive environment of the twenties, Socialist and Communist thinkers contributed little that was new to the idea of industrial democracy. Industrial unionism had long been advocated by leftists, and they therefore quickly and enthusiastically responded to the CIO movement with organizers, staff aides, publicity, finances, and political apparatus. Their hopes for an independent labor-farmer political party, however, were not realized. Nor were their ideas about the socialization of the major industries and resources of the country.

How much impact they had on the thinking of Lewis,

Murray, Hillman, and other nonradical leaders of the CIO is problematic—probably not very much, in any direct sense. Nevertheless, they were important critics and goads as well as sources of organizational energy in both labor and governmental institutions. All of the radical groups were early advocates of government unemployment insurance and other social security programs. Full employment was a major objective. They were in the forefront of the movement to organize unions and councils of unemployed workers and workers on government relief projects. They were vigorous advocates of worker freedoms and civil rights and played a significant role in the work of the La Follette Committee. They strongly attacked both company unionism and "sweetheart agreements" between employers and unscrupulous union officials. They were the most outspoken supporters of Negro rights in industry. They were among the most knowledgeable and perceptive critics of undemocratic practices within unions.

The radicals were, of course, not a homogeneous group in their views and tactics. The Communists, in particular, often thought and acted quite differently depending on the circumstances of their position and the degree of power or influence which they exercised. The published views of the radicals on industrial democracy, however, were more uniform than their tactics, especially since the old syndicalist-anarchist ideology of the IWW was not revived.

The most prominent of the Socialist party leaders in the thirties were Norman Thomas and Harry Laidler. Both spoke and wrote often about industrial democracy, stressing the public interest as distinct from the interests of managers and workers. In a 1931 book, Thomas declared that the whole subject of industrial government under socialism needed reexamination. He doubted that there would be one uniform plan. "I am less and less a believer on theoretical grounds in guild socialism to say nothing of that more extreme form of producers' control, syndicalism. The ultimate interest as I have already argued is the public interest; that is, the interest of workers as consumers. We want to build that up, rather than divisive craft or even industrial interests. . . ."[23]

Industrial democracy did not mean government by factory meeting or the election of foremen. That was likely to lead to the wrong sort of politics and favoritism. The election of directors was a different story. Nevertheless the workers did have special interests in administration, akin to those of the professions of law and medicine which were self-governing. These interests were in standards and working conditions. The union would be necessary even under socialism not only as a check on bureaucracy but as a positive form of organization. At least during a transitional period wages would be negotiated by collective bargaining. "Men fought and died for national independence and some voice in the nation. There is no reason why a similar desire for more industrial citizenship should not fill men's thoughts and somewhat dispossess the indifference of workers who now want more pay and more leisure rather than more responsibility. It will, however, be a calamity if men think not as workers primarily but as workers in one trade or craft."[24] A system of production for use also meant for Thomas national planning and coordination on democratic principles. His idea of industrial democracy, in short, encompassed the total national and ultimately the international society.

In a series of books and pamphlets during the latter half of the decade, Laidler restated and amplified socialist thinking. He noted in 1935 that organized labor had contributed to the cause of democracy in a number of industries by breaking down autocracy in the workshop, but he felt that in many cases it had substituted a "trade or industrial union autocracy whose chief

---

[23] Norman Thomas, *America's Way Out—A Program for Democracy* (New York: Macmillan Co., 1931), p. 166.
[24] Ibid., p. 169.

aim seems to be hold on to jobs, many of which have been made lucrative through racketeering and corruption."[25] The larger struggle for democracy lay ahead. Unions needed to gain a voice in the determination of the volume of production, prices, profits, and financial and sales policies. But as long as industry remained in private hands, labor was unlikely to obtain "a genuine place in management." Laidler stressed that socialism meant more than public ownership—it also meant democratic management, not of the kind called for by the syndicalists and early Bolsheviks but one in which all parties of interest (including workers, technicians, and consumers) would have their points of view represented. He noted that one reason why unions had been lukewarm about public ownership under capitalism was that the state had been substituted for the employer as the autocratic boss. The specific machinery for worker participation in management might vary as long as the spirit of democracy was infused in industrial life.

In a 1940 pamphlet,[26] Laidler reiterated the importance of democratic administration as well as public ownership. If the miners had complete administrative control of the mining industry, they could fix prices and production quotas, boost wages out of line with the workers in other industries, and exploit the consumers. Hence the administrative boards of public industries should include workers (because of their concern for work conditions), consumers (because of their interest in the quality, volume, and prices of the goods produced), and administrative and technical personnel (because of their expert knowledge). Readers of Sidney and Beatrice Webb will recall that virtually all of these ideas were expressed in Britain forty years earlier.

Since the early twenties, the master strategist of the Com-

[25] Harry Laidler, *Socializing Our Democracy* (New York: Harper and Bros., 1935), p. 179. See also *American Socialism—Its Aims and Practical Program* (New York: Harper and Bros., 1937).

[26] Laidler, *The Federal Government and Functional Democracy* (New York: League for Industrial Democracy, September 1940).

munists in labor relations had been William Z. Foster, the party's national chairman in the thirties. Leader of the unsuccessful steel strike of 1919, Foster had long supported industrial unionism as the proper basis for trade union organization. In summing up the Communist position in 1936, after the shift from their ineffective dual unionism policy to the popular front, Foster related industrial unionism to the broader framework of radical thought and strategy. "The Communists back the fight for industrial unionism to the fullest extent because it is a progressive step for the A.F. of L. But they point out that industrial unionism will be weakened in its effectiveness as a weapon in unifying the workers against the employers unless genuine trade union democracy is established in the A.F. of L., unless a fighting policy of class struggle is adopted, unless the unions rally behind and become the backbone of a Farmer-Labor Party which will elect real representatives of the workers to political office."[27] Three years later Foster voiced his approval of the trade-agreement system because the complex terms of workers' employment in modern industry required it. Such agreements should be adhered to by both sides. But, he added, the Communists did not share the illusions of conservative trade unionists that agreements meant a suspension of the class struggle. Employers used all kinds of tricks to violate and chisel away such agreements. Short-term agreements, not exceeding two years, were preferable, and under no circumstances were they to be used as the excuse for breaking the strike of another body of workers.[28]

An examination of the files of *The Communist*, the monthly journal of the Communist party of the USA throughout the thirties, provides valuable insights into Communist dialectics and tactics but little regarding their conception of the government

[27] William Z. Foster, *Industrial Unionism* (New York: Workers Library Publishers, April 1936), p. 42.

[28] Foster, *Your Questions Answered* (New York: Workers Library Publishers, June 1939), pp. 72–73.

of industry either under the capitalist system that they vigorously opposed or under the communist system which they hoped to establish. In 1935 Foster wrote an interesting analysis of the development of syndicalism in the United States, which he himself had once espoused, and concluded that it was no longer compatible with American conditions, particularly with the rise of the Communist party and its close ties with the Russian and world communist movements.[29]

The key to the new Communist approach at this time was "united front," and this was most fully developed by Earl Browder, the party's general secretary. In pursuance with instructions from the 1935 Seventh World Congress of the Comintern, Browder reported,[30] stress was to be placed on the formation of a broadly based Farmer-Labor party, the opening of closed factories and enterprises by the government at union wages, the adoption of unemployment and social insurance, the liberation of the Negro people, and most of all activity within the trade union movement to strengthen the forces of industrial unionism and to oppose class collaboration by the AFL leadership. The following year Browder's book, *What Is Communism?*, propounded the new theme—"Communism is the Americanism of the Twentieth Century!"[31] In a concluding chapter entitled "A Glimpse of Soviet America," Browder envisioned a communist society in which the major industries were nationalized, all available manpower was employed, and a highly centralized administrative system would be set up to produce maximum output. To the question whether a bureaucratic apparatus might grow up in control to become a new ruling class, he responded simply that this could not occur because of the absence of private ownership.

[29] Foster, "Syndicalism in the United States," *The Communist*, 14 (November 1935), 11:1044–1057.

[30] Earl Browder, "The United Front—The Key to Our New Tactical Orientation," *The Communist*, 14 (December 1935), 12:1075–1129.

[31] Browder, *What Is Communism?* (New York: Vanguard Press, 1936).

In commemorating the twentieth anniversary of the American Communist party in 1939, Browder and Foster, together with other party leaders and functionaries, traced the evolution of party tactics and policies over the two decades.[32] Despite the well-known gyrations in tactics and the shifts in slogans ("united front against Fascism" and "twentieth-century democracy" were in 1939 the favored terms) the long-run goal was unchanged— the fulfillment of the Marxist-Leninist program of international communism. On immediate issues Foster wrote:

Ever since our Party was formed twenty years ago, the Communists in the trade unions have carried on an indefatigable struggle to build the labor movement into a powerful and progressive instrument in the hands of the working class. During the whole period the Communists have been in the front line of every struggle for better wages, shorter hours, improved working conditions and against the speed-up; they have fought for industrial unionism, trade union democracy, the organization of the unorganized, national and international trade union unity, and a progressive trade union leadership; they have worked tirelessly for the organization of women, youth, Negroes, and foreign born; and they have struggled against bureaucracy, incompetency, racketeering, gangsterism and every form of corruption and reaction in the unions. The Communist trade unionists have carried on a resolute fight for the rights of the Negro people; against imperialist exploitation in Latin America; for the recognition of the Soviet Union by the United States government; for the defense of Tom Mooney, the Scottsboro boys and J. B. McNamara; for unemployment, old age, accident and sickness insurance; and for many other political demands of the masses. They have stood in the van in the struggle against fascism and for peace. Communist trade unionists have always carried on a policy of class struggle, fighting ceaselessly against capitalist illusions among the masses and against the class collaboration policies of reactionary labor leaders, urging alliances with other progressive forces, popularizing the lessons of the great

[32] *The Communist,* 18 (September 1939):9.

October Revolution, developing the class consciousness of the workers, helping to educate and lead the masses in organized political action, and propagandizing for the principles of socialism.[33]

Some Management Views

As in the past, employers viewed the idea of industrial democracy in a variety of ways. Most employers of the thirties continued to resist the idea in any form—they still regarded the enterprise as their private concern to be run, within limits, as they deemed best. These employers and their organizations— the Liberty League, the American Manufacturers Association, the U.S. Chamber of Commerce and many trade groups—were on the defensive and in opposition to the mainstream throughout the decade. They sought, wherever possible, to exclude the unions from the NRA codes; they opposed the labor boards and the several Wagner bills; they argued for proportional representation against the majority rule principle; they challenged the constitutionality of the Wagner Act and other New Deal labor laws; and in general they resisted collective bargaining in industry until they had no real choice.

The second main category of employers, including many of the largest, pursued the personnel program which had worked so successfully in the 1920's—with particular emphasis on employee representation or company unionism. Some of these, as in the twenties, used the company union purely as a device to discourage genuine unionism. Others sincerely believed that the plant work council or committee principle was much more conducive to industrial harmony than collective bargaining. Most of these employers adhered to their approach until strikes

[33] "Twenty Years of Communist Trade Union Policy," *The Communist*, 18 (September 1939), 9:408.

or a Labor Board decision coupled with a court order forced a change. Some were able to maintain an environment which permitted independent company unionism to survive despite the challenge of national trade unions of the AFL or CIO and NLRB tests.

The third employer category consisted of those who correctly assessed the temper of the times and the trend of events and decided to accept the collective-bargaining model of industrial democracy. These in turn fell into two groups. One of these accepted with some reluctance and regret, making the best of a situation which they would not have created if they had the choice. The other, a minority, saw merit in the model and decided to take the initiative in pursuing it. A few employers, as in previous decades, looked beyond collective bargaining.

EMPLOYER HOSTILITY

The auto employers (with a few exceptions) were in the forefront of the anti-union employers. William Knudsen, then vice-president and soon-to-be president of General Motors, put their views in a nutshell in a talk to the Advertising Club of New York on November 6, 1935.

> The advent of the National Recovery Act brought some complications in the way of attempts by government officials to plan for a business they knew nothing about, and apostles of the so-called social service gospel indulged in considerable finger-pointing which at first somewhat bewildered the industry.

> After having run its somewhat zigzag course, from preaching to damning, this died out from lack of practical results and again proved the fundamental principles that management functions belong to managements; that business belongs to the stockholders; that labor must be treated fairly and dealt with through the regular supervising organization and that no legislation can prevent

or settle labor disputes which can only be settled around the table on the principle that nobody ever won a strike.[34]

Two years later, Knudsen conceded to the Associated Industries of Massachusetts that collective bargaining had arrived and that "eventually" it would become orderly as both sides got to know the facts and were willing to present them. The manufacturers, he alleged rather plaintively, had tried to cooperate with the administration.

> I do not want ever to be in a position of criticizing our Administration, but I do think that all this hue and cry about collective bargaining could have been considerably less expensive if some ground rules had been set. As it was, the early stages of the conflict resembled very much a ball game without an umpire, and with everybody in the grandstands hollering advice.

> I think that with the Wagner Act in force, everything depends upon whether it will smooth out or lessen industrial stoppages. . . . To say that it is the Magna Charta of labor is all right, but it must prove its value in giving men uninterrupted work with consequent better earnings, or it will be a Magna Charta no longer.[35]

Both James Emery, general counsel of the National Association of Manufacturers, and Henry I. Harriman, president of the U.S. Chamber of Commerce, opposed the Wagner Act and attacked the majority rule principle as a violation of the fundamental principle of "liberty and property in labor"—the right to make a contract for yourself[36]—and as "un-American and unethical."[37] In 1935 the NAM adopted a platform entitled "Preserve Freedom of Enterprise" and opposing any regulation of employment relations or economic planning by the federal gov-

---

[34] *New York Times,* November 7, 1935, p. 25.

[35] Ibid., October 29, 1937, p. 6.

[36] U.S., Congress, Senate, Committee on Education and Labor, *National Labor Relations Board: Report on S. 1958,* 74th Cong., 1st sess., 1935, pt. 3:261.

[37] Ibid., p. 465.

ernment. As late as 1939 the Chamber of Commerce called for amendments to the Wagner Act eliminating majority rule.[38]

ADVOCATES OF EMPLOYEE REPRESENTATION

Paul Litchfield, president of Goodyear Tire and Rubber Company, had been a pioneer in the welfare-capitalist movement and employee representation going back to 1919 and before. Speaking about Goodyear's Industrial Assembly in late 1933, Litchfield claimed to be fifteen years ahead of the NRA. "Nothing more could be achieved by our workers under any other plan. And the particular beauty of the Assembly plan is that it is based upon self containment . . . we deal directly with our men and they deal directly with us. We all speak the same language and have a mutual understanding of each other's problems. Over the years we have learned to deal fairly and promptly with each other and the degree of reciprocal confidence thus engendered is indeed commendable as well as helpful to all."[39] Litchfield opposed the passage of the Wagner Act and attacked the assumptions on which it was based in the following terms:

1. It assumes the existence of an eternal conflict between employers and employees.
2. It presupposes that better working conditions for employees would result from its enactment.
3. Collective bargaining is to be established through attempted definition by law rather than by mutual cooperation and understanding.
4. It seems to presuppose that the majority of employers are exploiting labor or will do so whenever afforded an opportunity.
5. It assumes that most employees desired their relationship

[38] *Amendment of the National Labor Relations Act* (Washington, D.C.: Chamber of Commerce, March 23, 1939), pp. 8–9.
[39] Paul Litchfield, "Social Improvement . . . a By-Product of Industry," *The President Talks to the Men* (Akron: Goodyear Tire and Rubber Co., 1934), p. 73.

with employers to be based on conflict instead of on cooperation.

6. It prohibits employers from engaging in unfair labor practices but says nothing about protecting the rights of employers or of non-union employees.[40]

Ironically, during the second half of the decade the Akron plant of the Goodyear Company was the site of continuing conflict, surpassed by few other factories, and a major target of the sitdown strike movement that made headline news. Nearly a decade was to elapse before one of the prize examples of employee representation was transformed into an effective case of collective bargaining.

The steel industry was another center of employee-representation plans which strongly opposed the collective-bargaining model and experienced prolonged and bitter conflict before yielding to the dual pressure of union and government. A pamphlet by the Iron and Steel Institute in mid-1934 contrasted the virtues of employee representation, as industry saw them, with the evils of unions.

1. Employee representation builds harmony, confidence and understanding whereas union labor operates on the theory that the interests of capital and labor are inevitably antagonistic.

2. Under employee representation plans, employees are usually represented by men whom they know personally and who are thoroughly familiar with local conditions. The union officials are often men of little plant experience and no business training; they have no direct or immediate contact with the employees and their problems; they are more concerned with building personal and organizational power and with collecting dues than with the welfare of employees or plant conditions.

3. Employee representation contributes to productive efficiency on a day-to-day basis and in tune with local plant conditions. The

[40] U.S., Congress, Senate, Committee on Education and Labor, *National Labor Relations Board: Report on S. 1958*, 74th Cong., 1st sess., March-April 1935, 3:470–471.

unions are not inclined to make allowances for variation between different plants or cities. Strikes in one plant may foment conflicts in others and jurisdictional disputes create further problems.

4. Under employee representation, any employee has the right to raise his individual case at any time as well as being represented collectively. Union members have no rights as individuals. While a worker under the former plan may also belong to a union, a worker under the latter plan has no similar freedom; the union always seeks a closed shop, denying the fundamental right of contract.

5. Employee representation gives free play to individualism and encourages initiative, superior ability, and incentive plans. Union labor desires to bring all employees to the same level; it prevents men from working outside of a single trade classification and thereby prevents them from broadening their experience or increasing their usefulness.

6. Employee representation increases employee understanding of the employer's business whereas unions try to prevent employees from obtaining a reasonable understanding of the production and financial problems of the company.[41]

By 1938 one of the most bitter employer opponents of unionism, Tom M. Girdler of Republic Steel, was obliged to concede that collective bargaining was here to stay; but he was unalterably opposed to the closed shop, and he tried to limit the scope of bargaining. He agreed that wages, hours, working conditions, individual injustices, and seniority rights were valid subjects for joint discussion. He excluded from bargaining the right to hire and fire "except in certain cases which may be obvious grievances," the right to install equipment leading to improvement of quality and of the competitive position of the company, the right to make products by different methods, and the right

[41] American Iron and Steel Institute, *Collective Bargaining in the Steel Industry* (June 1934). See also the Institute pamphlet entitled *The Men Who Make Steel* (August 1936).

for men to work who do not belong to a particular organization.[42]

In tracing the evolutionary process of ideas about industrial government, it is interesting to note that even so staunch a later supporter of collective bargaining as Cyrus S. Ching, was, in April 1935, a defender of employee representation. Ching, then director of industrial and public relations of the U.S. Rubber Company, felt that under certain circumstances employee representation was "much better" than trade unionism. He did not understand, he said, why so much emphasis was placed on collective bargaining. Wages were, of course, important, but there were many other problems where management and employees have a lot in common and bargaining was not the best method of dealing. He agreed, however, that the threat of unionism had stopped many employers from exploiting workers.[43]

BEYOND EMPLOYEE REPRESENTATION
AND COLLECTIVE BARGAINING

A small group of employers, industrial engineers, management consultants, and academicians were impelled by the impact of the Depression to delve more deeply into the idea of industrial democracy. On May 26, 1932, they met in New York City under the rubric of Industrial Experimenters Association to discuss "Democratic Influences in Industry." In the words of Henry C. Metcalf, one of the founders, the organization was "designed to foster further experiment and development in methods of employer-employee ownership, control and management in industry."[44] Metcalf cited as an illustration of the underlying

[42] Tom M. Girdler, "Industry and Labor," *Fortune*, 17 (January 1938), 1:162.
[43] Cyrus Ching, "Collective Bargaining through Employee Representation," in *Collective Bargaining*, ed. Henry C. Metcalf (New York: Bureau of Personnel Administration, 1935), pp. 5–6.
[44] Henry C. Metcalf, "Introductory Remarks," in *Democratic Influences in Industry*, Proceedings of the First Annual Conference of Industrial Experimenters Association (May 26, 1932), p. 6. Cited hereafter as *IEA Conference Proceedings*.

philosophy of the association the following statement by Owen
D. Young, president of General Electric Company:

> I hope the day may come when these great business organizations
> will truly belong to the men who are giving their lives and their
> efforts to them. I care not in what capacity. They will then use
> capital truly as a tool, and they will be all interested in working
> it to the highest economic advantage. Then an idle machine will
> mean to every man in the plant who sees it an unproductive charge
> against himself. Then we shall have zest in labour, *provided* the
> leadership be competent and the division fair. Then we shall dis-
> pose once for all of the charge that in industry organizations are
> autocratic, not democratic. Then we shall have all the opportuni-
> ties for a cultural wage which the business can provide. Then, in
> a word, men will be free in cooperative undertaking, and subject
> only to the same limitations and changes as men in individual
> businesses. Then we shall have no hired men.[45]

He added that he knew of no better definition of sound democracy than Mazzini's "the progress of all through all, under the
leadership of the best and wisest."

Ordway Tead, editor of economic and business books for
Harper, who presided, stressed the basic assumption underlying
democracy—that human personality, the ultimate worth of each
individual in the community, is an ultimate good and end. Democracy was a process of achieving this goal for the generality
of people. It meant abundant life, not in material terms only,
but in spiritual values as well. It aimed at quality in individual
experience, self-choice of experience, communal organization
which fostered the cultivation of personal worth and happiness.
These principles must apply in industry as in all other phases of
life.[46]

Among the other speakers at the conference were William

---

[45] Statement attributed to Owen D. Young and quoted by Henry C. Metcalf in
his "Introductory Remarks," *IEA Conference Proceedings,* p. 7.

[46] Ibid., pp. 10–12.

Hapgood, president of the Columbia Conserve Company, who described the producers' cooperation organization in effect at that small enterprise since 1919,[47] and Banow Lyons of the Correlated Graphic Industries, Inc., a cooperative printing company of Seattle, Washington, which led to the establishment, in 1931–1932, of the Unemployed Citizens League—an effort to develop a widespread producers' and consumers' cooperative system.

The remainder of the conference talks were given by prominent members of the Taylor Society, including Harlow S. Person, managing director; Otto S. Beyer, author of the B. & O. Plan; and two consulting engineers, L. K. Comstock and Wallace Clark. Person offered three main propositions linking science and democracy in industry.

1. The impact of science on industry has made democracy in organization and procedure essential to the preservation of its fruitful results.

2. The development of democracy in industry is dependent upon and must be based upon the maximum use of science in every relationship. Democracy needs a reign of law and law must have the authority of scientifically validated facts rather than arbitrary power.

3. This interaction of science and democracy leads to new, workable concepts of democracy—for example, that individuals are not created equal but functional opportunities and responsibilities vary as much as do capacities, and it is therefore possible to match capacities to responsibilities and give every capacity its defined value. Science is also proving the organic nature of group efforts and the importance of every member to the whole.[48]

Beyer saw labor-management cooperation as the key to greater industrial democracy by enlarging the responsibility and status

[47] In 1926 W. Jett Lauck described this company as the most complete and perfect illustration of direct industrial democracy existing at that time. *Political and Industrial Democracy: 1776–1926* (New York: Funk & Wagnalls Co., 1926), p. 286.

[48] Harlow S. Person, *IEA Conference Proceedings*, pp. 39–40.

of the worker, increasing his benefits, and dignifying his position as well as benefiting society. Comstock pointed out the idealistic nature of industrial democracy and the great difficulty of translating ideal into reality. Endurance and persistence were essential. "Ideas and ideals in the workshops of industrial democracy are none too plentiful and must be clung to with the greatest tenacity, if one is to rise above discouragement."[49] And Clark closed the program by emphasizing that industrial democracy meant equality of opportunity rather than merely equal voting power. The future of democracy in industry depended on the experiments being made in terms of fundamentals, not financial success. "In any experiment in democratic industry, the ownership of the business must be constituted so as to secure complete cooperation from the workmen, the managing personnel and the shareholders, and upon that foundation must be developed a management which will secure the greatest results from the investment and the abilities of the workmen."[50]

The Industrial Experimenters Association soon disappeared from sight but a number of its members pursued related, although less far-reaching, ideas in the Bureau of Personnel Administration (established in 1918), also headed by Metcalf. In 1935 the Bureau sponsored a series of discussions on collective bargaining. At the first session Metcalf again sounded the industrial democracy theme. "The representation of interests is the key note of personnel administration—and expresses itself increasingly in the evolution of the democratic idea in industry." Democracy had been developed in the home, in school, in politics, in religious life. But "we are only beginning to get the feeling of democracy" in the workplace and "resistance to it is still great." For Metcalf the method (whether employee representation or collective bargaining) was not important; it was

[49] L. K. Comstock, *IEA Conference Proceedings*, p. 76.
[50] Wallace Clark, *IEA Conference Proceedings*, p. 92.

the spirit that counted. The principle of personality was central.[51]

Tead developed a related theme that was to attract considerable attention later. He looked at industrial self-government from a functional or administrative point of view—a full recognition of able management, a fair consideration of all the groups involved, and a fair control in the public interest of a bountiful productivity. The exercise of power cannot be left only to the business managers and the objective is not only making profits. From an administrative standpoint, major decisions will be sound only as they have the benefit of the judgment of the interested groups—through code authorities or any similar administrative units.[52]

The meetings of the American Management Association reflected the manner in which the more progressive and flexible personnel and management people were responding to the pressures of the time and the ideas which have just been described. In 1935, at a conference on collective bargaining, the director of personnel of Armour & Company indicated that while he favored employee representation, it was essential to avoid company control or domination; the plan must be fully accepted by a majority of the employees through a vote, and it must permit genuine collective bargaining. He also saw no reason why employees could not freely adopt other forms of organization and bargaining so that a variety of bargaining agencies prevailed in the same company or industry.[53]

The manager of industrial relations for U.S. Rubber Company felt that employee representatives should be given "every pos-

[51] Metcalf, "The Implications of Expanding Government Control over Employer-Employee Relations," in *Collective Bargaining*, pp. 3–4.

[52] Ordway Tead, "The Administrative Logic of Industrial Self-Government," in *Collective Bargaining*, pp. 2, 6–7.

[53] H. G. Allerd, "Collective Bargaining," American Management Association, *Personnel Series No. 19* (February 1935), pp. 7–8.

sible detail" of the business or industry in which they were in-terested and able to comprehend and assimilate. From this knowledge they would get a pride in the products of the com-pany which they helped to create.[54] The manager of the Socony-Vacuum Oil Company came out in favor of majority rule as long as "historic, logical, normal groups of employees, such as machin-ists, or car men in a railroad shop" were free to select their own representatives.[55]

At a similar conference held a year later an official of the Kimberly-Clark Corporation, a large Wisconsin paper manu-facturer, described the evolution of collective bargaining out of the company's employee-representation plan as a form of "con-stitutional government." "The essence of constitutional govern-ment," he stated, "is that there are specified boundaries to the executive's choice and discretion." He cautioned against reduc-ing too much of the human relations in industry to written law because this would lead to inflexibility and harmful delay in responding to changing conditions. But he thought that the merits of having well-written standardized policies, cooperative-ly developed by management and worker representatives, far outweighed the disadvantages. They "promote understanding, and uniformity, and consistency, and continuity. They give as much stability and certainty as is feasible under changing con-ditions. They encourage and make possible a feeling of assur-ance, and protection, and individual freedom."[56]

As the decade of the thirties approached its end, Ching re-flected the slowly changing attitude of management toward the collective-bargaining model of industrial democracy. After cau-tioning his audience, the annual meeting of the U.S. Chamber of Commerce, to take a more realistic view on labor relations

[54] Montague Clark, ibid., p. 18.
[55] C. R. Dooley, ibid., p. 5.
[56] C. G. Eubank, "Discussion: Management's Industrial Relations Problems," American Management Association, *Personnel Series No. 22* (1936), pp. 29–33.

in the light of recent developments, he urged: "Let us stop deal-ing with these relationships on the basis of our emotions, bias and prejudice. Let us deal with them on the basis of principles. We will meet with many discouraging situations, but it is not too late to at least make a start along the road to better relation-ships between employers and employees and between industry and organized labor. Let us stop calling names. Let us begin to realize, if we don't already know it, that the salvation of our whole industrial system lies in better coordination and better cooperation among the various factors which help to make it up."[57]

[57] Ching, "Responsibilities of Management and Workers," *Vital Speeches of the Day*, 4 (June 15, 1938), 17:542.

CHAPTER 13

TRIPARTISM DURING WORLD WAR II

J UST AS WORLD WAR I helped to crystallize the industrial-democracy movement that had been striving for a stable form during the preceding two decades, so World War II helped to solidify the new model of industrial democracy which the Great Depression and the New Deal had generated.

The outbreak of the war in Europe in 1939 signalled the end of the economic depression in the United States. In September 1939 the number of unemployed was about 9.5 million or 17 per cent of the civilian labor force. By January 1942, the first month after Pearl Harbor, the number of unemployed was under 4 million or about 7 per cent. The total involvement of the United States in the war quickly replaced the unemployment problem with a labor shortage problem. In Franklin Roosevelt's words, Dr. New Deal became Dr. Win-the-War.

Winning the war provided four major objectives for the industrial front. First was the production of sufficient goods and services to meet military needs and to keep the domestic economy going. Second, and an obvious corollary of the first, was the holding of industrial conflicts, as well as other interferences with production, to a minimum. Third was the need to prevent rapid inflation which might seriously disrupt the economy.

Finally it was necessary to fill all occupational and manpower requirements for essential industries.

Labor's Aspirations

From the attack on Pearl Harbor, December 7, 1941, until the Japanese surrender, August 14, 1945, organized labor was solidly and unswervingly behind the war effort. It agreed to give up the right to strike for the duration of the war and to submit unresolved disputes with management to decisions by the War Labor Board. It accepted the need for some sort of wage-control program, although it opposed an outright "freeze." It recognized that the labor force might have to be channeled to some degree in order to assure an adequate labor supply for essential war and domestic production. Had labor resisted such policies, the government would undoubtedly have attempted to impose them by fiat. In general, however, the spirit of voluntarism rather than compulsion prevailed.

In return for these contributions to the war effort, the labor leaders expected and obtained comparable contributions from other segments of the nation. Spokesmen for business and industry, for example, agreed to abandon the use of the lockout and to accept the decisions of the War Labor Board. They also concurred in the establishment of governmental controls over prices as well as wages, and in the planning and regulation of production.

The labor leadership was, of course, in a strong strategic position because of the needs for labor and labor cooperation and the shortage of labor in relation to the demand. They were unwilling to tolerate the hostility which they had experienced from many employers during the thirties, and they were determined to extend their share of industrial sovereignty as far as possible. In these respects they had the support of the Roosevelt Administration, and they were largely successful. From 1940 until the end of the war, one major corporation after another was obliged, because of union and government pressures, to abandon anti-union positions. Ford, Republic Steel, Remington Rand—these and many others fell in line. Union membership (excluding Canadian members) soared from 6.3 million in 1939 to 8.4 million in 1941 to 12.1 million in 1945. The union percentage of the civilian labor force rose from 11.5 to 22.4 and of the nonfarm employees from 20.7 to 29.9[1] Although much of the membership increase was due to increased employment in previously unionized plants and companies, a substantial proportion came in newly organized enterprises and industries.

Thanks to the NLRB and the courts, company unionism largely disappeared although a number of "independent" unions survived the challenge of the rival AFL and CIO organizations. The decision by the U.S. Supreme Court in the January 1941 *Heinz* case requiring that all agreements negotiated between unions and employers should be put into writing as a sign of good faith bargaining gave the collective-bargaining process a further boost. A few months later the Court held that it was illegal not only to dismiss an employee but also to refuse to hire a new employee because of union activity.[2] And in 1944 the Court held that an employer who made individual contracts with his employees, and refused to negotiate with representatives of a majority union was guilty of a refusal to bargain.[3]

In addition to extending unionization and collective bargaining, labor spokesmen sought to enlarge their participation in both private industry and in government agencies—in the name of democracy. The most imaginative and expressive advocates

[1] Estimates by Leo Troy, "Trade Union Membership, 1897–1962," *Review of Economics and Statistics* (February 1965), pp. 93–94.

[2] *Phelps Dodge Corp.* v. *N.L.R.B.*, 313 U.S. 177 (1941).

[3] *J. I. Case* v. *N.L.R.B.*, 321 U.S. 332 (1944).

of these ideas were Philip Murray, Walter Reuther, John Brophy, and Clinton Golden—all prominent CIO leaders.[4]

In the preceding chapter, reference has already been made to the Murray-Cooke volume calling for the collaboration of labor, management, and government in the development of a more rational and efficient economy. On December 14, 1940, Murray submitted to President Roosevelt an Industry Council Plan, based on these ideas, as a way of promoting the defense effort. The proposal provided that the President should establish a council "for each major basic and vital defense industry." Each council was to consist of an equal number of representatives of management and labor unions in the industry, with one government representative serving as chairman. The functions of the council were to:

1. Ascertain the domestic and armament requirements of the industry and coordinate and expand production facilities.

2. Reemploy unemployed workers in each area in which the industry operated and train workers for shortage occupations.

3. Achieve the greatest possible output as quickly as possible by bringing into use all the available production facilities.

4. Promote industrial peace through the perfection and extension of sound collective-bargaining relations between management and organized labor and the adherence to all laws affecting the rights and welfare of labor.

Each industry council was to be adequately staffed and all necessary information was to be made available to it.

The President would also establish a National Defense Board, composed of equal numbers of representatives for industry and organized labor, with the President as chairman. This board

---

[4] The focus on these men reflects, in part, the availability of their views in print. Comparable views were held by other CIO and AFL leaders, including Hillman, Dubinsky, and Harrison.

would assist the industry councils by providing pertinent data on the aims and scope of the defense program, by granting and reallocating armament contracts, by acting as an appeals agency, and by coordinating the work of the councils.

The objectives of the plan, according to the Murray memorandum, were:

1. To guarantee defense production in needed quantities and on time through the full and complete cooperation of industry, organized labor, and government.

2. To guarantee the production of nonmilitary goods and services so as to advance the American standard of living through a more equitable distribution of the national income and thereby improve the morale of the American people.

3. To preserve the basic democratic rights of the American people, namely, the freedom of speech, assembly, and worship, and the freedom to organize into independent associations for lawful purposes, such as the right to form unions and bargain collectively.

In bringing the plan before the 1941 CIO convention, Murray expressed labor's longtime aspiration for a greater participative role:

Do you know what is the matter with America today? Do you know why there is so much national disunity, so much national confusion? Obviously it is because labor does not trust the employer, the employer in too many instances does not trust labor, government doesn't trust either, and it seems to me that neither labor nor the employer trusts too much in government. Hence the need of using mechanisms of this description, devices such as are suggested in the Industry Council Plan, to bring all these elements together, working together in the common effort toward the attainment of our national objectives, whatever they may be. So far as labor is concerned, it gives to labor the thing that labor has been crying for down through the years in the United States of America.

It gives labor forthright administrative responsibility on each Board from the bottom right up to the top. It gives to labor equality of responsibility with that of management and with that of government. It brings labor squarely into the picture.[5]

At about the same time that Murray proposed his Industry Council Plan, Walter Reuther, then director of the General Motors Division of the United Auto Workers Union, applied the basic idea to the conversion of the auto industry for the mass production of airplanes. The Reuther Memorandum declared: "Labor offers its whole-hearted cooperation. All that Labor asks is intelligent planning, a voice in matters of policy and administration, recognition of its rights, and maintenance of its established standards.[6]

Neither the Murray nor the Reuther Plan was accepted by the Administration because of the intense opposition of the industrialists. But the joint production council idea continued to be advocated by these and other labor leaders. In 1944, when postwar reconversion was beginning to attract attention, Murray wrote: "Labor, agriculture and small business intend to have greater representation in the councils where basic decisions are being made on the program for production and on the planning of the demobilization of the American economy. We of organized labor demand similar representation for agriculture and small business, and for those larger businesses who believe in an economy of abundance—in short, representation for all groups in the community who have a direct stake in full employment."[7] In the same year, in speaking before the UAW convention, Murray called for both a tripartite National Production Board and separate industry councils in the basic mass-production indus-

[5] CIO, *Daily Proceedings of the Fourth Constitutional Convention* (November 17–22, 1941), p. 170.

[6] Walter Reuther, *500 Planes a Day* (Washington, D.C.: American Council on Public Affairs, 1944), pp. 9, 11.

[7] Philip Murray, "Reconversion and Post-War Needs," *Full Employment* (January 15, 1944), p. 63.

tries. The following year, shortly after the end of the war, John Brophy, a leading Murray aide, wrote an article advocating the adoption of the industrial council plan in order to prevent a post-war depression. But Brophy went much further than the earlier statements of the plan. This was not merely a device for union-management cooperation. It was a design for putting the nation on a comprehensive planning basis, in which minimum production goals would be set for all the basic industries to assure full production and prosperity for the entire population. The corporations would be expected to maintain minimum employment levels and to pay at least industry-wide minimum wages. A guaranteed annual wage, earlier called for by Murray, would naturally follow. The National Production Board and the industry councils would also be concerned with the capital investment policies of the large corporations, with plant location and utilization, with pricing policies, and with decisions on the items to be produced. Brophy saw his design as a fundamental revision of the American economy.

It asserts that the people of this country have a right, through their democratic government and their democratic unions, to participate in the major decisions made by the great corporations. It asserts that these corporations exist to serve the public interest, and not merely the private profit of industrialists and bankers.

I must insist that this is a very startling claim for the people of America to make, because, except with regard to the utilities, we have never asserted ourselves in this manner before; yet it is very obviously right and necessary. We are fully committed to the democratic process in our political activities. What we are now saying is that this democratic process must be extended to our economy. We are saying that America must become an economic as well as a political democracy, and that unless this happens then our political democracy itself is in grave danger.[8]

[8] John Brophy, "Phil Murray's Industry Council Plan," *Labor and Nation*, 1 (October 1945), 2:19–20.

The early rejection of the industry council idea did not discourage the union leaders from seeking a major participative role in the government agencies which ran the wartime program. For a short time in 1941, when Sidney Hillman, president of the Amalgamated Clothing Workers and labor's most influential advisor to President Roosevelt, was appointed associate director-general of the Office of Production Management, it seemed as if Murray's idea might be accepted—at least within the government. But the system of divided authority soon proved impractical and was abandoned. Labor representatives did play significant roles in the government throughout the war, but principally in agencies and divisions directly concerned with labor relations. The most important of these were the National War Labor Board, the War Manpower Commission, and the Labor Division of the War Production Board. The first of these agencies was composed of an equal number of representatives selected by labor (the AFL and CIO), management (the U.S. Chamber of Commerce and the National Association of Manufacturers), and the government (on behalf of the public). The labor members had a key role in both policy-making and administration at the national and regional levels of the board.

The Manpower Commission was made up of representatives from the major governmental departments and divisions concerned with the labor force and labor utilization. However, it established a National Management-Labor Policy Committee which, according to the official history of the Commission, "influenced the shaping of the policies and programs of the WMC, so much so that it was regarded by some as the strongest policy-forming influence in the WMC."[9] An Executive Order of December 5, 1942, made it mandatory for the WMC chairman to consult with the committee in carrying out his responsibilities,

[9] Technical Service Division, United States Employment Service, *A Short History of the War Manpower Commission*, preliminary draft, mimeographed (Washington, D.C.: Department of Labor, June 1948), p. 131.

thus giving the committee status coordinate with that of the commission itself.

Labor's role in the War Production Board proved to be one of its greatest disappointments. When the WPB replaced the Office of Production Management and Hillman was, in effect, demoted to head of the Labor Division, labor's voice weakened. When the WMC was set up and assumed responsibility for manpower policies, the Labor Division was further weakened. In the end the union representatives' role in WPB centered largely on providing assistance and advice in dispute or bottleneck situations and in furthering the voluntary establishment of joint labor-management production committees to increase plant output.[10]

In addition to their strong interest in widening labor's participative role in industry and government, the union leaders advanced ideas on a number of substantive items which had received minor attention in the preceding decade. Murray's speech to the UAW in 1944 placed particular emphasis on full employment and annual wage guarantees. He also listed dismissal pay, sick leave pay, paid vacations and holidays, paid insurance, veterans' funds, and the elimination of geographical differentials as necessary elements of future collective-bargaining contracts.

This view of the expanding nature of labor participation in relation to the idea of industrial democracy was reiterated and elaborated by Walter Reuther, who was soon to emerge as labor's most dynamic and imaginative contributor to thinking about industrial government. Reuther explored industrial democracy from many angles. About the union shop, for example, he wrote:

---

[10] See Bureau of Demobilization, Civilian Production Administration, *Industrial Mobilization for War: History of the War Production Board and Predecessor Agencies, 1940–1945*, 1 (Washington, D.C.: Government Printing Office, 1947), esp. 207, 235, 245, 417, 423.

The union shop is a phase of industrial democracy. The cardinal principle of democracy is majority rule. Refusal to grant a union shop on the pretense that such a step would be "unfair" to the non-union minority is in fact completely unfair to the majority in the plant. The unionist majority has struggled for years to raise wages, adjust working hours and set fair standards of work. The union workers feel that since every worker gains from the union's efforts, every worker should help pay the freight. The non-union shop is unfair to the union and the majority who are union members because it denies them sufficient authority to discharge their contractual obligations. Under a collective agreement the union workers assume responsibility for continuous operation, for maintenance of production standards preventing unauthorized strikes (in wartime, for preventing all strikes). It is an axiom that responsibility must be accompanied by a sufficient measure of authority. Unless there is a union shop clause, the union has no authority over any minority which chooses to assume a disruptive role.[11]

But Reuther recognized that the union shop could be a source of authoritarianism rather than democracy if it was not accompanied by safeguards. He therefore added that prerequisites for a union shop should include, in addition to majority determination in favor of a union through a labor board election, a democratic union constitution and administration, an honest accounting system and periodic audited financial reports to the union's membership. Reuther also called for the War Labor Board to establish a series of courts manned by impartial umpires to settle unresolved grievances wherever grievance arbitration was not already provided by collective-bargaining contracts.[12]

Throughout the war, Reuther felt that labor's potential had

[11] The article was erroneously titled, "For the Closed Shop," New York Times Magazine, August 2, 1942, pp. 7, 23.

[12] "Labor's Place in the War Pattern," New York Times Magazine, December 13, 1942, p. 36.

not been fully utilized. Despite labor representation in the War Production Board, "labor has not been accepted into full partnership in the war effort." Labor needed representation in production and strategy from the factory level to the President's cabinet. The least that unions could do, however, was to build labor morale by demanding equalization of wages through industrywide wage agreements based upon equal pay for equal work, guaranteed weekly wages, and a voluntary flow of manpower, under labor's direction, in response to production needs.[13] Reuther also saw the guaranteed annual wage as an economic necessity if the nation was to achieve the full postwar consuming power essential to maintain full production and full employment.[14]

A subject which greatly concerned both Murray and Reuther, as well as other CIO leaders, was discrimination against Negroes in industries and in unions. This was not a new subject. John L. Lewis had attacked it in the thirties and A. Philip Randolph, leader of the Pullman Porters, had repeatedly pressed the AFL to eliminate discrimination among its membership. Murray told the 1944 convention of the United Steel Workers that in almost every collective-bargaining contract of that organization provisions had been included to "protect the rights of colored workers against discrimination." He claimed that the only hope of the Negro worker was to affiliate with some CIO union. "We practice what we preach. We preach the elimination of all forms of discrimination and we practice that one thing. We do it in the shops. We do it in the factories. We do it wherever the CIO movement is."[15]

At the UAW convention of the same year, president R. J.

[13] Walter Reuther, "The Production Picture," *Ammunition*, 1 (September 1943), 6:7–8.

[14] Reuther, "Why an Annual Wage?" *Ammunition*, 2 (June 1944), 6:5–7.

[15] United Steel Workers of America, *Proceedings of the Second Constitutional Convention*, (May 9–13, 1944), p. 193.

Thomas reported that war tensions had accelerated social and economic antagonisms and that not all of the union's locals had accepted or understood the implications of the undemocratic policy of race prejudice and prejudice against other minority groups. He noted that the organization was extending its policy of nondiscriminatory contracts to all of its plants, that many of the locals had set up interracial and antidiscrimination committees to further educational programs, and that there had been an increase in elective and appointive positions held by Negro members. Nevertheless the problem persisted, and the union had decided to establish a staff position to deal with discrimination.[16] The following spring, a UAW representative told a Senate subcommittee that it heartily endorsed the proposed Fair Employment Practice Act and had established a fair practices committee of its own.[17]

One of the most interesting of labor's theoreticians and philosophers during the war period was Clinton Golden, a regional director of the Steel Workers Union. A remarkably broad-gauged man, Golden explored industrial democracy from many perspectives—psychological, economic, political, institutional, and social. In an early 1941 article for *Advanced Management,* a sophisticated journal of industrial engineers and personnel leaders, Golden told management what organized labor wanted of it: to discard its pretensions of infallibility, to grant labor the opportunity of full participation in productive processes, to recognize labor as an equal in productive processes, to assume its share of social responsibilities, to stop blaming its failures on labor and government, to get on with the job of national defense by getting on with labor, and to accept bona fide unions

[16] "Automobile Unionism (1944)," United Auto Workers, September 11, 1944, p. 64.

[17] U.S., Congress, Senate, Subcommittee of the Committee on Education and Labor, *Fair Employment Practice Act: Hearings on S. 101 and S. 459,* 79th Cong., 1st sess., 12–14 March 1945, p. 56.

and genuine collective-bargaining procedures completely and in good faith.[18]

In 1942 Golden and Harold Ruttenberg, director of research for the Steelworkers Union, published a book on the "dynamics of industrial democracy" in which they listed and supported by case materials thirty-seven principles—not as immutable rules but propositions which were the outgrowth of changing conditions and which were dependent "largely on the continued growth of industrial democracy."[19] Essentially these principles called for a high degree of union-management cooperation within a collective bargaining framework and without recourse to the government. But the final principle recognized that the future of industrial democracy depended upon the attainment and maintenance of full production and employment. As in the earlier Murray-Cooke volume, this book emphasized the importance of worker participation in management as an outlet for creative desires, as a means of improving productivity, and as a way of reducing costs.

Golden enthusiastically supported the program of labor-management production committees which was sponsored by the War Production Board, but he found a number of serious limitations, particularly in comparison with some of the systems established by unions and employers prior to the war. The committees should not be used as a substitute for regular union grievance committees. They were an extension, not a replacement, of collective bargaining. The program failed to provide for the equitable distribution of the proceeds of increased production to workers and owners alike. While not a problem during the wartime emergency, no provision was made for safeguarding the jobs of workers displaced as a result of tech-

[18] Clinton Golden, "What Labor Wants from Management," *Advanced Management,* 6 (January-March 1941), 1:7–8.

[19] Golden and Harold Ruttenberg, *The Dynamics of Industrial Democracy* (New York: Harper and Bros., 1942).

nological or other change in production methods. Finally, the absence of central planning was a serious defect in the effectiveness of the committees.[20]

In another analysis of industrial democracy, Golden stressed the distinction between union-management cooperation and labor-management cooperation. "The day of the town meeting is past. Politically our democracy is a representative democracy. So in the field of industry. Industrial democracy can operate only through the organization and representatives of the workers. . . ."[21]

Golden's most penetrating analysis of industrial democracy appeared in an article in the spring of 1944.[22] The foundation of industrial democracy, he asserted, rested upon the relation between the employer and employees in the plant, on the job. It cannot exist apart from a full and unqualified acceptance of the principles and procedures of collective bargaining. But these principles must be applied on a national basis and throughout given industries if they are to survive. Once established, industrial democracy means:

> that the employees in a plant enjoy good wages, hours and working conditions as the economics of the industry will permit, that they are protected against arbitrary dismissal, that there is machinery for securing a fair settlement of grievances, that they can meet and discuss their problems with their fellow workers without being spied upon or running the risk of employer displeasure, and that they can stand up like men and talk as equals with their foremen and supervisors. It means for both management and labor that there are a set of rules to guide their daily relations, which have been worked out together, and represent the best

[20] American Academy of Political and Social Science, "Collective Bargaining and Accelerated Production," *The Annals* (November 1942):98–101.

[21] Golden, "New Patterns of Democracy," *Antioch Review*, 3 (Fall 1943), 3:394.

[22] Golden, "The Meaning of Industrial Democracy," *Public Affairs*, 7 (Spring 1944):3.

kind of fair play and common justice the individuals concerned can develop. Industrial democracy has equal benefits to employers as well as employees, because it provides the law and order of industrial relationships which are equally essential to both sides, if they are going to live together in peace.[23]

Industrial democracy did not mean that labor was going to take over industry or deprive management of its prerogatives. It did mean that "there is a higher obligation which private owners and management must serve as well as their own interests." Beyond the plant and enterprise, it meant labor involvement with management and government in industrywide and national economic planning for the fullest use of the nation's resources, technology, and know-how. And last, it imposed a heavy responsibility upon labor. "A free man has to develop himself so that he can use his own initiative. Industrial democracy creates an environment in which both labor and management develop their best talents. Experience indicates that this training and development will have to take place in action." Unions, labor-management committees, and labor-management advisory committees were all schools in self-government.

The Contributions of the Federal Government

The primary concern of the Roosevelt administration was to win the war, not to promote industrial democracy. Nonetheless government leaders, including the President, were strongly imbued with the democratic ideology and wherever it was possible, voluntarism was stressed over compulsion. Although military conscription was adopted, both on the grounds of necessity and equity, Congress refused to enact national service legislation to draft men for work in shortage areas—even when finally requested by the President on the urging of the military. Wage

[23] Ibid., p. 134.

and price controls were introduced only gradually and after voluntary programs no longer seemed practicable. The no-strike, no-lockout policy was voluntarily adopted by the unions and employers; and while compulsion was used in a small number of cases of violation, punitive legislation was avoided. Dispute settlement machinery was based on tripartite cooperation of labor, management, and public representatives. As George W. Taylor stated: "Contrary to many gloomy expectations, the cost of victory did not include the acceptance of totalitarianism even while the war was being fought. One of the very great achievements of America at war was the integration of civilian strength into the war program largely on a voluntary nontotalitarian basis. In no area was voluntary cooperation more basic or more productive of results than in the labor relations program of war-time America."[24] The relevant question is to what extent governmental policy contributed to the continuing evolution of industrial democracy as distinct from solutions of the immediate problems of the wartime period. The answer is: considerable!

NATIONAL WAR LABOR BOARD

By far the greatest influence was exercised by the WLB because it was this agency which had primary responsibility for resolving union-management disputes and stabilizing wages. The board did not see itself as an innovator or trailblazer in industrial relations, but it was conscious of the need to base its decisions on the best of existing practice. And in some respects it had to introduce new principles and procedures in order to cope with the tremendous pressures which it encountered. On a case by case basis, in the tradition of the common law, the tripartite body forged a set of rules for industrial government. These may be summarized under the following five headings:

[24] *Termination Report of the N.W.L.B.* (Washington, D.C.: Government Printing Office, n.d.), p. xv.

1. *Union security.* The board majority was unwilling to accede to union pressures for the closed, union, or preferential shop where it did not already exist because this would have meant imposing unionism on nonmembers against their free choice. On the other hand, it recognized the validity of the union argument that it must be assured a measure of security beyond the status of exclusive bargaining representative under the National Labor Relations Act in order to fulfill its contractual responsibilities. This was all the more necessary because of the no-strike pledge. The answer which the board finally worked out as a compromise was the maintenance of membership clause that required union members to maintain their membership for the duration of an agreement, provided that they did not exercise their option to withdraw from the union during a fifteen-day escape period at the outset of the new agreement term. After the war many unions were able to convert their maintenance of membership clauses to union or agency shops, but the board's rule gave enduring support to the idea that responsible unions were entitled to union security.

The only basis for refusing to award maintenance of membership was evidence of some form of union irresponsibility. In an interesting decision, the board stated:

> There is a clear concensus of opinion in the Board that the maintenance of membership, with all its values, will not be granted to an irresponsible union which disregards the no-strike policy of the nation, or to a union which refuses to have reasonably frequent elections, or to a union which refuses to make reasonably regular financial reports to the members of the union. The War Labor Board, in standing for a few simple fundamentals of responsible democracy, will not sanction, on its own part or the part of management, any attempt to write the constitution and by-laws of the union, or to interfere in the responsible self-government of the union.[25]

[25] *Humble Oil and Refining Co. Case No.* 111–1819–0 (April 1, 1944).

2. *Grievance procedure.* Perhaps the greatest contribution of the board to industrial government was in the area of grievance handling. The necessity of providing employees effective due process when they had individual or group complaints during the lifetime of a contract had, of course, been recognized for many decades. The board subjected the grievance process to a thoroughgoing analysis and made the parties aware of the profound importance of clear, timely, and effective procedures. Beyond that it gave unqualified support to the idea of binding arbitration as the final step in the grievance handling process, extending it to numerous industries where it had been previously rejected.

In mid-1943, the board issued a policy statement in which it said:

The experience of the National War Labor Board in the administration of the no-strike no-lockout agreement has shown conclusively that proper grievance procedures under collective-bargaining agreements have:

1. Prevented abuse of the no-strike no-lockout agreement.

2. Removed obstacles to high morale and maximum production.

3. Preserved collective bargaining as a basic democratic institution in the total war effort.

These fundamental American values and aids to the successful prosecution of the war can be attained by grievance procedures which provide:

1. That prompt initial attention be given to the grievance by those in the plant who have intimate knowledge of the dispute. The exact steps and procedures for such attention to grievances must be adapted to the needs of the plant and can be best worked out by the parties themselves.

2. That the grievance procedure, whatever be its adaptation to the needs of the plant, should provide for the final and binding settlement of all grievances not otherwise resolved. For this purpose, provision should be made for the settlement of grievances

by an arbitrator, impartial chairman or umpire under terms and conditions agreed to by the parties.[26]

In its numerous decisions on grievance issues, the board helped to clarify the definition of a grievance, widening its scope to all complaints arising over the interpretation and application of the agreement; suggested ways of improving the structure of grievance procedures; prescribed, in conjunction with the NLRB and the courts, the conditions under which an individual might present and settle grievances apart from the union; discouraged the establishment of grievance procedures for minority unions; encouraged the use of time limits; distinguished the conditions under which grievances should be written or oral; considered the problems of the number of union grievance-men and payment to them for time spent in handling grievances; clarified the provisions for the investigation of grievances by union representatives; and provided guidelines for a number of problems relating to the arbitration stage, such as the scope of arbitration grievances, the use of permanent versus ad hoc arbitration, and the selection of arbitrators. Out of these wartime experiences emerged the distinctive American system of grievance settlement.

3. *Fringe benefits.* Although the concept of a wage freeze was never adopted, the War Labor Board did impose rather tight controls over wage increases under directives from the President, the Director of Economic Stabilization, and the Congress. Inevitably, considering the underlying inflationary forces in the economy, labor exerted strong pressures against the controls. One of the "safety valve" devices used by the board to contain these pressures was to approve (in voluntary cases) or award (in dispute cases) supplementary wage increases or so-called "fringe benefits" in lieu of basic wage increases. Although

[26] *Termination Report of the N.W.L.B.,* pp. 65–66.

these fringe benefits were cost items, their impact on prices was often less direct and immediate and they were generally viewed as less inflationary.

The board did not introduce new fringe benefits into industrial government. Paid vacations, paid holidays, shift differentials, Christmas and other nonproduction bonuses, sick leave, insurance plans, severance pay, paid meal periods, paid rest periods—these and other fringes had existed in industry previously, both under collective bargaining and individual employee relations. Board policies and wartime conditions led to a vast extension of such benefits. Gradually also the benefits were permitted to be enlarged. For example, initially, a one-week vacation after one year of service was allowed. Subsequently the standard policy became one week for one year and two weeks for five years of service. Likewise for shift differentials, the stabilizing limits of four cents per hour for the second shift and eight cents for the third shift on noncontinuous operations and four and six cents on continuous operations were gradually developed. Similar patterns evolved with respect to other benefits. By the end of the war the concept of fringe benefits was firmly established in industry.

4. *Wage structure.* The wage stabilization program (which involved nearly 440,000 applications for voluntary wage or salary adjustments) gave students as well as practitioners unprecedented information and understanding about the wage structures of American industry. For the first time the highly personal and essentially irrational character of many segments of the wage system began to be appreciated. The labor market in action was more often than not a far cry from the labor market in the economics textbook. Concern over rationalizing wage structures did not originate with the board. The pioneers in this respect had been the industrial engineers of the scientific management movement. But the board gave a great impetus to the

systematic rationalization of wage structures by its requirements that employers (and unions) justify any effort to correct so-called intraplant inequities. The board favored the correction of gross intraplant inequities by means of job evaluation. It gave a major boost to the old concept of equal pay for equal work. Most important of all, for the long-run, it made managers and union officials aware of the benefits to be derived from a wage structure which was based on some set of rational principles and which attempted to minimize the role of arbitrary personal judgment.

5. *Contracts and retroactivity.* Finally the board contributed to industrial government by strengthening the written contractual system and by applying the principle of retroactivity to new wage and fringe agreements. Again this was not a matter of innovation. The written agreement had a lengthy history and the National Labor Relations Board and the Supreme Court had made it a mandatory feature of collective bargaining. The idea of retroactivity had an equally long history. The War Labor Board elaborated and extended both practices. It was responsible for the shift from open-end to fixed-term contracts in the steel industry. It refused to modify the terms of unexpired contracts. It continuously stressed the sanctity of the contract in labor relations. It emphasized the value of retroactivity as an instrument for promoting peaceful wage negotiations while recognizing its limitations under certain conditions.

WAR PRODUCTION BOARD

The great concern over maximizing productivity and maintaining employee morale at a high level led to the initiation of the War Production Drive in March 1942 which encouraged employers and unions to set up joint management-labor production committees. The aim of these committees was to promote greater efficiency through consultation on absenteeism, health and safety, waste reduction, transportation, training, and other personnel matters. A leading student of the subject estimates that about 5000 committees were set up in plants employing some 7 million workers.[27] Not more than 3000 appear to have functioned at any one time and the level of performance ranged widely from a single patriotic rally to a quite elaborate continuing program. According to de Schweinitz, only a few hundred contributed significantly to improved productivity.

The successful cases achieved, among others, the following results:

1. They extended experience in union-management cooperation to a variety of industries—well beyond the boundaries of the earlier examples on the railroads, in the needle trades, and in a few other industries.

2. They increased output and improved quality in both large and small organizations which were already reasonably efficient.

3. They demonstrated that run-of-the-mill managers and union officers could cooperate on plant problems and the work did not depend on outstanding progressive leadership.

4. They showed that rank-and-file workers, machine operators, and others—not just skilled mechanics—have ideas to contribute.

5. As a result of separating production and bargaining functions they featured labor as a producer and operator, not only as a guardian of working conditions.[28]

Relatively few of the joint production committees continued long into the postwar period. Nevertheless, they helped to perpetuate a thin strand of American labor relations experience which, despite ups and downs, continues to suggest a model of industrial democracy with more elaborate dimensions than the typical collective bargaining case.

[27] Dorothea de Schweinitz, *Labor and Management in a Common Enterprise* (Cambridge: Harvard University Press, 1949), p. 19.
[28] See Ibid., pp. 154–155.

FAIR EMPLOYMENT PRACTICES

A much more powerful influence on the future was to be exercised by developments in the field of race relations within industry. Between 1940 and 1944 over one million Negroes moved from the farm to the factory. The war, in the words of Robert Weaver, gave many Negroes "their first opportunity to demonstrate ability to perform basic factory operations of skilled, single-skilled, and semi-skilled types in a wide range of industries and plants. It also permitted some Negroes to work alongside white workers in many individual establishments on the basis of industrial equality."[29] Training for these new jobs came from a number of sources, including the National Youth Administration and Civilian Conservation Corps of the thirties. But the discriminatory barriers did not begin to bend significantly until after 1942 when serious wartime labor shortages emerged and pressures from black groups and their white supporters reached unprecedented proportions.

The need for explicit executive and legislative policies against discrimination in employment and training became clear to the interested black and white groups as early as 1940. In August of that year the Office of Education, which was responsible for much of the defense training, was obliged, under pressure, to announce that "in the expenditure of Federal funds for vocational training for defense there should be no discrimination on account of race, creed or color."[30] The act appropriating funds for defense training in 1941 reaffirmed this policy although it also accepted the Southern pattern of segregated schools. Neither policy statement had much practical impact. Early in 1941 a group of Negro leaders, headed by A. Philip Randolph, threatened to hold a march of thousands of black people on Washing-

[29] Robert C. Weaver, *Negro Labor: A National Problem* (New York: Harcourt, Brace, 1946), pp. 78–79.
[30] Ibid., p. 57.

ton in order to dramatize the job discrimination situation of war industry. The threat seriously disturbed the Roosevelt Administration, and the march was not called off until the President met with the Negro leaders and agreed to issue an Executive Order (8802 of June 25, 1941) forbidding discrimination by employers and labor organizations in defense industries on the basis of race, creed, color, or national origin; ordering all federal departments and agencies concerned with vocational and training programs for defense production to administer such programs without discrimination; and providing that all defense contracts negotiated thereafter by contracting agencies of the federal government were to include a provision which obligated the contractor not to discriminate against any worker. The Executive Order was to be administered by a five-member committee on Fair Employment Practice within the Office of Production Management.

The history of the first FEPC and its reorganized successor, the second FEPC (Executive Order 9346 of May 27, 1943), has been traced in great detail in a number of works and need not be recapitulated here.[31] Although the two committees encountered bitter opposition (especially from Southern congressmen), had limited powers, and operated on inadequate budgets, they had far-ranging consequences. Within government, they served as continuing gadflies and, together with the War Manpower Commission and the military agencies, greatly improved the opportunities for black employees. In private industry the publicity which they gave to discriminatory practices and the corrective pressures which they were able to exert weakened barriers to the employment and advancement of Negroes. While discrimination continued on a wide scale, it was, for the first time, placed on the defensive. The federal FEPC failed to survive

---

[31] See, for example, Louis C. Kesselman, *The Social Politics of FEPC* (Chapel Hill: University of North Carolina Press, 1948) and Louis Ruchames, *Race, Jobs, and Politics* (New York: Columbia University Press, 1953).

the end of the war, but it left a legacy with great vitality. Within four years, eight states adopted FEPC laws with commissions to enforce them and twenty-eight cities adopted local ordinances. Weak as most of these laws were, they symbolized a new stage of industrial democracy as far as race relations were concerned.

Management Responses

The war enhanced the roles of both government and organized labor, but, strangely enough, this did not occur at the expense of management. On the contrary, management regained a good deal of the status and self-confidence which it had lost in the Great Depression and which it had failed to recover in the ensuing years. Management's prime interest was in the production sector and here, as has already been indicated, it succeeded in preventing the unionists from achieving the major role which they desired. As the war moved on, management representatives increasingly dominated the War Production Board and labor influence progressively declined. There is general agreement that the production job was brilliantly performed and management climbed appreciably in public esteem.

In the labor relations sector, management technically shared an equal role with organized labor and the public representatives on the War Labor Board. However, they tended to be on the minority side more often than the other two.[32] This is attributable in large measure to the trend of the times—the nation had accepted the new collective-bargaining model of industrial government and the board's decisions were based on it, rein-

[32] I draw on my personal observations and experiences for this analysis, having served in a research capacity with the board for three years and then having edited its Termination Report.

forcing the main features and filling in gaps. In addition, the management representatives as a whole failed to come up to the level of the labor and public representatives. The public representatives (e.g. William Davis, George Taylor, Lloyd Garrison, Wayne Morse) included most of the ablest labor relations experts in the country and their younger aides and staff members (e.g. W. Willard Wirtz, Theodore Kheel, John Dunlop, Clark Kerr) were to become their successors in the postwar years. The labor team included top-level officials and was strongly staffed. The management team, despite some outstanding members, was regarded as B-level and the staffing was comparatively weak.

During the war many management leaders gradually abandoned their long struggle against the collective-bargaining model and decided to accommodate to it—at least partly to better shape it more to their liking. They realized that resistance would be futile in the light of public attitudes and the distribution of political and economic power. But they also began to perceive, out of the intimate contact with the labor leaders and the educational experience of wartime relations, that most American unionists shared the same underlying values about the capitalist system and were reasonable and responsible men. Finally they saw that collective bargaining had advantages in terms of achieving industrial peace and stability which they had not earlier perceived. If they could maintain what they regarded as fundamental managerial prerogatives, they were willing to discard much of their earlier prejudice about dealing with unions.

These new attitudes were reflected in statements of the Chamber of Commerce and its enlightened president, Eric Johnston. In 1943 Johnston noted that unless managers accepted labor as an integral part of business and developed a system of self-government, the federal government would "rightly or wrongly . . . continue to inject itself into business, and into the affairs of labor."[33] In 1944 the Chamber, which had paid much less attention to the labor sector than the National Association of Manufacturers, set up its first Committee on Labor Relations. In early 1945 Johnston, speaking as Chamber president, proposed a "Charter for Industrial Peace" which was signed by William Green for the AFL and Philip Murray for the CIO but not by the president of the National Association of Manufacturers. The Charter[34] contained the following seven points:

1. Increased prosperity for all involves the highest degree of production and employment at wages assuring a steadily advancing standard of living. Improved productive efficiency and technological advancement must be constantly encouraged.

2. The system of private competitive capitalism is the foundation of the nation's economy.

3. Management's inherent rights and responsibility to direct the operations of an enterprise shall be recognized and preserved, without unnecessary Government restriction.

4. The fundamental rights of labor to organize and to engage in collective bargaining with management shall be recognized and preserved, without any negative Government interference.

5. The independence and dignity of the individual and the enjoyment of his democratic rights are inherent in our free American society. The system must protect the individual against the hazards of unemployment, old age, and physical impairments beyond his control.

6. An expanding economy at home will be stimulated by a vastly increased foreign trade. Foreign aid to devastated or underdeveloped countries must be arranged. Freer trade must be encouraged.

[33] Eric Johnston, "Management-Labor Cooperation in Wartime and After," *Public Opinion Quarterly,* 7 (Fall 1943), 3:366.

[34] Reproduced in Ludwig Teller, *A Labor Policy for America: A National Labor Code* (New York: Baker, Voorhis, & Co., 1945), pp. 309–310.

7. An enduring peace must be secured through the establishment of the United Nations.

The importance of this "Charter" lay in its humanistic and cooperative tone, its endorsement of full collective bargaining, and its "full employment" theme. In an explanatory article, Johnston said "It is good business to have good industrial relations."[35]

However, the NAM, which had for so long opposed unionism and collective bargaining, found it more difficult to change attitudes. While conceding the rights of workers to form unions and to engage in collective bargaining, it aggressively emphasized the rights of non-union employees, attacked the one-sided character of the Wagner Act, and insisted that management prerogatives must not be weakened. It was not yet ready to talk in terms of a working partnership with organized labor.

Although the point is difficult to document, it seems reasonable to suggest that in 1945 the NAM's approach to labor relations was somewhat to the right of many, if not most, of its larger corporate members whereas the Chamber's approach was somewhat to the left of most of its membership. These positions were to converge in the following decade.

President Truman's National Labor-Management Conference

The impact of the New Deal and the wartime experience on industrial democracy was effectively summarized in the Labor-Management Conference which President Truman convened on November 5, 1945, to lay the basis for a harmonious postwar era. Such a conference had been suggested in a letter to Labor Secretary Schwellenbach on July 30 by the influential Republi-

[35] "A Charter for Industrial Peace," *New York Times Magazine,* May 27, 1945, pp. 12, 37–38.

can Senator from Michigan, Arthur H. Vandenberg, who saw in the United Nations meeting at San Francisco a model for establishing peace at home. Vandenberg wrote:

> Responsible management knows that free collective bargaining is here to stay and that progressive law must continue to support it and that it must be wholeheartedly accepted. Responsible labor leadership knows that irresponsible strikes and subversive attacks upon essential production are the gravest threats to the permanent success of labor's bill of rights. The American public knows that we cannot rebuild and maintain our national economy at the high levels required by our unavoidable necessities if we cannot have productive peace instead of disruptive war on the industrial front.[36]

The idea of the conference had already been discussed within the administration. It had a precedent, although not a happy one, in President Wilson's conferences after World War I. Many of the mistakes of the earlier conferences were recognized and avoided.

The conference was prepared by a committee composed of representatives of the Chamber of Commerce, NAM, AFL, CIO, and the secretaries of labor and commerce. The delegates to the conference included, in addition to delegates selected by the four national organizations, representatives from the now independent United Mine Workers and the railroad Brotherhoods, and three public representatives—the secretaries of labor and commerce and Walter P. Stacy, chief justice of the supreme court of North Carolina, who served as conference chairman. George Taylor, a War Labor Board chairman, served as conference secretary. The representation for organized labor and industry was of the highest order.

In the message which he personally delivered to the conference, President Truman observed that the country was worried,

[36] Quoted in Division of Labor Standards, *The President's National Labor-Management Conference, November 5–30, 1945: Summary and Committee Reports,* Bulletin No. 77 (Washington, D.C.: Department of Labor, 1946), p. 29.

and justifiably so, about the state of industrial relations. Some difficulties in adjusting from war to peace had been expected, but not the amount of strife which had been threatened. Without industrial peace it would not be possible to achieve the goal of full employment and to raise the standard of living. Of the many considerations involved, the basic one is "not only the right, but the duty, to bargain collectively." If bargaining fails, there must be a willingness to use some impartial machinery for reaching decisions on the basis of proven facts and realities. It is equally essential to insure industrial peace during the lifetime of contracts—"there must be responsibility and integrity on both sides in carrying them out." Some substitute must be found for jurisdictional strikes, which are destructive of public confidence in unions. In turn, management must stop looking at labor "as a stepchild of its business, to be disregarded until the controversy has reached a point where real collective bargaining becomes very difficult—if not impossible."[37]

The agreements and disagreements recorded in the conference revealed the progress which had been made and the sources of conflict which remained. The main items of agreement were as follows:

1. All elements of labor and management were urged to adopt "the broad democratic spirit of tolerance and equality of economic opportunity in respect to race, sex, color, religion, age, national origin, or ancestry in determining who are employed and who are admitted to labor union membership.

2. Collective bargaining should be undertaken in good faith, looking forward to a signed agreement covering a defined period of time.

3. In the event of a failure to reach agreement, resort should be had to conciliation and then, if the parties agreed, to voluntary arbitration. Compulsory arbitration was rejected.

[37] See Division of Labor Standards, Bulletin No. 77, pp. 37–40.

4. Collective-bargaining agreements should contain effective grievance procedures, with arbitration as the final step, to resolve disputes involving the interpretation or application of the terms of an agreement, without resort to strikes, lock-outs, or any other interruption of normal operations. As guides to effective grievance procedure, some twenty elements were listed, including the use of time limits, the reduction to writing of the position of both sides if the initial informal discussions failed, and priority handling of grievances involving discharge, suspension, or other disciplinary action.

5. The Federal Conciliation Service should be strengthened and improved—in respect to its staff and resources, its arbitration service which should be kept separate from the conciliation service, and its technical services.

The items on which the parties in the conference failed to reach agreement related to three main subjects:

1. *The meaning of responsible and good faith bargaining and compliance with agreements.* The employers insisted on including a statement that bargaining was impossible "under conditions of force regardless of its source or nature." They also argued that each contract should provide for guarantees for compliance and that unions as well as employers should be subject to judicial proceedings for conduct in violation of contracts or legal requirements. The union delegates rejected these views.

2. *Management's right to manage.* The crux of this very complex issue was management's belief that labor must agree that certain specific functions and responsibilities of management are not proper subjects of collective bargaining and that failure to agree on such a listing implied that labor saw no end to its expansion into the field of management, with joint management as the only possible end. The union representatives agreed that "the functions and responsibilities of management must be preserved if business and industry is to be efficient, progressive,

and provide more good jobs." But they contended that the management list included some items which were already in the bargaining domain. More importantly, they argued that the "wide variety of traditions, customs, and practices that have grown out of relationships between unions and management in various industries over a long period of time" made it unwise to specify and classify the functions and responsibilities of management. This was a dynamic subject in which changes were inevitable. To erect fences around the management and the union would restrict flexibility and promote conflict. On a closely related topic, management wished to prohibit the unionization of foremen while the unionists preferred to leave the matter to the National Labor Relations Board where the issue was pending.

3. *Representation and jurisdictional questions.* The management side wanted to change the provisions of the Wagner Act in several respects—to make it possible for employers to question a union's majority status at the termination of any collective-bargaining contract, to make strikes and other forms of economic pressure illegal pending the determination of representation questions or in opposition to a determination of representation, and to restrict the ability of the NLRB to establish bargaining units wider than a single establishment unless all parties agreed or there was prior collective bargaining practice. The management group also wanted the NLRB to have authority over all jurisdictional disputes, including those between two unions belonging to the same federation. The union representatives at the conference objected to all of these points.

It is clear from the preceding summary that management had accepted the basic principles of collective bargaining but that it had moved from a defensive to an aggressive posture as to its format. The consequences of this shift were soon to be reflected in law.

CHAPTER 14

AN ASSESSMENT
AS OF 1945

PRESIDENT TRUMAN'S POSTWAR CONFERENCE revealed the progress in industrial democracy which had occurred in the dozen years between 1933 and 1945. At the start of the period most of the nation's major employers were still unwilling to accept collective bargaining with nationally affiliated unions. The employee-representation model of industrial government was a serious challenger to the trade-union model. By 1945 collective bargaining with trade unions was the established form of industrial government. The central issue of controversy was the scope of bargaining and the extent of union participation in the decision-making process. Management rights had replaced the more elementary question of worker representation.

The explanation for this shift in focus appears to be quite clear. The failure of business leadership in the Great Depression destroyed worker and public confidence in the employer approach to industrial democracy. The New Deal gave union-minded workers their first sustained political and legal encouragement to organize for bargaining purposes. The formation of the CIO provided a mechanism through which workers in mass-production industries could organize in a manner consonant with the technological, economic, and power attributes of the

400

enterprise. The reversal in Supreme Court policy on the meaning of interstate commerce under the Constitution removed one of the main barriers to labor organization and collective bargaining. A sympathetic public opinion and a favorable governmental program provided the necessary environment for the triumph of the trade-union model. The economic environment of the thirties, however, was not conducive to union organization. That the latter occurred on such a vast scale underlines the strength of the positive forces.

During the war, public attitudes toward unionism became relatively less favorable and attitudes toward the employers improved. But the governmental policy favoring and elaborating the trade-union model was still very positive, and it was strongly reinforced by the shift in economic conditions. As the World War I experience indicated, wartime economic conditions, including demands for labor exceeding the available supply, greatly enhance the bargaining power of unions and increase their attractiveness to potential members. Moreover employers are less inclined to resist organization, and added costs can normally be passed on to either the government or the private consumers. These forces were intensified during World War II, which was much longer than the earlier conflict and entailed a much more complete commitment of the nation's resources. Hence it is not surprising that the unions substantially increased their share of industrial sovereignty, worker participation in decision-making grew, and, notwithstanding the imposition of widespread government controls, industrial democracy was appreciably furthered.

Representation

Between 1933 and 1945 trade-union membership rose from about 2.8 million to slightly over 12 million. Even if allowance is made for the coverage of employee-representation plans in the earlier year, the increase was at least threefold. The ratio of union members to the civilian labor force went from about 5.4 to 22.4; the ratio of union members to nonfarm employees went from 11.8 to 29.9.

In 1933 the bulk of union strength was confined to the construction trades, coal mining, printing, the needle trades, and railroads. By 1945 union strength was not only much greater in these industries but had extended to most of the major manufacturing enterprises which had previously had no employee organization or only some form of company unionism. Union breakthroughs were not confined to manufacturing. Important gains were made in most branches of transportation and communication and some gains were made in trade and government. Leo Wolman has estimated that between 1930 and 1947 the percentage of nonfarm wage and salaried employees who were unionized rose from 8.8 to 41.9 for manufacturing; 23.4 to 64.2 for transportation, communication, and public utilities; 54.3 to 74.6 for building; 21.3 to 84.0 for mining, quarrying, and oil; 2.7 to 8.8 for services; and 8.3 to 11.9 for public service.[1]

The idea of shared sovereignty in industry through union representation became the law of the land during this period—as reflected in the passage of the National Labor Relations Act and in the decisions of the U.S. Supreme Court. The statistics cited above show that public policy and industrial practice were in reasonably close correspondence. There was, however, a marked discrepancy in other sectors of the economy, such as government, trade, or agriculture.

During the three years 1933–1935, the principle of majority rule for selecting union representatives was hammered out. This was a major innovation in industrial government. For the unions it meant the abandonment of their long-treasured concept of

[1] Industrial Relations Research Association, *Proceedings of Fifth Annual Meeting* (1952), p. 216.

voluntarism, that the nature of union representation and bargaining should be determined exclusively through union strength and action. For reluctant employers it provided a guideline on which union recognition could be based. Now both unions and employers were obliged to subject their differences over representation to a government agency, the National Labor Relations Board.

Majority rule had a number of other profound implications. It carried with it the idea of exclusive representation rights—that only the majority union could speak on behalf of the employees. The notion of proportional representation, which was briefly debated in 1934, was rejected. Minority unions were given no legal standing. Indeed it was made quite difficult for a minority rival union to become the majority representative since the main route open was to demonstrate to the board that it spoke for a substantial number of workers (normally 30 per cent of the total work-group) and that a secret-ballot election should be held to determine the will of the majority. Such a request normally could not be made more than once a year.

Majority rule also entailed the idea of an appropriate bargaining unit. The consequence of this corollary was that the structure of industrial government, as well as the designation of the employees' collective representative, was to be determined by the Labor Board. This function was particularly important in the cases of a conflict between a craft union and an industrial union and in a union-employer dispute over the coverage of a unit—whether it was to be a single enterprise, several or many enterprises belonging to the same employer, or the enterprises of many different employers.

The new principle raised the further question of whether special categories of employees should be included in the bargaining unit. In short, who were to be the citizens of the particular industrial community? The main group affected was the supervisors. Were they part of management, were they a separate group which should form their own organization, or should they be represented by a union composed mainly of employees under them? In some of the earlier craft unions—building, printing, and maritime, for example—the tradition had been to include the first-line and sometimes higher-level supervisors. The Labor Board did not attempt to disrupt these old relationships, but in new situations it tended to exclude supervisors from the bargaining unit. The question of separate unionism for supervisors was more troublesome and was not resolved until after 1945.

Finally, majority rule had an impact on the individual non-union employee. He was permitted by the law to pursue his own grievances. But if the grievance related in any way to the collective-bargaining agreement negotiated by the majority union, the company was obliged to inform and consult with the union so that the interests of the majority would not be adversely affected.

Participation

As the 1945 Labor-Management Conference demonstrated, once the basic issues of recognition had been resolved, the major subject of controversy was over managerial rights and the scope and depth of union involvement in management decision-making. In the older systems of industrial government, such as in construction, mining, railroads, printing, and garments, the already extensive patterns of participation did not change appreciably. In some cases, such as ladies garments, participation was extended somewhat. For example, the union expanded the work of its engineering department and carried on a nationwide publicity campaign for the sale of the industry's products. But, as Robinson concluded in 1949, the union had no desire to assume the major employer functions. In this industry of numerous small, highly competitive firms, "labor's interests are certain to bear more closely on the state of the industry as a whole rather than upon the direction of the individual firm."[2]

Among the newly established systems of industrial government, only a small number placed stress on union and worker participation beyond the conventional bargaining over wages, hours and working conditions, and the settlement of grievances. One of the outstanding examples was the TVA system of joint labor-management committees which developed after 1940. Some of the more successful wartime joint-production committees, combined with regular collective-bargaining arrangements, had a similar impact.

But in most of the mass-production industries, the struggle over participation was focused on issues which had previously been resolved in older systems. The issues came before the National Labor Relations Board under the heading of "refusing to bargain in good faith." The major issues inevitably were appealed to the Supreme Court. The outcome of this process was a gradual widening of the concept of participation, from both a procedural and substantive standpoint. Thus it was ruled that bargaining in good faith required that all agreements should be reduced to writing if requested by the union. Unilateral posting of the terms of an agreement by the company was not permissible; the union had to receive credit by a jointly signed document. Bargaining did not require the employer to make concessions or to accede to union demands. Management, however, did have to confer in reasonable fashion, make offers and counter-offers, and discuss "with an open and fair mind, and a sincere purpose to find a basis of agreement."[3] As to substantive issues, the board on a case by case basis made clear which ones

[2] Dwight Edwards Robinson, *Collective Bargaining and Market Control in the New York Coat and Suit Industry* (New York: Columbia University Press, 1949), p. 218.

[3] This assessment of board policy is based mainly on Harry A. Millis and Emily Clark Brown, *From the Wagner Act to Taft-Hartley* (Chicago: University of Chicago Press, 1950) especially pp. 112ff.

fell within the scope of bargaining—for example, holidays and vacations and merit increases. Insurance and pension plans were among the issues under study by the board at the end of the war. Essentially the board agreed with the position of the union spokesmen at the Truman postwar conference: "The appropriate scope of collective bargaining cannot be defined in a phrase; it depends upon the industry's custom and history, the previously existing employer-employee relationship, technological problems and demands, and other factors. It may vary with changes in industrial structure and practice." The NLRB, like the War Labor Board, tended to take a cautious and gradualist approach, following advanced practice rather than trying to pioneer.

The most important development in terms of participation in decision-making did not apply to the role of the union but rather to the role of the federal government. During the New Deal period—and this was, of course, reinforced during the war—the role of government in the establishment and administration of industrial democracy was significantly advanced. The great labor laws of the thirties—the Wagner Act, the Social Security Act, and the Fair Labor Standards Act—indicated that the government had accepted two new functions in the labor field. One was to assure a peaceful introduction of collective bargaining by specifying the rights of workers to organize and bargain collectively, the duties of employers in relation to these rights, and the machinery for the orderly determination of representation issues. For the most part, under the Wagner Act, the government role was confined to determining the rules of the game rather than the substantive results. Under the other two acts, however, the government undertook a second basic function—the establishment of minimum standards of employment. These standards applied most notably to the wage level, the basic workweek and the payment of premium wages for overtime, child labor, industrial home work, unemployment compensation, and retirement. Thus the government had become a good deal more than a keeper of the peace and the protector of certain "weak and defenseless" groups of employees, namely women and children.

Equal Rights and Opportunities

This was a period in which the equal-rights principle made some progress. Perhaps the greatest beneficiaries were the immigrants from non-English-speaking countries. Many of the workers in the mass-production industries fell in this category and when they became unionized, discrimination by foremen unquestionably declined. Union concepts of standardized work rules, strict seniority provisions, and an effective grievance procedure contributed. So did the War Labor Board's encouragement of arbitration as the last stage of the grievance machinery. The position of the immigrant in industry improved also because of the sharp decline in the volume of immigration. During the twenties, when the new immigration laws had not yet taken full effect, immigration totaled over 4 million. But the combination of the legal barriers and the depression reduced immigration in the thirties to only 500,000. Thus the Americanization process was able to proceed at a more rapid pace.

During the depression years, discrimination against women intensified rather than improved. Married women in particular were often subjected to discriminatory hiring rules so as to provide more job opportunities for men. When the war reversed the condition of the labor market, the position of the woman worker also improved. As in World War I, the War Labor Board reaffirmed the policy of equal pay for equal work and women occupied many jobs which previously had been filled by men.

The equal-pay principle began to be incorporated in collective-bargaining contracts, thus supplying a basis for a more enduring policy than in the past.

The Negro worker in the thirties was at the bottom of the industrial ladder. If he had employment, it was generally in the most menial and least desirable jobs. The one bright note for Negro workers who held jobs in the mass-production industries was the antidiscrimination policy of the leaders of the CIO unions. Several of the main CIO organizations actively sought to recruit black workers as members and, especially in the North, gave them a sense of participation which they had not previously had. But their seniority levels were low and their opportunities for advancement limited.

The war, as in the case of women, greatly enhanced the opportunities for Negro workers and drew large numbers of blacks from the rural South to jobs in the industrial areas. The new situation, for the first time, gave the Negro leadership a measure of bargaining power to break down discriminatory barriers. The threat of a massive march on Washington produced the Fair Employment Practices Committee. FEPC represented the first important effort by the federal government to eliminate industrial discrimination against blacks. Concurrently the new collective-bargaining agreements, negotiated especially by the CIO unions but also by some of the AFL internationals, contained antidiscrimination provisions which improved the Negro position. But it was only a start. The Negro was far from a full industrial citizen in 1945.

Right of Dissent

The issue of right of dissent or, more broadly, freedom of speech, followed contradictory paths during the New Deal era. From the standpoint of worker freedom in relation to management, there was a major advance. The growth in union organization, the regulations of the Wagner Act on employer unfair practices, and the findings of the La Follette subcommittee were responsible for a vast extension of freedom of speech within industry. For the first time in American history, it seems safe to conclude, the bulk of industrial workers could openly criticize their employers and publicly dissent from employer policies without fear of being disciplined or fired.

From the standpoint of worker expression within their unions, the picture was more mixed.[4] Autocratic rule by some union leaders has had a rather long history. Sometimes the reason has been corrupt leadership; sometimes it has been a factional struggle for power, with the in-group trying to stave off its opposition; sometimes it has been a response to insecurity in a hostile environment and concern for the survival of the union organization. As the national union grew in strength and size, another element was added—the centralization of authority and the shift in power from the local union to the national leadership. This phenomenon had attracted attention by the early twenties; it became a matter of considerable concern by the early forties. This concern was reflected in a number of writings by men and organizations sympathetic to unionism.[5] As Seidman noted, "Real and formidable obstacles must be overcome, moreover, if unions are to be run in a democratic fashion, for some national unions include more than half a million members, and some local unions, as in the automobile industry in Michigan,

[4] As Selig Perlman had written in 1928, frequently workers were willing to resign themselves to "boss control" in their union for the sake of liberty in the shop. See Perlman, *A Theory of the Labor Movement* (New York: Macmillan Co., 1928), p. 275.

[5] See, for example, Will Herberg, "Democracy in Labor Unions," *Antioch Review*, 3 (Fall 1943), 3:405–417; Joel Seidman, *Union Rights and Union Duties* (New York: Harcourt, Brace, 1943); American Civil Liberties Union, *Democracy in Trade Unions* (New York: ACLU, November 1943).

embrace tens of thousands of members. A political science of the labor movement is needed to study its structure and appraise various devices in the light of democracy and efficiency."[6]

The split in the labor movement seems to have had a dual impact on the right of minority groups to dissent. On the one hand, the availability of rival organizations gave workers the possibility of shifting membership if they were dissatisfied with the way a union was run. On the other hand, where inter-union rivalry existed, union leaders were inclined to be less tolerant of dissenters whom they often regarded as traitors to their cause.

Labor Secretary Perkins and Senator Wagner in the thirties and Frank Graham and other NWLB members in the forties had suggested the desirability of developing a code of ethical behavior for unions in return for the benefits and protections which the government was providing organized labor. But nothing significant came from their suggestions at that time.

A wholly new freedom of speech issue arose in the thirties as a result of the passage of the Wagner Act and its prohibition of employer interference with the worker right to organize. In the early period of the act, as Millis and Brown have observed,[7] the board and the courts required the employer to maintain strict neutrality on the grounds that any indication of employer preference might have a coercive effect on the employees. Employer organizations and many congressmen strongly criticized these decisions as violative of the employer's constitutional right, and efforts were made to amend the act to guarantee employer free speech. In a major decision in 1941, in the *Virginia Electric and Power Company* case, the Supreme Court began to distinguish between employer words which were coercive and those which were not. The employer had the right to express views on labor matters to employees but the board had the obligation to judge

[6] Seidman, *Union Rights and Union Duties*, p. 22.
[7] Millis and Brown, *From the Wagner Act to Taft-Hartley*, p. 176ff.

whether words, like actions, interfered with the worker right to organize. Critics of the board continued to attack many of its decisions in this area.

Due Process

This was another aspect of industrial democracy in which major gains were made. As unionization advanced in the thirties, perhaps the central demand beyond recognition was the establishment of effective grievance machinery. Where employee-representation plans had functioned reasonably well, the procedures already in existence served as a useful foundation. But unionism involved the role of the international union representatives, in addition to the committmen and stewards in the shop, and these representatives tended to be much more skilled and sophisticated in grievance handling than the shop men. As a result, management found it necessary to improve its own organization for dealing with grievances.

The picture was often complicated where unionism had been opposed by the company and where grievances were often used as a harassment technique by the union to put pressure on hostile foremen as well as on higher management. Frequently the foremen became the frustrated "man in the middle" uncertain whether to seek friendly relations with his men or to follow a tough company policy. One of the consequences was that many employers found it necessary to shift responsibility for grievance administration from the line officials to the personnel office. The foreman who, until the twenties and even later, had been the source of authority in the shop now found himself relegated to an almost exclusively production role, pressured on the one side by the shop stewards and on the other by the personnel staff. This "crisis" for the foreman was a major factor in the strong drive among supervisors during the war to form their own union and was not to be resolved until some time after the war.

Grievance procedures and grievance administration reached a new level of maturity under the policies and decisions of the War Labor Board. The board not only recognized the importance of effective grievance handling for industrial government but also was concerned about its own work load—it did not want to be swamped by thousands of grievance disputes. Consequently it encouraged and directed the parties to establish sound procedures, and it was instrumental in the provision of binding arbitration as the final step in grievance settlement. Although, as earlier chapters have indicated, formal grievance machinery has evolved over a long period of time, the impact of the board in this area was perhaps its greatest and most enduring achievement. The board made another contribution of long-range significance in this regard. It provided the training ground for an entire generation of labor relations specialists, including the leading arbitrators of the next two decades.

Responsibility

During the hectic conflicts of the thirties, the concept of responsibility in industrial government took a back seat. As Seidman noted, the older unions, except for the racketeering or antisocial fringe, were seldom charged with lack of responsibility, although they were often criticized for "loose financial practices and undemocratic procedure."[8] Their leaders had many years of experience with collective bargaining, industrial economics, and labor agreements; they had learned how far they could push without severely jeopardizing employment in the industry or trade, and they had a long tradition of respecting the terms of an agreement. In the newly organized sectors of the

[8] Seidman, *Union Rights and Union Duties,* chapter 1.

economy, the situation was different. Even where the leadership was experienced, the expansion of organization was so vast and so rapid that these leaders were overwhelmed with their duties. Below them were a large number of young, ambitious, power-seeking, and aggressive men who often were impatient and as often lacked seasoned judgment and understanding. In the learning process, mistakes and misjudgments were common. Agreements were often violated, sitdowns and other forms of economic pressure were resorted to frequently. Such actions were, of course, encouraged by anti-union employer behavior and the reluctance of many employers to accept collective bargaining as an on-going process. As Cyrus Ching told many groups of fellow employers, a company gets the kind of labor relations which it deserves. And while this is only a partial truth, in common with many similar maxims, it had special relevance to the period under discussion. Aggression begot aggression; suspicion begot suspicion.

During the war, improvements in responsible behavior occurred. For one thing, the Supreme Court decision in the *Heinz* case made written collective-bargaining agreements a legal requirement. Whereas the initial agreements were often brief and general statements, with each new bargaining period they became more comprehensive and explicit compilations of working rules—matching the older contracts. The pledge of labor and management organizations to refrain from strikes and lockouts during the war had a stabilizing effect even though almost 4600 work stoppages occurred between January 1942 and August 1945. In comparison with World War I, and the thirties, the results were very favorable. Moreover with a few notable exceptions, the top union leaders made serious efforts to live up to the pledge, and most of the disputes were of short duration. The wartime experience contributed to more responsible union-management relations from another angle. During the nearly four years of intimate association on the board (in the regions as well as the Washington office), union and management representatives developed a mutual understanding and appreciation which almost certainly promoted responsible action on both sides.

Minimum Standards

As earlier indicated, the idea of creating a set of socially acceptable minimum standards for industry through government legislation and administrative agencies has a long history. The earliest concerns were with child labor and with the hours and work conditions of women. Later the safety conditions of men in particularly hazardous employments, such as mining, maritime, and railroads, were the subject of regulation; the AFL opposed most other types of legislation for adult males. Except for federal employees and certain branches of transportation, almost all of the protective legislation was enacted by the states. Most federal legislation was declared unconstitutional by the Supreme Court.

One of the major achievements of the New Deal was to make minimum standards for industrial employees a national policy. The Supreme Court yielded to Presidential and public pressure and reinterpreted the constitutional meaning of "interstate commerce" so as to embrace virtually all of manufacturing and large segments of the rest of the economy. The AFL reversed its tradition of voluntarism and supported, with increasing vigor, the principle of national minimum standards. The new CIO was a staunch supporter of the principle from the outset. And much of industry and business—especially the larger firms—gradually acquiesced with various degrees of enthusiasm or reluctance.

Minimum standards were set for wages, the basic workweek and the payment of premium overtime rates, child and adolescent labor, the working hours of women, unemployment insurance, retirement age and benefits, industrial accidents and illness, and industrial homework. A few major areas were left uncovered, of which the most important was probably protection against illness or accident not incurred on the job. One economic sector was exempted from practically all of the protections although its employees were perhaps the most needy— the farm workers.

In contrast to practice in many European countries, certain fringe benefits were not included in the legislative program but left to collective bargaining. In this category were paid vacations, paid holidays, and severance pay. These and other fringe benefits for the first time began to be embodied in collective-bargaining agreements on a significant scale in the late thirties. They were given an enormous boost by the War Labor Board as a safety valve for the wage-stabilization program. By 1945, the lines between the publicly protected items and the privately negotiated ones were becoming a subject for study.

Information

The traditional attitude of business and industry was to treat much of the information about production costs, earnings, and plans as confidential, partly out of fear that competitors might otherwise gain some advantage, partly out of the belief that the private-property owner had no obligation to publicize his financial affairs (beyond certain minimum legal requirements for corporations), not even to his employees. This attitude had been somewhat modified during the first quarter of the century as a result of the anti-monopoly attacks of the Progressives and the federal government's involvement in business during World War I. The growth of the public corporation at the expense of the unincorporated family enterprise also had some impact, as did the employee-representation plan movement with its emphasis on more information for employees in the twenties. Nevertheless the old approach clearly dominated.

During the 1933–1945 period, a major shift in attitude about industrial information occurred. Several factors were responsible. One was the revelation of financial irregularity in a number of highly respectable industries and firms, leading to public investigations and regulations of banks, the stock market, and utilities. The depression which drove many businesses to the wall and weakened many others required greater exposure of the private company's economic affairs. The National Industrial Recovery Act and other New Deal programs affecting business called for huge amounts of economic information. The work of academic and government statisticians on the basic concepts and applications of the gross national product and the labor force proved extremely useful as tools of analysis to business and encouraged business cooperation in providing the necessary input data.[9] The World War II experience, in which the government became concerned with virtually all of industry, made even further demands on the provision of information. Finally the growth of unionism and collective bargaining brought intensified pressure from the unions on management to give them information for more effective bargaining—a process encouraged by the NLRB in its gradually evolving conception of bargaining in good faith.

The sharing of information was extended rather quietly in many industries. It was dramatized in the General Motors dispute of late 1945 when Walter Reuther insisted to the Presidential Fact-Finding Commission that the company should "open its books" to the union so that the latter could verify its claim that the company had the resources not only to meet the union's economic demands but also to reduce the price of autos and still make a substantial profit. The company did not deny

[9] I am indebted to Professor Irving Bernstein for this idea which he conceives of as the "statistical revolution" of the thirties and forties.

its ability to pay (it opposed the union's demands on other grounds) and therefore contended that it had no obligation to permit the union to examine its records on costs and plans. The union was not successful in this "open the books" campaign; but it is clear that for practical as well as theoretical reasons, the degree of secrecy in corporate affairs had been greatly reduced.

Concomitant with the pressure to make more company information available, pressures also began to mount on the unions to provide a more adequate accounting of their finances. Apart from the minority of corrupted unions, whose leaders naturally preferred secrecy, many of the new unions in the thirties had kept membership and financial information secret on the grounds that they were still struggling for survival and the information might aid hostile employers. This argument became less persuasive in the forties as the unions grew in power and acceptability and, indeed, a number of the newer unions did begin to provide comprehensive financial statements to their general conventions.

Personal Dignity

Prolonged depression inevitably reduces the dignity of the individual; rising employment opportunities tend to enhance the sense of the worker's dignity. The successful struggle for unionization and the generally hopeful tone of the New Deal helped to offset, to some degree, the fact that unemployment remained a major problem throughout the thirties and job security was a major concern of those workers who were fortunate enough to have jobs. The situation, of course, changed remarkably after the outbreak of the European war and especially after Pearl Harbor. Full employment, strong unions, a sympathetic government all combined to elevate the position of the ordinary man in American society and industry. The change was not total.

Discrimination persisted—especially against black workers. Many workers, urban as well as rural, remained unorganized or only weakly organized. But the general trend was very favorable. It was perhaps confirmed by the relatively small reliance upon mandatory legislation in the labor market and in the government of industry.

Some Interpretive Conclusions

Industrial democracy had come a long way by 1945. As noted above, it was far from complete; but for the mass of industrial workers, whether newly organized or longtime members of revitalized unions, progress had occurred in almost every dimension of industrial government. Many sectors of the economy which had not adopted the trade-union model were, nonetheless, influenced by the latter's advance. Although some sectors continued to lag badly, levels of aspiration were rising everywhere and the autocratic employer was generally on the defensive.

This did not mean that the unions were in a dominant role. Wartime and immediate postwar strikes had aroused considerable public resentment and employers, through a brilliant performance in production, had regained much of the status lost during the 1929–1933 depression. Apart from strikes, abuses by some union leaders of the power which they had gained, as well as corrupt practices, had built up sentiments for imposing curbs on the unions.

Organizational success also created new problems which had significant implications for the future of industrial democracy. The country was now directed by three powerful institutional forces, popularly identified as Big Government, Big Business, and Big Labor. Bigness brought new degrees of bureaucratization. As the institutions worked out an accommodation, the individual within the institutions was confronted by the problem of retaining individual freedom within a collective setting. A new technology, stimulated by the war, posed threats to the existence of traditional industries and occupations as well as promise of a brave new world. The spector of a stagnating, if not declining, American society was replaced by the vision of an expansionist power with international perspectives and responsibilities.

THE GROWTH IN LEGALIZATION, 1945–1965

CHAPTER **15**

THE NEW ECONOMICS
AND THE RULE
OF LAW

MAJOR WARS invariably have powerful, if not revolutionary, effects on the course of a society, and World War II had
consequences for the United States matched only by the Civil
War and the War of Independence. These effects appeared over
the two decades which followed the war's end in 1945. Perhaps
the most significant developments, as far as industrial democracy was concerned, occurred in the areas of economic policy,
industrialization and technology, urbanization and education,
internationalization, and race relations. Each of these developments merits a brief comment as part of the changing environment of industrial government.

The Changing Environment

ECONOMIC POLICY

In the thirties, despite the buoyancy of Roosevelt's outlook,
many economists, other social scientists, and politicians adopted
the view that the growth of the American population and econ-

423

omy was largely over and that we were approaching a stable long-run plateau. The wartime production record destroyed this pessimism and replaced it with a new vision of unlimited growth through a full-employment economy. The federal government was seen as a prime force in the achievement of this economy. The Employment Act of 1946 symbolized the change in economic attitudes, although it did not go as far as its sponsors had hoped when they originally proposed a "full employment" bill. Essentially the act stated that it was the policy of the federal government to do everything possible "to promote maximum employment, production, and purchasing power"; it imposed upon the President the responsibility of reporting to the Congress each January on the state of the economy; and it established a Council of Economic Advisers to gather necessary data for the President and to recommend national economic policies to achieve the objectives of the act.[1] In each of the economic reports made by the President, beginning in 1947, the national commitment to a high-production, high-employment expanding economy was asserted. This commitment was a profound change from the policy of government in previous decades, including the New Deal period in which recovery efforts never came close to full employment.

As a result of the new economic policy as well as international economic and political circumstances, the two decades between 1945 and 1965 were years of tremendous economic growth. Gross national product, in 1958 dollars, rose from $355 billion to $609 billion. Employment of civilian labor rose from about 52.5 million to over 72 million.

The growth rate was not uniform and there were several periods of recession—in 1948–1949, 1953–1954, 1957–1958, and 1960–1961. Indeed during the second half of the fifties, much

[1] In the Manpower Development and Training Act of 1962, the President was also asked to transmit to the Congress an annual report by the secretary of labor on manpower requirements, resources, use, and training.

public discussion was devoted to the slackening of the growth rate (especially in comparison with other industrial countries) and to the fact that the level of unemployment was higher after each recovery from the three consecutive recessions. The ratio of unemployment to the civilian labor force was 3.1 in 1952, 4.2 in 1956, and 5.5 in 1959. The trend indicated by these statistics led the Senate to establish a Special Committee on Unemployment Problems in September 1959, and economists argued about whether the rising unemployment was primarily due to structural defects in the economy, resulting from technological change, or to an insufficiency of aggregate demand.

Nevertheless, the general economic tone was one of high expectations. Although the unemployment rate reached a high of 6.8 per cent (in 1958), this figure was well below the minimum level achieved during the 1930's. The fact that unemployment rates in excess of 5 per cent excited national attention and that 3.5 or 4 per cent was regarded a desirable target was a sign of the new economic outlook. In 1961 under President Kennedy, the nation began a recovery that was to last longer than any previous period in American economic history. In his first Economic Report, Kennedy stated: "As a declaration of national purpose and as a recognition of Federal responsibility, the (Employment) Act has few parallels in the Nation's history. In passing the Act by heavy bipartisan majorities, the Congress registered the consensus of the American people that this Nation will not countenance the suffering, frustration, and injustice of unemployment, or let the vast potential of the world's leading economy run to waste in idle manpower, silent machinery, and empty plants."[2]

INDUSTRIALIZATION AND TECHNOLOGY

The war demonstrated production potentials which relatively few people, even trained economists and business executives,

[2] *Economic Report of the President* (January 1962), p. 3.

had appreciated. It also gave a stimulus to the development of earlier scientific and technological ideas in such fields as electronics, aerospace, atomic energy, and chemistry. This stimulus was later reinforced by the competition from the Soviet Union symbolized by Sputnik in 1957. As a result, the postwar period saw the birth of a host of new industries which seemed to herald another industrial revolution. For example, commercial aviation which employed 22,000 persons in 1940 had 207,000 in 1965.[3] The manufacturers of aircraft increased their employment from about 50,000 in 1939 to 619,000 in 1965. The unmanned aerospace industry which was nonexistent before the war became a major governmental enterprise, with its nondefense potential only starting to be realized. The atomic energy field, equally new, employed over 133,000 in 1966.

In electronics, which overlapped some of the above industries, comparable developments and potentials were observed. The commercial television industry, which was still in the experimental stage before the war, was a major employer in 1965 at both the manufacturing and communications levels. The electronic computer industry, although in its infancy, made "automation" a household word and, in a number of fields, transformed production, office, and distributional patterns.

Developments of this type were possible only as a result of the expenditure of vast sums of money on organized research—in the universities, in government, and in private industry. Prior to the war the expenditure on such research was probably under a billion dollars—largely by a few major corporations in the petroleum, chemical, electrical, and communications industries. By 1965 it was estimated at over $20 billion.[4] The number of scientists and engineers in private industry alone was estimated at 890,000 in 1964; in 1940 the number was under 400,000.

While science and technology produced spectacular new in-

[3] *Statistical Abstract of the United States, 1967*, p. 586.
[4] Ibid., p. 537.

dustries, their impact was also felt in virtually every important older field—steel production, auto manufacture, fabrics, food production, household appliances, banking, shipping, insurance. They increased the size and complexity of corporations, required companies to draw more of their supervisory personnel from the universities rather than from the lower work force, greatly reduced the need for unskilled heavy labor, and made many traditional work practices obsolete.

The quickening pace of industrialization speeded up the long-time shift in the labor force from production to service. In 1956 the Labor Department reported that for the first time the number of white-collar workers exceeded the number of blue-collar workers.[5] Between 1945 and 1965, manufacturing employment rose from about 15.5 million to 18 million, mining declined from 840,000 to 630,000, and transportation and utilities were virtually stable around the 4 million mark. In contrast, trade rose from 7.3 to 12.7 million; finance, insurance, and real estate from 1.5 to 3; services from 4.2 to 9.1; and government (mostly state and local) from 6 to over 10 million. The only predominantly blue-collar field to match the white-collar growth was contract construction which went from 1.1 to 3.2 million.[6]

URBANIZATION AND EDUCATION

The urbanization process, which is so closely related to industrialization, also continued at a rapid pace. In 1940 urban inhabitants (in places of 2500 and up) comprised about 56.5 per cent of the nation's 132 million; in 1960 they comprised about 63 per cent of the 180 million;[7] and by 1965 as the population soared to 194 million, the percentage was still rising. The standard metropolitan area—the city of 50,000 or more with an

[5] See *Manpower Report of the President* (March 1963), p. 26.
[6] *Statistical Abstract, 1967*, p. 224.
[7] Under a revised definition, it was 69.9 per cent.

increasingly large suburban population—became the principle site of American life.

The overall increase in population was more than double the rate of the 1930's. Moreover, it was largely the result of a markedly higher birth rate rather than through increased immigration. Although the nation continued to attract foreign immigrants, legal restrictions kept the net figure down to under 400,000 per year. Earlier industrial problems stemming from foreign language and cultural differences were therefore considerably reduced.

The urbanization-industrialization process necessitated and resulted in a rapid increase in educational levels. In 1940, 14 per cent of persons 25 years and older had completed high school and under 5 per cent had completed college. In 1960, the comparable percentages were 25 and nearly 8, and in 1966 they were 31 and 10.[8] More important, there was a growing and widespread belief that education "paid off" in occupational and income achievement terms and that the high school "dropout" was doomed to a lower status in the economic system. It was not mere coincidence that during the 1950's an important new branch of economics emerged under the label of investment in human capital and that the decade of the sixties witnessed an unprecedented public interest in occupational training and re-training.

INTERNATIONALIZATION

Prior to World War II, the United States had played a relatively minor role in world affairs. Despite involvement in World War I, the country had refused to join the League of Nations and, apart from trade, its main foreign concerns seemed to be to stay out of European politics and to keep the European nations out of Western hemispheric matters. Pearl Harbor changed

[8] *Statistical Abstract, 1967,* p. 114.

all that. With the defeat of the Nazis and the Japanese, and a Europe half destroyed and exhausted by war, the United States became the number-one power of the world in economic and, for a considerable period, in political terms. American business and labor, as well as the government, turned their eyes and a considerable share of resources to overseas industry and politics.

The remarkable recovery of the Soviet Union and its Communist allies soon led, however, to a challenge to American hegemony. The world was split into non-Communist, Communist, and neutralist blocs, and the international scene was chilled by a "cold war" which burst into a "hot war" in Korea in the early fifties and in Vietnam in the mid-sixties.

A development of less dramatic proportions but one with important implications for industrial government was the huge investment by American corporations in foreign industry and the emergence of firms which might realistically be considered international enterprises. At the same time the labor movement extended its activities and relationships abroad through the formation of the International Confederation of Free Trade Unions, through various international federations of unions in particular industries, and in the International Labour Organization.

RACE RELATIONS

Another of the environmental factors affecting industrial democracy in this period was the intensified struggle of the black community for full political, social, and economic status in the nation. During the war a vast migration of Negroes from the rural South to northern cities and industries occurred. Between 1940 and 1960, it is estimated there was a net migration of over 3 million Negroes from the South, about twice the number migrating between 1910 and 1940.[9] In 1966 almost 70 per cent of

9 These statistics are taken from the *Report of the National Advisory Commission on Civil Disorders* (New York: Bantam Books, 1968), pp. 239ff.

all Negroes lived in metropolitan areas. The industrial employment of Negroes increased and so did their pressure for fair employment practices which would enable them to obtain higher-level jobs, more job security, and greater opportunities for advancement. Increasing pressure was exerted not only against employers but also against the trade unions, especially the skilled trades. Even unions which had been regarded as proponents of Negro rights, like the International Ladies Garment Workers Union, were charged with discriminatory practices in higher-paying jobs and the filling of union leadership positions. The fight for civil rights and later for black power encompassed the job market as well as other aspects of American life—education, housing, transportation, voting, etc.

Closely related to race problems in industry was the problem of poverty, of which the nation became acutely conscious in the sixties—mainly because of its black dimension. Statistically speaking there were many more poor whites than blacks in the nation, but the poverty of the black urban ghettoes in the midst of seeming white urban affluence commanded special attention. Government, industry, and organized labor were challenged to respond.

LABOR, MANAGEMENT, AND THE SOCIO-PSYCHOLOGICAL CLIMATE

During the 1930's labor was still viewed as the underdog in American society and, especially after the Great Depression, the union movement enjoyed a considerable amount of public sympathy and favor. By 1939 the growth in union strength and the large volume of strikes and sitdowns had begun to alter these public attitudes. The continued expansion of labor power during the war and the great outburst of strikes for higher wages and fringe benefits immediately after the war (1945–1946 reached a new peak) further changed the socio-psychological climate within which the labor movement operated. Labor was no longer seen as the perennial underdog but rather as a center of national power. Big Labor ranked with Big Business and Big Government. This did not mean that the right to unionize and engage in collective bargaining was threatened, but it did mean that serious voices were being raised as to whether the unions had not gained too much power and whether "union monopoly" was not as bad as "business monopoly."

In contrast to the post–World War I decade, however, the unions continued to grow in membership after 1945. Excluding Canadian members, it is estimated by Leo Troy[10] that membership totaled 12.1 million in 1945 and 16.6 million in 1957. But most of this increase merely reflected the growth in population and the labor force—the union percentage of the civilian labor force was 22.4 in 1945, reached 25.7 in 1953, and was 24.5 in 1957. After 1957 there was a slow decline in both absolute numbers and percentages until 1963 when, according to the BLS, the absolute membership began to rise to a new peak of 17.9 million in 1966. But the ratio to the civilian labor force was only 22.7, showing a lag behind the growth in the labor force.

During and after the war, ideological differences between the AFL and the CIO narrowed appreciably. At the same time both groups found the public climate turning against them, especially just before and after passage of the Taft-Hartley Law in 1947. Inter-union competition, which had been a valuable stimulating force in the thirties, seemed now to work chiefly to the detriment of the unions. In 1949 and 1950, reacting to cold war conditions, the CIO expelled eleven allegedly Communist-dominated unions. Finally, Eisenhower's election in 1952 and what was regarded as an unfriendly national administration set the stage for the AFL-CIO merger of 1955.

[10] Leo Troy, "Trade Union Membership, 1897–1962," *The Review of Economics and Statistics,* February 1965, pp. 93–94. These figures differ somewhat from the statistics of the Bureau of Labor Statistics which show 1956 as the peak in the fifties with 17.5 million and a ratio of 25.2.

As noted earlier, management recovered much of its lost prestige during World War II but, despite the decline in union public appeal, it was no longer the guiding light of the twenties. The public was impressed by the productive power of industry but had qualms about the size and wealth of the leading corporations. John Galbraith's thesis of capitalism as a system of countervailing power among large business, labor, and government institutions made sense to many observers of American life. Sensitive to these public views, the professional managers of the large corporations adopted much more sophisticated approaches to both the unions and the public. The idea of an accommodation with responsible union leadership became the key to sound employee relations. In fact, despite some major strikes and policy conflicts, many observers concluded that big business and organized labor had joined arms with the politicians of the two main parties to form the new American establishment.

The New Legal Framework

Perhaps the single most important postwar development in industrial democracy was the further involvement of the federal government. This new involvement was essentially a continuation of the dramatic change in governmental role instituted in the thirties and elaborated during the war. Its effect was to make the American system of industrial relations the most legalistic in the non-communist, industrialized world except, perhaps, for Australia and New Zealand.

As in the past, the evolving model of industrial government was not a product of planning or philosophic thought or ideological dogma. It was an organic growth generated by the interaction of major interest groups under a peculiar set of environmental conditions, such as those described above. Thus the nature and rationale of the model are best found in the legislation which created it and in the actions and statements of the government officials (executive, legislative, administrative, and judicial) who produced and implemented the legal framework.

THE TAFT-HARTLEY LAW

The first and most significant of the postwar laws was the Labor Management Relations Act of 1947, popularly known after its congressional sponsors as the Taft-Hartley Law. In contrast to the Wagner Act, which was a relatively short and simple law, the Taft-Hartley Law was long and complex. To the unhappy union leadership of the time it was a "slave labor law"; but although it was intended to alter the power balance between labor and management, the epithet was undeserved. Organizing non-union establishments, especially in the South, became more difficult; but it was not impossible and relations in industries already unionized were not seriously affected.

The law's declaration of policy offered a good clue to its goal and spirit: "Industrial strife which interferes with the normal flow of commerce and with the full production of articles and commodities for commerce, can be avoided or substantially minimized if employers, employees, and labor organizations each recognize under law one another's legitimate rights in their relations with each other, and above all recognize under law that neither party has any right in its relations with any other to engage in acts or practices which jeopardize the public health, safety, or interest." The law maintained virtually all of the basic elements of the Wagner Act, but to the list of employer unfair labor practices, it added a comparable list of union unfair labor practices. Among the latter provisions was a protection for union members against excessive initiation fees and a protection for employers against payment for work not performed. The earlier controversy over employer free speech was treated in a clause which expressly permitted such speech provided it "contains no threat of reprisal or force or promise of benefit." The NLRB's discretion in determining bargaining units was qualified with respect to professional employees and craft groups, giving these categories more autonomy. Supervisors, who had begun to develop a strong independent union organization, were removed from the protection of the law. Procedures were included to improve the effectiveness of the conciliation process in labor disputes and to settle disputes which appeared to imperil national health or safety.

From a conceptual standpoint Section 301 of the act had special interest because, for the first time, a federal statute made the collective-bargaining agreement a contract whose violation was subject to suit in the U.S. district courts. Prior to this point, such suits were entertained only under common law. It was provided, however, that judgments against unions were to be enforceable only against the organization as an entity and not against any individual member.

The implementation of Taft-Hartley continued to have important implications for the content of collective bargaining as well as the process, largely because of the way in which the NLRB interpreted terms like "bargaining in good faith" and "bargaining in respect to rates of pay, wages, hours of employment, or other conditions of employment." Despite employer objection, the board gradually widened the scope of bargaining to include such items as pensions, employee stock purchase, Christmas bonuses, welfare plans, the price of cafeteria food, and subcontracting. Almost every employer decision which had a direct effect on employment conditions became an appropriate bargaining subject.

The act also led to further legal treatment of grievance arbitration to which the War Labor Board had given so much stimulus. For example, in a landmark set of decisions involving three steel industry cases, which came to be known as the "Trilogy," the Supreme Court held in 1960 that the functions of the arbitrator and of the court must be clearly separated.[11] It was the function of the arbitrator to resolve all questions of interpretation and application of the collective-bargaining agreement; the function of the court was to safeguard the arbitration system, provided it was clear that there was a valid agreement and that arbitration was embodied by the parties in it. It was felt that the court lacked the expertise of the arbitrator and therefore should not go into the merits of a grievance.

THE LANDRUM-GRIFFIN ACT

Another pillar was added to the legal framework with the passage of the Labor-Management Reporting and Disclosure Act of 1959 (known as the Landrum-Griffin Act). This act was largely the result of the investigations of the Senate Committee on Improper Activities in the Labor or Management Field, chaired by Senator McClellan, although the McClellan committee itself was created because of prior complaints and findings— i.e., the investigations of the New York State Crime Commission in the longshore industry, the studies by the New York State Department of Insurance and the Douglas committee of the

[11] *United Steelworkers of America* v. *Enterprise Wheel and Car Corp.*, 363 U.S. 593 (1960); *United Steelworkers of America* v. *American Manufacturing Company*, 363 U.S. 564 (1960); and *United Steelworkers of America* v. *Warrior and Gulf Navigation Co.*, 363 U.S. 574 (1960). The Trilogy was a sequel to and elaboration of an earlier court decision, *Textile Workers Union of America* v. *Lincoln Mills of Alabama*, 353 U.S. 448 (1957) which held that the federal district courts may take jurisdiction over suits to enforce arbitration provisions in collective bargaining agreements under Section 301 of the Taft-Hartley Act. These cases are discussed in the *Proceedings* of the Twelfth and Fourteenth Annual Meetings of the National Academy of Arbitrators (Washington, D.C.: BNA, 1959, 1961).

U.S. Senate in the mishandling of private health and welfare funds, and the findings of corrupt practices among a number of member organizations by the AFL and the CIO.

For the first time the federal government undertook regulation of the internal structure and functioning of trade unions. The argument that unions were private institutions subject only to self-regulation was rejected. As the preamble to the law stated, since it was in the public interest for the Congress to protect the rights of employees to organize and bargain collectively, to achieve this goal—as well as to maintain a free flow of commerce—"it is essential that labor organizations, employers, and their officials adhere to the highest standards of responsibility and ethical conduct in administering the affairs of their organizations." Thus the Landrum-Griffin Act set forth a bill of rights for union members, including equal voting and participation rights, freedom of speech and assembly, reasonable dues and fees, protection of the right to sue the organization or its officers, safeguards against improper disciplinary action, and the right to obtain copies of collective-bargaining agreements. Labor organizations were required to file with the Labor Department copies of their constitutions and bylaws, the names of officers, information on dues and fees, and detailed annual financial reports. National union trusteeships imposed on local unions had to be justified; union election procedures had to meet certain minimum standards; officers of labor organizations had to meet certain rules to assure fiduciary responsibility.

WAGES, HOURS, AND SOCIAL SECURITY

In the area of so-called protective labor legislation, older principles were revised and extended and one major new program that had been recommended in the mid-thirties was finally enacted on a partial basis. Thus the minimum wage levels of the Fair Labor Standards Act were increased in 1949, 1955, 1961, and 1966 (mainly to keep pace with inflation) and the coverage of the act was extended to additional groups of workers, finally including in 1966 some 9 million workers in trade and service, in schools, hospitals, and on large farms. The Davis-Bacon Act standards were redefined to include certain fringe benefits in the concept of prevailing wages. A new minor statute, the Service Contract Act of 1965, extended similar principles on wages and fringe benefits to employees of federal contractors furnishings services to federal agencies.

In the social security field, benefits as well as tax payments were increased and a variety of other adjustments were made to bring more people under the coverage of the retirement and other programs. A major breakthrough came in 1965 with the adoption of the so-called Medicare program giving hospitalization and medical benefits to persons over the age of 65. Health insurance had long been regarded as the principal gap in the nation's social security system, especially in view of the half-century's experience with workmen's compensation for accidents and diseases incurred on the job. Medicare represented a significant start at filling the gap.

MANPOWER AND EQUAL OPPORTUNITY

Legislation to eliminate discrimination because of race, color, religion, national origin, sex, or age was another important product of the postwar period. The FEPC of World War II had illuminated the problems and the remedies. When its authority expired, a number of states and local communities adopted their own programs with limited effectiveness. At the federal level, President Truman in 1951 and President Eisenhower in 1953 set up committees on government contracts to promote nondiscrimination in this sector, but these committees lacked enforcement powers. It was not until the 1960's, under Kennedy and Johnson, that a significant measure of compliance by federal contractors and unions was achieved through a combination of Justice Department legal action and a "plan for progress" based on persuasion. In the last analysis it was the pressure of the Civil Rights movement that breached the barriers of discrimination. The Civil Rights Act of 1964 extended government control to all industry within the federal jurisdiction. An increasing number of state acts, such as those in New York, Massachusetts, and Illinois, slowly and imperfectly covered the nonfederal jurisdictions.

The main focus of the equal-opportunity movement was on the black worker. In a 1964 Executive Order, President Johnson extended the nondiscrimination rule in federally assisted areas to the factor of age. Title VII of the Civil Rights Act did not include the age factor but did include sex—as did a number of the state acts. The Equal Pay Act of 1963 prohibited discrimination against women in the payment of wages.

During the Kennedy regime, the widespread concern over unemployment, poverty, and discrimination resulted in pioneering government programs to train or retrain unemployed workers. The Area Redevelopment Act of 1961 and the Manpower Development and Training Act of 1962 were the initial major actions; they were followed by the Vocational Education Act of 1963, the Education Acts of 1964 and 1965, and the Economic Opportunity Act of 1964. As the Labor Department's fourth annual Manpower Report stated:

> These innovations reflected a recognition that large numbers of persons would benefit from enlightened fiscal policy only as they were freed from the effects of unenlightened racial prejudice, lack of education and training, and the more dynamic nature of industry than of people. The concept of an active manpower policy geared to the individual and the locality, was recognized as a necessary component of overall national economic policy. It has

become steadily clearer that economic growth and stability require increasing the employability of workers and reducing to a minimum the human dislocations of a changing economy.[12]

PUBLIC EMPLOYEES

Legislation governing the rights of organization and collective bargaining for public employees had been virtually nonexistent prior to 1945. For most employee categories, the right to form organizations and to petition their employers or legislative bodies was recognized, but the employers were under no obligation to engage in collective discussions or agreements and most of them chose not to. The TVA was an outstanding exception. A flurry of strikes by public employees after the war, despite almost universal court and executive declarations prohibiting the strike, led to the enactment of numerous state laws banning public-employee strikes, often with harsh penalties. In 1947 eight states, including New York, Pennsylvania, and Michigan, adopted such legislation; the Taft-Hartley Law of the same year contained a similar prohibition for federal employees.

This negative approach proved to be a failure, particularly as the wages and employment conditions of public employees lagged behind those in the private sector. Restlessness grew in the federal service and militant organizations appeared at the state and local levels among teachers, nurses, social workers, sanitation workers, and security employees. The spokesmen of these public employees contended that they had become second-class citizens. In response to these developments, a new, more positive public policy began to emerge. In January 1962 President Kennedy issued Executive Order 10988 giving federal employees organizational and limited bargaining rights. Among the states, first Wisconsin in 1959 and 1961 and then several other states—including Michigan, Connecticut, Massachusetts,

---

[12] *Manpower Report of the President* (March 1966), p. 2.

and Oregon—adopted laws of a comparable nature for municipal and/or state employees. What was to become a new major strand of American employee-employer life had begun.

The final area in which the federal government became newly involved was that of wage-price levels. Except for a short period during World War I, the idea of directly controlling or influencing these relations through government action had attracted little attention before 1940. Monetary and, to a lesser extent, fiscal measures were seen as the chief economic tools to deal with business cycle fluctuations and other variations. During World War II there was, however, general recognition that a direct control program was necessary to prevent runaway inflation and disruption of the wartime economy. But when the War Labor Board was succeeded for about a year by a National Wage Stabilization Board, whose main objective in conjunction with a parallel price program was to provide an orderly reconversion to a free wage system, the effort at a peacetime wage-price policy proved ineffectual. Another wage-price stabilization program was instituted during the Korean War period, but the limited character of the war and the pervasiveness of normal domestic activities also subjected this program to frustration and defeat.

A continuing series of wage-price rounds, however, kept the issue of stability high on the public agenda. For the first time the theme of wage-push inflation as opposed to the more traditional demand-pull inflation was hotly debated by economists, politicians, journalists, businessmen, and labor officials. In 1962 the Council of Economic Advisers explicitly enunciated and proposed a policy of national wage-price guideposts.[13] This policy did not contemplate legally enforced controls but suggested standards to which the leading corporations and unions would

[13] For a historical summary, see the 1967 Economic Report.

voluntarily adhere in collective bargaining. The general rule
was that wages should advance in accordance with the national
increase in productivity. Underpaid workers might rise more
rapidly, overpaid groups should rise more slowly than the average. Other variations might occur because of labor surpluses
or shortages in an industry or because of agreements furthering
productivity by relaxing or eliminating restrictive work rules.
The aim was to stabilize unit labor costs. Similarly prices were
to be kept stable in industries whose productivity about equaled
the average for the economy, they were to fall where productivity was above average, and they could rise where productivity
was below average. The council did not attempt to recommend
a specific general wage guidepost until 1966, but the figure of
3.2 per cent then suggested was roughly in accord with the
postwar trend of annual productivity increments.

The years between 1962 and 1965 proved to be remarkably
stable in terms of prices and, except for construction and a few
other important industries, the guideposts seemed to be working well. Whether the suggested policy was really a serious influence, outside of a handful of cases in which the federal
government became involved, was widely disputed. A few years
later, under the pressures of the Vietnam War, the guidepost
policy was to be deliberately challenged by organized labor and
ignored by business. As of 1965, however, they seemed to symbolize the establishment of a national incomes policy and a new
role for government in industrial democracy.

ENTANGLEMENTS IN THE RULE OF LAW

The new legal framework for industrial government in the
United States was, as the above summary demonstrates, comprehensive and consequential. It was, however, neither tightly
integrated nor stable. For one thing the three national administrations of the period—Truman (1945–1952), Eisenhower

(1953–1960), and Kennedy-Johnson (1961–1965)—differed in outlook as to the degree of government involvement in employee-employer relations and in national economic policy. The first and third were, of course, much closer together than either was to the second; but even they differed because of differing circumstances and personalities. Organized labor had less influence on the Eisenhower regime, and Eisenhower and his main advisors were less inclined to intervene in labor disputes and other business and economic affairs.

Administrative agencies also complicated the rule of law. This was especially true of the NLRB experience. The Eisenhower board was clearly more sensitive to the complaints of business on such issues as free speech by employers, the fragmentation of bargaining units, or subcontracting. One board showed little hesitancy in modifying or reversing the policies of its predecessor. The Supreme Court, in ruling on NLRB matters, also exercised considerable discretion—reversing board decisions on a number of occasions and laying down new lines of legal thought regarding such important elements of industrial government as the arbitration process, union discrimination against racial and other minority group members, and contracting out.

As the legal framework grew in size and complexity and went through frequent changes of interpretation and administration, the role of the lawyer in industrial government inevitably increased. Lawyers had played relatively minor roles in industrial relations prior to the New Deal, although there were some distinguished exceptions—for example, the part which Louis Brandeis, Louis Marshall, and Julius Henry Cohen played in constructing the famous Protocol of Peace in the New York garment industry. But mostly lawyers had been used by employers and unions in court-related and legislative controversies rather than in negotiations or grievance handling. In this respect, as in many others of the early period, British practice was followed.

But as the federal government increased its involvement, so did the legal profession. Lawyers participated increasingly in the negotiation, as well as the drafting, of collective-bargaining contracts, in the handling of grievances, especially but not exclusively at the arbitration stage, and as representatives of labor and business before congressional committees, administrative agencies like the NLRB, and on the lecture platform. Lawyers also took on the functions of arbitrator and conciliator in many disputes.

The effects were mixed. The legal mind brought a measure of clarity and analytical ability to industrial government. But it also brought unnecessary legalism and technicality, the struggle to win the individual case rather than to consider the long-run living implications, and to some extent the displacement of the organic labor and employer leadership in the rule-making and decision-making process.

Governmental Views and Perspectives

Although the general trend of industrial democracy entailed a growing involvement by the federal authorities and an increasing legalization, some important differences in ideology characterized the three administrations of the 1945–1965 period. It may be desirable, therefore, to depict separately the evolving model as conceived by leaders of these administrations—the presidents, their labor secretaries, their NLRB chairmen, and other key officials. Since space limitations must not be ignored, the statements which are selected will be only illustrative of a much greater body of available literature.

THE TRUMAN ADMINISTRATION, 1945–1952

President Harry Truman's central concern was to fill the gaps in the New Deal model—to round it out, so to speak. He strongly favored unionism and collective bargaining—too much so in the views of his critics. He believed that unions and managements had the right to conduct their affairs without active government intervention, but that they had the obligation to stay within bounds which would safeguard the national interest. This meant restraint in the use of strikes and lockouts, moderation in the size of wage and price increases, justice in the operation of their internal rules. The government's job was to insure fair play and to protect the national interest when one or both parties acted contrary to it. The government had the further responsibility to maintain a stable and prosperous economy, to provide jobs for all who needed them, and to eliminate the insecurities of unemployment, old age, disability, illness and accidents, substandard wages, and discrimination because of race, creed, or sex.

In a radio address on wages and prices in the reconversion period, Truman stated: "The country is entitled to expect that industry and labor will bargain in good faith, with labor recognizing the right of industry to a fair profit, and industry recognizing labor's need to a decent and sustained standard of living—and with both of them realizing that we cannot have either deflation or inflation in our economy."[14]

When Congress in 1946 passed the Case bill restricting the right to strike, Truman issued a veto statement that the way to prevent strikes was not by oppressive legislation but by enacting measures (adequate unemployment insurance, health and medical benefits, and a fair minimum wage) to correct the major causes of insecurity. At the same time in vetoing (unsuccessfully) the Taft-Hartley bill of 1947, he warned against the excessive injection of government into private economic affairs. In this latter message, he listed the criteria on which he measured the bill:

[14] October 30, 1945. *Public Papers of the Presidents of the United States: Harry S. Truman*, 1945 (Washington, D.C.: Government Printing Office, 1961), p. 449.

1. Would it result in more or less government intervention in our economic life? He favored industrial self-government with freedom of contract and free collective bargaining. The bill would have the opposite effect, in his judgment.

2. Would it improve human relations between employers and their employees? He felt that it would remove the settlement of differences from the bargaining table to courts of law. Instead of learning to live together, employers and unions would be encouraged to engage in costly, time-consuming litigation, embittering both parties.

3. Is the bill workable? He thought that it was not because (a) the emergency dispute procedure would require an immense and fruitless amount of government effort, (b) the NLRB would be overburdened by its new tasks and hobbled in its efforts to carry them out, and (c) restrictions on the board's procedures would increase the backlog of unsettled cases and drive the parties to the use of economic force.

4. Is the bill fair? He regarded it as unfair because it would require the board to give priority to charges against workers over related charges against employers, and it would unduly penalize workers for all critical strikes.

5. The most fundamental test was whether the bill would strengthen or weaken American democracy. He concluded that it would weaken our democratic society. In striking at union abuses, it seriously threatened the entire trade union movement. By raising barriers between labor and management and by injecting political considerations into normal economic decisions, it would invite the parties to gain their ends through direct political action. He believed that it would be exceedingly dangerous to the country to develop a class basis for political action.

Subsequent experience under Taft-Hartley did not validate the dire predictions in Truman's message, although some of the defects which he noted were correctly diagnosed. While the

President was a strong supporter of organized labor, he was by no means blind to its faults and he would not tolerate action which he regarded as detrimental to the national welfare. In the railroad strike emergency of May 1946 he stated:

> I am a friend of labor. You men of labor who are familiar with my record in the United States Senate know that I have been a consistent advocate of the rights of labor and of the improvement of labor's position. I have opposed and will continue to oppose unfair restrictions upon the activities of labor organizations and upon the right of employees to organize and bargain collectively. It has been the basic philosophy of my political career to advocate those measures that result in the greatest good for the greatest number of our people. I shall always be a friend of labor. But in any conflict that arises between one particular group, no matter who they may be, and the country as a whole, the welfare of the country must come first.[15]

In his State of the Union message of January 6, 1947, Truman identified a number of labor practices which he thought were abuses and needed legislative correction. These included jurisdictional strikes, certain secondary boycotts, and the use of economic force by either labor or management to decide issues arising out of the interpretation of existing contracts. In a comment on the 1952 steel dispute, Truman reemphasized his overriding concerns: "The parties must realize that collective bargaining is a precious liberty, enjoyed by both employers and workers, and that the possession of liberty involves not only right but also duties on the part of both employers and workers —including the duty so to exercise freedom that it does not encroach upon the freedom of others. The freedom of all the people is at stake in the current emergency, and the production of steel is essential to the support of that freedom."[16]

But Truman, like Roosevelt, always looked at a wider field

[15] *Public Papers: Truman*, p. 276.
[16] Ibid., p. 497.

than that of collective bargaining. In a speech in 1950, he stated simply and directly: "I think it is the responsibility of Government to help those who, because of old age or other disability, are unable to work, and those who, through no fault of their own, are unable to find work. I believe that the strong should help the weak, and I make no apologies for that belief, either. But for men who are able to work, I want jobs—and not idleness. That's what they want, too—an opportunity to earn their own living."[17] And in his annual budget message of the same year, he recommended legislative proposals on training and safety, a permanent Fair Employment Practice Commission to eliminate not only unjust discriminatory practice but also to promote the best use of available manpower, and a labor extension service in the Department of Labor to make available to wage earners educational programs designed to promote sound labor-management relations.

President Truman effectively articulated his administration's views on industrial democracy. Similar and related views were also expressed by other high government officials whom he appointed. Thus NLRB chairman Paul M. Herzog told a Senate committee in opposing the Taft-Hartley bill, "We believe in collective bargaining because we believe in democracy. It provides the surest means of giving employees a voice in fixing the conditions under which they work, of erecting the industrial equivalent of government by consent of the governed. . . . The problem is one of establishing conditions under which newly won power will not be indiscriminately used, without recreating that ancient system of individual bargaining under which the word of the employer was law."[18]

Cyrus Ching, a former industrial spokesman but now director of the Federal Mediation and Conciliation Service, put the same

[17] Ibid., p. 389.
[18] U.S., Congress, Senate, Committee on Labor and Public Welfare, S. 55 and S. J. Res. 22, 80th Cong., 1st sess., 5–8 and 13 March 1947, pt. 4.

theme in these words: "Free collective bargaining, in my opinion, can be one of the cornerstones of our democratic form of government. That statement is predicated on the assumption that both labor and management will accept their full responsibility in making free collective bargaining work. And if labor and management do not accept their full responsibility for making it work, then collective bargaining will fail and, because of the profound effect on the whole national scene of the relationship between employer and employees, it is conceivable that our government may be torn down by its failure."[19]

THE EISENHOWER ADMINISTRATION, 1953–1960

James Mitchell, one of the ablest of the secretaries of labor, was the chief spokesman for the Eisenhower Administration in the labor field. The President himself had little personal knowledge or experience in this area.[20] When Mitchell was asked by a journalist in 1956 to describe the essential differences between this administration and its predecessor, he made two distinctions:

1. The Eisenhower Administration looked upon labor as meaning all people who work, whether they were organized or not. The previous administration seemed to regard labor as exclusively organized labor.

2. The Eisenhower Administration regarded the labor-management problem as exclusively the responsibility of labor and management to solve, without government interference, except where the national health or safety was involved.

[19] "The Future of Labor-Management Relations," *Vital Speeches of the Day,* 15 (July 15, 1949):19.

[20] His first appointee as labor secretary, Martin Durkin, General President of the Plumbers Union, was not a sound choice and resigned after nine months in office.

Mitchell went on to comment that increasingly the negotiations over the big labor contracts had wound up in Washington, with the government tending to favor labor in the bargaining. The aim of the Eisenhower government was to encourage responsibility by the parties and to maintain a neutral position. However he also hoped that the unions would participate more actively as labor representatives in the Labor Department and on various boards.[21]

In a series of speeches and articles between 1953 and 1959, Mitchell delineated his model of industrial government. The basic assumption was one of full faith in the free institutions of labor and management. Collective bargaining worked best for the nation when it was based on a broad mutuality of interest among management (the employer), labor (the employees), and the public (consumers). Government had three important, practical functions in the labor-management area. One was to create, through fitting legislation, a framework of laws within which collective bargaining could freely operate to the best advantage of all. A second function was to render service and assistance to collective bargaining by providing mediation services and by describing the general economic situation of the nation through fact-gathering and publishing. The third function was the promotion of goodwill and understanding between the interested parties. In addition, the government was the guardian of the public interest and had to intervene actively in those cases in which the national interest was clearly endangered.

Mitchell noted that government promoted sounder labor-management relations indirectly when, in the protection of the rights and skills of individual workers, it encouraged industrial safety standards, discouraged discriminatory hiring practices,

[21] "Should Labor Unions Be Partisan," *U. S. News & World Report*, 41 (September 7, 1956):10.

or developed ideas for more effective training of workers. Furthermore, as part of the governmental responsibility to provide a healthy environment for free collective bargaining, it was necessary to adopt legislation curbing the abuse and misuse of power in the labor-management relations field.[22]

It is important to observe that the Eisenhower administration made no effort to eliminate existing laws on labor relations adopted in the Truman and Roosevelt periods or to weaken union power by supporting the "right-to-work" movement. However, with some minor changes, it supported the Taft-Hartley Law and actively encouraged the Congress in the passage of the Landrum-Griffin Act. With respect to the latter, Mitchell said: "The program we are proposing is designed to raise the general standard of responsibility and accountability of unions and employers in labor-management relations and at the same time to keep Government out of undesirable direct interference with union or employer matters."[23] At the administrative level, two differences from the Truman period were observable. The government did refrain from intervening as often in national disputes although cases like the 1959 steel strike were examples of intense involvement by government leaders, including the labor secretary and the Vice President. In interpreting the Employment Act of 1946, more emphasis was placed on price stability and less on full employment.

THE KENNEDY-JOHNSON ADMINISTRATION, 1961–1965

In principle, the Kennedy Administration's policy on labor-management relations did not differ appreciably from its predecessor's just as the latter was not fundamentally different from

[22] See "Government and Labor in the Eisenhower Administration," *Current History,* 37 (September 1959):217.

[23] U.S., Congress, Senate, Subcommittee on Labor and Public Welfare, *Union Financial and Administrative Practices and Procedures,* 85th Cong., 2d sess., 26 March 1958.

Truman's. All extolled free collective bargaining, played down government intervention, criticized labor and management abuses, encouraged industrial peace, asserted the need to protect the public interest in emergency situations, endorsed social security and the elimination of discriminatory practices, and proclaimed a goal of a prosperous and growing America. The differences were partly a matter of style, partly a matter of rhetoric, and partly a matter of interpretation.

Neither President Kennedy nor his dynamic and imaginative first labor secretary, Arthur Goldberg, former labor counsel for the United Steelworkers Union, favored passivity or feared interventionism. The President was determined to keep the country moving; the secretary was a prime mover. Within a month of assuming office, Kennedy sent a special message to Congress in which he highlighted the problems of technology and unemployment and announced the establishment of a President's Advisory Committee on Labor-Management Policy composed of nationally prominent representatives of labor, management, and the public. The message stated: "Rapid technological change is resulting in serious employment dislocations, which deny us the full stimulus to growth which advancing technology makes possible. Labor and industry have demonstrated cooperative initiative in working out solutions in specific plants and industries. Government action is also necessary, not only to maintain an environment favorable to economic growth, but also to deal with special problems in communities and industries suffering from economic dislocations and to help those who through unemployment are bearing an unfair share of the burden of technological change."[24]

The new advisory committee, which Goldberg had advocated in a public address prior to his appointment as secretary of labor, was directed to advise the President with respect to actions that

[24] *Public Papers of the Presidents of the United States: John F. Kennedy, 1961,* p. 52.

might be taken by labor, management, and the public to promote "free and responsible collective bargaining, industrial peace, sound wage policies, sound price policies and stability, a higher standard of living, increased productivity, and America's competitive position in world markets."[25]

In his 1961 Labor Day message, Kennedy stressed two themes —individual dignity and economic growth. He saw them as closely interrelated because of the dynamic and dislocative character of technology and industry.

Full employment through wider opportunity for the occupationally displaced and the minority group member rests ultimately, as do all of our ambitions for higher economic life, upon the ability of the economy to grow. This Labor Day we can find satisfaction that our government, this Administration and the Congress, have been successful in enacting legislation such as the Temporary Extended Unemployment Compensation Act, the new Minimum Wage Law, the Area Redevelopment Act, improved Social Security, and the Housing Act that contributes to the economic welfare of all of our people. The guide-posts to the further and greater progress we seek are these:

Wage and price policies that contribute to expansion without impairing our competitive posture in world markets; great productivity from a wide use of scientific discovery and the exertion of dedicated individual effort; the proper utilization of increased resources for the fulfillment of urgent national needs; statesmanship in collective bargaining that acknowledges the public interest.[26]

In speaking to the Auto Workers Union convention of May 1962 about the new wage-price guidepost policy, the President stressed that his administration would not undertake to fix prices and wages, intervene in every labor dispute, or "substitute our judgment for the judgment of those who sit at the local bargaining tables across the country." Nonetheless, "we can suggest

[25] Ibid.
[26] Ibid., pp. 571–572.

guidelines for the economy. . . . We can and must, under the responsibilities given to us by the Constitution, and by statute and by necessity, point out the national interest. And where applicable we can and must and will enforce the law—on restraints of trade and national emergencies."[27] Thus he did not hesitate to urge a noninflationary and peaceful settlement in the forthcoming aircraft and missile industry negotiations, or later to hardpress railway management and labor for a settlement of their national work-rules dispute, or on another occasion to publicly chastise and threaten the management of Big Steel for increasing prices.

As exponents of action programs, Kennedy and Goldberg sought to extend the scope and applicability of the industrial democracy model to areas where it had lagged. These efforts were reflected in the encouragement given to organization and negotiations by federal employees through Executive Order 10988, in support for the Equal Pay Act for women, and directives and agreements aimed against employment barriers based on racial discrimination.

This widened perspective was expressed in many of Goldberg's speeches. In a 1962 statement to the United Auto Workers, Goldberg said: "The actions you take in collective bargaining no longer affect only your industry. They affect the nation, they affect the economy and they also affect, as the President has said, such esoteric questions as balance of payments, foreign trade, and our position in a competitive and a busy world. No longer can any trade-union movement satisfy itself that by handling bread and butter issues, important as they are, that they discharge their responsibility as trade unionists and as citizens."[28] Similarly in addressing the Executives' Club of Chicago, the secretary stated: "It is time that labor and management embark

[27] Ibid., p. 365.
[28] United Auto Workers, *Proceedings of the Eighteenth Constitutional Convention* (May 4–10, 1962), p. 426.

together for the new world of the economic future, and leave behind the old hostilities and inadequate ideas and misconceptions that have so long delayed a needed mutual effort."[29]

One result of this concern for "the new world of the economic future" was the emergence of questions from a variety of groups as to whether collective bargaining was really adequate to meet the major problems of the time—such as long-term unemployment for workers displaced by technological development and maintenance of high standards of living for American workers in the face of foreign competition or race discrimination and poverty in the urban ghettoes. W. Willard Wirtz, then undersecretary of labor, and, after September 1962, an outstanding successor to Goldberg as secretary of labor under Kennedy and Johnson, directed himself to this challenge. In a speech at the International Trade Fair in Chicago in August 1961, he observed that "unless collective bargaining does have room to accommodate them, and answers to offer, it will be relegated in the future to matters of housekeeping in the plant, administering procedures for handling discharge cases, establishing safety programs, devising seniority systems that don't cover the crucial cases, and dividing up pies whose size is determined someplace else."[30] Wirtz suggested three propositions:

1. The continuation of private collective bargaining as an important force depends on the decisions of the bargainers to exercise, or not to exercise, responsibility for the concerns that affect the whole economy.

2. It also depends on whether the motive power and procedures of collective bargaining can be adjusted and revised to permit a larger recognition and reflection of the common national interests, particularly those in the achievement of stability

[29] "Labor-Management Relations," *Vital Speeches of the Day*, 28 (March 15, 1962), 11:330–333.
[30] W. Willard Wirtz, "The Future of Collective Bargaining," *Monthly Labor Review*, 84 (November 1961), 11:1206.

and growth. In this connection, he noted the spreading view that essential industries cannot be shut down by strikes and lockouts and that substitutes for work stoppages must be found. In addition, there was the increasing use of neutral third parties as integral agencies of the collective-bargaining process, not just as arbitrators or as "agreement brokers" but as exponents of more factual, more rational, and more responsible approaches.

3. Finally, the effectiveness of future collective bargaining will depend upon the working out of significantly new forms of coordinated private and public administrative processes. This means more reliance in collective bargaining on the principles of government, more use in government of the resources and procedures of collective bargaining, and coordination of the two processes to enhance the effectiveness of both.

Another of President Kennedy's appointees, Solicitor-General Archibald Cox, took a related position in an address to the American Bar Association's Section on labor law:

1. The need for collective bargaining continues as a way of enabling industrial workers to share in the governance of industrial lives, of extending the rule of law, and of increasing their bargaining power, but the job is rounding out and maintaining what has been accomplished rather than creating new ideals and institutions.

2. There will be much greater governmental activity not only in the field heretofore occupied by collective bargaining but also in the areas of employment and industrial relations now of dominant concern to industrial workers.

3. Despite the increased participation of government, we will continue to rely upon essentially voluntary methods. Compulsion is not an inescapable ingredient of all government participation. There is a wide range of possibilities between non-intervention and public regulation through orders backed by the force of law.

4. If we adhere to voluntarism, as indeed we must, then plainly collective bargaining will be the base upon which there is built much wider cooperation with government.

5. The labor movement will be under pressure to devote more time, effort and financial support to political activity.[31]

When Lyndon B. Johnson assumed the Presidency following the assassination of President Kennedy in November 1963, he followed much the same lines in labor policy, with Secretary Wirtz continuing as Labor Department head. Since this volume concludes with the Kennedy term, the Johnsonian innovations of the second term will not be discussed here. It need only be noted that Johnson's declaration of war on poverty in his first State of the Union Message (January 8, 1964) and his subsequent enunciation of The Great Society were entirely consistent with the Kennedy approach. As he told the Congress in the State of the Union Message, "Let us carry forward the plans and programs of John Fitzgerald Kennedy—not because of our sorrow or sympathy, but because they are right."

[31] Bureau of National Affairs, "The Future of Collective Bargaining," *Labor Relations Reference Manual*, 48 (May 1–October 31, 1961).

CHAPTER **16**

NEW IDEAS AND
PRACTICES IN INDUSTRY
AND OUTSIDE

THE EXPANDING ROLE of government in the framework of industrial democracy was largely the conception of political, legal, and academic thinkers although labor and management practitioners contributed significant elements through the interplay of their often conflicting ideas and objectives. The industrial democracy model was also reshaped, however, by new thoughts about the roles of the management and employee organizations, the procedures to be pursued, and the substantive working rules. Creative thinking came from labor's ranks, from management, and from academic and other outside sources. As in previous periods, while the mass of employers and labor leaders were slowly (and often with great difficulty) accommodating themselves to changing conditions and views, a small number of more imaginative individuals and groups were trying to formulate and implement new ideas.

Organized Labor

With John L. Lewis' decline in power after 1945 and with the death of Sidney Hillman in 1946 and of Philip Murray and Wil-

liam Green in 1952, the postwar leadership of the union movement devolved to two men[1]—George Meany, Green's successor
as president of the AFL and later of the merged AFL-CIO, and
Walter Reuther, Murray's successor as president of the CIO and
head of the giant Auto Workers Union. Meany represented the
mainstream of business unionism adjusted to the Big Government environment of his day. Reuther was the rare combination of successful pragmatist and pioneering social idealist. The
radical voice, so prominent in earlier years, was virtually ex-
tinguished after expulsion by the CIO of eleven Communist-
dominated unions in 1949 and 1950. There were, of course, other
able and thoughtful spokesmen for labor, but they fell within
the Meany or Reuther streams of thought and do not merit separate discussion.

GEORGE MEANY

In early 1955, shortly before the AFL-CIO merger took place,
Meany gave *Fortune* magazine his overview of organized labor's
goals and methods.[2] "Our goals as trade-unionists are modest,
for we do not seek to recast American society in any particular
doctrinaire or ideological image. We seek an ever rising standard
of living." It was still Sam Gompers' "more," Meany stated. The
way to achieve "more" was through the flexible method of voluntary collective bargaining, of free decision-making outside
the coercions of government. Collective bargaining can exist
only in the environment of political freedom. "And so we are
dedicated to freedom, not only political but also economic. . . .

[1] A third outstanding union figure, James Hoffa of the Teamsters, was a master of organizational and economic tactics but stood outside of the industrial
democracy tradition. Hoff's union career was halted in 1967 when he was sent
to prison on two separate convictions of jury bribing and misuse of union funds.

[2] George Meany, "What Labor Means By 'More'," *Fortune*, 5 (March 1955),
3:92–93; 172–176.

We believe in the American profit system. We believe in free competition." The AFL had relied upon the judgment of free men, unimpeded by the interference of government, to reach private agreement. "On its philosophical side, collective bargaining is a means of assuring justice and fair treatment. In the economic realm it is a means of prodding management to increase efficiency and output, of placing upon trade unions great responsibilities to limit their demands to practical realities."

For Meany co-determination or seeking a voice in management or having a union representative on the company board of directors was not a realistic goal. On the other hand, there was no reason why the scope of collective bargaining should not continue to expand. It had once included largely wages, hours, and health and safety conditions; later it had applied to hiring, firing, and promotion; now it includes medical care, pensions and the like. And some unions are beginning to question the unilateral right of management to set production standards and the location of a plant. "A union exists to protect the livelihood and interest of a worker. Those matters that do not touch a worker directly, a union cannot and will not challenge. These may include investment policy, a decision to make a new product, a desire to erect a new plant so as to be closer to expanding markets, to re-invest out of earnings or seek new equity capital, etc. But where management decisions affect a worker directly, a union will intervene." The guaranteed annual wage was a good objective but the nature of some industries limited its application, and in other industries it was highly impractical.

Labor had become involved with government, according to Meany, only when industry had failed to accept its social responsibility. The heavy hand of government is always a threat to freedom. But government has an obligation to help people do what they cannot do for themselves. Yet "we still believe that government alone should not be called upon to provide complete social security." The inadequacies of the government system give unionists an added incentive to press for realistic security through private health, welfare, and pension plans.

Like Gompers, Meany had a strong sense of what was needed and feasible. He was to the fore of most of his members and supporters but not a long distance ahead. Thus as public criticism of corruption in certain unions built up in the fifties, he took an active leadership role in seeking internal reform partly out of conviction and partly to forestall, if possible, governmental regulation of unions. Under his regime, the trade union movement for the first time established codes of ethical practices and expelled such unions as the longshoremen, the bakery workers, and the teamsters for corruption and racketeering. In 1958 he told a Senate committee that the union movement was founded on the democratic tradition; freedom and democracy were its essential attributes. "The AFL-CIO is in favor of, is committed to, and will support without reservation every piece of necessary and adequate legislation that will help the legitimate trade-union movement combat corruption, communism and racketeering. On the other hand . . . the AFL-CIO is opposed to and will fight any piece of legislation which, under the guise of meeting the above-stated test, in reality has as its purpose the weakening or the destruction of either trade unions or the process of free collective bargaining."[3] Meany's approach to the problem of race discrimination had many of the same elements as his approach to union corruption. He was personally opposed to discrimination. As a leader of the construction trades which resisted black members and apprentices more strongly than most other union groups, he exerted gradual and increasing pressure for internal reform as he himself felt the pressures of the environment move in this direction.

[3] U.S., Congress, Senate, Subcommittee on Labor of the Committee on Labor and Public Welfare, *Union Financial and Administrative Practices and Procedures*, 85th Cong., 2d sess., 22 May 1958, p. 1345.

Meany was a staunch advocate of union-management cooperation. Workers, he asserted, were responsive to programs to increase productivity if they were given a share of responsibility for them, if their standards were safeguarded against the abuses of the "stretch-out" and the "speedup," and if they got a fair share of the economic benefits accruing from higher output and reduced unit costs. Unions also had a long history of cooperation with management in apprenticeship and other industrial training programs. Much more training of men in skilled work of high precision could be done jointly to meet the needs of an atomic age.[4]

The challenge of union critics that the AFL-CIO had gotten complacent, self-centered, and unresponsive to the needs of the time incensed Meany but also served to extend his horizons. At the 1965 constitutional convention of the AFL-CIO, he indicated how far beyond Gompersism he had moved in a decade of national leadership.[5] Listing recent union gains in pension benefits, health and welfare plans, job security provisions and supplemental unemployment benefits, programs to humanize the effects of automation and technical change, and reduced work hours, he stated:

> These gains do not represent perfection nor are they economic cure-alls. All of them represent a degree of compromise, essential to the bargaining process. But they are solid, practical achievements on which a trade union builds from day to day and year to year—increased buying power for improved living standards, better job security, gains in pensions for workers when they retire, improved health and welfare plans for workers and their dependents when they are sick, orderly procedures for the handling of grievances, better and safer working conditions at the work place,

[4] Meany, "Basic Concepts for Peaceful Labor Management Relations," *Vital Speeches of the Day*, 22 (February 15, 1956), 9:273–274.

[5] American Federation of Labor-Congress of Industrial Organizations, *Proceedings of the Sixth Constitutional Convention*, 1 (December 9, 1965), pp. 24–29.

and increased leisure time to spend with their families and in their own private pursuits.

That is what free collective bargaining was meant to do and that is what it is doing effectively and well. Far from being obsolete or on its way out—as some of our "way-out" friends on the sidelines predict—it is being extended and expanded into new and broader areas of employment and in the resolution of new issues confronting workers in their relations with their employers.

However, this was not enough. Labor also had broader goals and larger responsibilities. Millions of people were underpaid and underprivileged. "They are poor. They are hungry. Their children suffer. They need our help, now, today." Although for the most part they were not union members, "they are our brothers and our responsibility. Their needs cannot wait until we organize them and undertake to make decent citizens out of their inhuman employers." And he concluded:

> The AFL-CIO is going to continue to fight for these and many other important programs in the Congress. We are going to continue to fight for a better share for those who work for wages, along every possible line—in organizing, at the collective bargaining table, at the ballot box, in the legislative field and anywhere else that the opportunity and the means present themselves.
>
> We are going to continue to support, here and abroad, the kind of policies and the kind of environment that open up these avenues of progress and keep them open, that give us the chance to campaign and fight to improve the society in which we live as free people.

WALTER REUTHER

If George Meany epitomized the gradual evolution of the traditional unionist, Walter Reuther represented the spirit of dynamic change. Reuther was the most imaginative and creative union leader of the postwar period as well as labor's most eloquent spokesman. He set forth his general conception of industrial democracy in the following words:

> The strength and solidarity of the UAW has brought about a great change. Our economic gains—higher wages, paid vacations, overtime, pensions, hospital-medical insurance program, and others—are important; but most important is the fact that we have won a measure of industrial democracy within our industries. We have won recognition of workers' rights. A worker is no longer a mere clock-card number; he is now a person—a human being, who can hold his head high and demand the respect and consideration to which he is entitled. We have in truth given substance to the old phrase, "the dignity of labor."
>
> The UAW-CIO has worked and fought hard to raise collective bargaining above the level of a struggle between competing economic pressure groups, and to gear it to the good of the whole community. We have clearly understood that we live in an interdependent world in which labor cannot raise itself by its own economic bootstraps. The UAW-CIO has had the strength and has generated the loyalty and enthusiasm that have made possible our great gains, because we abandoned the old slot-machine kind of unionism and instead developed the kind of progressive and dynamic program that reflects the needs of all the American people.[6]

Dealing with some of the most powerful and efficiently managed corporations in the nation, Reuther incessantly explored and tested out the potentialities of collective bargaining as an instrument for extending industrial democracy. He was not always successful but he invariably produced some change.[7] In the great strike against General Motors of 1945–1946, he raised (unsuccessfully) the issue of union access to the company books as well as the national economic policy argument that the union

[6] American Academy of Political and Social Science, "Practical Aims and Purposes of American Labor," *The Annals*, 274 (March 1951):64-74.

[7] The following listing is derived from the BLS *Wage Chronology of General Motors Corp., 1939–1966*, Bulletin No. 1532, October 1966.

demands could be met without a price increase. In 1948 the escalator clause (the automatic quarterly adjustment of cost-of-living allowances) and an annual "improvement factor" (based on long-range productivity gains) were introduced. In the early 1950's pension and insurance plans were negotiated because the national social security system was proving inadequate. There were also experiments with five-year contracts. In 1955 the supplemental unemployment benefit program was worked out as an initial step toward the guaranteed annual wage. At the same time the union called for the negotiation of a profit-sharing plan. In 1958 the union offered to forego wage increases under the annual improvement clause in return for improvements in the supplemental unemployment benefit program and a company reduction in auto prices. In 1961 a wide array of fringe benefits were upgraded, and provisions were made for severance pay and for worker moving allowances in case of transfer. In 1964 one of the major innovations was an early retirement program.

Reuther repeatedly conceptualized collective bargaining as part of a broad economic framework. In 1953 he told the Economic Club of Detroit: "Just as the American economy is the key to much of the economic future of the free world, so the question of collective bargaining is an important and essential key to the future of the American economy. I would like to touch briefly on a number of basic principles that I think labor and management must keep in mind, as they approach their joint responsibilities at the bargaining table. I call these principles the common denominators of democratic survival."[8] The five principles he posed were as follows:

1. In a free society there can be no legislative substitute for good faith at the bargaining table.

[8] Walter Reuther, "How Labor and Management Can Cooperate," *Vital Speeches of the Day*, 20 (March 1, 1954), 10:309–317.

2. The welfare of the whole of society transcends the economic interest of any segment of that society.

3. Industrial peace is possible only as a by-product of economic and social justice.

4. Collective-bargaining decisions must flow from mutual exploration of economic facts, and not by the exercise of economic power.

5. Industry must operate on a single, not a double, set of economic and moral standards. If pensions are good for company executives, they are also appropriate for low paid workers.

In response to a challenge from the audience, Reuther noted changes from some earlier views. He no longer favored a national council to regulate the industry and he strongly opposed nationalization. But the union was entitled to scrutinize production schedules and to protest extreme variations which would at one point attract large numbers of new recruits from outside communities and then dump them as unemployed on the streets of the new communities.

The guaranteed annual wage issue was, for Reuther, not a panacea, not a cure-all, but an essential, dynamic, economic tool yet unused in our society. "We don't believe that any American is automatically entitled to economic security. We have no sympathy for a worker who can find a job but who is unwilling to work. What we do believe is that every American is entitled to an opportunity to earn his economic security. In other words, the guaranteed annual wage is directed toward the objective of full employment and full production."[9]

In discussing the problems arising from automation, Reuther made it clear that he favored technological change which would eliminate the drudgery of many jobs and vastly enhance the

[9] Reuther, "Industry Can Afford Guaranteed Annual Wage," *Vital Speeches of the Day*, 21 (July 1, 1955), 18:1314–1318.

standard of living. But the adjustment problems were not to be ignored. The shutting down of a plant, the displacement of thousands of workers, the dislocation of whole communities cannot be justified by potential profits to the corporation. Industry must pay for the social costs of automation, including retraining, the cost of moving and new housing, early retirement, reduced workweeks, and extended vacations. Some of this could be handled through collective bargaining. But a national approach would be needed to make certain that the costs and benefits of automation were equitably shared.[10]

Reuther did not want the government to be a third party at the bargaining table. "I believe that the less the Government interferes in disputes involving management and labor the better . . . the necessity for, and extent of, government intervention in industrial disputes depends upon the extent to which the parties to such disputes assume their social responsibility."[11]

He saw collective bargaining reaching out for more complex and challenging objectives rather than government moving into the bargaining area.[12] "Collective bargaining is the most effective, practical, democratic, economic tool with which a free people can work to translate this new abundance into practical and tangible human progress." But collective bargaining was not the narrow private concern of management and labor. It was everybody's business and had a relation to the problems of our entire society. "We can't solve the problems of unemployment, the crisis in education that robs our children of adequate educational opportunities, the challenge of providing older people a fuller measure of security or other problems in isolation."

[10] U.S., Congress, Subcommittee on Economic Stabilization of the Joint Committee on the Economic Report, *Automation and Technological Change,* 84th Cong., 1st sess., 14-28 October 1955, pp. 101ff.

[11] Reuther, "What Labor Wants Next," *The American Magazine,* 161 (January 1956), 1:107.

[12] Reuther, "Our Greatest Challenge," Address at First Annual Industrial Relations Conference of I.U.D., IUD Publication No. 12, June 6, 1957.

To contribute effectively and rationally to the achievement of these ends, collective bargaining must be based upon economic facts. In 95 per cent of the collective-bargaining sessions of America, the economic facts are not at the bargaining table. The UAW, he observed, had proposed management-union study committees to take a joint look at the facts prior to bargaining, but management was reluctant to do so. Industrial managements, by and large, had not comprehended the dimensions of our present economic abundance. "Our job is to develop a practical formula that will permit the economics of distribution to catch up with the economics of abundance on the production end of our economic equation."

Two years later he reiterated the need to reevaluate and redefine the role collective bargaining must play in this growing complex society. "We have been trying to get people to understand that collective bargaining is a democratic tool with which free labor and free management must work together in finding answers to common problems; that collective bargaining transcends the question of equity between the worker and stockholder and consumer. It gets to the very core of the basic unsolved problem in the American economy, namely how do we work out these competing and relative equities between the basic economic groups in our free society?"[13]

Despite his faith in a broadened collective bargaining, Reuther was well aware that it could not cope by itself with the serious economic problems of the nation. Government had a major responsibility to eliminate cycles of recession and boom and to promote full utilization of the country's economic potential. It also had to take actions to supplement the inadequate efforts of the so-called private economy. Among the measures which he thought the government ought to take were: amend-

[13] Industrial Union Department, AFL-CIO, "Collective Bargaining Today," *Proceedings of the 3rd Annual Industrial Relations Conference* (June 15, 1959), p. 9.

ment of the Fair Labor Standards Act to provide for flexible workweeks, a national program for retraining displaced workers, the subsidizing of relocation expenses, public reinsurance for private pensions plans, and improvements in unemployment insurance benefits. Government must also apply new ground rules to corporations which dominate whole industries. One new measure would require a form of public investigation in instances of proposed price increases in administered price sectors of the economy. Another would relate to the location of new plants so as to discourage the movement of industry into areas of labor shortage and encourage its location in areas of higher than average unemployment.[14]

For Reuther the labor movement had responsibilities "for improving every aspect of the quality of American life." In 1965 he outlined a program to the Industrial Union Department of the AFL-CIO which mirrored President Johnson's view of the Great Society. "There are neighbors in need of jobs, children trapped in the quicksand of poverty, old folks burdened by insecurity, youngsters dropping out of school and into delinquency—there are cities to be rebuilt, rural towns to be revitalized, rivers and lakes to be cleaned, air to be made sweet and pure again, forests and meadows to be saved. There are exciting visions to be made real and a Great Society to be built."[15]

Reuther considered internal union democracy an essential element of industrial democracy. He was in the forefront of the civil-rights movement and strongly supported the efforts of Negroes to advance not only in society at large but within the auto industry, other industries organized by the UAW, and within the union itself. He was a leader in the effort to rid the AFL-CIO of corruption and gangsterism and played a major

[14] American Academy of Political and Social Science, "Policies for Automation: A Labor Viewpoint," *The Annals*, 340 (March 1962):107ff.

[15] AFL-CIO, *Proceedings of the Sixth Constitutional Convention* (November 18, 1965), pp. 1–3.

part in the formulation of the codes of ethical practice. In 1957 the UAW established, at his initiative, a unique Public Review Board consisting of seven prominent clergymen, lawyers, and academicians, with the authority to hear and make binding decisions on the appeals of union members or subordinate bodies against decisions of the International Executive Board or complaints of violations of the union's ethical practices code.

Management Views

There were no voices in industry which spoke with the mark of leadership and influence on industrial government comparable to those of George Meany and Walter Reuther. This was perhaps inevitable because of the wider dispersion of employer organization and because few of the industrial and business leaders devoted their primary thoughts and energies to the subject of employer-employee relations. Although a small number of top leaders accepted membership on such bodies as Truman's postwar Labor-Management Conference, Kennedy's Advisory Committee on Labor-Management Policy, and Johnson's National Commission on Technology, Automation, and Economic Progress, for the most part the development and public expression of management views were delegated to specialists who had, on a widespread and growing scale, been elevated to vice presidents of industrial relations in major corporations and in employer associations. Apart from these individuals, the principal source of management views consists of statements and reports of the Chamber of Commerce, the National Association of Manufacturers, the Committee on Economic Development, and other employer groups.

If there is a single unifying thread which runs through employer thinking of the 1945–1965 period, it is the belief that management must defend with the utmost vigor and imagination its right to manage. This belief was the rock on which management stood most firm in the 1945 Labor-Management Conference; it was a central concern behind management advocacy of the Taft-Hartley Law; and it was reflected in many management statements dealing with collective bargaining. The belief, however, was imbedded in a number of different conceptions of industrial government. For many, perhaps most, employers it was primarily a continuation of the defensive or containment posture of previous years. For others, it entailed a more sophisticated form of collective bargaining that accepted and encouraged "welfare capitalism" economic benefits for the workers in return for reduced pressure on the managerial function. For some, influenced by the idea of human relations of Elton Mayo and his Harvard Business School colleagues, it was linked to an emphasis on management skill in developing teamwork and high morale in the enterprise. For still others it meant a powerful management initiative in relation to both the union and the employees, with particular emphasis on communications. Each of these conceptions will be discussed briefly.

CONTAINMENT

This approach is illustrated in policy declarations and leadership statements of both the Chamber of Commerce and the National Association of Manufacturers. Except for the brief period (1944–1945) of Eric Johnston's presidency of the Chamber, the two organizations differed mainly in tone—the NAM being somewhat more outspoken.[16] The Chamber, for example, stated in its policy declaration on management responsibilities:

> The successful and efficient conduct of an enterprise requires individual responsibility for its management. Thus the right and duty

[16] See Clark Kerr, "Employer Policies in Industrial Relations, 1945 to 1947," in Colston E. Warne, ed., *Labor in Postwar America* (New York: Remsen Press, 1949).

of management to manage must not be curtailed; and management opposes any proposal which would limit or divide its authority to direct the enterprise, such as has been suggested by those advancing the industry council or similar concepts of co-management.

Similarly, the right and responsibility of management to encourage wholesome cooperative relations with employees must not be curtailed by restrictions imposed on speech, conduct, or other legitimate managerial activities. All employees with supervisory responsibilities are members of management and should be acknowledged and accepted as such.[17]

The Chamber endorsed the right of employees to organize and bargain collectively, but most of its eleven basic principles, when read in the context of the times, had a defensive quality. They were directed at restricting or diminishing union power.

1. Equitable application and impartial administration of labor laws.

2. Employees should have the right to organize and bargain collectively.

3. The right to work should not be dependent upon union membership or nonmembership.

4. Management should be free to manage without unwarrented government restrictions on their speech and conduct.

5. Employers, employees, and labor organizations should be equally accountable for breach of contract.

6. The right to strike should not be permitted if adversely affecting the safety, health, and welfare of the people.

7. Strikes should not be permitted against government.

8. Secondary boycotts are harmful.

9. Violence, intimidation, mass picketing and other coercive methods are against the public interest.

[17] Chamber of Commerce of the United States of America, *1963–1964 Policy Declarations*, Washington, D.C., p. 69.

10. Monopolistic practices by labor organizations should be subject to legal controls similar to those on monopolistic practices by employers.

11. The states should have maximum freedom to establish labor laws.[18]

NAM statements convey a similar outlook. In January 1946 Ira Mosher, chairman of the NAM board, told the Senate Committee on Education and Labor: "Management subscribes to the principle of collective bargaining. But collective bargaining will promote industrial peace only under conditions in which both labor and management stand equal before the law; conditions which require that both labor and management assume full responsibility for their acts; and finally, conditions in which both parties recognize the importance of the public interest."[19] These are, of course, unexceptionable principles, but Mosher was arguing (successfully, as passage of the Taft-Hartley Law soon revealed) that for a decade the law had favored labor at the expense of management and a change was needed. Thus he illustrated his general proposition by references to the antitrust regulation of monopolistic employers but not of unions, restrictions on management's right of free speech, enforcement of contract breaches against labor, the harmful impact of jurisdictional disputes, etc.[20]

Ten years later, NAM Board Chairman Charles R. Sligh presented a similar view in his proposed Code of Conduct for both organized labor and industry. It contained the following five planks:

1. A recognition of the right of every individual to join a union or to refrain from joining, as he chooses.

[18] Ibid., pp. 63–69.
[19] U.S., Congress, Senate, Committee on Education and Labor, *Labor Fact-Finding Boards Act: Hearings on S. 1661*, 79th Cong., 2d sess., 25 January–11 February 1946, p. 399.
[20] Ibid., pp. 399–402.

2. No interference with this right through violence, retaliation, subterfuge or coercion of any sort.

3. A striving for the utmost efficiency and productivity and the elimination of economic waste of every type.

4. An end to monopoly, whether on the part of organized labor or of industry.

5. Keep politics out of labor-management relations and avoid trying to obtain by political pressure that which cannot be justified economically.[21]

WELFARE CAPITALISM THROUGH COLLECTIVE BARGAINING

Writing about 1950 on the philosophy of American labor, Selig Perlman observed that "For the present, the role of experimenter in that great industry [autos] seems to have fallen less to Reuther than to the General Motors management, bent on bringing back the welfare capitalism of the twenties, with the sophisticated change of a national union in the place of a company union."[22] There was a powerful insight in this observation as the unfolding events of the postwar period indicated. On control over managerial functions, the nation's major corporations yielded very little additional ground. More graphically than in words, this was revealed in such major conflicts as the 1945–1946 General Motors strike, the 1959 steel strike, and the prolonged railroad work rules dispute of the early 1960's. It was also reflected in the "hardening of antagonistic attitudes" reported by E. Wight Bakke of Yale University in his December 1958 presidential address to the Industrial Relations Research Association.[23]

[21] Charles R. Sligh, "What Industry Expects of Organized Labor," Address before the Congress of American Industry, December 4, 1955 (New York: National Association of Manufacturers, 1956), p. 19.

[22] American Academy of Political and Social Science, *The Annals*, 174 (March 1951):63.

[23] E. Wight Bakke, "Mutual Survival after Twelve Years," *Proceedings of Eleventh Annual Meeting of Industrial Relations Research Association* (December 28–29, 1958), pp. 2–18.

At the same time General Motors and many of the other leaders of Big Business (for whom neither the NAM nor the Chamber of Commerce really spoke) were prepared to go a long way in providing welfare and insurance benefits, in grappling with the problem of variations in employment and unemployment, in raising wage levels and supplemental payments like paid vacations and holidays. They accepted unionism not merely as a reality which was unavoidable but as a source of positive value in large-scale industry. The grievance procedure with final and binding arbitration was perceived as indispensable, but grievance avoidance was preferable to grievance settlement.

This conception was well expressed by Malcolm L. Denise, vice president of labor relations for the Ford Motor Company, in a talk to the Pittsburgh chapter of the Society for the Advancement of Management in March 1963. "Collective bargaining is a continuous, never-ending, enormously complicated process. Yet, for all its complexity, collective bargaining works —by and large, year in and year out—rather well. Despite some exceptions, and for all the well-publicized friction it generates, it performs some fundamentally important services for represented employees, for management and for the public. In fact, I cannot think of any other workable way to settle disagreements between organized employees and management that would be consistent with the values of a free society."[24] Denise noted that different observers have described collective bargaining as a contest, a crusade, a hold-up, a seminar, an exercise in democracy, a debate, and a ritual. He thought that it embraced all of these characteristics "with a large dash of gamesmanship thrown in." But at bottom were five fundamental concerns for management:

1. To evaluate all proposals in terms of both their short and long-range implications to the enterprise.

[24] Malcolm L. Denise, "An Approach to Labor Relations," *Labor Relations Reference Manual,* 52 (January 1–April 30, 1963):25ff.

2. To secure relationships of mutual confidence, respect and accommodations with employees and their unions on a basis of equity and reasonable adjustment to legitimate problems.

3. To seek with earnestness and ingenuity sound bases for avoiding prolonged interruptions to production.

4. To confine cost increases to dimensions that recognize the interests of shareholders, and that will not impair the firm's ability to compete in tomorrow's as well as today's markets.

5. To protect to the utmost the vital rights and flexibility that go to the heart of management's ability to manage.

Denise stressed that collective bargaining entailed far more than the negotiation of a contract. The bulk of the labor relations task was concerned with day in and day out relationships in the plant, requiring appropriate measures to insure goodwill and cooperation from employees as well as union officials and informal as well as formal channels of communication.

The model of industrial government reflected in the statements and behavior of companies like General Motors and Ford is also to be found in the policy statements of the Committee for Economic Development, a group of some 200 prominent businessmen commonly identified with the more liberal or progressive segment of Big Business that was set up in 1942 to sponsor research and policy discussions on national economic affairs. In March 1964 the CED issued a national policy statement entitled *Union Powers and Union Functions: Toward a Better Balance.* Its central theme was summed up in a few introductory sentences. Unions, when desired by workers, have useful functions in our society, and to perform these functions unions need certain kinds and degrees of power. The problem is how to permit unions the powers they need without allowing them power to injure others. Taken as a whole, the national labor legislation adopted in the past generation has been constructive. According to Eric Johnston, one of the early CED leaders, it was a CED committee which he chaired in 1946 and 1947 that originally recommended a permanent council of management and labor appointed by the President to confer regularly with cabinet officers and Congressional leaders and to make an annual report to the President on the state of the nation's industrial relations.[25]

HUMAN RELATIONS

One of the major academic influences on management thought in the first postwar decade was the "human relations" ideology of Mayo and his associates at the Harvard Business School, stemming from the famous Hawthorne studies of the 1920's.[26] Mayo concluded that the major source of industrial conflict and malaise was the failure of management to develop the requisite skills in building teamwork (i.e., spontaneous collaboration) in industry. By the proper use of communications with informal work groups, management could raise worker morale, enhance productivity, and eliminate labor conflict. The key was sound leadership and administration. Mayo gave the personnel management movement a tremendous boost by his emphasis on interpersonal relationships within the plant rather than on the traditional concern with economic issues. Communications and social psychology became new watchwords in industry. Although Mayo himself virtually ignored unionism, some of his colleagues, like Ben Selekman, and followers, like William Whyte, made persuasive cases for the application of human relations ideas and techniques to grievance handling and contract administration. They served as a useful counterbalance to the economists, engineers, and lawyers. "Human relations" as a slogan began to fall into disfavor among managers during the

[25] Eric Johnston, "To Give Labor a Sense of Dignity," *New York Times Magazine,* March 30, 1947, p. 551. See also "For a New Approach to the Labor Issue," *New York Times Magazine,* January 29, 1950, p. 7.

[26] See particularly Elton Mayo, *The Social Problems of an Industrial Civilization* (Cambridge: Harvard University, 1945).

late fifties on the grounds that it indicated softness and senti-
mentality and detracted from a hard-nosed attention to costs,
profits, and managerial responsibility. But it had a permanent
impact on corporate personnel practice.

BOULWARISM

The emphasis in human relations thought on communications
was wedded to collective bargaining in highly distinctive and
controversial fashion by Lemuel R. Boulware, vice president of
employee relations for General Electric Company from 1946 to
1961. According to Herbert Northrup, author of a full-length
study of Boulwarism and for several years a member of the GE
employee relations staff, the essence of Boulwarism was the
application of the tools of marketing to employee relations—
market research, product planning, market development, and
merchandising.[27] It was management's responsibility to take
and maintain the initiative in employee relations. Employees,
the company found, wanted good pay and other material benefits, good working conditions, good bosses, a fair chance to get
ahead, steady work, respectful treatment, full information, important and significant work, and rewarding associations on the
job. The company had tried to supply these elements but had
failed to provide full information to the employees on what its
objectives were and what had been done. An effective system of
communications was essential.

This applied equally to collective bargaining. The company
had to thoroughly research every issue and determine the best
possible package for the satisfaction of its employees and cus-

[27] Herbert Northrup, *Boulwarism: The Labor Relations Policies of the General Electric Company. Their Implications for Public Policy and Management
Action* (Ann Arbor: Bureau of Industrial Relations, University of Michigan,
1964). See especially chapter 4.

tomers. It had to listen fully and carefully to the union demands and be prepared to make changes if new information or thinking were provided by the union. Otherwise it should remain firm on what it believed to be right. And it should, throughout negotiations, as well as at other times, keep the employees fully informed about company thinking and actions.

Boulwarism, as applied by General Electric, proved to be a formidable challenge to the unions in the company. It was attacked before the NLRB as unfair bargaining and the board found that aspects of it were contrary to the National Labor Management Relations Act. It was criticized by some academic students of collective bargaining as reflecting a posture that only management's perception of the facts was valid and therefore was violative of a joint participative system of rule-making. In any event it was not widely imitated, perhaps because few employers had the economic and human resources of General Electric to apply it effectively.

Some Creative Experiments

Economic necessity, the search for conflict-free relationships, the challenge of new technology, and the desire for greater employee participation—these and other factors led, as they had in previous decades, to a small number of more or less novel experiments in industrial government.

THE SCANLON PLAN

One of the earliest and most publicized of such experiments was a plan devised by Joseph Scanlon, accountant, steelworker and union official, and finally member of the faculty of Massachusetts Institute of Technology. Scanlon's idea emerged in the late 1930's but it began to command serious attention only after its successful adoption at the Lapointe Machine Tool Company at the end of 1947.[28] The essence of the plan was to enlist the participation of workers in the shop in the improvement of productivity, the reduction of costs, and the elimination of waste. This was to be accomplished through (a) a system of joint labor-management committees to discuss production problems and to consider ways of dealing with them and (b) a plantwide incentive system in which workers would receive monthly bonuses based on the savings achieved through cost reduction. The plan was to operate separately from collective bargaining but was conceived to be wholly compatible with it.

As Scanlon, Lesieur, McGregor and other supporters of the plan saw it, engaging the interest and participation of workers in a creative and mutually beneficial enterprise with management had important psychological as well as economic consequences. It helped to integrate the worker, job, and supervisor. It was psychologically satisfying. And it reduced the likelihood of conflict in the collective-bargaining sphere.

Although the Scanlon Plan proved highly successful at Lapointe and a number of other companies, it did not achieve wide acceptance. Like some earlier cases of union-management cooperation, it seemed to have greater appeal to companies in economic distress than those which were prospering. It appeared to be more manageable in small establishments than in large ones (i.e., with over a thousand employees). Workers were pleased to get the monthly bonuses but were unhappy when the bonuses declined or were not forthcoming at all. The connection between the bonus and the workers' contributions

[28] The Scanlon experience is described in a work by his colleague and successor, Frederick G. Lesieur, *The Scanlon Plan: A Frontier in Labor-Management Cooperation* (Cambridge: Technology Press of MIT, 1958). It was subsequently given strong support in the writings of MIT industrial psychologist, Douglas McGregor.

often appeared distant and unclear. Few managements wished to involve the workers to the degree contemplated in the plan or were willing to make the sustained efforts to maintain the plan over time.

A number of similar programs were developed to increase productive efficiency through improved communications, greater involvement of employees, and a sharing of the benefits of productivity gains. One of the most widely known was the Long Range Sharing Plan of the Kaiser Steel Corporation and the United Steelworkers Union at Fontana, California, formulated between 1959 and 1963.[29] The Kaiser Plan was partly the result of the company president's unwillingness to participate in a prolonged strike with the other major steel producers over an issue that had little significance for his enterprise and partly the result of suggestions by Arthur Goldberg, then counsel for the union, who hoped to see the progress-sharing idea adopted throughout the steel industry. The nine-member Long Range committee, which worked out the details, included three top company men, three top union officials, and three distinguished labor relations specialists. The latter were George W. Taylor of the University of Pennsylvania, David L. Cole, labor attorney and arbitrator, and John T. Dunlop of Harvard University. The composition of the committee gave the plan a significance which its details might otherwise not have merited, for in its broad approach it did not differ much from the Scanlon idea. Its basic elements were a sharing of cost savings and a scheme for protecting workers displayed by technological or methods changes from losing company employment. Although it did not provide, as the Scanlon Plan did, for joint suggestion or cost-cutting committees, a large number of such committees emerged spontane-

[29] For an interesting account of the origination of this plan, see James A. Henderson et al., *Creative Collective Bargaining* (Englewood Cliffs, N.J.: Prentice-Hall, 1965), chapter 8.

ously and there was, reportedly, a marked improvement in worker attitudes.

A program which stemmed directly from the original Scanlon experience was introduced into a number of companies by Harold J. Ruttenberg, director of research for the steelworkers union from 1934 to 1946, a steel manager and employer for fifteen years, and then head of an industrial consulting firm called Humanation Associates. Ruttenberg's aim was "to discover in each plant the best way of recognizing the mutual interests of employee and employer in the survival and success of the enterprise."[30] He felt that the union was using its power to price itself out of the market and that unless earnings were related to productivity, the workers would pay a heavy cost in unemployment. His alternative was to demonstrate to unionized, financially profitable companies that by a total approach to productivity, by developing managers and workers into an integrated competitive team, and by using a plantwide incentive system, it was possible to raise productivity by 15 to 33 per cent. Most important was the fact that the unionist would develop an interest in the problems in a specific plant, in a specific business, facing a specific market.

Ruttenberg was much influenced in his thinking by the ideas of Allen Rucker, who in 1931–1932 worked out a formula tying wages to productivity.[31] Rucker identified what he called "production value" or what the Census Bureau calls "value added" (the difference between net sales and the cost of raw materials, supplies and outside services) and determined that for many firms whose output is relatively stable and product changes are evolutionary, the relation between wage costs and production value is almost a constant. With this relationship as its base, the

---

[30] Harold J. Ruttenberg, *How to Save and Create Jobs in the Pittsburgh Area* (Pittsburgh: Humanation Associates, 1964), p. 5.

[31] Ibid., pp. 72–75.

Rucker Plan called for labor-management cooperation to raise output and cut costs, sharing the gains through group incentives.

DISCUSSION COMMITTEES AND COLLECTIVE BARGAINING

A development of some interest also occurred in the relationship between the chief negotiators in several major industries about 1959 and 1960. For the most part the collective-bargaining model entailed only periodic interactions between the national union leaders and the key management spokesmen—at contract negotiation time and in "crisis" situations. The growing complexity of bargaining issues and the difficult new problems which rapid technological change produced led to the realization that these periodic interactions were insufficient. Collective bargaining at the policy-making level was seen to necessitate a continuing exchange of ideas and information as much as the implementation of contracts at the plant level. If the bargaining process was to avoid regular prolonged breakdowns, the parties had to undertake a great deal of preliminary preparation and mutual education.

The result of this new awareness was the establishment in many of the major industries—meat packing, steel, longshore, autos, and electrical products—of special committees to carry on a continuing exploration and discussion of troubling problems in an educational rather than a bargaining context. One of the first was the Armour Automation committee, set up by the Armour Company and the two main meat-packing unions. The committee, composed of management, union, and "public" representatives, sponsored a series of studies dealing with the problems of unemployment, reemployment, training, transfers, and the like which were created by the shutdown of a number of old plants that had become obsolescent technologically as well as geographically. Actually the term *automation* in the title of the committee was inaccurate, but the situation was much the same as if the displacement had been created by automation.

No two experiments along this line worked the same way. In the West Coast longshore industry, the parties engaged in studies (assisted by an expert from the Bureau of Labor Statistics) which led to a far-reaching agreement that permitted the employers to make major revisions of work methods and techniques in return for wage and employment guarantees, early retirements with substantial termination pay, as well as increased benefits and pay increases. In effect a heritage of restrictive work rules was "bought out." The employers got enhanced efficiency; the employees got economic benefits, security, and an enlarged body of information about the industry. In the steel industry the parties set up a Human Relations committee, which was to make its own studies (outsiders were not used) and to carry on discussions on contract problems in a quiet, unpublicized manner— a considerable contrast to the fish-bowl manner in which the contract negotiations had increasingly been conducted.

PROFIT SHARING

It would hardly be appropriate to refer to profit-sharing developments as experiments, considering the long history of the profit-sharing movement. But after World War II the character of the movement changed dramatically. While there was some extension of the traditional approach, which considered profit sharing primarily as the basis for a comprehensive system of industrial government, the main emphasis in the postwar period was on plans designated as deferred profit sharing that were akin to pension and retirement programs. The deferred plan is believed to have received its initial stimulus from an investigation and report in 1938–1939 by a subcommittee of the U.S. Senate under the chairmanship of Michigan Senator Arthur Vandenburg. The Vandenburg committee reported only about 728 plans in existence, but it strongly endorsed the idea of profit sharing as a symbol of the free enterprise system and as a means of improving employee-employer relations. Favorable tax legislation for deferred plans was recommended. During the war, profit sharing, like many fringe benefits, was given additional encouragement by the War Labor Board as long as it did not serve as a subterfuge for wage increases and did not result in any price increases. In the postwar decades of generally high and profitable economic activity, the deferred plans, together with pension plans, were promoted by banks, mutual funds, insurance companies, and other trustee groups.

Because of the differences in conception, statistics on profit-sharing plans vary. In 1957 the Council of Profit Sharing Industries, which had been formed in 1947 with the support of a number of longtime practitioners of profit sharing, estimated that the number of plans had grown to between 1500 and 2000.[32] But a study by the Profit Sharing Research Foundation which was an outgrowth of a Council committee estimated that there were 8200 qualified deferred and combination (deferred and cash) plans in 1955. The Foundation study reported over 20,000 plans by 1960 and nearly 43,000 by 1965.[33]

For the most part, organized labor remained "consistently cautious or overtly hostile" to profit sharing.[34] The plans were seen as management tools, installed unilaterally by management, and controlled by management. Some modification in union attitudes was reflected in the plans worked out by Eric Johnston and several AFL unions at his four West Coast establishments and by the Adamson Company of East Palestine, Ohio, and the steelworkers union, the first of the Scanlon efforts. Perhaps the most

[32] Joseph B. Meier, ed., *Profit Sharing Manual* (Chicago: Council of Profit Sharing Industries, 1957), p. 18.

[33] B. L. Metzger, *Profit Sharing in Perspective*, 2nd ed. (Evanston, Ill.: Profit Sharing Research Foundation, 1966), p. 17.

[34] Kenneth M. Thompson, *Profit Sharing: Democratic Capitalism in American Industry* (New York: Harper and Bros., 1949), p. 43.

significant change in union attitudes occurred when Walter Reuther announced that profit sharing had become a major goal of the UAW in 1958, although only one auto firm—American Motors—agreed (in 1961) to establish what was called a "progress sharing fund." The agreement provided that two-thirds of the portion of profits set aside for the employees would be distributed either as wages or other benefits, as determined by a joint management-union committee, and the remaining third would be placed in a trust fund for each individal worker in the form of stocks. At the 1959 UAW convention, Reuther told the delegates that "when we proposed profit sharing last year we were fully aware that we were going counter to a long-standing position of the bulk of the American trade union movement." But the old fears and objections were no longer justified. The union was strong enough to prevent speedups or other abuses, and it would not permit profit sharing to substitute for proper basic wages. "Legitimate cooperation" Reuther said, "between workers and employers for mutual objectives, without sacrifice of the workers' basic rights and interests, has never been opposed by the UAW and, to the extent that profit sharing would foster such cooperation, the effect would be a desirable one."[35] Two years after the American Motors progress-sharing pact, however, widespread employee discontent was expressed and neither side claimed any improvement in relations.[36] In 1964 the plan was sharply revised and restricted.

Contributions and Challenges from the Intellectuals

During World War II a large number of academicians participated in governmental labor programs or assumed industrial relations positions with employers and unions. When the war

[35] UAW-CIO, *Report of the President*, Submitted to the Seventeenth Constitutional Convention (October 9, 1959), pp. 50–52.
[36] Henderson et al., *Creative Collective Bargaining*, pp. 48–49.

ended and they returned to the universities, they brought back with them firsthand experiences and insights which greatly enriched the study of industrial government. The establishment of industrial and labor relations centers, institutes, and schools in more than two dozen of the major universities gave a strong institutional base for research and teaching. In several universities—Cornell, Illinois, Wisconsin, Minnesota, Michigan State —specialized postgraduate degrees in industrial relations were also introduced.

Most of these academicians accepted the new version of the collective-bargaining model and searched for ways of making it work better. A popular topic of research in the first postwar decade was how to reduce industrial conflict and to create industrial peace and harmony.[37] A second subject of relevant interest was management and union organization and administration— how to achieve organizational goals through effective leadership, communications, and teamwork. And a third area of interest was the web of rules in the workplace that developed in the process of industrialization.

These researchers helped considerably to illuminate the governmental process in industry. Industrial sociologists, like William Whyte and Melville Dalton, following the lead of Elton Mayo, revealed the informal group network underlying the formal structure and showed how the behavior of these informal groups often led to profound deviations from formal agreements and procedures. Psychologists like Douglas McGregor and Rensis Likert suggested that the quality of plant relations depended in considerable measure on the theories which managers held (consciously or not) of the worker's attitude toward work. Other psychologists, like Ross Stagner, emphasized the perceptual aspects of group interaction as a source of conflict. The multi-

[37] For references on this and the following topics, see Milton Derber, *Research in Labor Problems in the United States* (New York: Random House, 1967), chapter 5.

plicity of interest groups within the workforce was demonstrated by Leonard Sayles and George Strauss; James Kuhn showed how this diversity created "fractional bargaining" in the shop within the more unified and homogeneous bargaining at the formal level. The effectiveness of leadership was traced by Fred Fiedler and others to situational as well as trait characteristics. John Dunlop, in his conceptualization of the industrial-relations system, stressed the importance of the technological, budgetary, and power elements of the environment for the working rules which the system produced. Numerous other scholars threw light on the collective-bargaining process, contract administration, grievance handling, and arbitration. While few definitive principles emerged from these studies, they suggested how more effective leaders, better communications, greater understanding of the other person's goals and standards, clearer appreciation of the economic and political environment, stronger organizational lines, etc. could improve industrial democracy.

Some intellectuals, however, began to raise searching questions about the new model and the system in which it operated. These critiques emanated from several very different perspectives, and their authors often differed with one another. One type of challenge came from organizational students who saw a growth in industrial bureaucracy which seemed incompatible with industrial democracy. For example, Seymour Lipset, Martin Trow, and James Coleman, in their penetrating analysis of one of the most democratic of unions, the International Typographical Union, reached a conclusion that for most organizations the iron law of oligarchy formulated in 1911 by the German sociologist, Robert Michels, probably still held. Chris Argyris, looking at management organization, contended that the goals of the individual and the goals of the large organization were basically incompatible. During the fifties many writers expressed concern over the homogenizing impact of the organization on the individual; the "organization man" was widely bemoaned.

The Fund for the Republic established a Center for the Study of Democratic Institutions, and this center in turn sponsored a series of discussions and research projects on the problems of achieving and maintaining democracy within the corporation, the trade unions, religious institutions, and political institutions.

An unusual development was the alienation and disaffiliation of a considerable number of intellectuals who had served the labor movement for many years. Men like George Brooks, Solomon Barkin, and Paul Jacobs, as well as intellectuals on the outside, launched broadsides at what they perceived to be stagnation and complacency in the labor movement, a lack of social consciousness and interest, and an unwillingness to help the poor and discriminated. They also argued that collective bargaining was losing much of its relevancy in the modern world, that the great economic and industrial problems of the day no longer could be dealt with effectively through collective bargaining.

Solomon Barkin, concerned with what he perceived as a crisis for trade unionists and for American democracy, asked a series of perceptive questions:

> What is sapping the vitality of this essential institution of our democratic society? Is the answer to be found in the success with which employers have been able to liquidate unions; in the contraction of employment in unionized industries; in the increased aggressiveness and frank opposition of employers; in the misbehavior of individual union leaders; in the sullied image of unionism resulting from the propaganda of its opponents and from Congressional hearings; or in the disillusionment of former supporters? Have unions lost their appeal because of anachronistic goals, aspirations, and policies, because of inadequate and unsophisticated performance?

> Why are the unorganized workers unreceptive to the call for collective action and loath to fight for its attainment? Must the country wait, as it did in the past, for a new cycle of revulsion against social conditions to usher in a new upsurge in union organization?

Is the saturation of our culture and our school instruction with the concepts of frontier individualism so antagonistic to unionism that only profound personal and social disturbances can awaken employees to the needs of collective organization? Must we look to another event like the adoption of the Wagner Labor Relations Act before the legitimacy of unionism is reestablished for the great mass of the white collar workers? Will a new National Labor Relations Board and staff more understanding of the protection needed by employees seeking to organize unions and ready to combat employers' anti-union tactics prove sufficient to change the trends? Do the difficulties lie within the movement, or among the employees, or in the environment, or in all three?[38]

For Paul Jacobs the answer lay in two fundamental alterations in industrial society. The system of collective bargaining was less and less adequate for the solution of basic problems facing unions and management, such as the particular unemployment that automation brings to a particular plant and the operation of the growing "cold war industries." Secondly, an increasing number of workers, due to technological unemployment and to the shift from manufacturing to service and government, remained outside the system with very little possibility that they would ever come into it.[39]

Daniel Bell offered a different explanation in an article entitled provocatively "The Capitalism of the Proletariat: A Theory of American Trade-Unionism."[40] He saw job-conscious or market unionism becoming an "ally" of its industry, a part of the establishment, the manager of worker discontent. Union membership had reached its upper limit; unions had achieved the limits of collective bargaining; the proletariat was being re-

[38] Solomon Barkin, *The Decline of the Labor Movement: And What Can Be Done about It* (Santa Barbara, Calif.: Center for the Study of Democratic Institutions, 1961), pp. 7–8.

[39] Paul Jacobs, *Old before Its Time: Collective Bargaining at 28* (Santa Barbara, Calif.: Center for the Study of Democratic Institutions, 1963), pp. 9–11.

[40] Daniel Bell, *The End of Ideology: On the Exhaustion of Political Ideas in the Fifties*, 2nd rev. ed. (New York: Collier Books, 1962), chapter 10.

placed by a salariat; and labor had lost its élan and public favor. To Bell the unions' only hope for revival lay in the resurgence of organized labor as a social movement—not in the direction of radical socialism but rather in the form of a more emphatic version of "laborism" that insisted on "such benefits as better housing, more schools, adequate medical care, the creation of a more 'humanistic' work atmosphere in the factory, and the like."

A final challenge to the industrial-democracy model came from students of industrial society who envisioned, with considerable misgiving, the automated and bureaucratized society of the future. The sentiments of this group were perhaps best reflected in the work of a French social philosopher, Jacques Ellul, entitled *The Technological Society*. Ellul's book was originally published in 1954 but did not receive an English translation or much attention in the United States until 1964. One of the Americans most impressed by this book, and a stimulating commentator in his own right on the problems of the automated society, Robert Theobald, wrote in a review article that Ellul "convincingly demonstrates that technology, which we continue to conceptualize as the servant of man, will overthrow everything that prevents the internal logic of its development, including humanity itself—unless we take the necessary steps to move human society out of the environment that 'technique' is creating to meet its own needs."[41]

Thus at a time when the collective-bargaining model of industrial democracy was reaching a high point of sophistication, the validity of its very foundation was being seriously questioned.

[41] Robert Theobald, *The Nation*, 199 (October 19, 1964), 11:249. John Galbraith's *The New Industrial State* (Boston: Houghton Mifflin, 1967) adds some important insights on the changing character of the large corporation and its emerging "technostructure." I have not attempted to discuss this work because it appeared after my closing date, 1965.

CHAPTER **17**

PROGRESS AND
DOUBTS, 1965

BETWEEN 1945 AND 1965 the collective-bargaining model of industrial democracy attained its highest level of acceptability up to that point in American history and, paradoxically, at the same time began to be subjected to serious doubts and questions from supporters as well as opponents. The level of acceptability is indicated by the extent to which collective bargaining was practiced in the nation's major industries, by the legal framework which Congress and the courts had erected to support and regulate it, and by the policy statements of every important governmental and employer body as well as those of organized labor. President Kennedy's tripartite Advisory Committee on Labor-Management Policy began its report on "Free Collective Bargaining and Industrial Peace" with the declaration: "Collective bargaining is an essential element of economic democracy. The freedom-of-choice elements in collective bargaining derive from the basic principles of the free society and must be carefully preserved to help achieve our national goals."[1]

[1] Advisory Committee on Labor-Management Policy, "Report to the President, May 1, 1962." *Labor Relations Reference Manual,* 50 (Washington, D.C.: Bureau of National Affairs, Inc., 1962):11.

President Eisenhower's Commission on National Goals stated in a section on "The Democratic Economy": "Collective bargaining between representatives of workers and employers should continue as the nation's chief method for determining wages and working conditions. Conferences among management, union leaders, and representatives of the public can contribute to mutual understanding of problems that affect the welfare of the economy as a whole."[2]

Concurrent with these affirmations, however, was the critique. As an Independent Study Group (composed of academicians and arbitrators) reported to the Committee for Economic Development:

> A generation ago, industrial relations in the United States were undergoing an historic transformation, moving from unilateral decision-making by management toward joint decision-making by management and organized workers. Collective bargaining . . . was in process of becoming a truly national institution. In the quarter century that has elapsed since the mid-1930's, this form of industrial relations has been widely accepted in principle but is now being criticized more and more in practice. In recent years particularly, collective bargaining has been the target in a cross-fire of mounting complaints about its past and present consequences and of increasing reservations about its future serviceability.[3]

It is therefore important in assessing the balance sheet for the final period covered in this study to carefully depict and weigh both the elements of gain and the elements of loss or insufficiency.

---

[2] *Goals for Americans: The Report of the President's Commission on National Goals* (New York: Prentice-Hall, Spectrum Book edition, February 1963), p. 9.

[3] Committee for Economic Development, *The Public Interest in National Labor Policy,* by an Independent Study Group (New York: CED, 1961), p. 7.

Representation

The principle of union representation in industry reached a high point of development just before the end of the first postwar decade and then appeared to settle into something of a plateau. (In terms of percentage of civilian labor force organized, the BLS reported a decline from 25.2 in 1956 to 22.4 in 1965.) The conventional index (ratio of union membership to civilian or nonfarm labor force) was misleading, however. Wherever the unions had become established—in manufacturing, transportation, construction, mining, etc.—collective bargaining continued uninterrupted; the number of workers covered declined only because of a shift in the composition of the labor force from the more strongly unionized blue-collar to the less strongly unionized white-collar occupations and industries.

But in the late 1950's and particularly in the 1960's a dramatic change in attitude and behavior began to occur among white-collar workers. Teachers, nurses, social workers, and civil servants started to turn to the collective-bargaining model. They were abetted in this move by President Kennedy's Executive Order 10988 encouraging unionization among federal employees and by public employee laws favoring organization in a number of states from Connecticut, Massachusetts, and Rhode Island on the East Coast to Wisconsin, Michigan, and Missouri in the Midwest to Washington, Oregon and California on the West Coast. The drive of the AFL-CIO unions in the public and private white-collar sectors stimulated the conversion to trade-union behavior of many other employee organizations that had formerly functioned solely as professional or semiprofessional societies. Such changes occurred in the million-member National Education Association, the American Nurses Association, the Civil Service Associations of New York and Oregon, and many other groups. Thus the organizational economy grew rather than declined.

Some sectors of the economy continued to reject the principle of representation. Employee organization made little headway in the finance and insurance fields outside of some Eastern insurance firms. The large and growing engineering profession failed to listen to union appeals outside of a few isolated enterprises, such as the Tennessee Valley Authority and some aircraft plants. Farm employees made a small breakthrough in the California vineyards but, being exempted from the protection of the National Labor Management Relations Act, had great difficulty in overcoming employer opposition to unionization. In rural sections of the South, anti-union sentiments still reigned. But all of these unorganized sectors reflected a posture which was out of keeping with the main trend in American industrial life.

The selection of exclusive bargaining representatives by majority rule became firmly established in the 1930's and, as a general principle, encountered no serious challenges in the postwar period. The only legislative alternative adopted was the idea of proportional representation embodied in a 1965 California law giving public school teachers the right to meet and confer with school boards on economic and instructional matters. This revival of proportional representation won little support elsewhere and had little practical consequence in California. Under the Kennedy Executive Order 10988, three types of union recognition were made available to federal employee organizations: (a) informal, allowing a minority organization to present its views to officials on matters of concern to its members, (b) formal, giving organizations with a membership of no less than ten per cent of the unit the right to be consulted by management on the formulation and implementation of personnel policies and practices, and matters affecting working conditions that were of concern to its members, and (c) exclusive, giving sole bargaining rights to a majority union as under the National Labor Management Relations Act for private employees. Federal employee unions were generally dissatisfied with the deviation from private sector practice and pressed for a change. In the private sector there continued to be controversies over appropriate bargaining units, although the Taft-Hartley Law gave professional and craft groups protection against being included in wider units contrary to their will.

The major representational issue of the period had to do with the closed and union shops. Taft-Hartley prohibited the closed shop and permitted the union shop requiring all employees to become union members in thirty days after employment only if a majority of the employees specifically voted for it. The requirement for a separate ballot on the union shop was subsequently eliminated as unnecessary. In some twenty states opponents of the union shop succeeded in getting legislation enacted which prohibited compulsory union membership. This so-called "right-to-work" legislation was passed mainly in southern and central nonindustrial states—it was adopted in only one industrial state, Indiana, and subsequently revoked there. The unions were successful in their revocation drives in only one other state, Louisiana; but on the other hand, they were able to defeat right-to-work campaigns in other states as well as at the level of the federal government. A strong union effort to amend the federal law to establish the federal preemption doctrine and thereby void the state right-to-work laws was unable to muster enough congressional support despite the backing of Presidents Kennedy and Johnson.

Participation

The problem of containing or even reducing union participation in management decision-making was a central concern to unionized employers as a whole. This concern was evident in President

Truman's postwar labor-management conference as well as in the employer-supported amendments to the Taft-Hartley Law which were designed to reduce union power. By and large the employers were successful in their containment movement—for three reasons. One was the resurgence in employer strength and popular prestige following the debacle of the thirties. A second factor was the self-limiting nature of most American unions— union leaders and members gave no sign of wishing to assume parity in decision-making with employers outside of job-related matters; they preferred the role of critic. Third, many unions were willing to give up what employers regarded as restrictive work rules or abstain from pressing for new rules in return for substantial economic benefits. The latter phenomenon is illustrated by the agreements reached in the railroad and longshore industries; it is also indicated in the auto industry where the powerful UAW achieved major advances in wages and fringe benefits but yielded considerable leeway to the companies on work standards and the speed of the assembly lines.[4]

It is true that during this period the NLRB and the courts gradually extended the concept of the scope of bargaining to include such items as pensions, year-end bonuses, and contracting out. But these decisions simply affirmed practices which had long existed in the garment industries, in coal mining, and other well-established collective-bargaining systems.

Perhaps the most interesting participation issues arose in some of the newly unionized sectors like public education and social work where employee organizations sought to forge a new amalgam between their professional interests and their economic objectives. The American Federation of Teachers, for example, wished to have a decision-making voice not only in salaries and class size but also in the location and quality of schools, in the character of new school programs, and in the mission of the

---

[4] I am indebted to my colleague Bernard Karsh for this observation.

school system. Similarly the social workers were concerned with the standards for their relief clients as well as their own job standards. Still in process of crystallization were the lines to be drawn between the subjects that were appropriate for bargaining and those that were in the domain of consultation (i.e., the union would be given the right to express its views but would not have a determinative voice in the final decision).

Worker participation in decision-making, as distinct from the role of their organizational representatives, was given some stimulus by the adoption of the Scanlon and Rucker Plans. But the joint production committees of World War II did not survive and, apart from the extension of suggestion systems and the establishment of some joint safety and health committees, the worker participation movement did not make much headway.

While management was relatively successful in limiting union and worker participation in decision-making, it was unable to prevent the federal government from assuming an increasing role in many important industries. Such a role emerged primarily from the newly assumed responsibilities of the government for the maintenance of high level employment, strong economic growth, and stable prices. But it also stemmed from the ever-widening interests of the government in military-related industries; in research and development; in space, missiles, atomic energy, and communication systems—all reflective of the new technological society. The crises in race relations and urban living, as well as the international military scene (Korea, Vietnam, etc.), also promoted a greater governmental role in industrial-relations decisions.

Government participation took a variety of forms. In the major disputes in steel, railroads, longshore, and airlines, the White House became directly involved in working out a settlement; and in the case of the railroads, Congress took the unprecedented peacetime step of imposing binding arbitration. The wage-price guideposts, although they were hortatory and not legally binding, were another major move by government to participate in the collective-bargaining process. President Kennedy's assault on the steel companies for a general price increase in 1962, forcing a cutback, was the most extreme and overt example, but more subtle pressures were exerted on other occasions. The activities of the National Labor Relations Board, the Equal Employment Opportunity Commission, the Labor Department in the implementation of the Landrum-Griffin Law—all had important effects on enterprise and industrial administration.

Equal Rights and Opportunities

The gap between principle and practice with respect to equal rights narrowed to a greater extent than in any previous period. First through Executive Order and then through federal and state legislation a vigorous attack was made on discrimination because of race, sex, and other traditional reasons.

Major progress was made in the fight against discrimination toward female employees. The century-old issue of equal pay for equal work was finally subjected to legal regulation by an amendment to the Fair Labor Standards Act of 1963. Discrimination in employment because of sex was banned under Title VII of the 1964 Civil Rights Act. Discrimination because of age was also proscribed, with varying degrees of effectiveness, in a number of state laws. The Civil Rights Act (Section 715) directed the secretary of labor to make a comprehensive study of the factors which might tend to result in discrimination in employment because of age and of the consequences of such discrimination on the economy and individuals affected. This report, which was issued in June 1965, recommended, among other things, a federal antidiscrimination law; but no congressional action had been taken by the closing date of this volume.

The race barrier was the most difficult to penetrate because of the depth of racism in American culture. By the 1960's many of the top leaders of corporate and union organizations seemed to be genuinely convinced that discrimination had to be eliminated from industry to prevent widespread disorder and disunity in the nation. Nonetheless, despite laws, policy statements, and agreements, achievement of equal rights was slow. The difficulties in the construction industry to open apprenticeship opportunities to black youth were not surprising because of the decentralization of power and the numerous ways in which reluctant white workers and business agents could evade or delay compliance. But even in industries where the unions had developed a favorable reputation for opposing discrimination, such as in the needle trades, autos, and steel, militant black groups charged continued discrimination and pressed for greater opportunity and voice.

A significant index of the gains that were achieved was the fact that much of the struggle for black equality shifted from the issue of hiring (although that remained serious, especially for black youth) to the issue of advancement to higher-level positions in the skilled trades, in management, in white-collar occupations, and in union leadership. Perhaps the greatest advances came in the federal government itself, which, having assumed a key role in the equal rights fight, felt a special obligation to implement the policies that it advocated. The 1968 report of the National Advisory Commission on Civil Disorders stated, however, that Negro men were more than twice as likely as whites to be in unskilled or service jobs which pay far less than most and estimated that upgrading the employment of Negro men to make their occupational distribution identical with that of the labor force as a whole in 1965 would have shifted wage and salary income upwards by 30 per cent.[5]

[5] *Report of the National Advisory Commission on Civil Disorders* (New York: Bantam Books, 1968), pp. 253–256.

NLRB and court decisions contributed to the advancement of equal rights for black workers who were employed. The death blow was given to discriminatory union constitutional provisions and bylaws, to segregated or Jim Crow locals, and to grievance procedures which did not treat all employees on an equal basis.

Right of Dissent

The freedom of the individual worker to express views different from those of his supervisor or of the company increased appreciably with the growth in union power. Selig Perlman's observation in 1928 of the importance to the worker of not having to kowtow to his boss in the shop was validated in many unionized enterprises. This pattern carried over to many non-unionized situations as well. It was well illustrated by the change in the position of the public school teacher who had traditionally been severely restrained by school board rules and administrative directives.

For the dissenting worker within the union, the 1959 Landrum-Griffin Law marked a major step forward. In its report for fiscal 1965,[6] the Labor Department noted that all but 21 of the trusteeships established prior to the LMRDA had been terminated by the end of the 1965 year and that 18 of the remainder of this group (in the jurisdiction of the United Mine Workers) were being challenged in the courts. Trusteeships by the national unions often served useful functions in eliminating local corruption, but they had also served as a device in some unions to curtail local freedom. Now the Labor Department helped to separate the two types. On June 30, 1965, there were only 226 active trusteeships compared with 488 in mid-September, 1959.

[6] U.S., Department of Labor, *1965 Summary of Operations, Labor-Management Reporting and Disclosure Act* (Washington, D.C.: Government Printing Office, 1965).

Another area affected by the law was union elections. Claims of irregularities were investigated in 119 cases in fiscal 1965. More than two-thirds of the cases were closed because no violations were found or there was insufficient evidence or for other similar reasons. But in the national elections of the International Union of Electrical, Radio, and Machine Workers, the reelection of an incumbent president was found to be fraudulant, and his opponent was installed in his place. The 1965 election of the huge Steelworkers Union was supervised by the Labor Department under agreement between the two slates of candidates. The department also supervised eight court-ordered elections during the year because of minority group charges of irregularity. Since the act's passage, 54 national unions with over 13 million members had changed their constitutional rules on local elections to bring about conformity with one or more of the act's requirements.[7]

The act was instrumental in correcting other abuses by union leaders. For example, sixteen members of a Philadelphia Teamsters local were enabled to end the use of union funds to defend union officers in several criminal cases. In another type of situation, a court ordered the reinstatement of a union member who had been expelled for "malicious vilification" of union officers, holding that the act protected the right of a member to express views critical of union officers and their policies at a union meeting—even if the statements were false and libelous.[8]

Formal proceedings under Landrum-Griffin involved only a small proportion of the nation's unions and union members. But the few important cases had a widespread effect, reinforcing the Ethical Practices Codes which the AFL-CIO had adopted and the public review boards which the Auto Workers and a few other unions had established.

One of the issues of the late 1930's was the restrictions which

[7] Ibid., p. 9.
[8] Ibid., p. 22.

the NLRB imposed on employer speech in union representation and bargaining situations. Employer organizations complained that their constitutional freedom to speak was being curtailed. This complaint was largely remedied by an amendment in the Taft-Hartley Act. However, the concept of coercive and therefore illegal speech was retained and arguments continued in specific cases as to whether employer speech was legitimate or whether it threatened worker and union self-organizational rights.

Due Process

The idea of effective grievance machinery including binding arbitration by a neutral third party, which the National War Labor Board had so vigorously endorsed, became almost universal practice in the postwar period. Many of the public representatives on the board and its various agencies were the skilled arbitrators of the succeeding period. Arbitration of grievances became a distinctive profession and in 1947 the National Academy of Arbitrators, which grew to some 300 members, was formed. The arbitration process was given strong support by the U.S. Supreme Court in the *Lincoln Mills* and the steel *Trilogy* cases, with the holding that arbitration awards were enforceable in the courts under Section 301 of the Taft-Hartley Law.

Although the principle of due process was widely accepted by non-unionized as well as unionized enterprises, its implementation was not free from criticism or challenge both within industry and by outsiders. These criticisms took a variety of forms. One had to do with the delays which often occurred in the handling of grievances, despite time limits at various steps, and the consequent piling up of large backlogs. Such backlogs were reflected in local strikes in the auto and steel industries after company or industrywide contracts had been negotiated. One of the more ingenious attacks on the backlog problem was initiated at the International Harvester Company in 1959 which emphasized the elimination of paperwork and focused on the immediate joint union-management investigation of new grievances on an oral basis. Informality and problem-solving were substituted for legalism.[9] But this approach was not widely imitated.

Attacks were also made against the arbitration stage. It was alleged that arbitrators often exceeded their authority by interpreting contracts in ways not contemplated by the parties, that some arbitrators prolonged cases in order to increase their fees, that arbitration cost too much for small employers and unions, that arbitrators often were ignorant of the practices and problems of an industry, that the parties sometimes rigged the cases as a face-saving device, and that arbitrators tended to compromise decisions rather than to award a just decision in order to maintain favor with the parties.

In a series of lectures at Yale Law School in 1964, Judge Paul R. Hays aroused the ire of many arbitrators by attacking the philosophy of the Supreme Court decisions in *Lincoln Mills* and the *Trilogy* cases as well as the competency of the great majority of arbitrators.[10] Hays opposed the Court decision to make arbitration decisions legally enforceable. He believed that, if they were to be given legal sanction, labor agreements should be treated as contracts and not as industrial codes or systems of self-government. In this event, he felt that judges were better qualified and courts were more competent arenas than private

[9] An interesting account of the background of this new approach is given in James A. Henderson et al., *Creative Collective Bargaining* (Englewood Cliffs, N.J.: Prentice-Hall, 1965), chapter 8.

[10] Paul R. Hays, *Labor Arbitration: A Dissenting View* (New Haven: Yale University Press, 1966). Hays thought that the Court had been persuaded by such outstanding arbitrators and legal authorities as Harry Shulman of Yale and Archibald Cox of Harvard to idealize the arbitration process. Only a handful of arbitrators had the ability and character of a Shulman or Cox, he observed, to be good judges and therefore good arbitrators (p. 112).

arbitrators in an informal setting to enforce contracts. He suggested that some sort of labor court system, modeled after German or Swedish practice, might be desirable.

Hays' basic views, as he recognized, were not widely shared. But there were members of the National Academy of Arbitrators who were sensitive to the abuses occurring in the arbitration process and who sought ways of remedying them.

Responsibility

Throughout its history complaints had been made about irresponsibility in collective bargaining on the part of a minority of its practitioners. Unionists had been accused of abuse of power, illegal methods of coercion, and disregard for the economics of a firm or industry. Employers had been accused of utilizing labor spies, fomenting dissension in worker ranks, and cutting corners on agreed rules to save costs. The responsible leadership on both sides had strongly stressed the sanctity of agreements and had often exerted pressure on their own people to secure compliance.

The concept of responsibility was given added emphasis in the post–World War II period because of the growth in union strength and the temptations to abuse from the vast new retirement and welfare funds to be administered. Passage of the Landrum-Griffin Law, which was formally entitled the Labor-Management Reporting and Disclosure Act, was preceded by Congressional investigations into abuses in the administration of welfare funds as well as other corrupt practices. Financial responsibility was one of the main concerns of the law. This was equally true of the Ethical Practices Codes adopted by the AFL-CIO.

The most significant innovation with respect to the agreement system was the provision of the Taft-Hartley Law and the Supreme Court decisions, referred to above, which made collective-bargaining agreements legal contracts enforceable in the courts. Previously, contract violations were subject to legal proceedings in the states, but state practice varied widely and there was much confusion over the law in this respect. Even though relatively few cases went to the courts, the possibility of legal action undoubtedly reduced gross contract violations. The strengthening of the grievance arbitration system clearly had a similar effect since work stoppages during the contract period appear to have declined appreciably.

The issue of union economic responsibility was the most complex and contentious of the responsibility issues. Although unions in the past had been charged with demanding excessive wage increases, this was the first period in which "cost-push" (meaning wage increases in excess of productivity increases) became a subject of national debate. This charge of economic irresponsibility underlay a fairly strong (but unsuccessful) drive by some major employer groups to prohibit industrywide bargaining and to subject organized "monopoly" labor to the controls of the antitrust laws. Most studies of wage-price relationships tended to conclude that the union impact on inflation was relatively small but that under conditions of high level or full employment, union demands could have inflationary consequences. The wage-price guideposts policy was a government effort to reduce this possibility. The remarkable stability of the price level between 1962 and 1965 gave rise to the hope that the guideposts were a solution to the full-employment-inflation problem, but this optimism was soon to be shattered by the inflation of the Vietnam War years.

Minimum Standards

The principle of establishing socially acceptable minimum standards through legislative enactment was reinforced during the period. The Fair Labor Standards Act was amended not only to raise minimum wages to levels consistent with rising prices but also to extend its coverage to millions of low-paid farm, hospital, restaurant, laundry, and retail trade workers who had previously been exempted. The prevailing wage concept was enlarged for construction workers on public contracts to include a number of fringe benefits as well as wage rates; it was extended to service workers on government contracts and to the federal government's civil service employees whose salaries were to be placed on a parity with those of comparable office and professional workers in private industry. The social security system underwent the dual process of improved benefits and extended coverage which the minimum wage system experienced. The most important advance in social security standards was the provision of medicare for older persons.

Fewer changes were made in other traditional areas of protective labor law. Standard work hours remained generally unchanged at forty, although during the late 1950's and early 1960's the desirability of reducing the workweek below forty hours in order to cope with technological unemployment was widely discussed. In the job accident and illness area, the limitations of the long-established state workmen's compensation programs were exposed, and for the first time in half a century the principles of workmen's compensation were reexamined. The changes provided liberalized benefits for job-related sickness as well as accidents. The need to improve factory inspection and to establish national safety standards was not to be seriously advocated until 1968.

The standards of education for successful job careers were subjected to a "new look" in the 1960's. The Soviet sputnik challenge jarred the complacency of the public and the educational authorities as never before. But from the standpoint of industrial government, the recognition that technological advance and

automation were making uneducated people increasingly obsolete was at least as important. A major segment of the elaborate
job training programs approved by the Congress involved basic
general education for illiterate and semiliterate blacks and
whites alike. The need to raise educational levels was acknowledged as relevant for the prospective black auto worker from
Mississippi as well as for the prospective white auto worker from
Appalachia.

The "interrelationship of public and private programs in labor
relations" became, for the first time, a matter of practical as well
as theoretical concern.[11] Two key questions were involved. One
entailed determination of the areas which were appropriate
for governmental action. The other had to do with the level of
government standards. The strongly organized unions not only
bargained for higher private pensions and supplemental unemployment benefit programs to enrich federal programs but also
filled in the gaps in the social security program with hospitalization and medical benefits that the government had failed to fill.
Collective bargaining was seen as a way of pressuring employers to try to influence Congress when the latter was reluctant
to adopt protective labor legislation. The traditional view of
legislation as a protection for the marginal or submarginal worker applied mainly to unorganized manual and service occupations and to some of the fields predominantly employing women
or Negroes.

The plight of the poor, a theme common in American history,
was discussed in a new light. Earlier discussions had always been
cast in terms of poverty within a scarcity economy. Now the subject was over how to eradicate poverty in an affluent society. The
answers offered by the President's National Commission on
Technology, Automation, and Economic Progress (1965) were

---

[11] See the proceedings of a meeting of the Industrial Relations Research Association on this topic, Boston, Massachusetts, May 1–2, 1959.

an index of the extraordinary changes in thought which had taken place.[12] For those unsuccessful in the regular job market, the commission recommended that the government serve as the employer of last resort. For those who cannot or should not participate in the job economy, the commission recommended an adequate system of income maintenance, guaranteeing a floor of income at an acceptable level. The commission envisioned a variety of steps which both the government and the private parties (chiefly management and unions) could take to soften the blows of unemployment. The government could make improvements in education, retraining, and relocation assistance. The private decision-makers could utilize severance pay, early warning, company assistance in retraining and placement, more flexible work schedules, and vesting of pension rights. The possibilities for action by the collective-bargaining system were substantial; the actions taken were only a small portion of the potential.

Information

Walter Reuther lost his battle to force General Motors to "open its books" in 1945, but the movement for less secrecy and more information in economic affairs made appreciable headway after 1945 as compared with practice prior to 1940. The extensive involvement of the federal government in the life of private industry during the New Deal decade represented a major breakthrough. The even greater wartime involvement carried the process further. As the three principal institutions—the federal government, the corporation, and the national union—grew in size, it was perhaps only natural that they would scrutinize

[12] National Commission on Technology, Automation, and Economic Progress, *Technology and the American Economy,* 1 (February 1966).

each other and be scrutinized by the general public with increased concern.

The main contributor to the informational flow was the government. Starting in 1947 the annual reports of the President and the Council of Economic Advisers on the state of the economy provided the general framework. The President's annual Manpower Reports from 1963 onward threw much additional light on the labor force and the labor market. Both reports depended upon the primary data collections of other agencies, such as the Census Bureau, the Labor Department, and the Federal Reserve Board. The Bureau of Labor Statistics alone expanded to some 700 employees and was probably the largest compiler of labor relations data in the world. In contrast to the census, most of the BLS data were gathered through the voluntary cooperation of employers.

The Presidential, Council, Census, and BLS reports provided general economic data, broken down into industrial and occupational categories. Congressional investigations and the government's regulatory agencies produced vast amounts of information about individual corporations and unions. The McClellan committee hearings of the 1950's did to the unions, on a more limited scale, what the La Follette committee hearings of the 1930's did to the corporations—they exposed some of the sordid elements and created an atmosphere for reform. The result in 1959 was the Labor-Management Reporting and Disclosure Act, which among other things required unions to make available extensive information on their internal government, finances, and collective agreements to their members and to the public. The NLRB compelled employers to make available to majority unions data relevant to bargaining issues, such as seniority lists and the bases for subcontracting, although they did not go as far as some unions desired. The Securities and Exchange Commission, the Interstate Commerce Commission, and similar regulatory agencies were responsible, even more than in the past, for a great deal of information on corporate economic activities.

The informational expansion was not entirely the result of pressure and compulsion. During the 1920's the larger corporations had begun to recognize that in order to win and maintain the loyalty and effective service of their employees, it was necessary to give them an understanding of the economics of the enterprise and to establish good two-way communication channels. Corporations found that most employees had serious degrees of misunderstanding and ignorance about costs and profits. They learned that grievances were often caused by insufficient or misleading information. They also learned that management often did not know what was on the workers' minds. The informational and communications problems in the twenties was complicated by the fact that so large a proportion of the employees was foreign-born and from non-English-speaking countries. In the fifties and sixties, the educational level of the predominantly native-born work force was considerably higher than in the previous generation, and their leaders were economically more sophisticated. The informational level therefore had to be higher and the communications process more developed. Spurred on by the "human relations" proponents, communication became a major personnel function, most notably in a firm like General Electric which adopted management-to-worker communication as an essential tool during contract negotiations as well as in day-to-day plant relations.

Corporations had to communicate not only with more sophisticated workers and union leaders but also with a vastly enlarged body of stockholders. Between 1956 and 1965, for example, the estimated number of adult civilian shareholders rose from 8.3 to 18.5 million.[13] To carry out this dual system of communication effectively, company financial and other reports were made

[13] National Industrial Conference Board, *Economic Almanac, 1967–1968* (New York: Macmillan Co., 1967), p. 402.

much more attractive in format, more data were provided, and the style of writing became much more readable. Skilled journalists and public relations writers were employed by many of the larger firms to produce these reports as well as to enhance their "house organs."

For some critics, the line between providing useful information and propagandizing or manipulating the employees was often questionable. C. Wright Mills accused the communications advocates of the Mayo school of seeking to transform workers into "contented cows." L. Baritz warned of social scientists who had become "servants of power." There can be no doubt, however, that ordinary workers, union officials, and management were all better informed about their enterprises and unions and had available to them better channels of communication than ever before.

Personal Dignity

Whether the conditions for personal dignity advanced or retrogressed between 1945 and 1965 is perhaps the most difficult of the questions raised in this attempted assessment of industrial democracy. In purely physical respects the majority of workers were clearly better off. Their real earnings were higher, they enjoyed unprecedented fringe benefits, they worked in more attractive work places, they had more job protection, and they had more and better opportunities to state their grievances. Some work groups, of course, lagged behind the others—Negroes, migrant farm laborers, some categories of public employees—but even most of these were better off than their equivalents in the thirties or earlier.

Yet, despite the gains, the position of the individual within the corporation, within the trade union, and within government was being questioned as it had never been questioned before.

The Fund for the Republic, in announcing the establishment of the Center for the Study of Democratic Institutions, asserted: "Everywhere questions are being raised about the possibility of maintaining faith in democracy and making it effective in an industrialized, scientific, bureaucratic, polarized world."[14] Some writers worried about the "organization man," the problem of conformity, and the difficulty of individuals expressing themselves in ways that ran contrary to the interests of the organization. Others were concerned about the dehumanizing effects of the "second industrial revolution" which they perceived in computer technology. The National Commission on Technology, Automation, and Economic Progress stated: "Despite the contributions of technology to higher standards of living, we have not yet found ideal solutions to the monotony and drudgery of some work processes."[15] President Eisenhower's National Commission warned that to achieve the democratic economy, "corporations and labor unions must limit the influence they exert on the private lives of their members."[16]

These comments suggest that the dignity which the average worker was gaining through certain forms of organization was being endangered by the changes occurring in other aspects of institutional life.

Interpretations

How shall we account for the gains, setbacks, and gaps in industrial democracy described above? In the conceptual framework presented in Chapter 1, six sets of determinant factors were suggested—worker-manager attitudes, abilities of the parties, com-

[14] Fund for the Republic, *Bulletin*, November 1959.
[15] National Commission on Technology, Automation, and Economic Progress, p. 89.
[16] President's Commission on National Goals, p. 9.

munity climate, the political system, the economic situation, and technology. Each of these merits brief discussion.

As far as one can determine from opinion polls, attitude surveys, votes in NLRB elections, and other forms of overt behavior, the attitudes of most manual workers strongly favored the collective-bargaining model of industrial democracy. Union leaders who had gone through the struggles of the thirties sometimes complained about worker apathy and lack of appreciation of the tumultuous history of the labor movement; they criticized members who viewed unions like a slot-machine, i.e., evaluating the unions in terms of how wage increases compared with dues payments. But overall, union ranks held firm or expanded among the manual groups. Among white-collar employees, there was a dramatic shift from the traditional individualist attitude to the organizational, bargaining approach—especially among teachers, nurses, and other public employee groups. Major exceptions were professional engineers and financial employees. Thus, while it was by no means universal, the will of the workers was generally and strongly favorable to industrial democracy. Futhermore there was more uniformity of thought about the collective-bargaining model. The chief rivals to this model in the past—various forms of socialism or syndicalism—virtually disappeared from the scene after 1950.

On the employer side, attitudes similarly were conducive to the bargaining model, although this was probably more true of the large corporations than of small employers. By the end of World War II, the employer hope that the employee-representation model could supplant the collective-bargaining model was gone; most large employers reconciled themselves to living with the unions and directed their main efforts to protecting their managerial functions. Their relative success in this latter regard reinforced their attitude, particularly as they came to perceive the anti-radical nature of the American trade-union movement. Accommodation with the unions did not mean the absence of strife, but such accommodation was feasible. Among smaller employers, the fear of union domination and interference was greater and the unions were more often resisted. The response took a variety of forms, ranging from authoritarian hostility, as among farm employers, to quite sophisticated alternatives of a paternalistic nature, such as profit sharing and active communication programs.

The failure of the collective-bargaining model to advance more rapidly than it did in private industry must be attributed in considerable measure to the resistance tactics of smaller employers. Resistance in the public sector was rooted in traditional ideas about state sovereignty and was declining. However, among engineers and some other white collar groups—an expanding portion of the labor force—the predominant attitude appeared to remain more individualistic.

The rapidly increasing educational level of the labor force must be considered another factor in the spread of industrial democracy. The educated man is more likely to resist authoritarianism or paternalism because he views himself the equal of his employer (or his work superior) in thinking for himself. This attitude, resulting from education, may lead to individualism rather than reliance on a collective approach, but such individualism seemed to be discouraged by other elements in the modern organizational society. The educational upgrading of the Negro worker (although still in an early stage by 1965) added to the democratizing force because the Negro in the past had often been used by employers as a divisive instrument in resisting collective bargaining.

Although the problems of the city were coming to a head during the postwar period and racial conflicts were mounting in intensity, the community environment surrounding industrial enterprise also tended to support democratic movements within industry. With a few notable exceptions, the old-style political machines, which had relied on the manipulation of diverse new immigrant groups, had become obsolete. The struggle of the black community for a share in political power was democratizing in itself. City affairs were constantly exposed to the spotlight of publicity; civic groups were better organized and more sophisticated; the peccadillos of politicians were more quickly detected and assailed. Both union and employer organizations were increasingly involved in the public life of the city and thus there was a strong interchange of ideas between community and industry, reinforcing the democratic process in both. The company town still survived in some parts of the South, but it was a declining force.

The distribution of power in American society at large, especially as reflected in Washington, was also favorable to the collective-bargaining model of industrial democracy. The Taft-Hartley and Landrum-Griffin Acts had imposed restraints on union power but had not challenged the model's basic principles and in important respects had strengthened them. Union and employer forces were indeed in an unusual balance. This was shown in the conflict over the right-to-work issue. The employers who supported right-to-work legislation at the federal level and the unions who wished to restore the federal preemption clause to nullify state right-to-work laws were equally unsuccessful. The most significant change was in the role of the government. While organized labor and management had attained a position of approximate balance, the federal government greatly increased its role in American economic life. But in exercising its new functions and responsibilities, it had, for the most part, strengthened and not weakened industrial democracy in the nation.

The trend of the economy and of national economic policy in the postwar period was also favorable to industrial democracy. For the first time in American history, the government adopted a policy of full or near-full employment consistent with rapid economic growth and stable prices. Although the policy was not entirely realized, economic growth achieved unprecedented levels of affluence. The existence of a large minority of poor people (perhaps a fifth of the population) seriously marred the record; yet in comparison with the American past and with other large countries, the economic achievement was impressive. In any event, the economy facilitated industrial democracy because it made it possible for the parties to raise their minimum standards to generally acceptable levels, and it enabled industrial government to function on a profitable basis for all its participants.

The forces favorable to industrial democracy were confronted, however, with counterforces which threatened to undermine the system. These counterforces have been identified by a number of observers as technology, organizational size and complexity, and centrally-dominated bureaucracy. These three elements are not isolated. As technology becomes more and more sophisticated, it requires increasingly large concentrations of capital and scientific expertise. The organizations to manage such technology grow in size and develop characteristics commonly associated with bureaucracy—specialization of function, formal rules, an authority hierarchy, and a wide spread between the policy-makers and the mass of employees. Since union structure invariably adapts to the business structure, it too develops bureaucratic traits. Power becomes more centralized in fewer institutions and fewer hands. The result is a society dominated by Big Business, Big Unions, and Big Government in which the ordinary individual is dwarfed into a punchcard and democratic participation is reduced to minute proportions.

That such counterforces were at work in postwar America and that they were more extensive than in previous periods seems incontrovertible. But they were not new forces; they had been evolving over many decades. That they would make the concept of industrial democracy meaningless and unworkable was therefore not yet accepted doctrine. But they were the subject of growing fears and deepening consideration.

SECTION **VII**

EPILOGUE

CHAPTER **18**

FUTURE PROSPECTS

THE AMERICAN IDEA of industrial democracy which has
evolved over the past hundred years is the distinctive product
of the American people and the American environment. Important features of the collective-bargaining model were influenced
by British thought and experience, particularly during the nineteenth century. Marxist thinking, brought over by German and
Jewish intellectuals and workers, helped modify the model. But
mostly the formulation was the outcome of an organic process
in which one slowly evolving set of concepts competed with and
surpassed a number of rivals in the struggle for acceptance and
survival. The struggle was reflected in both theory and practice.
The collective-bargaining model triumphed over its rivals (paternalism, profit sharing, socialism, syndicalism, employee representation) because it worked in the American environment
better than they did and was more congenial in ideology to national sentiment.

The struggle was not an easy one; the environment contained
many hostile forces. Until well into the twentieth century, the
majority of the population was rural and small-town, sharing few
interests with the industrial workers in the cities. Farm-labor
movements were short-lived and achieved limited success. The
cities were controlled by businessmen and politicians who enun-

ciated and preached the doctrine of individual freedom to make contracts and to otherwise use their private property as they pleased, with a minimum of interference from the state. The judicial system long favored dominance by the business community. Worker challenges to the freedom of the businessmen proved successful only when they were able to marshall sufficient collective economic force. But worker collective organization was hindered by the diversity of the immigrant population whose ethnic differences in culture and language made manipulation by the politician and the businessman more feasible. The influx of immigrants in separate waves enabled the earlier immigrant groups to move up the socio-economic ladder at the expense of the later groups, adding an element of ethnic mobility to the natural economic mobility of a rapidly expanding society and thus promoting divisiveness.

In the early decades skilled craftsmen matched their relatively small employers in mental resources, shared interests and goals, and, given favorable economic circumstances, could deal with them on a fairly even (and sometimes superior) basis. It was in these sectors of the economy that the collective-bargaining idea of industrial democracy first took a firm hold. The mass of semiskilled and unskilled labor, however, was largely dependent on the paternal goodwill or the authoritarian rule of the employer. The larger the firm, the less voice for the body of workers.

Industrialization and urbanization—the concentration of capital and people—expanded the need for a collective approach to industrial democracy, provided its major obstacles, and in the end laid the basis for its achievement. With the growth of large-scale enterprise that widened the gap between employer and employee and with rapid and massive technological change that undermined traditional job skills, the nature of industrial government was profoundly altered. Individualism and informality were insufficient. Either the management had to develop effective formal administrative machinery on its own initiative or it had to be compelled by worker organization or government to share its sovereignty. Much of the conflict between 1865 and the 1940's was over these alternatives. The outcome was a bilateral employer-union system with an increasingly participant role for the government.

The change in public attitudes favoring the collective-bargaining model occurred slowly and erratically. The first positive shift took place around the turn of the century and during the following decade as a result of strong popular reaction to corporate monopoly power, the glaring inequities caused by unregulated abuses of such power, and concerns over the violence emerging from the prevailing conditions. The second major advance occurred during and immediately after World War I within the international context of democratization. The climax came with the labor legislation of the New Deal in the thirties and the reversal in the orientation of the U.S. Supreme Court. The most significant positive employer initiative—the employee-representation movement between 1915 and 1935—won widespread public approval until the collapse of employer power and prestige in the Great Depression. Following World War II the union movement lost its long-held role as economic and social underdog, and public sentiments approved legislative changes which restored some employer powers and regulated various aspects of union behavior in relation to the employers, individual workers, and internal union government. But these changes were seen as furthering industrial democracy, not negating it.

The industrial-democracy model was imbedded in the law of the land and in the social fabric during a period of deep depression and radical reform. Its position was solidified during a period of war and full employment. After 1945, under continuing favorable economic conditions, it was modified and elaborated but not fundamentally challenged. Yet as it matured and extended its roots, it began to encounter new challenges and new doubts resulting from new environmental conditions.

Some New General Considerations

The doubts and challenges and the evironmental conditions which projected them may be summarized in the following questions:

1. In a society newly committed to maintaining full or nearly full employment, rapid economic growth, the eradication of poverty, and price stability, is the collective-bargaining model of industrial government capable of coping with the major issues and problems, or must it be increasingly subordinated and subjected to government control and direction?

2. In a society undergoing revolutionary technological changes, typified by the electronic computer, automated production lines, atomic energy, the displacement of manual by white-collar workers, and the growth of professionalism, can the collective-bargaining model based on independent trade unionism and largely autonomous managers perform its functions without drastic alteration?

3. In a society dominated by huge organizations of men and capital, can industrial democracy with a concern for the rights, opportunities, and personal dignity of the individual employee operate at a level that is compatible with technological and bureaucratic requirements of efficiency and effectiveness?

Virtually every informed look into the future supports the relevancy of these questions for the decades immediately ahead. The welfare state, the technological revolution, the mass organizational society must be the assumptions for any assessment of future prospects in industrial government in the United States. What are the implications of these assumptions for the collective-bargaining model overall?

One implication is that the enterprise cannot be treated as a self-contained and isolated unit. The rules of the enterprise must not only be accommodated to the constraints of the external society but must be positively integrated with the community's and nation's objectives and goals. For example, relocation of a plant must be related to the old community's employment and fiscal situation as well as to the new community's resources. Job training for the culturally disadvantaged must be provided. Workers displaced by technological change must be given maximum transfer opportunities, retraining programs, and adequate severance pay so that they do not bear all of the costs of technical progress.

A second implication is that as the level of education and skill of the work force rises, it will become increasingly more difficult for the rule-makers not to share their sovereignty with all segments of the employee group, and to involve them in policy- and decision-making. This is illustrated by the experience of the skilled craftsmen who formed the first unions and of the professionals who associated in societies to advance the standards of their profession. It is interesting that these two categories have displayed the greatest concern in controlling their work conditions.

A third implication is that as the new technology brings about changes in the occupational structure and in the management structure, the units of government may have to be altered to make them compatible. For example, rapid-speed information systems will allow closer central controls over corporate units while permitting decentralized decision-making with respect to different products and geographic locations. Coalitions and mergers among unions will be necessary to keep pace with the spread of multiproduct companies and conglomerates.

Many scholars have agreed with Robert Michels on the oligarchical tendencies of modern mass institutions. Few American corporations have developed democratic managerial organizations; the typical management has been hierarchical and centrally controlled by a single head or by a small committee. The leadership has normally been free to alter the managerial structure and its composition at will, without restriction. Unions started out as highly democratic organizations; but as they grew in size and complexity, many of the national unions and some of the larger local unions lost their democratic character and became dominated by small cliques or factions. Whether either management or union can be made more democratic by voluntary reforms or through legislative edict, such as the Landrum-Griffin Act, remains to be seen. On the other hand, it has been argued persuasively that regardless of the outcome of intra-institutional democracy, the existence of counteracting organizations within industry may be sufficient to make the democratic process a reality. The problem then becomes one of impelling the leadership to fulfill their proper roles and to avoid collusion at the expense of the rank-and-file.

The Nine Dimensions

If we consider the future prospects of industrial democracy in terms of the nine separate dimensions, the following picture emerges:

REPRESENTATION

The upsurge of organization and collective economic action among teachers, nurses, civil service employees, and other white-collar workers suggests that the sharing of industrial sovereignty between managements and organized employees is destined to spread. However, the traditional unions may not be the most successful organizations in the professional and semiprofessional categories, particularly where professional societies already exist. Even in the factories, the growth of professional employment may lead to new organizational units. It is doubtful, over the long run, that an increasingly more sophisticated management and the new social-psychology can prevent the representation movement from expanding.

For the selection of employee representatives, majority rule seems assured of continuation. In the management area, the professionalization process should lead to a broadening of the group determining top leadership. Stock ownership no longer is the key to the selection of industrial leaders; management tends to be self-controlling. While it is unlikely that leadership will be determined by majority vote, either by employees or managerial staff, more of the managers are likely to be involved in the selection process.

PARTICIPATION

This aspect of industrial government has been the most controversial and the most uncertain. Its future prospect remains equally murky until more understanding is obtained on its fundamental elements. How much and what types of participation do employees want in decision-making and what kinds of participation are they most capable of? Psychologists and psychoanalysts like Maslow, McGregor, Likert, and Fromm have contended that the human desire for self-expression is very strong and that if employees are given the proper conditions and opportunities, they will participate to good advantage in the government of their enterprises. Studies in the United States and abroad of participative programs, however, give a very mixed picture, suggesting that many employees are content to leave the decisions to others as long as they are reasonably satisfied with their jobs. The increasing complexity of enterprise technology and organization may also have a limiting effect on employee participation. The more specialized tasks become, the more limited the participation opportunities would seem to be. Job enlargement may serve to counteract this factor.

Organizational considerations likewise have a bearing on the participation issue. To what extent can union officials share in decision-making and fulfill their roles as the "loyal opposition" or the critical watchdog or the spokesmen for grievants? Can employee representatives serve on boards of directors or on management committees without jeopardizing their influence with the people who elected them? American trade unions have tended to be self-limiting in their participation goals. They have preferred the posture of bargainers and grievers to the role of co-partners.

The attitude of managers is another essential element in the participation area. Will the managers be desirous of encouraging and facilitating employee and union participation in decision-making, or will they insist on maintaining their functions and responsibilities for themselves? The distinction between joint determination and joint consultation becomes relevant. In the latter case, employees are given the opportunity of expressing their views but not of deciding issues. Managers have often been willing to consult with employee groups before making important decisions affecting them directly or indirectly, but have been reluctant to share decision-making responsibility. Most managers have resisted mandatory consultation, apart from the traditional bargaining areas, as unnecessary, time-consuming, and wasted energy—and an infringement on their prerogatives.

American experience in the post–World War II period supports the idea of a gradual continuing enlargement of the range of bargaining items under union pressure and a more rapid extension of voluntary consultation by the more sophisticated managers. As professionalization grows throughout industry, both consultation and joint decision-making will grow because, as the fields of education, social work, and entertainment have already shown, the professional employee and the professional organization have both the competency and the desire for a substantial degree of participation.

The involvement of government in the administration of industry is also likely to be extended. Having accepted responsibility for full employment, the elimination of poverty, the reduction of discrimination, and national economic development, the government must continue to be concerned about income and employment policies. Such a concern will inevitably increase the role of government as a factor, if not a direct participant, in the larger and more important enterprises just as the minimum-wage law has made it a factor in the less advanced enterprises. For example, the hitherto unrestricted freedom of firms to move from one location to another without regard for the effects on either location may be curtailed.

EQUAL RIGHTS AND OPPORTUNITIES

The principle of nondiscrimination because of race, color, sex, creed, or national origin achieved firm legal status in the 1945–1965 period. The idea of equal opportunity for the white male has been part of the national ethos for generations; its extension to the white female came after World War I. For the black community it was clearly enunciated only after the civil-rights movement of the 1950's and 1960's. The gap between principle and practice has, of course, been wide and difficult to bridge. That it will continue to be narrowed in industry seems assured—unless the nation has the misfortune of succumbing to a general racist solution, the two-community alternative which the 1958 National Commission on Civil Disorders warned would materialize if discrimination were not eliminated.

RIGHT OF DISSENT

The freedom of belief and expression within the enterprise was substantially advanced by the rise of unionism and the adoption of the National Labor Relations Act. The dissenter's ability to speak his mind within unions was enhanced by the passage of the Landrum-Griffin Act. The employer's freedom was curtailed to some extent under the NLRA if his words had a coercive effect upon worker organizational rights. This curtailment was reduced somewhat by the Taft-Hartley Law, to make sure that there was no abridgment of the employer's constitutional rights.

The dissenting individual in industry, however, has often experienced difficulties in making himself heard if he has challenged the existing leadership without support from a strong faction or group. Only one national union—the typographical union—has formalized the party system found in state and national politics, although informal factions have functioned more or less successfully in other unions. Once a group has secured control over the treasury, the secretariat, the communication channels, and the field staff, the odds against minority positions and efforts to dislodge the majority become very strong. Notwithstanding the oligarchic tendencies described by Michels, the tradition of free speech varies widely in practice—from the most exemplary to the most repressive.

The outlook for the future seems to be relatively favorable for the dissenter within unions as well as within industry. The legal supports have been greatly strengthened in the postwar years. The relative expansion of organization among white-collar and professional employees and their growing importance in the economy provide more favorable conditions for dissent. The improved facilities for exposing repression through public communications channels make such repression more difficult.

DUE PROCESS

The concept of due process and the machinery for implementing the concept were firmly rooted by 1965. Although criticisms have been lodged against misuses of the private arbitration system, and suggestions have been made for the adoption of a labor court system in its place, there seems no reason to expect any major change. Many unorganized enterprises have recognized the virtues of grievance machinery, and although the use of voluntary arbitration is mainly restricted to organized establishments, it continues to spread. The next main sector to adopt arbitration on a wide scale as a part of the process of settling grievances will undoubtedly be public employment. Civil service boards have long provided public employees an opportunity to appeal charges of discrimination and unjust treatment. Unions, however, have viewed these boards as arms of management and have called for procedures used in private industry. This call is almost certain to be effectuated in many public jurisdictions—local, state, and federal.

RESPONSIBILITY

In the sense of adhering to the provisions of an agreement, the idea of responsibility became firmly engrained during the postwar period. Moreover, the Taft-Hartley Law (Section 301) made the violation of labor contracts suable in federal court. There is no reason to believe that retrogression would occur in the future. Fiscal responsibility of union and company officials had also been reinforced by the passage of the Landrum-Griffin Act and the prospects for continued improvements in this respect were strong. Responsibility in the more general sense of a concern for the public welfare as well as economic self-interest is less easily predictable. The behavior of most union and management officials between 1962 and 1965 under the guidepost policy appeared to be exemplary—the only serious deviation occurred in the construction industry. In subsequent years, however, the government was unable to secure voluntary compliance with the guideposts and inflationary pressures, fueled by the Vietnam War, spread throughout the economy. In view of the decentralization of power in industry and labor circles, it is probably safer to expect organizational self-interest to prevail. Hence if economic restraints are in order, the government will have to achieve them through legislative compulsion or through indirect monetary and fiscal policy rather than through exhortation.

MINIMUM STANDARDS

The principle of the national minimum, imposed by legislation to assure socially acceptable standards on wages, hours, overtime, social security, child labor, and other employment conditions, was well established by 1965. But the agenda of items had not yet been entirely dealt with. Among the next steps that were being suggested for national action were the extension of medicare to those below the age of sixty-five, adoption of a guaranteed annual income through the negative income tax or other devices, establishment of a national system of industrial safety and health standards, and the raising of farm work standards to a level of parity with the factory. Action on one or more of these items seemed to be a good future prospect.

Meantime, it was to be expected that, as in the past, unions in individual industries would seek to raise their minimum standards above the national standards through collective bargaining and to establish some new standards. The reduction of the workweek below forty hours was likely to spread to a number of industries. So too were the guaranteed annual wage and the payment of blue-collar workers on a salaried basis rather than on an hourly, piece, or daily basis. The historic lines between blue-collar and white-collar employees, between manual and mental workers, were blurring rapidly and were likely to become dimmer in the future.

INFORMATION

It is significant that one of the earliest demands of American labor was for the establishment of federal and state bureaus of labor statistics so that reliable facts would be available for the improvement of worker conditions through legislation and collective bargaining. By 1965 labor statistics were available to a degree unmatched in earlier decades and probably unmatched elsewhere in the world. Under the Reporting and Disclosure Act (Landrum-Griffin), union members were assured information on the internal affairs of their organizations as well as on collective-bargaining agreements which they sometimes had not been able to obtain. And employers got access to information on the unions which they formerly gained through the use of labor spies. Although cases continued to come before the NLRB involving union desires for such information as the names and home addresses of all workers in a bargaining unit, these were relatively minor. The chief issue that remained in collective-bargaining situations was union access to detailed company cost data. Although managements insisted on a certain degree of secrecy for competitive reasons and to protect technological and marketing developments, company financial reporting seemed likely to continue the strong trend to general availability resulting from the conversion of family firms to public corporate status, the spread in stockholding, the growth of the big corporation and the conglomerate, and the increased government regulation of and involvement in the affairs of private industry.

PERSONAL DIGNITY

For much of the past century, the worker struggled against the concept of labor as a commodity whose value was set by the operations of market forces. Thus the declaration in the Clayton Act of 1914 that labor was not a commodity or an article of commerce was hailed by Gompers as labor's Magna Charta. When management turned to "welfare capitalism," the worker's struggle focused on equal citizenship against paternalistic human relations. The continued growth of Big Business, especially after World War II, converted the struggle for personal dignity into a new phase—the struggle against depersonalization. In this latest phase, the worker was not considered a commodity; the problem was, rather, that in the vast bureaucratic structure of the modern corporation (and to a lesser extent in the large union) he tended to become a number on a key punch card or a series of electric impulses on an electronic tape. This problem may become the most serious of the new automated age—how to give the individual worker a sense of significance and involvement in large enterprises and industries on whose rules and decisions and ultimate products he has, seemingly, a minimal impact. The union gave the worker a feeling of security and power vis-a-vis his supervisor and even top management. It has not yet addressed itself to the problem of depersonalization.

Pragmatic Adaptability

One of the principal lessons to be learned from the history of the collective-bargaining model of industrial democracy is the strength that it derives from its flexibility and adaptability. Because it is an idea developed out of pragmatic experience, it has the capacity for change as conditions change. Unlike more rigid ideologies which are the product of a single man's thought, it

permits, indeed encourages, experimentation. Some practitioners have tended to mythologize "free collective bargaining" but
even these have been more rigid in their rhetoric than in their
behavior. Thus we can expect in the years ahead that the model
will be no more fixed than it has been in the past, that new methods and procedures will be tried and new rules formulated. In
particular it is likely that government will assume more of a
third-party role, that organizational structures will conform to
the requirements of automation, and that in many occupations
and industries a new amalgam will emerge between worker professional interests and standards on the one hand and economic
and job control interests on the other.

INDEX

A Note on the Author

Milton Derber is professor of Labor and Industrial Relations at the University of Illinois. He received his Ph.D. in 1940 from the University of Wisconsin, where he was a Social Science Research Council Fellow from 1936–39. Since then he has been a labor economist with the U.S. Bureau of Labor Statistics (1940–41 and 1946–47), a field examiner with the National Labor Relations Board (1941–42), an economist at the Office of Price Administration in Washington, D.C. (1942–43), and economist and Research Director of the National War Labor Board (1943–45). From 1958–61 he served on the Executive Board of the Industrial Relations Research Association. He was vice-chairman and project director of the Governor's Advisory Commission on Labor-Management Policy for Public Employees in Illinois from 1966 to 1967 and was a member of the Task Force on State and Local Government Labor Relations for the National Governor's Conference in 1967–69. His previous publications include *Research in Labor Problems in the United States* (1967), *Plant Union Management Relations: From Practice to Theory*, with W. E. Chalmers and Milton T. Edelman (1965), *Labor and the New Deal*, with Edwin Young (1958), and *Labor-Management Relations at the Plant Level under Industry-Wide Bargaining* (1955).

UNIVERSITY OF ILLINOIS PRESS

]